Nick Vandome

MacBook

In easy steps is an imprint of In Easy Steps Limited
Southfield Road · Southam
Warwickshire CV47 0FB · United Kingdom
www.ineasysteps.com

Notice of Liability
Every effort has been made to ensure that this book contains accurate
and current information. However, In Easy Steps Limited and the
author shall not be liable for any loss or damage suffered by readers
as a result of any information contained herein.

Trademarks
Mac, Mac OS, MacBook and MacBook Air are trademarks of Apple
Inc., registered in the U.S. and other countries. All other trademarks
are acknowledged as belonging to their respective companies.

In Easy Steps Limited supports The Forest Stewardship Council (FSC),
the leading international forest certification organisation. All our titles
that are printed on Greenpeace approved FSC certified paper carry the
FSC logo.

MIX
Paper from
responsible sources
FSC® C020837

Printed and bound in the United Kingdom

ISBN 978-1-84078-408-4

Contents

8 Sharing OS X 129

9 MacBook Networking 139

10 MacBook Mobility 151

1 Introducing MacBooks

Mobile computing has taken off in recent years, to the extent that laptops are now selling at a comparable rate to desktops. Apple are a major player in this area, and their MacBook range is one of the most stylish and user-friendly notebook computers on the market.

About MacBooks

When Apple Computers introduced their iMac range of desktop computers in 1998 it was a major breakthrough. It was an innovative design for a desktop computer that captured the public's imagination and helped revive the commercial fortunes for the company: without the iMac Apple may never have been in the position to dazzle us with the iPod, iPhone and iPad.

To try and match the success of the iMac, Apple began working on a new range of Notebook computers. They first entered this market seriously with the Macintosh Portable in 1989. However, like many laptops during this period it was very expensive and not portable in the way that we would expect today. In 1991, Apple introduced the PowerBook range of laptops, which was essentially the forerunner to the MacBook range. The PowerBooks were aimed at the professional market and, although relatively expensive, they were quickly adopted by professions such as designers and graphic artists. The PowerBooks were also used by Apple to develop technologies that would be incorporated into their subsequent Notebook ranges.

After the iMac the new range of Apple laptops were introduced the following year, 1999. These were the iBook range aimed firmly at the consumer market. The first version of the iBook was an innovative rounded clamshell design, which in some ways mirrored the novel design of the iMac, including the range of bright colors for the casing.

The iBook was a major success for Apple, particularly with students and school pupils. After the initial clamshell design the iBook then appeared in an all-white design.

Don't forget

iBooks had a lot of media coverage in terms of appearing in popular TVs shows and movies.

In May 2006 the MacBook range first appeared, replacing both the iBook and PowerBook ranges. The two main reasons for this consolidation were:

- Simplifying Apple's laptop range under one banner

- It was during this period that Apple were moving from Power PC processors for their computers to Intel processors

The MacBook range has now produced at least eight different models. There are also two other variations of the standard MacBook:

- MacBook Pro. This is the professional version of the MacBook and is aimed more at the market previously covered by the PowerBook range

- MacBook Air. This range pushes the idea of thin, light and portable laptops even further than the standard MacBook. It is billed as an ultraportable notebook computer and claims to be the thinnest on the market, currently at 0.76 inch

Although previous Apple Notebooks have been offered in various monitor sizes, the MacBook now comes in one standard size of 13.3 inches. The MacBook Air is the same, but the MacBook Pro comes in three sizes, 13, 15 and 17 inches.

Although the MacBook is similar in design to its predecessor, the iBook, it is thinner, more rectangular and has smoother edges.

MacBooks v. iMacs

When considering buying a MacBook, one of the first considerations is how it will perform in comparison with a desktop iMac. In general, MacBooks are more expensive than an iMac with a comparable specification. The reason for this is purely down to size: it is more expensive to fit the required hardware into a MacBook than the more generous physical capacity of an iMac. However, with modern computing technology and power, MacBooks with lower specifications than their desktop cousins will be able to handle all but the most intensive computing needs of most home and business users. The one situation where MacBooks will have to have as high a specification as possible, is if you are going to be doing a lot a video downloading and editing, such as converting and editing old family movies.

Some of the issues to consider when looking at the differences between MacBooks and iMacs are:

- Portability. Obviously, MacBooks easily win over iMacs in this respect but, when looking at this area, it is worth thinking about how portable you actually want your computer to be. If you want to mainly use it in the home then you may think that a desktop is the answer. However, a MacBook gives you portability in the home too, which means you can use your computer in a variety of locations within the home and even in the garden, if desired

- Power. Even the most inexpensive MacBooks have enough computing power to perform most of the tasks the majority of users require. If you are looking for the optimum amount of power from a MacBook then the MacBook Pro range should be considered

- Functionality. MacBooks now contain similar functionality to iMacs in terms of CD/DVD SuperDrive and iSight web-cam. This allows for similar functions to be performed with either a MacBook or an iMac. When it comes down to making a choice it may be a question of how portable you want your computer to be, either when you are traveling or in the home

MacBook Specifications

All computing technology moves at a break-neck speed, and specifications are always getting better and better. However, these are the specifications for the range of MacBook released in the summer of 2010.

MacBook

- Display: 13.3-inch (diagonal) LED-backlit glossy widescreen display with support for millions of colors

- Battery life: Up to 10 hours

- Height: 1.08 inches (2.74 cm)

- Width: 13.00 inches (33.03 cm)

- Depth: 9.12 inches (23.17 cm)

- Weight: 4.7 pounds (2.13 kg)

- 2.4GHz Intel Core 2 Duo processor with 3MB on-chip shared L2 cache

- 250GB 5400-rpm Serial ATA hard disk drive; optional 320GB or 500GB 5400-rpm drive

- 2GB (two 1GB SO-DIMMs) of 1066MHz DDR3 SDRAM; two SO-DIMM slots support up to 4GB

- AirPort Extreme 802.11n Wi-Fi wireless networking; IEEE 802.11a/b/g compatible

- Bluetooth 2.1 + EDR (Enhanced Data Rate) wireless technology

- 8x slot-loading SuperDrive (DVD±R DL/DVD±RW/CD-RW)

- NVIDIA GeForce 320M graphics processor with 256MB of DDR3 SDRAM shared with main memory

- Gigabit Ethernet port

- Mini DisplayPort

- Two USB 2.0 ports (up to 480 Mbps)

- A range of energy saving features

MacBook Air

The specifications for the MacBook Air are slightly below those of the standard MacBook, which is unsurprising given its revolutionary thinness. One of the main differences is that there is no inbuilt CD/DVD SuperDrive. However, an external SuperDrive can be used in conjunction with the MacBook Air.

- Display: 13.3-inch (diagonal) LED-backlit glossy widescreen display with support for millions of colors

- Battery life: Up to 5 hours

- Height: 0.16-0.76 inch (0.4-1.94 cm)

- Width: 12.8 inches (32.5 cm)

- Depth: 8.94 inches (22.7 cm)

- Weight: 3.0 pounds (1.36 kg)

- 1.86GHz or 2.13GHz Intel Core 2 Duo processor with 6MB on-chip shared L2 cache

- 120GB 4200-rpm Serial ATA hard disk drive or 128GB solid-state drive

- 2GB of 1066MHz DDR3 SDRAM onboard

- Built-in AirPort Extreme Wi-Fi wireless networking (based on IEEE 802.11n specification); IEEE 802.11a/b/g compatible

- Built-in Bluetooth 2.1 + EDR (Enhanced Data Rate) wireless technology

- Optional external USB MacBook Air SuperDrive (separate)

- NVIDIA GeForce 9400M graphics processor with 256MB of DDR3 SDRAM shared with main memory

- Mini DisplayPort

- One USB 2.0 ports (up to 480 Mbps)

- A range of energy saving features

MacBook Pro

- Display: 13.3, 15.4 or 17-inch (diagonal) LED-backlit glossy widescreen display with support for millions of colors

- Battery life: 8-9 hours

- Height: 0.95 inch (2.41 cm)

- Width: 14.35 inches (36.4 cm)

- Depth: 9.82 inches (24.9 cm)

- Weight: 5.6 pounds (2.54 kg)

- 2.4GHz or 2.53GHz Intel Core i5 processor with 3MB shared L3 cache; or 2.66GHz Intel Core i7 processor with 4MB shared L3 cache

- 320GB or 500GB 5400-rpm Serial ATA hard drive; optional 500GB 7200-rpm hard drive, or 128GB, 256GB, or 512GB solid-state drive

- 4GB (two 2GB SO-DIMMs) of 1066MHz DDR3 memory; two SO-DIMM slots support up to 8GB

- AirPort Extreme Wi-Fi wireless networking (based on IEEE 802.11n specification); IEEE 802.11a/b/g compatible

- Bluetooth 2.1 + EDR (Enhanced Data Rate) wireless technology

- 8x slot-loading SuperDrive (DVD±R DL/DVD±RW/CD-RW)

- NVIDIA GeForce GT 330M graphics processor with 256MB of GDDR memory

- Gigabit Ethernet port

- One FireWire 800 port (up to 800 Mbps)

- Mini DisplayPort

- Two USB 2.0 ports (up to 480 Mbps)

- A range of energy saving features

MacBook Jargon Explained

Since MacBooks are essentially portable computers, a lot of the jargon is the same as for other computers. However, it is worth looking at some of this jargon and the significance it has in terms of MacBooks.

- Processor. Also known as the central processing unit, or CPU, this refers to the processing of digital data as it is provided by programs on the computer. The more powerful the processor, the quicker the data is interpreted. As with the rest of Apple's computers, MacBooks use Intel processors

- Memory. This closely relates to the processor and is also known as random-access memory, or RAM. Essentially, this type of memory manages the programs that are being run and the commands that are being executed. The greater the amount of memory there is, the quicker programs will run. With more RAM they will also be more stable and less likely to crash. In the current range of MacBooks, memory is measured in megabytes (MB) or gigabytes (GB)

- Storage. This refers to the amount of digital information the MacBook can store. It is frequently referred to in terms of hard disk space and is measured in gigabytes. The minimum storage space on a standard MacBook is 250GB

- Trackpad. This is an input device that takes the place of a mouse (although a mouse can still be used with a MacBook, either with a USB cable or wirelessly). Traditionally, trackpads have come with a button that duplicates the function of the buttons on a mouse. However, the glass trackpad on a MacBook has no button, as the pad itself performs the functions of a button

Don't forget

Memory can be thought of as a temporary storage device, as it only keeps information about the currently-open programs. Storage is more permanent, as it keeps the information even when the MacBook has been turned off.

14

- Graphics card. This is a device that enables images, video and animations to be displayed on the MacBook. It is also sometimes known as a video card. The faster the graphics card, the better the quality relevant media will be displayed at. In general, very fast graphics cards are really only needed for intensive multimedia applications, such as video games or videos. On a MacBook this is the NVIDIA card

- Wireless. This refers to a MacBook's ability to connect wirelessly to a network, i.e. another computer or an Internet connection. In order to be able to do this, the MacBook must have a wireless card, which enables it to connect to a network or high-speed Internet connection. This is known as the Airport Extreme Wi-Fi wireless networking card

- Bluetooth. This is a radio technology for connecting devices wirelessly over short distance. It can be used for items such as a wireless mouse, or for connecting to a device, such as an iPhone for downloading photos

Don't forget

For more on using wireless technology see Chapter Nine.

15

- Ports. These are the parts of a MacBook external devices can be plugged into, using a cable such as a USB or a FireWire. They are located on the side of the MacBook

- USB. This is a method for connecting a variety of external devices, such as digital cameras, MP3 music players, scanners and printers

Don't forget

USB stands for Universal Serial Bus and is a popular way of connecting external devices to computers.

- Ethernet. This is for connecting an Ethernet cable to a router, for accessing the Internet, rather than doing it wirelessly

...cont'd

- FireWire. This is a similar method of data transfer to USB but it is much faster. For this reason, it is generally used for devices that need to transfer larger amounts of data, such as digital video cameras. FireWire ports are only available on the MacBook Pro

- Mini-display. This is a port for connecting a MacBook to a larger, stand-alone monitor

- CD/DVD players or re-writers. On a MacBook this is known as a SuperDrive, and is a thin slot at on the side of the MacBook. Discs are inserted by simply pushing them into the SuperDrive slot. The SuperDrive can be used to play music CDs, watch DVDs, copy data from CDs or DVDs, and copy data from your MacBook onto CDs or DVDs

- Web-cam (iSight). This is a type of camera fitted into the MacBook and it can be used to take stills photographs or communicate via video with other people. On the MacBook, it is known as the iSight camera and it works with the iChat program. The iSight camera is built-in at the top, middle of the inner casing

Don't forget

When the iSight camera is on, a green light appears next to it.

Getting Comfortable

Since you will probably be using your MacBook in more than one location, the issue of finding a comfortable working position can be a vital one, particularly as you cannot put the keyboard and monitor in different positions, as you can with a desktop computer. Whenever you are using your MacBook, try and make sure that you are sitting in a comfortable position, with your back well supported, and that the MacBook is in a position where you can reach the keyboard easily, and also see the screen, without straining your arms.

Despite the possible temptation to do so, avoid using your MacBook in bed, on your lap or where you have to slouch or strain to reach the MacBook properly:

Don't forget

Working comfortably at a MacBook involves a combination of a good chair, good posture and good MacBook positioning.

Hot tip

If possible, the best place to work at a MacBook is at a dedicated desk or workstation.

17

Seating position

The ideal way to sit at a MacBook is with an office-type chair that offers good support for your back. Even with these types of chairs it is important to maintain a good body position so that your back is straight and your head is pointing forwards.

If you do not have an office-type chair, use a chair with a straight back and place a cushion behind you for extra support and comfort as required.

Hot tip

One of the advantages of office-type chairs is that the height can usually be adjusted, and this can be a great help in achieving a comfortable position.

...cont'd

MacBook position

When working at your MacBook it is important to have it positioned so that both the keyboard and the screen are in a comfortable position. If the keyboard is too low you will have to slouch or strain to reach it:

If the keyboard is too high, your arms will be stretching. This could lead to pain in your tendons:

Beware

Take regular breaks when working with a MacBook and stop working if you experience aches, or pins and needles in your arms or legs.

The ideal setup is to have the MacBook in a position where you can sit with your forearms and wrists as level as possible while you are typing on the keyboard:

Adjusting the screen

Another factor in working comfortably at a MacBook is the position of the screen. Unlike with a desktop computer, it is not feasible to have a MacBook screen at eye level, as this would result in the keyboard being in too high a position. Instead, once you have achieved a comfortable seating position, open the screen so that it is approximately 90 degrees from your eye line:

One problem with MacBook screens is that they can reflect glare from sunlight or indoor lighting:

If this happens, either change your position, or block out the light source using some form of blind or shade. Avoid squinting at a screen that is reflecting glare, as this will make you feel uncomfortable and quickly give you a headache.

Don't forget

Find a comfortable body position and move your MacBook to accommodate this, rather than vice versa.

Beware

MacBooks have high quality anti-glare screens. However, even this will not be very effective against bright sunlight shining directly onto the screen.

19

Trackpad and Keyboard

MacBooks have the same data input devices as most laptops: a keyboard and a trackpad. However, the trackpad has an innovative feature that makes it stand out from the crowd: there is no button, the trackpad itself performs the functions of a button. To use the trackpad:

- One-finger click. Click anywhere on the trackpad to perform one-click operations

- Right-click. Right-click functions (such as accessing contextual menus) can be performed by clicking on a corner of the trackpad or clicking anywhere with two fingers

- Scrolling. The can be done on a page by dragging two fingers on the trackpad either up or down

When using the keyboard or trackpad, keep your hands and fingers as flat as possible over the keyboard and trackpad

Keyboard and Trackpad options

Options for the functioning of the keyboard and trackpad can be set within the System Preferences. To use this:

Don't forget

Contextual menus are ones that have actions that are specific to the item being viewed.

Don't forget

System Preferences can be accessed from the Dock. For more details on this see Chapter Two.

1 Click on the Keyboard & Mouse button

Keyboard & Mouse

2 Click on the Keyboard or Trackpad tabs to set options for each

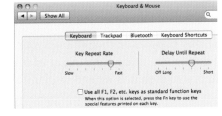

Using an External Mouse

Not everyone likes trackpads as a means of moving the cursor on a MacBook, and it is true that they can sometimes be slightly fiddly and prone to erratic movement if you are not used to them. The good news is that it is perfectly possible to use a conventional mouse with a MacBook to move the cursor.

A mouse can be connected to a MacBook via one of the USB ports on the side of the MacBook.

Once the mouse has been connected to the MacBook it can be used in exactly the same way as with a desktop computer. It is possible to add a wireless mouse, which can be used without needing a cable:

Hot tip

If using an external mouse, a wireless one is a good option because you can use it easily on either side, whereas a cable one is more restricted in its position.

21

MacBook Power Cable

All MacBooks need a power cable, in the form of an AC Adapter, that can be used to recharge the battery, and it can also be used when the MacBook is not being used in a mobile environment. This can save the battery and, if possible, the adapter should be used instead of battery power.

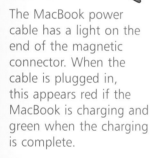

The MacBook adapter also has a built-in safety feature known as the MagSafe power port. This consists of a magnetic connection between the power adapter and the power port on the side of the MacBook. When the connection is made it is a magnetic one rather than a physical one. This means that if the power cord is accidentally pulled or kicked out the magnetic connection will be broken without dragging the MacBook with it. This is safer for both the user and the MacBook itself.

Cleaning a MacBook

Like most things, MacBooks benefit greatly from a little care and attention. The two most important areas to keep clean are the screen and the keyboard.

Cleaning the screen

All computer screens quickly collect dust and fingerprints, and MacBooks are no different. If this is left too long it can make the screen harder to read and cause eye strain and headaches. Clean the screen regularly with the following cleaning materials:

- A lint-free cloth, similar to the type used to clean camera lenses (it is important not to scratch the screen in any way)

- An alcohol-free cleaning fluid recommended for computer screens

- Screen wipes, that are again recommended for use on computer screens

Cleaning the keyboard

Keyboards are notorious for accumulating dust, fluff and crumbs. One way to solve this problem is to turn the MacBook upside down and very gently shake it to loosen any foreign objects. Failing this, a can of condensed air can be used, with a narrow nozzle to blow out any stubborn items that remain lodged between the keys.

Don't forget

The outer casing of a MacBook can be cleaned with the same fluid as used for the screen. A duster or a damp (but not wet) cloth and warm water can be equally effective. Keep soap away from MacBooks if possible.

23

Spares and Accessories

Whenever you are going anywhere with your MacBook there are always spares and accessories to consider. Some of these are just nice things to have, while others could be essential in ensuring that you can still use your MacBook if anything goes wrong while you are on your travels. Items to consider putting in your MacBook case include:

- Spare battery. This is probably the most important spare if you are going to be away from home or work for any length of time, and particularly if you think you may be unable to access a power supply for a long period of time, and be unable to charge your MacBook battery. Like all batteries, MacBook batteries slowly lose power over time and do not keep their charge for as long as when they are new. It is a good idea to always keep an eye on how much battery power you have left and, if you are running low, to try and conserve as much energy as possible. Although MacBook batteries are relatively bulky and heavy, this could mean the difference between frustration and relief, if you are left with no battery power

- Multi-card reader. This is a device that can be used to copy data from the cards used in digital cameras. If you have a digital camera, it is possible to download the photographs from it directly onto a MacBook with a cable. However, a multi-card reader can be more efficient and flexible

- Headphones. These can be used to listen to music or films if you are in the company of other people and you do not want to disturb them. They can also be very useful if there are distracting noises from other people

- Pen drive. This is a small device that can be used to copy data to and from your MacBook. It connects via a USB port and is about the size of a packet of chewing gum. It is an excellent way of backing up files from your MacBook when you are away from home or the office

- Cleaning material. The materials described on page 23 can be taken to ensure your MacBook is always in tip-top condition for use

- DVDs/CDs. Video or music DVDs and CDs can be taken to provide mobile entertainment, and blank ones can be taken to copy data onto, similar to using a pen drive

Hot tip

It is important that headphones are comfortable to wear for extended periods of time. In general, the types that fit over the ears are more comfortable than the "bud" variety that are inserted into the ear.

2 Around a MacBook

This chapter looks at getting started with your MacBook: from opening it up and turning it on through to keyboard functions. It also covers burning information to CDs/DVDs and connecting external devices, such as printers and pen drives.

Opening Up

The first step towards getting started with a new MacBook is to open it ready for use.

There is no physical latch on the front of a MacBook so there is nothing obvious in terms of how to open it.

Beware

Open the screen of a MacBook carefully, so as not to put any unnecessary pressure on the connection between the screen and the main body of the MacBook.

Instead of a latch, a MacBook has a magnetic closing mechanism, which engages when the monitor screen is closed onto the main body of the MacBook. To open it, raise it firmly upwards from the center, where there is a smooth groove.

Once the MacBook has been opened the screen should stay in whatever position it is placed

Turning On

The button for turning on a MacBook, ready for use, is round and is located at the top-right corner of the keyboard:

Beware

Press the button for turning on with one firm, definite motion. If you accidentally press it twice in quick succession, the MacBook may turn on and then shut down immediately.

The MacBook can be turned on by pushing this button firmly. The MacBook will then make the Apple "chime" to indicate that it has been turned on and has begun the startup process. Once the MacBook has completed this process the opening screen should be displayed. At this point the MacBook is ready for use.

MacBook Desktop

The opening view of a MacBook is known as the Desktop. Items, such as programs and files, can be stored on the Desktop but, in general, it is best to try and keep it as clear as possible.

At the top of the Desktop is the Apple Menu and the Menu bar. This contains links to a collection of commonly used menus and functions, such as copy and paste.

Don't forget

The menus on the Menu bar are looked at in detail in Chapter Six.

At the bottom of the Desktop is the Dock. This is a collection of icons that are shortcuts to frequently used programs or folders.

One of the items on the Dock is the Finder. This can be used to access the main area for programs, folders and files and also organize the way you work on your MacBook.

Apple Menu

The Apple Menu is accessed from the Apple symbol at the left-hand side of the Menu bar:

The options on the Apple Menu are:

- About this Mac. This provides general information about the processor, the amount of memory and the OS X version

- Software Update. This can be used to view and install available software updates

- Mac OS X Software. The takes you to the Downloads page on the Apple website

- System Preferences. This is a shortcut to System Preferences

- Dock. This can be used to access settings for the Dock

- Location. This lists available network locations

- Recent Items. This displays the items you have most recently used and viewed

- Force Quit. This can be used to manually quit a program that has frozen or will not close

- Sleep. This puts the MacBook into a state of hibernation

- Restart. This closes down the MacBook and restarts it

- Shut Down. This shuts down the MacBook

- Log Out. This logs out the current user

Hot tip

Force Quit can be used to close down a program that is frozen or is not responding.

Keyboard Buttons

As shown on the previous page, the Apple Menu has options for Sleep, Restart and Shut down. Sleep saves your current session and puts the MacBook into a state of hibernation. This is useful if your MacBook is going to be inactive for a period but you do not want to close it down.

Shortcut keys can also be used to put the MacBook to sleep.

To do this, press the Alt and Command keys and the Eject key simultaneously. (The Alt and Command keys are located on the left-hand side of the space bar and the Eject key is at the top-right of the keyboard.)

Fn (Function) Keys

A MacBook keyboard has a number of keys that can be used for shortcuts or specific function. Four of them are located at the left of the space bar. They are (from left to right):

- The Function key. This can be used to activate the function (f) keys at the top of the keyboard. To activate the operation of a function key, press it while holding down the Fn key

- The Control key. This can be used to access contextual menus

- The Alt (Option) key. This is frequently used in conjunction with the Command key to perform specific tasks, such as above with Sleep

- The Command key. As above

At the top of the keyboard there are keys for changing some of the settings on your MacBook. These are (from left to right):

- F1: Decrease brightness

- F2: Increase brightness

- F3: Show all open windows (Exposé)

- F4: Show/Hide Dashboard widgets

- F7: Rewind a video

- F8: Play/Pause a video

- F9: Fast forward a video

- F10: Mute volume

- F11: Decrease volume

- F12: Increase volume

- Eject button. Remove CDs/DVDs from the SuperDrive

Don't forget

By default, the F keys operate without having to simulataneously press the Fn key. If you want to use the Fn key in conjunction with the F keys, this can be specified in the System Preferences. To do this, open System Preferences and click on the Keyboard & Mouse button. Under the Keyboard tab, check on the box that says "Use all F keys as standard function keys".

System Preferences

In OS X there are preferences that can be set for just about every aspect of the way your MacBook operates. This gives you great control over how the interface looks and how the operating system functions. To access System Preferences:

1 Click on this icon on the Dock or in the Applications folder in the Finder

2 The available System Preferences are displayed in this window

Don't forget

For more information about the Dock, see Chapter Five, and for the Finder, Chapter Six.

3 Click once on an item to view its options

Personal preferences

Appearance. Options for the overall look of buttons, menus, windows and scroll bars.

Desktop & Screen Saver. This can be used to change the desktop background and the screen saver.

Dock. Options for the way the Dock looks and functions.

Exposé and Spaces. This can be used to specify keystrokes for the different Spaces and Exposé functions.

Language & Text. Options for the language used on the computer.

Security. This enables you to secure your Home folder with a master password, for added security.

Spotlight. This can be used to specify settings for the OS X search facility, Spotlight.

Hardware preferences

CDs & DVDs. Options for what action is taken when you insert CDs and DVDs.

Displays. Options for the screen display, such as resolution.

Energy Saver. Options for when the computer is inactive.

Keyboard. Options for how the keyboard functions and also keyboard shortcuts.

Mouse. Options for how the mouse functions.

Print & Fax. Options for selecting printers and handling faxes.

Sound. Options for adding sound effects and playing or recording sound.

Internet & Network preferences

MobileMe. Options for setting up your online MobileMe membership and also for configuring your iDisk. This is looked at in more detail in Chapter Ten.

Network. This can be used to specify network settings for linking two or more computers together. This is looked at in more detail in Chapter Nine.

...cont'd

Bluetooth. Options for attaching Bluetooth wireless devices.

Sharing. This can be used to specify how files are shared over a network. This is also looked at in Chapter Nine.

System preferences

Accounts. This can be used to allow different users to create their own accounts for use on the same computer.

Date & Time. Options for changing the computer's date and time to time zones around the world.

Parental Controls. This can be used to limit access to the computer and various online functions.

Software Update. This can be used to specify how software updates are handled. It can be set so that updates are automatically downloaded when the computer is connected to the Internet, or they can be done manually.

Speech. Options for using speakable commands to control the computer. This can be useful for users who find it uncomfortable using the keyboard or the mouse as it enables them to perform some tasks by speech alone.

Startup Disk. This can be used to specify the disk from which your computer starts up. This is usually the OS X volume, or in some cases, a previous version of the Mac operating system.

Time Machine. This can be used to configure and set up the OS X backup facility.

Universal Access. This can be used to set options for users who have difficulty with viewing text on screen, hearing commands, using the keyboard or using the mouse.

CD and DVD SuperDrive

The SuperDrive on a MacBook can be used to copy data from a CD or DVD onto the hard drive, or vice versa. As with many of the functions of a MacBook there are settings that can be applied within the System Preferences. To do this:

1 Open System Preferences and click on this icon under the Hardware section

Hardware

CDs & DVDs

2 There are various options for what happens when you insert blank CDs/DVDs and also for music, picture and video CDs/DVDs

Burning a CD/DVD

The process of copying data onto a CD/DVD is known as burning. This can be done with data, (such as a Word document), presentations, photos, music or videos. To do this:

1 Insert a CD/DVD into the SuperDrive. A window will ask you what action you want performed. For burning, keep the default as Open Finder and click OK

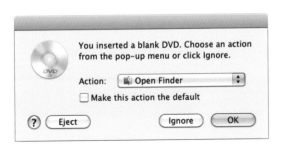

...cont'd

2 The other options are for opening different progams. Use Open iDVD if you want to create a DVD menu to go with a home video, or Open iTunes if it is a music disk

✓ 🖥 Open Finder
◎ Open iDVD
🎵 Open iTunes
🖥 Open Disk Utility

Open other application...

Run Script...

3 For burning a disk, the CD/DVD will show up in the Finder, with no title

💿 Untitled DVD ☢

4 Ctrl+click on the untitled disk name and select the Rename option from the contextual menu

Open

Open Enclosing Folder

Eject

Get Info

Rename "Untitled DVD"
Remove from Sidebar

Open Sidebar Preferences...

5 The disk name will be highlighted

💿 **Untitled DVD**   ☢

6 Overtype the name with one that you want

💿 Photos   ☢

7 Within the Finder, locate and select the items that you want to burn onto the CD/DVD

8 Drag the selected items onto the CD/DVD name in the Finder navigation pane

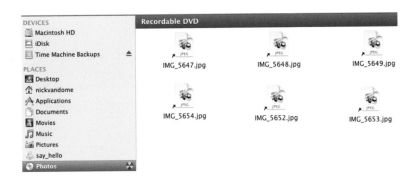

9 Click on the Burn button or click on the burn icon next to the CD/DVD name in the Finder

Hot tip

When burning a CD or DVD use a slower burn speed to ensure that the recording process works as smoothly as possible.

10 Select options for the name of the CD/DVD and the burn speed. Click on the Burn button to copy the items from the MacBook to the CD/DVD

Connecting a Printer

Using a printer on any computer is essential and MacBooks allow you to quickly add a printer to aid your productivity. To do this:

1 Open System Preferences and click on this icon under the Hardware section

2 Any printers that have been added are shown in this window. If there are no printers it will be empty

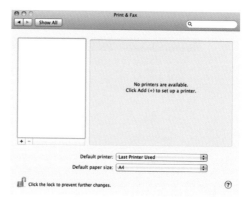

3 Click on the + button to add a new printer

4 Any printers that are connected by a cable or wirelessly will be recognized

5 If the MacBook does not have a driver for the specific printer it will use a generic one instead

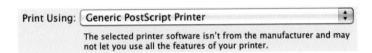

Print Using: Generic PostScript Printer

The selected printer software isn't from the manufacturer and may not let you use all the features of your printer.

6 Click on the Add button to add the selected printer

Add

Don't forget

Printer drivers are programs that enable the printer to communicate with your computer. Printer drivers are usually provided on a disk when the printer is purchased. In addition, MacBooks will have a number of printer drivers pre-installed. If you MacBook does not recognize your printer, you can load the driver from the disk.

7 The new printer and its details are added in the Print & Fax System Preference window

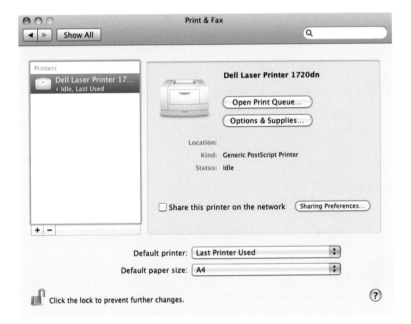

39

8 The added printer will be available when you next select Print, when you want to print a document or picture. If you add more than one printer, one will be set as the default while the others will have to be selected when you want to print something through them

External Drives

Attaching external drives is an essential part of mobile computing: whether it is to backup data as you are travelling or for downloading photos and other items. On MacBooks, external drives are displayed on the Desktop once they have been attached and they can then be used for the required task. To do this:

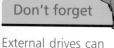

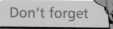
1 Attach the external drive. This is usually done with a USB cable. Once it has been attached it is shown on the Desktop

2 The drive is shown under the Devices section of the Finder

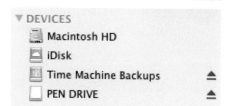

3 Perform the required task for the external drive (such as copying files or folders onto it from the hard drive of your MacBook)

4 External drives have to be ejected properly, not just pulled out or removed. To do this, click on this button next to the drive in the Finder window, or drag its icon on the Desktop over the Trash icon on the Dock. This will then change into an Eject icon

3 Battery Issues

Battery power is crucial to a MacBook. This chapter shows how to get the best from your battery and how to deal with any problems.

Power Consumption

Battery life for each charge of MacBook batteries is one area engineers have worked very hard on since MacBooks were first introduced. For the latest models of MacBooks the average battery life for each charge is approximately 10 hours. However, this is dependent on the power consumption of the MacBook, i.e. how much power is being used to perform particular tasks. Power-intensive tasks will reduce the battery life of each charge cycle. These types of tasks include:

- Watching a DVD

- Editing digital video

- Editing digital photographs

- Listening to music

When you are using your MacBook you can always monitor how much battery power you currently have available. This is shown by the battery icon that appears at the top right on the Apple Menu:

As the battery runs down, the monitor bar turns red as a warning.

Because of the vital role the battery plays in relation to your MacBook, it is important to try and conserve its power as much as possible. To do this:

- Where possible, use the mains adapter rather than the battery when using your MacBook

- Use the Sleep function when you are not actively using your MacBook (see Chapter 2)

- Use power-management functions to save battery power (see the next pages)

Power Management

To access power management options, click on the battery icon on the Apple Menu. Select an option for how you want the battery to operate, i.e. Better Battery Life, Normal or Better Performance. For each option the relevant settings are automatically made in the Energy Saver System Preference. This can be accessed by clicking on the Open Energy Saver link, or:

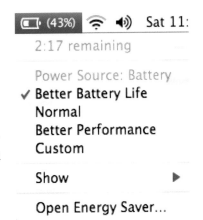

1. Access the System Preferences and click on the Energy Saver button

Energy Saver

2. The Energy Saver window has a number of settings for the operation of your MacBook battery

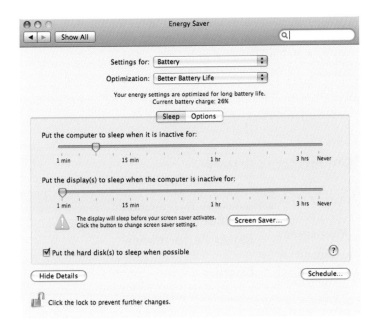

Beware

If you are undertaking an energy-intensive task, such as watching a DVD, try and use the external AC/DC power cable rather than the battery. Otherwise the battery may drain quite quickly and the MacBook closes down completely.

Energy Saver

MacBooks have options for how the battery is managed, within the Energy Saver System Preference. These allow you to set things like individual power settings for the battery and to view how much charge is left in the battery. To use the Energy Saver:

1 Access the System Preferences and click on the Energy Saver button

Energy Saver

2 At the top of the Energy Saver window, the amount of the current battery charge and the amount of time left that it can run on are shown below the "Settings for" and "Optimization" options

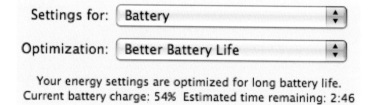

Settings for: Battery

Optimization: Better Battery Life

Your energy settings are optimized for long battery life.
Current battery charge: 54% Estimated time remaining: 2:46

3 Click on the "Optimization" option. Select a setting for the operation of your battery

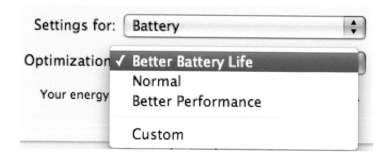

Settings for: Battery

Optimization ✓ Better Battery Life
Normal
Better Performance

Your energy
Custom

4 Click on the Sleep tab to access settings for putting the MacBook to sleep

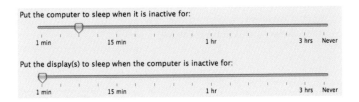

5 Drag these sliders to determine how long until the computer and the monitor go to sleep if the MacBook is not used. These are set automatically for each Optimization setting in Step 3

Put the computer to sleep when it is inactive for:

1 min   15 min   1 hr   3 hrs   Never

Put the display(s) to sleep when the computer is inactive for:

1 min   15 min   1 hr   3 hrs   Never

6 Click on the Option tab to access the settings for additional battery settings

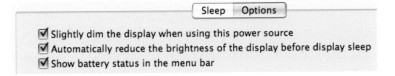

Sleep   Options

☑ Slightly dim the display when using this power source
☑ Automatically reduce the brightness of the display before display sleep
☑ Show battery status in the menu bar

7 Under "Setting for," select the Power Adapter option. This has the same Sleep options as for Battery power

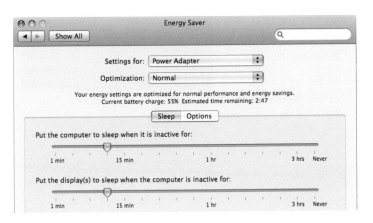

Energy Saver

◄ ► Show All

Settings for: Power Adapter
Optimization: Normal

Your energy settings are optimized for normal performance and energy savings.
Current battery charge: 55% Estimated time remaining: 2:47

Sleep   Options

Put the computer to sleep when it is inactive for:

1 min   15 min   1 hr   3 hrs   Never

Put the display(s) to sleep when the computer is inactive for:

1 min   15 min   1 hr   3 hrs   Never

...cont'd

8 Click on the Options tab and select the required settings for when your MacBook is plugged into the adapter

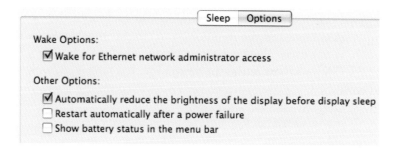

9 For Screen Saver settings click on this button in the Sleep section

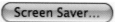

10 Select Screen Saver settings for the type of screen saver (left-hand panel) and the amount of time until the screen saver is activated (underneath Preview window)

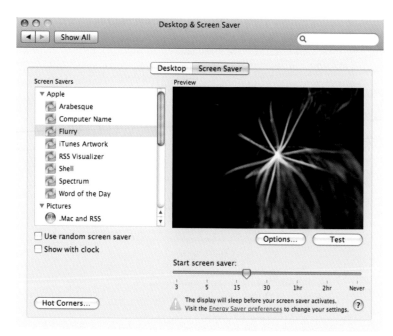

Charging the Battery

MacBook batteries are charged using an AC/DC adapter, which can also be used to power the MacBook instead of the battery. If the MacBook is turned on and is being powered by the AC/DC adapter, the battery will be charged at the same time, although at a slower rate than if it is being charged when the MacBook is turned off.

The AC/DC adapter should be supplied with a new MacBook and consists of a cable and a power adapter. To charge a MacBook battery using an AC/DC adapter:

1   Connect the AC/DC adapter and the cable and plug it into the mains socket

2   Attach the AC/DC adapter to the MacBook and turn it on at the mains socket. When it is attach this battery icon is displayed on the Apple Menu, including the amount the battery is charged

3   Click on the battery icon to view how long until the battery is charged, the power source and also the current energy saving setting

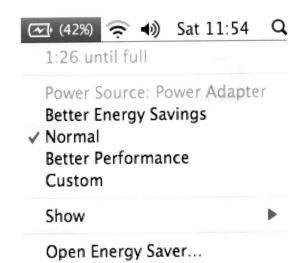

47

Don't forget

A MacBook battery can be charged whether the MacBook is turned on or off. It charges more quickly if the MacBook is not in use.

Beware

When you are warned about a low battery, save all of your current work and either close down or switch to using an external AC/DC cable for powering your MacBook.

Removing the Battery

Although a MacBook's battery does not have to be removed on a regular basis, there may be occasions when you want to do this. These include:

- If the MacBook freezes, i.e. you are unable to undertake any operations using the keyboard or trackpad and you cannot turn off the MacBook using the power button

- If you are traveling, particularly in extreme temperatures. In situations like this you may prefer to keep the battery with you to try and avoid exposing it to either very hot or very cold temperatures

To remove a MacBook battery:

48

1 With the MacBook turned off and the lid closed, turn the MacBook upside down

2 Locate the battery compartment and with a small coin turn the lock button from closed to open

3 Gently slide or pull the battery out of its compartment

Dead and Spare Batteries

No energy source lasts forever and MacBook batteries are no exception to this rule. Over time, the battery will operate less efficiently until it will not be possible to charge the battery at all. With average usage, most MacBook batteries should last approximately five years, although they will start to lose performance before this and become less efficient. Some signs of a dead MacBook battery are:

- Nothing happens when the MacBook is turned on using just battery power

- The MacBook shuts down immediately if it is being run on the AC/DC adapter and the cord is suddenly removed

- The following window appears a few minutes or immediately after you have charged the battery and then started to use your MacBook on battery power

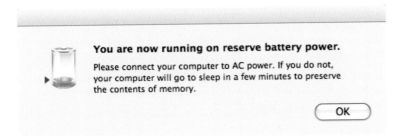

You are now running on reserve battery power.

Please connect your computer to AC power. If you do not, your computer will go to sleep in a few minutes to preserve the contents of memory.

OK

Beware

If you think that your battery may be losing its performance, make sure that you save your work at regular intervals. Although you should do this anyway, it is more important if there is a chance of your battery running out of power.

Spare battery

Depending on how and where you use your MacBook it could be worth considering buying a spare battery. Although these are not cheap, it can be a valuable investment, particularly if you spend a lot of time traveling with your MacBook and you are not always near a source of mains electricity. In situations like this, a spare battery could enable you to keep using your MacBook if your original battery runs out of power.

MacBook batteries can be bought from the Apple website or from an Apple store..

Battery Troubleshooting

If you look after your MacBook battery well it should provide you with several years of mobile computing power. However, there are some problems that may occur with the battery:

- It won't keep its charge even when connected to an AC/DC adapter. The battery is probably flat and should be replaced with a new one. (Even if the battery is flat the MacBook will still operate using the AC/DC adapter)

- It only charges up a limited amount. Over time, MacBook batteries become less efficient and so do not hold their charge so well. One way to try and improve this is to drain the battery completely before it is charged again

- It keeps its charge but runs down quickly. This can be caused by using a lot of power-hungry applications on the MacBook. The more work the MacBook has to do to run applications, such as those involving videos or games, the more power will be required from the battery and the faster it will run down

- It is fully charged but does not appear to work at all when inserted. Check that the battery has clicked into place properly in the battery compartment and that the battery and MacBook terminals are clean and free from dust or moisture

- It is inserted correctly but still does not work. The battery may have become damaged in some way, such as becoming very wet. If you know the battery is damaged in any way, do not insert it, as it could short-circuit the MacBook. If the battery has been in contact with liquid, dry it out completely before you try inserting it into the MacBook. If it is thoroughly dry it may work again

- It gets very hot when in operation. This could be caused by a faulty battery and it can be dangerous and lead to a fire. If in doubt, turn off the MacBook immediately and consult Apple. In some cases, faulty batteries can be recalled, so keep an eye on the Apple website to see if there are any details of this if you are concerned. Even in normal operation, MacBook batteries can feel quite warm. Get to know the normal temperature of your battery, so you can judge whether it is getting too hot or not

Don't forget

If there is no response from your MacBook when you turn it on in battery mode, try removing the battery and re-inserting it. If there is still no response, the battery is probably flat and should be replaced.

Hot tip

If you are not going to be using your MacBook for an extended period of time, remove the battery and store it in a safe, dry, cool place.

50

4 Introducing OS X

Snow Leopard is the latest
operating system from
Apple and is pre-installed
on MacBooks. It is secure,
fast and fun to use. This
chapter introduces the OS X
interface and shows how to
get started with it.

About OS X

In 1984 Apple Computers introduced a new operating system (OS) for its Macintosh computers and, at the time, it was revolutionary. Instead of having to access programs and files through lines of lengthy computer code commands, users could navigate their way through Apple computers using a new Graphical User Interface (GUI). This produced the same results as the previous method, but it was much easier for the user: instead of having to type in lines of computer coding it was possible to access files and programs by clicking on buttons, icons and drop down menus. This ease of use was a major factor in the mass adoption of personal computers and this type of operating system soon began to appear on all personal computers, not just Macs.

Over the years Apple has refined its OS and added more and more functions with each new release. However, like any operating system the Mac OS was not without its problems: it was as prone to crashes as any other operating system and it had its own quirky idiosyncrasies, such as extension conflicts (when two programs refused to cohabit on the same machine).

When Apple decided to upgrade their OS from version 9 they were faced with two choices: add more code to what was becoming an incredibly complicated structure for the Apple programmers to work with, or, create an entirely new program from scratch. Thankfully, they chose the second option, and the result is OS X (pronounced "ten").

In some ways OS X is a contradiction of Apple's original philosophy: while it retains and enhances its traditional ease of use, it is also based on the UNIX programming language, the very type of thing that Apple was trying to get away from in 1984. The reason it is based on UNIX is that this is a very stable operating environment and it ensures that OS X is one of the most stable consumer operating systems that has ever been designed. However, most users can be blissfully unaware of the very existence of UNIX if they want and just enjoy its benefits, while using the new Aqua interface of OS X and all of the advantages that this brings. For the programming expert, there is also an option for delving into UNIX itself and getting to grips with this side of the program. Snow Leopard is the sixth version of OS X and is one of the most advanced operating system seen to date.

Don't forget

UNIX is an operating system that has traditionally been used for large commercial mainframe computers. It is renowned for its stability and ability to be used within different computing environments.

Installing OS X

The first step in installing OS X is to insert the CD-ROM into the CD drive. The disk should run automatically and the installation can then proceed as follows:

1 Double-click on the Install Mac OS X icon to begin the installation process

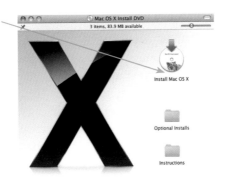

2 Click on the Continue button to access the installation wizard

Don't forget

Make sure you read any documentation before you install OS X. These documents, which are usually in PDF format, can contain useful general information and also any late news about the program that was released after it was produced.

3 Click on the Install button to complete the installation

About Snow Leopard

In the world of operating systems Snow Leopard is something of a novelty: the majority of its improvements and enhancements over earlier version are in its performance rather than new features or functionality. Some of the programs have been improved but, again, these improvements are largely to do with speed of performance. Some of the improvements in Snow Leopard are:

Smaller and faster
Snow Leopard has a much smaller footprint than any of its predecessors: it uses up to 50% less hard disk space, which can equate to GB on your Mac. Also, the installation of Snow Leopard can be up to 50% faster, which is a significant increase on previous versions, which could take several hours to install. Continuing this theme, Snow Leopard is also faster at waking up and shutting down. This can be particularly useful for MacBook users, as it can be up to 80% faster to wake up or shut down when on the move.

Technology
For those who are concerned about the technology behind their computers, Snow Leopard delivers by providing the transition from 32-bit technology to 64-bit technology. This is the next development in computing technology that enables computers to run faster and for programs to improve their performance. This also enables Snow Leopard to be fully prepared for future computing developments and it allows for more security measures to be built-in. Within Snow Leopard, programs such as Finder, Mail, Safari, iCal and iChat have been rewritten with 64-bit technology. This does not change their functionality but it makes them run faster and more efficiently.

Program refinements
Although improvements are not necessarily immediately visible in Snow Leopard there are a number of improvements behind the scenes. One of these is the speed at which the backup feature, Time Machine, works. It is now up to 80% faster than the previous version and it is also quicker at creating the initial backup, thus freeing up more time for general computing.

Microsoft Exchange

For users of Microsoft Exchange in a working environment Snow Leopard provides built-in support. This means that users can use the Mail, Address Book and iCal (calendar) programs with the latest version of Microsoft Exchange Server. To do this, you can use the Exchange Autodiscovery feature, on the Exchange Server, and then enter your Exchange details in the Mail, Accounts section. This may require obtaining the relevant details from your IT department and then entering them in Mail.

Finder

The Finder function in Snow Leopard is one of the most crucial ones, as this is where you can access all of the applications, documents, pictures, videos, music and connected devices. In Snow Leopard this has been simplified so that each element is clearly labelled so you can access each element as quickly and efficiently as possible.

The OS X Environment

The first most noticeable element about OS X is its elegant user interface. This has been designed to create a user friendly graphic overlay to the UNIX operating system at the heart of OS X and it is a combination of rich colors and sharp, original graphics. The main elements that make up the initial OS X environment are:

Apple menu   Menu bar   Windows   Disk icons

Don't forget

The disk icons sit on the desktop and identify which disks are connected to the computer. This includes the Mac hard drive and any external devices that are connected, such as a CD/DVD drive.

The Dock   Desktop

The Apple menu is standardized throughout OS X, regardless of the program in use

Don't forget

The Dock is designed to help make organizing and opening items as quick and easy as possible. For a detailed look at the Dock, see Chapter Five.

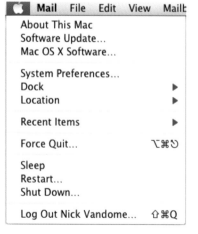

Aqua Interface

The name given by Apple to its OS X interface is Aqua. This describes the graphical appearance of the operating system. Essentially, it is just the cosmetic appearance of the elements within the operating system, but they combine to give OS X a rich visual look and feel. Some of the main elements of the Aqua interface are:

Menus

Menus in OS X contain commands for the operating system and any relevant programs. If there is an arrow next to a command it means there are subsequent options for the item:

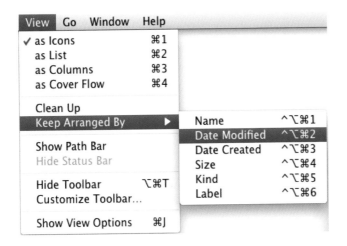

Window buttons

These appear in any open OS X window and can be used to manipulate the window.

Option buttons

Whenever a dialog box with separate options is accessed, OS X highlights the suggested option with a pulsing blue button. This can be accepted by clicking on it or by pressing Enter. If you do not want to accept this option, click on another button in the dialog box.

Don't forget

The graphics used in OS X are designed in a style known as Quartz. This design means that some elements, such as menus, allow the background behind them to show through.

Don't forget

The red window button is used to close a window, the amber one to minimize it, and the green one to expand it.

Changing the Background

Background imagery is an important way to add your own personal touch to your MacBook. (This is the graphical element upon which all other items on your computer sit.) There are a range of background options that can be used. To select your own background:

1 Click on this icon in the System Preferences folder

Desktop &
Screen Saver

2 Click on the Desktop tab

Desktop

3 Select a location from where you want to select a background

▼ Apple
  Apple Images
  Nature
  Plants
  Black & White
  Abstract
  Solid Colors
  Pictures Folder

4 Click on one of the available backgrounds

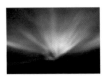
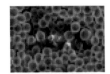

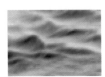

5 The background is applied as the desktop background imagery

Changing the Screen Saver

A screen saver is the element that appears when the MacBook has not been used for a specified period of time. Originally this was designed to avoid screen burn (caused by items being at the same position on the screen for an extended period of time) but now they largely consist of a graphical element. To select your own screen saver:

1 Click on this icon in the System Preferences folder

Desktop & Screen Saver

2 Click on the Screen Saver tab

Screen Saver

3 Select a location from where you want to select a screen saver

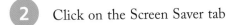

Screen Savers

🔄 Computer Name

🔄 Flurry

🔄 iTunes Artwork

🔄 RSS Visualizer

🔄 Shell

4 Click the Test button to preview the selected screen saver

Test

5 Drag this slider to specify the amount of time the Mac is inactive before the screen saver is activated

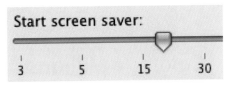

Start screen saver:

3   5   15   30

Changing the Resolution

For most computer users the size at which items are displayed on the screen is a crucial issue: if items are too small, this can make them hard to read and lead to eye strain; too large and you have to spend a lot of time scrolling around to see everything.

The size of items on the screen is controlled by the screen resolution, i.e. the number of colored dots displayed in an area of the screen. The higher the resolution the smaller the items on the screen, the lower the resolution the larger the items. To change the screen resolution:

 Don't forget

A higher resolution makes items appear sharper on the screen, even though they appear physically smaller.

1 Click on this icon in the System Preferences folder

Displays

2 Select a resolution setting to change the overall screen resolution

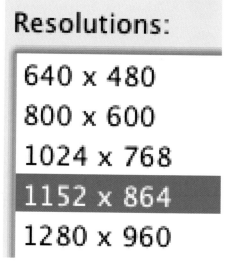

Resolutions:

640 x 480

800 x 600

1024 x 768

1152 x 864

1280 x 960

3 Click here to select the number of colors displayed on the screen (the higher the better)

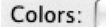 Colors: Millions

Universal Access

In all areas of computing it is important to give as many people access to the system as possible. This includes users with visual impairments and also people who have problems using the mouse and keyboard. In OS X this is achieved through the functions of the Universal Access System Preferences. To use these:

1 Click once here on the Dock to access the System Preferences

2 Click on the Universal Access button

Universal Access

3 Click on the Seeing tab for help with issues connected with visual impairment

Seeing

4 Check on the Zoom On button to enable zooming in on specific areas of the screen

Zoom:
⊙ On ○ Off

5 Check on the White on Black display button to invert the default settings for your system display

Display:
○ Black on White
⊙ White on Black

Don't forget

Experiment with the VoiceOver function (in the Seeing window), if only to see how it operates. This will give you a better idea of how visually impaired users access information on a computer.

...cont'd

6 Click on the Hearing tab to adjust settings for an audio problem

7 Click on this button to adjust the system volume

8 In the System Preferences click on the Mouse button

Mouse

9 Drag these sliders to change the speed at which the mouse moves and how quickly you have to press it to achieve a double-click operation

Don't forget

Under the Keyboard tab there are options for the time it takes for a keystroke to appear on the screen and how long before a keystroke is repeated if a key is held down for a few seconds.

5 Getting Up and Running

This chapter looks at some of the essential features of OS X. These include the Dock for organizing and accessing all of the elements of the computer, the system preferences for the way the computer looks and operates and items for arranging folders and files.

Introducing the Dock

The Dock is one of the main innovative elements of OS X. Its main function is to help organize and access programs, folders and files. In addition, with its rich translucent colors and elegant graphical icons, it also makes an aesthetically pleasing addition to the desktop. The main things to remember about the Dock are:

- It is divided into two: programs go on the left of the dividing line; all other items go on the right

- It can be edited in just about any way you choose

By default the Dock appears at the bottom of the screen

Programs go here   Dividing line   Open items

Setting Dock Preferences

As with most elements of OS X, the Dock can be modified in numerous ways. This can affect both the appearance of the Dock and the way it operates. To set Dock preferences:

1 Select Apple Menu>Dock from the Menu bar

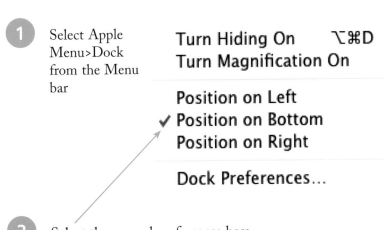

| Turn Hiding On | ⌥⌘D |
| Turn Magnification On | |

Position on Left
✓ Position on Bottom
Position on Right

Dock Preferences...

2 Select the general preferences here

Dock Preferences...

3 Click here to access more Dock preferences (below)

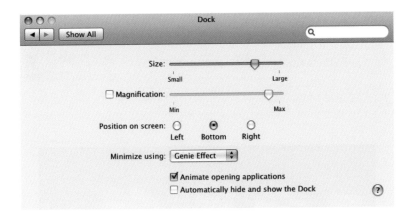

Hot tip

The Apple Menu is constantly available in OS X, regardless of the program you are working in. The menu options are also constant in all applications.

Beware

You will not be able to make the Dock size too large preventing some of the icons from not being visible on the desktop. By default, the Dock is resized so that everything is always visible.

...cont'd

The Dock Preferences allow you to change its size, orientation, the way icons appear and effects for when items are minimized:

The "Position on screen" options enable you to place the Dock on the left, right or bottom of the screen

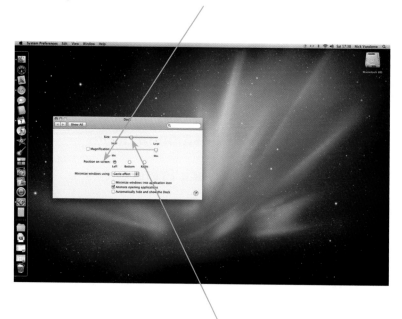

Drag the Dock Size slider to increase or decrease the size of the Dock

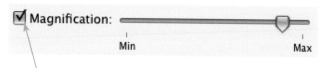

Check on the Magnification box and drag the slider to determine the size icons are enlarged to when the cursor is moved over them

The effects that are applied to items when they are minimized are one of the features of OS X (it is not absolutely necessary, but it sums up the Apple ethos of trying to enhance the user experience as much as possible).

The Genie effect shrinks the item to be minimized, like a genie going back into its lamp

Manual resizing

In addition to changing the size of the Dock by using the Dock Preference dialog box, it can also be resized manually:

Drag vertically on the Dock dividing line to increase or decrease its size

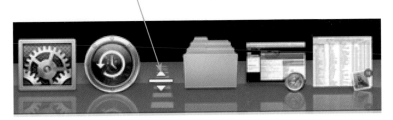

Stacks on the Dock

Stacking items

To save space on the Dock, it is possible to add folders to the Dock, where their contents can be accessed. This is known as Stacks. By default, Stacks for documents and downloaded files are created on the Dock. To use Stacks:

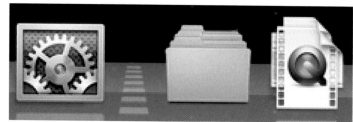

1 Stacked items are placed at the right-hand side of the Dock dividing line

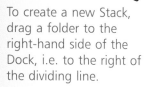

Hot tip

To create a new Stack, drag a folder to the right-hand side of the Dock, i.e. to the right of the dividing line.

2 Click on a Stack to view its contents

3 Stacks can be viewed as a fan, or

4 As a grid

5 Click on an item within a Stack to open it

6 To create a new Stack, drag a folder onto the Dock. Any new items that are added to the folder will also be visible through the Stack

Hot tip

The appearance of a stack can be toggled between fan or grid by Ctrl+clicking on the stack and selecting an option from the menu.

Dock Menus

One of the features of the Dock is that it can display contextual menus for selected items. This means that it shows menus with options that are applicable to the item that is being accessed. This can only be done when an item has been opened.

 Click and hold here to display an item's individual menu

2 Click on Show in Finder to see where the item is located on your computer

Working with Dock Items

Adding items

As many items as you like can be added to the Dock; the only restriction is the size of monitor used to display all of the Dock items (the size of the Dock can be reduced to accommodate more icons, but you have to be careful that all of the icons are still legible). To add items to the Dock:

Locate the required item and drag it onto the Dock. All of the other icons move along to make space for the new one

Don't forget

Icons on the Dock are shortcuts to the related item, rather than the item itself, which remains in its original location.

Keep in Dock

Every time you open a new program, its icon will appear in the Dock for the duration the program is open, even if it has not previously been put in the Dock. If you then decide that you would like to keep it in the Dock, you can do so as follows:

Beware

You can add as many items as you like to the Dock, it will automatically shrink to display all of its items if it becomes too big for the available space.

1 Click and hold on the icon underneath an open program

2 Click on Keep In Dock, to ensure the program remains in the Dock when it is closed

Removing items

Any item, except the Finder, can be removed from the Dock. However, this does not remove it from your computer, it just removes the shortcut for accessing it. You will still be able to locate it in its folder on your hard drive and, if required, drag it back onto the Dock. To remove items from the Dock:

Drag it away from the Dock and release. The item disappears in a satisfying puff of smoke, to indicate that it has been removed. All of the other icons then move up to fill in the space

Removing open programs

You can remove a program from the Dock, even if it is open and running. To do this:

1 Drag a program off the Dock while it is running. Initially the icon will remain on the Dock because the program is still open

2 When the program is closed its icon will be removed from the Dock (unless Keep in Dock has been selected from the item's Dock menu)

Trash

The Trash folder is a location for placing items that you do not want to use anymore. However, when items are placed in the Trash, they are not removed from your computer. This requires another command, as the Trash is really a holding area before you decide you want to remove items permanently. The Trash can also be used for ejecting removable disks attached to your MacBook.

Sending items to the Trash

Items can be sent to the Trash by dragging them from the location in which they are stored:

① Drag an item over the Trash icon to place it in the Trash folder

② Click once on the Trash icon on the Dock to view its contents

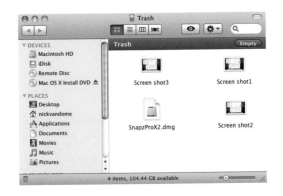

Don't forget

Items can also be sent to the Trash by selecting them and then selecting File>Move to Trash, from the Menu bar.

Don't forget

All of the items within the Trash can be removed in a single command: Select Finder>Empty Trash from the Menu bar to remove all of the items in the Trash folder.

Useful Applications

Within OS X Snow Leopard there are a number of useful applications that can be used to perform everyday tasks. These are located within the Applications folder within the Finder, but they can also be accessed directly from the Dock by clicking on their relevant icons. The most commonly used applications available from the Dock are:

- Safari. This is the default OS X web browser

- Mail. This is the OS X email program. It can be used with an email service provided through your Internet Service Provider (ISP) or with the online MobileMe service. This provides an online email account that can also be used directly on your MacBook

- Address Book. This can be used to store all of your contact information. It can include items like people's names, addresses, phone numbers and email addresses. Groups of contacts can also be created within Address Book, e.g. for work or social groups

- iCal. This is a calendar function that can be used to store important dates, events, birthdays, etc. Different types of events can be specified by a specific color and there is also a To Do list for personal reminders

- Dashboard. This is a collection of widgets that can be added to perform a multitude of tasks. There is a default set that comes with OS X, but more can be added through Dashboard, via the Apple website at www.apple.com/

- iChat. This is the text/video messaging program that enables MobileMe users (and subscribers to other messaging services such as AOL) to chat in real-time using text or video messaging

- Preview. This program can be used to view a variety of different file formats such as jpgs for images or pdf documents. If no other programs have been specified for opening these types of file formats, Preview will act as the default

- iTunes. The iLife suite of programs is one that contains programs to make managing your digital lifestyle as easy and enjoyable as possible. It covers music, photographs, video, creating music and creating web galleries. The most well known program is iTunes, which can be used to download music from CDs, buy music from the iTunes store and add music to an iPod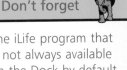

Don't forget

The iLife program that is not always available on the Dock by default is iWeb. This can be used for creating photo galleries for the Web that can be viewed through the MobileMe online service (for more details on this, see Chapter Ten).

- iPhoto. This is the iLife program for downloading, storing, editing and sharing photos. It is not the most powerful image editing program on the market but it is excellent for storing and viewing images

- iMovie. This is the iLife program for downloading your own video footage and then creating and editing home movies

- GarageBand. This is the iLife program for creating your own music. There are pre-recorded samples that can be used as the basis for a track and also input devices so that you can play your own tunes and have them recorded by GarageBand

Desktop Items

If required, the Desktop can be used to store programs and files. However, the Finder (see Chapter Six) does such a good job of organizing all of the elements within your computer, the Desktop is rendered largely redundant, unless you feel happier storing items here. The Desktop also displays any removable disks connected to your computer.

Hot tip

Icons for removable disks, i.e. pen drives, CDs or DVDs, will only become visible on the Desktop once a disk has been inserted into the appropriate drive.

By default, the Desktop displays the Macintosh HD icon

If a removable disk is connected to your computer, double-click the Desktop icon to view its contents

Don't forget

Any removable disks connected to your computer can also be viewed by clicking on them in the Sidebar in the Finder.

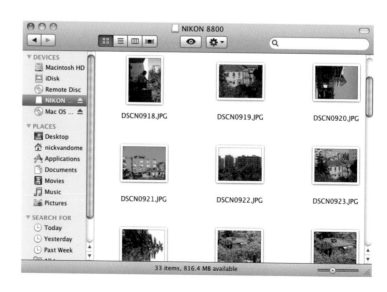

Ejecting Items

If you have removable disks attached to your MacBook it is essential to be able to eject them quickly and easily. In OS X there are two ways this can be done:

1 In the Finder, click on the icon to the right of the name of the removable disk

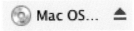

2 On the Desktop, drag the disk icon over the Trash. This turns the Trash icon into the Eject icon and the disk will be ejected

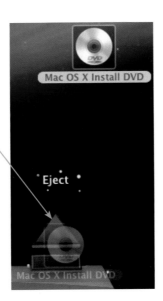

3 Some disks, such as CDs and DVDs, are physically ejected when either of these two action are performed. Other disks, such as pen drives, have to be removed manually once they have been ejected by OS X. If the disk is not ejected first the following warning message will appear:

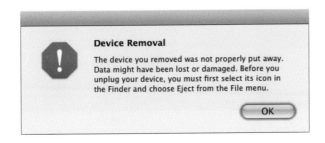

Spaces

A new way for organizing and viewing items with OS X is the Spaces feature. This enables you to specify certain areas of the screen that will contain specific content items. For instance, you can specify a space for Web content and another for photo editing programs. To use Spaces:

1 Click on the System Preferences icon on the Dock

2 In the System Preferences folder, click on the Exposé & Spaces icon

Exposé & Spaces

3 Click on the Spaces tab

4 Check on the Enable Spaces box

5 Check on this box to view the Spaces icon in the Finder Menu bar

☑ Show Spaces in menu bar

6 Select the number of rows and columns you want to be displayed by Spaces

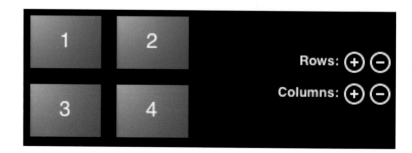

7 In the Application Assignments window, click on the Plus button

8 Select a program to be included in that assigned Space

9 Select the way you want to activate Spaces

10 Click on the assigned activation key to view the items in your Spaces

Don't forget

When you click on an area within Spaces, that content is then displayed full screen.

Organizing with Exposé

A similar organizational feature to Spaces is known as Exposé. This can quickly let you see what you have open on your desktop, or hide everything from view. To use Exposé:

1 Click on the System Preferences icon on the Dock

2 In the System Preferences folder, click on the Exposé & Spaces icon

Exposé & Spaces

3 Click on the Exposé tab

Exposé

4 Using Exposé, the four corners of the screen can be set to perform certain actions, such as showing the Desktop or all open windows. Select the functions in the top section of the Exposé window

Don't forget

Select the - sign if you do not want any action performed when you move the cursor over a specific corner.

5 Click on the arrows next to an item and select the action that is performed when the selected screen corner is activated

All Windows
Application Windows
✓ Desktop
Dashboard

Spaces

Start Screen Saver
Disable Screen Saver

Put Display to Sleep

-

... cont'd

6 Move the cursor into a corner for the specified action to be performed. In the example below, moving the cursor to the right screen corner displays all open windows. Click on one to make it the active window

Hot tip

Pass the cursor over an item that has been revealed by Exposé to see its name.

7 Below the screen corners option, select actions for the F keys (hold down the Fn key for this)

All windows:	F9
Application windows:	F10
Show Desktop:	F11

Hot tip

Click once on any window to activate it and return it to its original size.

8 Click on the arrows next to an item to select a different key or action

...cont'd

9 The final section of the Exposé window covers accessing the Dashboard. This is a collection of widgets that can be used for numerous functions such as a dictionary, calendar, checking airline times, weather forecasts and many, many more. By default the Dashboard is accessed using the F12 key, but this can be amended within the Exposé window. Click on the "Hide and show" box to select a different key for accessing the Dashboard widgets

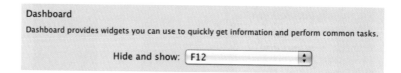

Dashboard

Dashboard provides widgets you can use to quickly get information and perform common tasks.

Hide and show: F12

10 When they are accessed, the Dashboard widgets appear above the Desktop. Click on one to access its function

6 Finder

The principal program for moving around OS X is the Finder. This enables you to access items and organize your programs, folders and files as efficiently as possible. This chapter looks at how to use the Finder and how to get the most out of this powerful tool at the heart of navigating around OS X. It covers accessing items through the Finder, how to customize the interface and numerous options for working with folders in OS X.

Working with the Finder

If you were only able to use one item on the Dock it would be the Finder. This is the gateway to all of the elements of your computer. It is possible to get to selected items through other routes, but the Finder is the only location where you can gain access to everything on your system. If you ever feel that you are getting lost within OS X, click on the Finder and you should then begin to feel more at home. To access the Finder:

Don't forget

The Finder is always open (as denoted by the graphic underneath its icon on the Dock) and it cannot readily be closed down or removed.

Click once on this icon on the Dock

Overview

The Finder has its own toolbar, a Sidebar from which items can be accessed and a main window where the contents of selected items can be viewed:

Don't forget

The Action button has options for displaying information about a selected item and also options for how it is displayed with the Finder.

Forward and back   View options   Action box   Search

Static and removable volumes

Folders are displayed here

Sidebar

Main windows

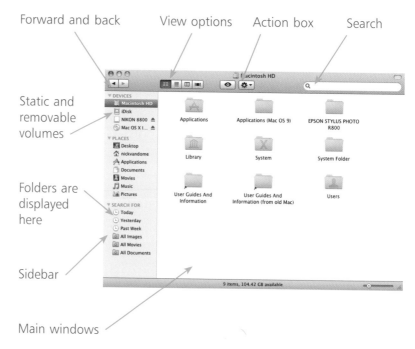

Finder Folders

Home

This contains the contents of your own home directory, containing your personal folders and files. OS X inserts some pre-named folders it thinks will be useful, but it is possible to rename, rearrange or delete these as you please. It is also possible to add as many folders as you want.

1 Click on this link in the Finder Sidebar to access the contents of your Home folder

2 The Home folder contains the Public folder that can be used to share files with other users if the computer is part of a network

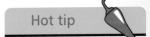

Hot tip

Your Home folder is a good one to add to the Dock, so that all of your own programs, folders and files are accessible with a single click.

Hot tip

When you are creating documents OS X, by default, recognizes their type and then, when you save them, suggests the most applicable folder in your Home directory to save them in. So, if you have created a word processed document, OS X will suggest that you save it in Documents, if it is a photograph it will suggest Pictures, if it is a video it will suggest Movies, and so on.

...cont'd

Applications

This folder contains some of the programs on your computer. However, by default, it is only the programs that come installed with OS X, not every program on your system. If you had programs that you used under a previous Mac operating system, these will be contained within the Applications (Mac OS 9) folder, which can be accessed directly from your hard drive in the Finder. However, it is possible to add any of these programs to your Applications folder by opening the Applications (Mac OS 9) folder and then dragging items into the Applications folder.

Hot tip

The Applications folder is another one that is worth adding to the Dock for easy access.

1 Click on this link in the Finder Sidebar to access the contents of your Applications folder

2 Double-click on an application icon to open the relevant program. This will open in its own new window

Finder Views

The way in which items are displayed within the Finder can be amended in a variety of ways, depending on how you want to view the contents of a folder. Different folders can have their own viewing options applied to them and these will stay in place until a new option is specified.

Back button

When working within the Finder each new window replaces the previous one, unless you open a new program. This prevents the screen from becoming cluttered with dozens of open windows, as you look through various Finder windows for a particular item. To ensure that you never feel lost within the Finder structure, there is a Back button on the Finder toolbar that enables you to retrace the steps that you have taken.

1 Navigate to a folder within the Finder (in this case the "For printing" folder contained within Pictures)

2 Click on the Back button to move back to the previously visited window (in this case, the main Pictures window)

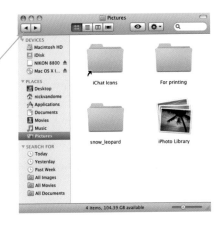

...cont'd

Icon view

One of the viewing options for displaying items within the Finder is as icons. This provides a graphical representation of the items in the Finder. It is possible to customize the way that Icon view looks and functions:

The Arrange By options can be used to arrange icons into specific groups, e.g. by name or type, or to snap them to an invisible grid so that they have an ordered appearance.

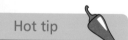

1 Click here on the Finder toolbar to access Icon view

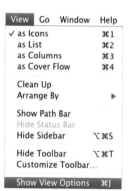

2 Select View from the Menu bar, check on "as Icons" and select "Show View Options" to access the options for customizing Icon view

A very large icon size can be useful for people with poor eyesight, but it does take up a lot more space in a window.

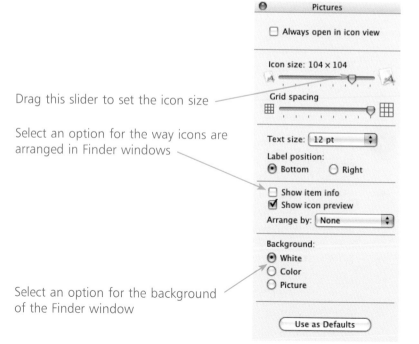

Drag this slider to set the icon size

Select an option for the way icons are arranged in Finder windows

Select an option for the background of the Finder window

List view

List view can be used to show the items within a Finder window as a list, with additional information shown next to them. This can be a more efficient method than icon view if there are a lot of items within a folder: List view enables you to see more items at one time and also view the additional information.

1 Click here on the Finder toolbar to access List view

2 The name of each folder or file is displayed here. If any item has additional elements within it, this is represented by a small triangle next to them. Additional information in List view, such as file size and last modified date, is included in columns to the right

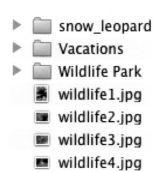

Column view

Column view is a useful option if you want to trace the location of a particular item, i.e. see the full path of its location, starting from the hard drive.

1 Click here on the Finder toolbar to access Column view

2 Click on an item to see everything within that folder. If an arrow follows an item it means that there are further items to view

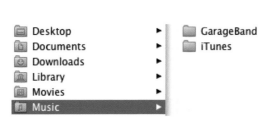

Covers

Covers is another innovative feature on the MacBook that enables you to view the contents of a folder without having to open the folder itself. Additionally, each item is displayed as a large icon, this enables you to see what a particular item contains, such as images. To use Covers:

1 Select a folder and at the top of the Finder window click on this button

2 The items within the folder are displayed in their cover state

3 Drag on each item with the mouse to view the next one, or click on the slider at the bottom of the window

Quick Look

Through a Finder option called Quick Look, it is possible to view the content of a file without having to open it first. To do this:

1 Select a file within the Finder

- hwp12.jpg
- hwp13.jpg
- hwp14.jpg
- hwp16.jpg
- hwp17.jpg

2 Press the space bar

3 The contents of the file are displayed without it opening in its default program

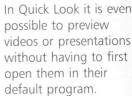
4 Click on the cross to close Quick Look

Finder Toolbar

Customizing the toolbar

As with most elements of OS X, it is possible to customize the Finder toolbar:

Beware

Do not put too many items on the Finder toolbar, because you may not be able to see them all in the Finder window. If there are additional toolbar items, there will be a directional arrow indicating this. Click on the arrow to view the available items.

1 Select View>Customize Toolbar from the Menu bar

2 Drag items from the window into the toolbar, or:

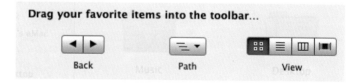

3 Drag the default set of icons into the toolbar

4 Click Done at the bottom of the window

Finder Sidebar

Using the Sidebar

The Sidebar is the left-hand panel of the Finder, which can be used to access items on your MacBook:

1 Click on an item on the Sidebar

2 Its contents are displayed in the main Finder window

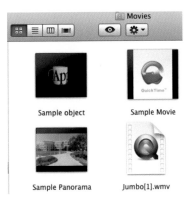

Sample object Sample Movie

Sample Panorama Jumbo[1].wmv

Adding to the Sidebar

Items that you access most frequently can be added to the Sidebar. To do this:

1 Drag an item from the main Finder window onto the Sidebar

Library

Downloads

2 The item is added to the Sidebar. You can do this with programs, folders and files

Finder Search

Searching electronic data is now a massive industry, with companies like Google leading the way in online searching. On MacBooks it is also possible to search your folders and files, using the built-in search facilities. This can be done either through the Finder or with the Spotlight program.

Using Finder

To search for items within the Finder:

Don't forget

Try and make your search keywords and phrases as accurate as possible. This will create a better list of search results.

1 In the Finder window, enter the search keyword(s) in this box

2 The results are shown in the Finder window

3 Select the areas where you want the search performed

Don't forget

Both folders and files will be displayed in the Finder as part of the search results.

4 Double-click on a folder to see its contents

5 Double-click on a file to open it

6 Click once on an item to view its file path on your computer (i.e. where it is actually located)

Creating Aliases

Aliases are shortcuts to the actual version of items. This can include programs, folders and files. Aliases take up virtually no disk space and numerous aliases can be created for a single item and then placed in various locations for ease of access. To create an alias:

1   Select an item in any open window, by clicking on it once

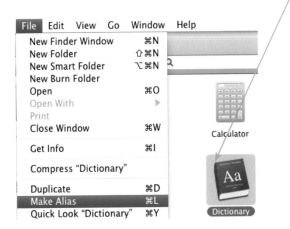

2   Select File>Make Alias from the Menu bar

3   Once an alias has been created, it can then be moved to any location (in this case the Desktop)

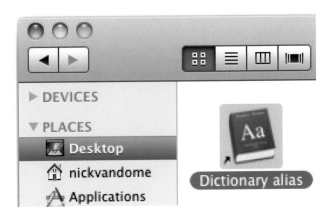

Copying and Moving Items

Items can be copied and moved within OS X by using the copy and paste method or by dragging:

Copy and paste

1 Select an item and select Edit>Copy from the Menu bar

2 Move to the target location and select Edit>Paste Item from the Menu bar. The item is then pasted into the new location

Dragging
Drag a file from one location into another to move it to that location

Working with Windows

OS X has a much better method of managing open windows than any of the previous Apple operating systems. Whenever a new item is accessed from within the Finder, it replaces the existing window, rather than opening a new one. This means that the screen does not become cluttered with a lot of open windows. The exception to this is programs, which always open in their own, new window.

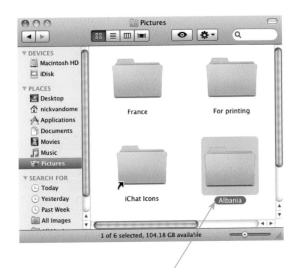

Don't forget

Use the Back button to move back to the most recently accessed window.

From within the Finder, if you select a new item (except a program) it replaces the existing item, rather than opening in a new window

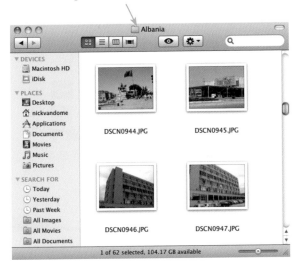

...cont'd

When you are working with a lot of open windows, it can sometimes be confusing which is the active window and how you can then quickly switch to other windows.

1 The active window always sits on the top of any other open window. There can only be one active window at any one time

2 Click on any window behind the currently active one, to bring it to the front and make it active

3 At the top left of any active window, click on the red button to close it, the amber button to minimize it and the green button to enlarge it

Working with Folders

When OS X is first installed, there are various folders that have already been created to hold programs and files. Some of these are essential (i.e. those containing programs) while others are created as an aid for where you might want to store the files that you create (such as the Pictures and Movies folders). Once you start working with OS X, you will probably want to create your own folders, to store and organize your documents in. This can be done on the desktop or within any level of your existing folder structure. To create a new folder:

1 Access the location where you want to create the new folder (i.e. your Home folder) and select File>New Folder from the Menu bar

2 A new, empty folder is inserted at the selected location (named "untitled folder")

Desktop

untitled folder

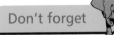
Don't forget

Folders are always denoted by a folder icon. This is the same regardless of the Finder view selected. The only difference is that the icon is larger in Icon view than in List or Column views.

99

...cont'd

3 Overtype the file name with a new one. Press Enter

Snow Leopard

Snow Leopard

4 Double-click on a folder to view its contents (it should be empty at this point)

Smart Folders

When working on any computer it is inevitable that you will soon have a number of related files in different locations. This could be because you save your images in one folder, your word processing documents in another, web pages in another and so on. This can cause difficulties when you are trying to keep track of a lot of related documents. OS X overcomes this problem through the use of Smart Folders. These are folders that you set up using Finder search results as the foundation. Then when new items are created that meet the original criteria they are automatically included within the Smart Folder. To create a Smart Folder:

Hot tip

Numerous different Smart Folders can be created, for different types of files and information.

1 Conduct a search with the Finder search box

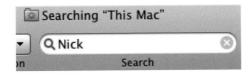

2 Once the search is completed, click the Save button to create a Smart Folder

Save

3 Enter a name for the new Smart Folder and click Save

Specify a name and location for your Smart Folder

Save As: Nick

Where: Saved Searches

☑ Add To Sidebar

Cancel   Save

4 The Smart Folder is added to the Finder Sidebar. Click the Smart Folder to view its contents

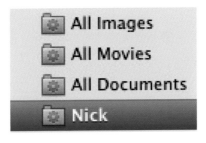

All Images

All Movies

All Documents

Nick

...cont'd

5 Create a new item that matches some, or all, of the original search criteria

6 The new item is automatically included within the Smart Folder

Don't forget

If you set a very precise criteria for a Smart Folder this will result in a fewer number of items being included within it.

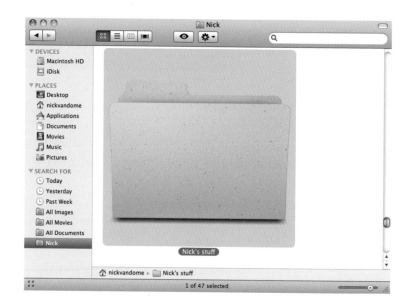

7 Click on an item to view its full path

Spring-loaded Folders

Another method for moving items with the Finder is to use the spring-loaded folder option. This enables you to drag items into a folder and then view the contents of the folder before you drop the item into it. This means that you can drag items into nested folders in a single operation. To do this:

1 Select the item you want to move

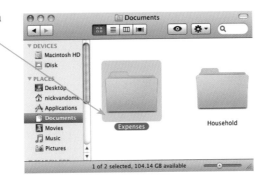

2 Drag the selected item over the folder you want to place it in. Keep the mouse held down

3 The folder will open, revealing its contents. The selected item can either be dropped into the folder or, if there are sub-folders, the same operation can be repeated until you find the folder where you want to place the selected item

Burnable Folders

With the increasing use of images, digital video and music files, computer users are frequently copying data from their computers onto CDs. In some cases this can be a frustrating process but in OS X the use of burnable folders can make the process much quicker. These are folders that can be created specifically for the contents to be burned onto a CD or DVD. To do this:

1 In the Finder, select File>New Burn Folder from the Menu bar

Burn Folder

104

2 The burn folder is created in the Finder window, which was active when Step 1 was performed. Click on the folder name and overtype to give it a unique name

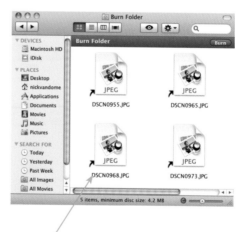

3 Select the items that you want to burn and drag and drop, or copy and paste them into the burn folder

4 Click here to burn the disk

Selecting Items

Programs and files within OS X folders can be selected by a variety of different methods:

Selecting by dragging

Drag the cursor to encompass the items to be selected. The selected items will become highlighted.

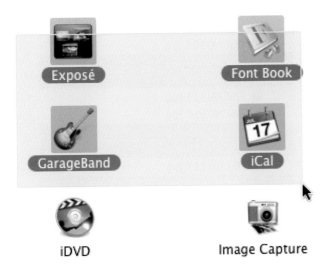

Selecting by clicking

Click once on an item to select it, hold down Shift and then click on another item in a list to select a consecutive group of items.

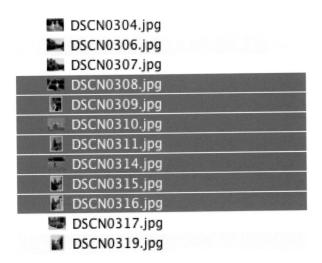

Don't forget

Once items have been selected, a single command can be applied to all of them. For instance, you can copy a group of items by selecting them and then applying the Copy command from the Menu bar.

...cont'd

To select a non-consecutive group, select the first item by clicking on it once, then hold down the Command key (the one with the Apple symbol on it) and select the other required items. The selected items will appear highlighted.

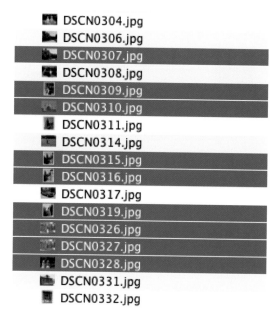

Don't forget

The Select All command selects all of the elements within the active item. For instance, if the active item is a word processing document, the Select All command will select all of the items within that document; if it is a folder it will select all the items within that folder.

Select All

To select all of the items in a folder, select Edit>Select All from the Menu bar:

Labeling Items

With the Finder it is possible to label items (including files, folders and programs) so that they can be easily identified for specific purposes. This could be items created on a certain date or to quickly identify a particular type of document. To do this:

1 Select an item, or group of items, to which you want to apply labels

Labels are visible regardless of the View option selected in the Finder.

2 Click the Actions button and select a color for the label, or labels

File	Edit	View	Go	Window
New Finder Window				⌘N
New Folder				⇧⌘N
New Smart Folder				⌥⌘N
New Burn Folder				
Open in New Window				^⌘O
Open With				▶
Print				
Close Window				⌘W
Get Summary Info				^⌘I
Compress 2 Items				
Duplicate				⌘D
Make Alias				⌘L
Quick Look 2 Items				⌘Y
Show Original				⌘R
Add To Favorites				^⌘T
Move to Trash				⌘⌫
Eject				^⌘E
Burn 2 Items to Disc...				
Find				⌘F
Label:				

3 The colored labels are applied to the selected items. Other items can then have other label colors applied to them

Menus

The main Apple Menu bar in OS X contains a variety of menus, which are consistent regardless of the program in operation:

- Apple Menu. This is denoted by a translucent blue apple and contains general information about the computer, a preferences option for changing the functionality and appearance of the Dock and options for closing down the computer

- Finder menu. This contains preferences options for amending the functionality and appearance of the Finder and also options for emptying the Trash and accessing other programs (under the Services option)

- File menu. This contains common commands for working with open documents, such as opening and closing files, creating aliases, moving to the Trash, ejecting external devices and burning discs

- Edit menu. This contains common commands that apply to the majority of programs used on the Mac. These include undo, cut, copy, paste, select all and show the contents of the clipboard, i.e. items that have been cut or copied

- View. This contains options for how windows and folders are displayed within the Finder and for customizing the Finder toolbar

- Go. This can be used to navigate around your computer. This includes moving to your Home folder, your iDisk, your Applications folder, recently opened items and remote servers for connecting to other computers on a network

- Window. This contains commands to organize the currently open programs and files on your desktop

- Help. This contains the Mac Help files, which contain information about all aspects of OS X

7 Internet and Email

This chapter shows how to get the most out of the Internet and email. It covers connecting to the Internet and how to use the OS X Web browser, Safari, and its email program, Mail. It also covers text and video chatting, accessing your favorite websites and the use of RSS news feeds.

Getting Connected

Access to the Internet is an accepted part of the computing world and it is unusual for users not to want to do this. Not only does this provide a gateway to the World Wide Web but also email.

Connecting to the Internet with a MacBook is done through the System Preferences. To do this:

110

1 Click on the System Preferences icon on the Dock

2 Click on the Network icon

Network

3 Check that your method of connecting to the Internet is active, i.e. colored green

4 Click on the Assist me button to access wizards for connecting to the Internet with your preferred method of connection

Assist me...

5 Click on the Assistant button

Assistant...

6 The Network Setup Assistant is used to configure your system so you can connect to the Internet

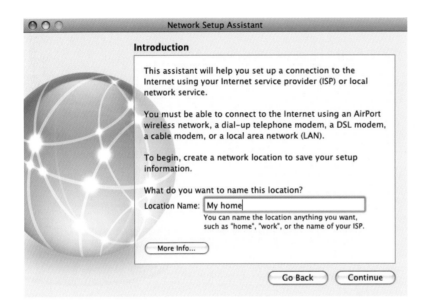

Network Setup Assistant

Introduction

This assistant will help you set up a connection to the Internet using your Internet service provider (ISP) or local network service.

You must be able to connect to the Internet using an AirPort wireless network, a dial-up telephone modem, a DSL modem, a cable modem, or a local area network (LAN).

To begin, create a network location to save your setup information.

What do you want to name this location?

Location Name: My home

You can name the location anything you want, such as "home", "work", or the name of your ISP.

More Info...

Go Back   Continue

7 Enter a name for your connection

Location Name: My home

8 Click on the Continue button

Continue

...cont'd

9 Select an option for
how you will connect
to the Internet, e.g.
wireless, cable or
telephone modem

10 Click on the Continue button

11 For a wireless connection, select an available wireless
network. This will be the router that is being used to
make the connection

12 Enter a password for the router (this will have been
created when you connected and configured the router)

Password: Selected network requires a password

••••••

More Info...

Go Back   Continue

13 Click on the Continue button

14 The Ready to Connect window informs you that you are about to attempt to connect to your network

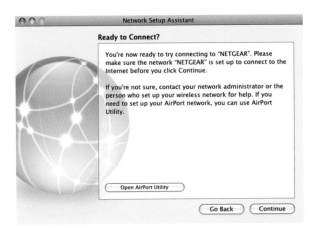

15 Click on the Continue button

16 You are informed if the connection has been successful

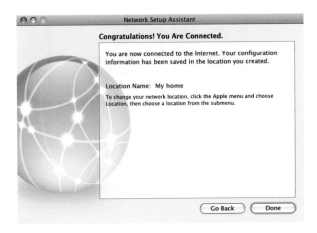

17 Click on the Done button

Safari

Safari is a Web browser that is specifically designed to be used with OS X. It is similar in most respects to other browsers, but it usually functions more quickly and works seamlessly with OS X.

Safari overview

1 Click here on the Dock to launch Safari

Hot tip

If the Address Bar is not visible, select View from the Menu bar and check on the Address Bar option. From this menu you can also select or deselect items like the Back/Forward buttons and the Stop/Reload buttons.

Back and forward   Address bar   Refresh   Search

Bookmarks bar

Page content

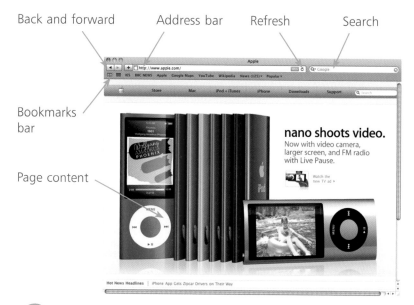

nano shoots video.
Now with video camera, larger screen, and FM radio with Live Pause.

2 Select Safari>Preferences from the Menu bar to specify settings for the way Safari operates and displays Web pages

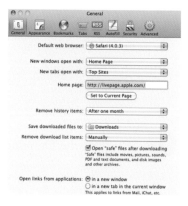

Adding bookmarks

Bookmarks are a device by which you can create quick links to your favorite Web pages or the ones you visit most frequently. Bookmarks can be added to a menu or the Bookmarks bar in Safari, which makes them even quicker to access. Folders can also be created to store the less frequently used bookmarks. To view and create bookmarks:

1 Click here to view all bookmarks

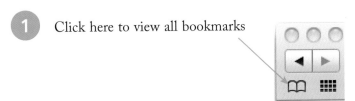

2 All of the saved bookmarks are displayed in the Bookmarks window

115

3 Click here to create a bookmark for the page currently being viewed

4 Enter a name for the bookmark and select a location to store it at

5 Click on the Add button

Type a name for the bookmark, and choose where to keep it.

Apple

Bookmarks Bar

Cancel   Add

Safari Top Sites

Within Safari there is a facility to view a graphical representation of the websites that you visit most frequently. This can be done from a button on the Safari Menu bar. To do this:

1 Click on this button to view the Top Sites window

2 The Top Sites window contains thumbnails of the websites that you have visited most frequently with Safari

3 Click on the Edit button to change the properties of the Top Sites thumbnails

4 Click on the cross to delete a thumbnail from the Top Sites window. Click on the pin to keep it there permanently

5 Click on a thumbnail to go to the full site

6 To add a new site to the Top Sites, open another window and drag the URL (website address) into the Top Sites

Safari RSS

RSS, which stands for Really Simple Syndication, is a method of producing regularly updated information on websites. It works by using XML (Extensible Markup Language) and is most frequently seen on news websites: the RSS feed displays the latest news. In order for a RSS feed to be viewed, the browser has to support the RSS technology. Safari does this and, when it comes across a website with RSS, this icon is displayed in the Safari address bar:

Once an RSS enabled site has been located the news feeds can be accessed by clicking on the RSS icon.

RSS preferences

The way that RSS feeds are dealt with can be set within the Safari preferences by selecting Safari>Preferences from the Menu bar:

Don't forget

RSS is becoming increasingly popular and more and more websites are now using it for areas like news.

118

1 Click here to access RSS settings

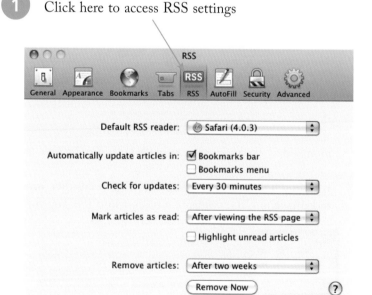

2 Specific settings can be made in the RSS window

Mail

Email is an essential element for most computer users. MacBooks come with their own email program called Mail. This covers all of the email functionality that anyone could need.

When first using Mail you have to set up your email account. This information will be available from the company who provides your email service, although in some cases Mail may obtain this information automatically. To view your Mail account details:

Don't forget

If you have an online email account with the MobileMe service, this will appear in your Mail accounts too. You can use this to download email directly from your MobileMe account, without having to logon first. See Chapter Ten for details.

1 Click on this icon on the Dock

2 Select Mail>Preferences from the Menu bar

119

3 Click on the Accounts tab

Don't forget

If you are setting up a new email account, you will need to get the details to enter from your Internet Service Provider (ISP).

4 If it has not already been included, enter the details of your email account in the Account Information section

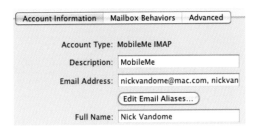

5 Click on this button to close the Mail Preferences window

Adding Mailboxes

Before you start creating email messages it is a good idea to create a folder structure (mailboxes) for your emails. This will allow you to sort your emails into relevant subjects when you receive them, rather than having all of them sitting in your Inbox. To add a structure of new mailboxes:

1 Mailboxes are displayed in the Mailboxes panel

2 At the bottom of the Mailboxes panel, click on this icon

+

3 Select where you want the mailbox to be created (by default this will be On My Mac)

4 Enter a name for the new mailbox

5 Click on the OK button

6 The new mailbox is added to the current list

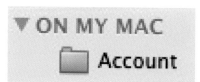

Creating Email

Mail enables you to send and receive emails and also format them to your own style. This can be simply formatting text or adding customized stationery.

To access Mail and start creating email messages:

1 Click on this icon on the Dock

2 Mail contains options for creating, receiving and formatting email messages

Hot tip

If you Forward an email with an attachment, the attachment is included. If you Reply to an email, the attachment will not be included.

3 Click on this button to create a new email message

Hot tip

When entering the name of a recipient for a message, Mail will display details of matching names from your Address Book. For instance, if you type DA, all of the entries in your Address Book beginning with this will be displayed, and you can then select the required one.

4 Enter the email address of the recipient in the To box

To: robin.vandome@mac.com

5 Enter a title for the email in the Subject box

Subject: Well done

...cont'd

6 Enter the content of the email here

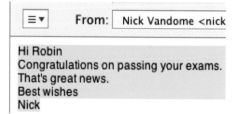

Hi Robin
Congratulations on passing your exams.
That's great news.
Best wishes
Nick

7 To format the text in the email, select it first

From: Nick Vandome <nick

Hi Robin
Congratulations on passing your exams.
That's great news.
Best wishes
Nick

8 Click on the Fonts button

9 Select formatting options for the text

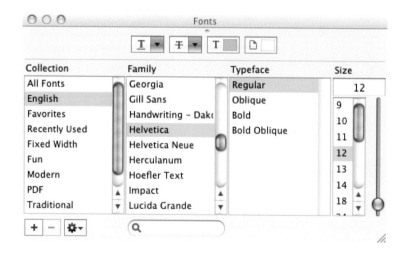

10 Click on the Send button to send the email to the selected recipient

Dealing with Junk Email

Spam, or junk email, is the scourge of every email user. It is unwanted and unsolicited messages usually sent in bulk to lists of email addresses. In Mail there is a function to try and limit the amount of junk email you receive in your Inbox. To do this:

1 When you receive a junk email, click on this button on the Mail toolbar (initially this will help to train Mail to identify junk email)

2 Once Mail has recognized the types of junk that you receive it will start to filter them directly into the Trash Mailbox

Hot tip

It is worth checking in your Junk Mailbox occasionally, in case something you want has been put there.

3 To set the preferences for junk email select Mail>Preferences from the Menu bar and click on the Junk tab

4 Junk email is displayed in the Junk Mailbox

●	✎	From	Subject
○		WebProNews	If They're Searching, Give …
●		Maricela Goddard	Let yourself look really swell!

Attaching Photos

Emails do not have to be restricted to plain text. Through the use of attachments they can also include other documents and photos in particular. This is an excellent way to send photos to family and friends around the world. There are two ways to attach photos to an email:

Attach button
To attach photos using the Attach button:

1 Click on this icon on the Mail toolbar

2 Browse your hard drive for the photo(s) you want to include in your email. Select the photos you want

3 Click on the Choose File button

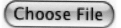

4 The photo is added to the body of the email

Photo Browser

To attach photos using the Photo Browser:

1 Click on this icon on the Mail toolbar

2 Browse the Photo Browser for the photo(s) you want to include

Don't forget

The Photo Browser is available from a variety of other applications.

3 Drag the selected photo(s) into the open email to include them in the message

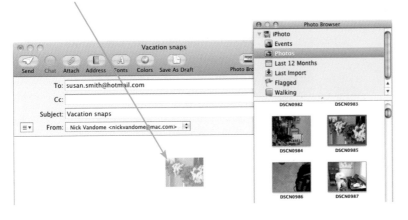

Email Stationery

You do not have to settle for conservative formatting options in emails, Mail offers a variety of templates that can give your messages a creative and eye-catching appearance. It can also be used to format any photos you have attached to your message. This is done through the use of the Stationery function within Mail. To use this:

1 Click on this icon on the Mail toolbar

2 Select a category for the stationery

3 Double-click on a style to apply it to the email

4 The stationery incorporates any photos attached to the email

iChat

One issue with email is that you can never be sure when the recipient receives the message, or when they will reply to it. For a more immediate form of communication, instant messaging or video messaging can be used. This is done with the iChat program. To use this:

1   Click on this icon on the Dock

2   In order to chat to someone you have to add them as a buddy. To do this, click on this button:

3   Enter the required details in the buddy window and then click on the Add button

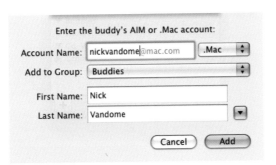

4   Select a buddy in the iChat window

5   Click on this button to start a text chat

6   Click on this button to start a video chat

iChat AV

iChat AV operates in the same way as iChat, except it uses video for communication rather than text. To use iChat AV you require a cable or broadband Internet connection and the built-in iSight video camera. To use iChat AV:

1 Open iChat and select a buddy

2 Click here to invite the buddy to a video chat

3 Click here to view your own video screen

4 Before the video chat starts your image appears here. Once the chat starts this is minimized, but is still visible, and the other person's image takes up the main part of the screen

5 Click here to select preferences for the way iChat AV operates

Preferences...

6 Preferences can be selected for the type of camera used, the microphone and the type of connection

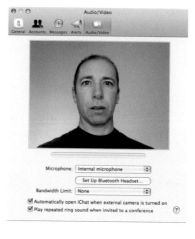

8 Sharing OS X

This chapter looks at how to set up different user accounts and how to keep everyone safe on your Mac by using parental controls.

Adding Users

OS X enables multiple users to access individual accounts on the same computer. If there are multiple users, i.e. two or more, for a single machine, each person can sign on individually and access their own files and folders. This means that each person can log in to their own settings and preferences. All user accounts can be password protected, to ensure that each user's environment is secure. To set up multiple user accounts:

Don't forget

Every MacBook with multiple users has at least one main user, also known as an administrator. This means that they have greater control over the number of items they can edit and alter. If there is only one user on a computer, they automatically take on the role of the administrator. Administrators have a particularly important role to play when computers are networked together. Each computer can potentially have several administrators.

1 Click on the System Preferences icon on the Dock

2 Click on the Accounts icon

3 The information about the current account is displayed. This is your own account, the information is based on details you provide when you first set up your MacBook

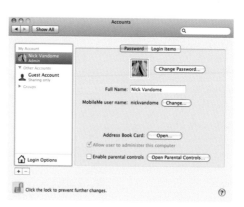

Don't forget

Each user can select their own icon or photo of themselves.

4 Click on this icon to enable new accounts to be added (the padlock needs to be open)

Click the lock to prevent further changes.

5 Click on the plus sign icon to add a new account

6 Enter the details for the new account holder

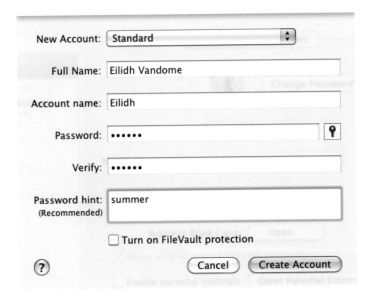

Don't forget

By default, you are the administrator for your MacBook. This means that you can administer other user accounts.

7 Click on the Create Account button

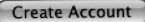

8 The new account is added to the list in the Accounts window, under Other Accounts

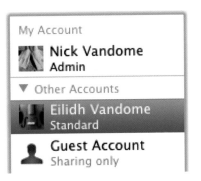

Hot tip

If an administrator forgets their password, insert the OS X CD while holding down the C key. Once this opens, select Installer>Reset Password from the Menu bar. Then select the correct user and enter a new password. Click on Save to apply the changes.

Deleting Users

Once a user has been added, their name appears on the list in the Accounts preference dialog box. It is then possible to edit the details of a particular user or to delete them altogether. To do this:

1 Select a user from the list

2 Click here to remove the selected person's user account

3 A warning box appears to check if you really do want to delete the selected user. If you do, select the required option and click on OK

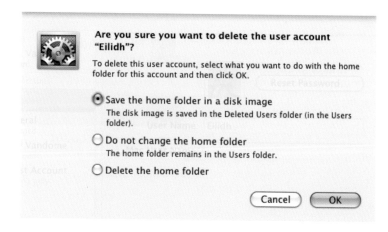

Fast User Switching

If there are multiple users using OS X it is useful to be able to switch between them as quickly as possible. When this is done, the first user's session is retained so that they can return to it if required. To switch between users:

1. In the Accounts window, click on the Login Options button

2. Check on the Enable Fast User Switching box

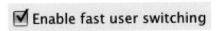

3. At the top-right of the screen, click on the current user's name

Don't forget

When you switch between users, the first user remains logged in and their current session is retained intact.

4. Click on the name of another user

5. Enter the relevant password (if required)

6. Click on the Log In button

Viewing User Accounts

It is possible for individual users to see the overview of another user's account. They can also exchange files with other users by placing them in a folder called a Drop Box. This means that the user can then access these files the next time they log in to their own account. (Under normal circumstances they would not be able to view any folders or files in someone else's account). To view another user's folders and share files in the Finder:

Don't forget

The Users folder also contains the folders of any users that have been deleted. This is where their documents are stored. A system administrator would be able to access these documents and return them to their owner.

1 Select the hard drive and double-click on the Users folder

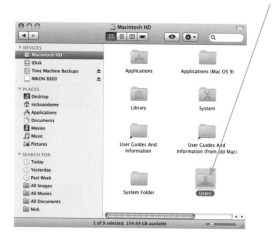

2 Double-click on another user's folder to view its contents

3 Folders with a No Entry icon indicates that they cannot be accessed

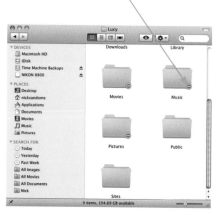

OS X for the Family

Many families share their computers between multiple users and, with the ability to create different accounts in OS X, each user can have their own customized workspace. However, if children are using the computer, parents may want to restrict access to certain types of information that can be viewed, particularly in relation to the Internet and email. Controls can be set within the Accounts system preference. To do this:

1 Access the user Accounts (as shown on page 130)

2 Click on a username and check the Enable Parental Controls box, then click on the Open Parental Controls button to access the Parental Controls

System controls

1 Click on the System tab

2 Check on the Use Simple Finder box to show a simplified version of the Finder

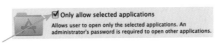

3 Check on this box if you want to limit the types of program a user can access

4 Check off the boxes next to the programs you do not want used

Hot tip

To check which sites have been viewed on a Web browser, check the History menu, which is located on the main Menu bar.

135

...cont'd

Content controls

1 Click on the Content tab

2 Check on this box to prevent any profanities in the Mac Dictionary from being displayed

3 Check on this button and click on the Customize button to edit the type of Web content that can be viewed

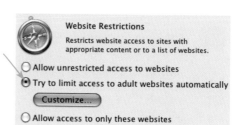

4 Enter the Web addresses for sites that are acceptable

Always allow these sites:
http://www.ineasysteps.com

5 Enter the Web addresses for sites that are not acceptable

Never allow these sites:
http://www.badcontent.com

Mail and iChat controls

1 Click on the Mail & iChat tab

Mail & iChat

2 Check on the Limit boxes to limit the type of content in email messages and iChat text messages

Limit Mail   Limit iChat
This user can exchange email and chat with only the addresses added to the list.

Time Limits controls

1   Click on the Time Limits tab   **Time Limits**

2   Check this box to limit the amount of time the user can use the MacBook

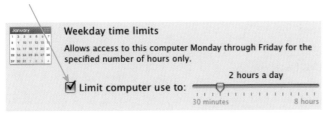

3   Check these boxes to determine the times at which the user cannot access their account

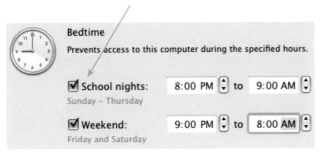

Log controls

1   Click on the Logs tab   **Logs**

2   The logs can be edited to show activity over a certain time period and content type

OS X for Windows Users

General sharing

One of the historical complaints about Macs is that it is difficult to share files between them and Microsoft Windows computers. While this may have been true with some file types, in years gone by, this is an issue that is becoming less and less important, particularly with OS X. Some of the reasons for this are:

- A number of popular file formats, such as PDFs (Portable Document Format) for documents and JPEGs (Joint Photographic Experts Group) for photos and images, are designed so that they can be used on both Mac and Windows platforms

- A lot of software programs on the Mac have options for saving files into different formats, including ones that are specifically for Windows machines

- Other popular programs, such as Microsoft Office, now have Mac versions, so the resulting files can be shared on both formats

Sharing with Boot Camp

For people who find it hard to live without Microsoft Windows, help is at hand even on a Mac. Macs have a program called Boot Camp, which can be used to run a version of Windows on a Mac. This is only available with Snow Leopard. Once it has been accessed, a copy of Windows can then be installed and run. This means that, if you have a non-Mac program you want to use on your Mac, you can do so with Boot Camp.

Boot Camp is set up with the Boot Camp Assistant, which is located within the Utilities folder within the Applications folder. Once this is run, you can then install either Windows XP, Vista or Windows 7, which will run at its native speed. If you need drivers for specific programs, these can be obtained from your Snow Leopard installation disc.

Hot tip

A lot of file formats can be opened on both Mac and Windows PCs. Even Word, Excel and Powerpoint files can be exchanged, as long as each user has the relevant version of Office.

9 MacBook Networking

This chapter looks at how to use your MacBook to create and work with networks between other computers for sharing information.

Networking Overview

Before you start sharing files directly between computers, you have to connect them together. This is known as networking and can be done with two computers in the same room, or with thousands of computers in a major corporation. If you are setting up your own small network it will be known in the computing world as a Local Area Network (LAN). When setting up a network there are various pieces of hardware that are initially needed to join all of the required items together. Once this has been done, software settings can be applied for the networked items. Some of the items of hardware that may be required include:

- A network card. This is known as a Network Interface Card (NIC), all recent MacBooks have them built-in

- An Ethernet port and Ethernet cable. This enables you to make the physical connection between devices. Ethernet cables come in a variety of forms, but the one you should be looking for is the Cat5E type as this allows for the fastest transfer of data. If you are creating a wireless network, you will not require these

- A hub. This is a piece of hardware with multiple Ethernet ports that enables you to connect all of your devices together and let them communicate with each other. However, conflicts can occur with hubs if two devices try and send data through it at the same time

- A switch. This is similar in operation to a hub but is more sophisticated in its method of data transfer, thus allowing all of the machines on the network to communicate simultaneously, unlike a hub

Once you have worked out all of the devices you want to include on your network you can arrange them accordingly. Try and keep the switches and hub within relative proximity of a power supply and, if you are using cables, make sure they are laid out safely.

It is perfectly possible to create a simple network of two computers by joining them with an Ethernet cable.

Ethernet network

Hot tip

If you have two Macs to be networked, and they are in close proximity, this can be achieved with an Ethernet crossover cable. If you have more than two computers, then this is where an Ethernet hub is required. In both cases, there is no need to connect to the Internet to achieve the network.

The cheapest and easiest way to network computers is to create an Ethernet network. This involves buying an Ethernet hub or switch, which enables you to connect several devices to a central point, i.e. the hub or switch. All MacBooks, and most modern printers, have an Ethernet connection, so it is possible to connect various devices, not just computers. Once all of the devices have been connected by Ethernet cables, you can then start applying network settings.

AirPort network

The other option for creating a network is an AirPort network. This is a wireless network, and there are two main standards used by Apple computers: AirPort, using the IEEE 802.11b standard, which is more commonly known as Wi-Fi, which stands for Wireless Fidelity, and the newer AirPort Extreme, using the newer IEEE 802.11g standard, which is up to 5 times faster than the older 802.11b standard. Thankfully, AirPort Extreme is also compatible with devices based on the older standard, so one machine loaded with AirPort Extreme can still communicate wirelessly with an older AirPort one.

One of the issues with a wireless network is security, since it is possible for someone with a wireless-enabled machine to access your wireless network, if they are within range. However, in the majority of cases, the chances of this happening are fairly slim, although it is an issue you should be aware of.

The basics of a wireless network with MacBooks is an AirPort card (either AirPort or AirPort Extreme) installed in all of the required machines, and an AirPort base station that can be located anywhere within 150 metres of the AirPort enabled computers. Once the hardware is in place, wireless-enabled devices can be configured by using the AirPort Setup Assistant utility found in the Utilities folder. After AirPort has been set up, the wireless network can be connected. All of the wireless-enabled devices should then be able to communicate with each other, without using a multitude of cables.

Don't forget

Another method for connecting items wirelessly is called Bluetooth. This covers much shorter distances than AirPort and is usually used for items like printers and cellphones. Bluetooth devices can be connected by using the Bluetooth Setup Assistant in the Utilities folder.

Network Settings

Once you have connected the hardware required for a network, you can start applying the network settings required for different computers to communicate with one another. There are settings for both wireless and Ethernet connections:

1 In System Preferences, double-click on the Network icon

Network

2 For a wireless connection, click on the Airport button

3 Details of wireless settings are displayed

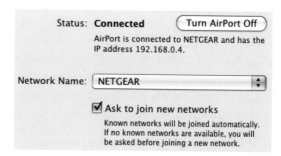

4 For a cable connection, click on the Ethernet button

5 Details of the cable settings are displayed

Status: **Connected**

Ethernet has a self-assigned IP address and may not be able to connect.

Configure: Using DHCP

IP Address: 169.254.122.252

Subnet Mask: 255.255.0.0

6 Click on the Advanced button to see the full settings for each option

Advanced...

Network Preferences

Before you can share files on a network, or access the Internet, the appropriate network settings have to applied on your MacBook so that the network is prepared. This is done by creating a new named network. To do this:

1 In System Preferences, double-click on the Network icon

Network

2 Network details are displayed in the same way as for connecting to the Internet (as shown in Chapter Seven)

3 If you are already connected to a network, this will be shown in the Status section. If you are connected to a wireless network the connection will be via Airport

Status: **Connected**   **Turn AirPort Off**

AirPort is connected to NETGEAR and has the IP address 192.168.0.2.

4 The network name is shown here

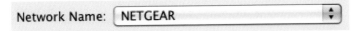

Network Name: NETGEAR

Beware

If you turn off the Airport function, this will disconnect you from your Network and also the Internet.

...cont'd

5 Check this box if you want to be notified before joining a new network

☑ **Ask to join new networks**

Known networks will be joined automatically. If no known networks are available, you will be asked before joining a new network.

6 When a new network is available (for instance, if you are in a Wi-Fi area) you will be prompted for the network you want to join

144

7 If required, enter a password for the network (this is a security measure for the router that provides the network). Click on the Join button

☐ **Remember this network**

Password: ●●●●●●●●|

☐ Show password

(Other...)   (Cancel)   (Join)

Network Diagnostics

If your network is unavailable you can check to see what the problem is. To do this:

1 If you cannot connect to the Internet, Safari will return to a page with this button on it. Click on it to try and find the problem

2 Select the network name you are using

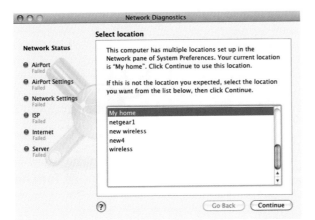

Beware

Over time, you may end up with a number of network names, not all of which are still used. Delete any names that are redundant so that the list does not become too long.

145

3 Click on the Continue button

4 The status of the network is shown in the left-hand panel. Select the method you want to connect to a network with, e.g. Airport (wireless). Click on the Continue button

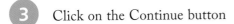

...cont'd

5 Airport needs to be turned on for the network diagnostics to continue

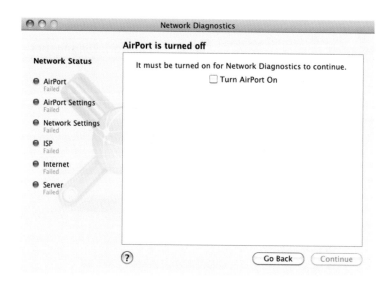

6 Check the Turn Airport On box and click the Continue button

☑ **Turn AirPort On**

7 Select an available network. The left-hand panel will display the status for each required element

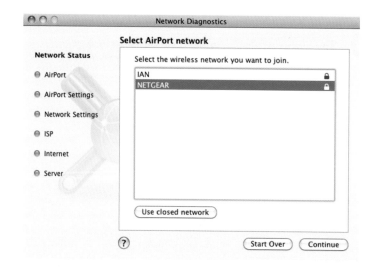

Connecting to a Network

Connecting as a registered user

To connect as a registered user (usually as yourself when you want to access items on another one of your own computers):

1 Other connected computers on the network will show up in the Shared section in the Finder. Click on a networked computer

2 Click on the Connect As button

3 Check on the Registered User button and enter your username and password

Don't forget

Your username and password is specified in the Accounts section of System Preferences.

4 Click on the Connect button

5 The hard drive and home folder of the networked computer is available to the registered user. Double-click on an item to view its contents

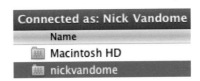

Don't forget

You can disconnect from a networked computer by ejecting it in the Finder, in the same way as you would a removable drive, such as a DVD.

...cont'd

Guest users

Guest users on a network are users other than yourself, or other registered users, to whom you want to limit access to your files and folders. Guests only have access to a folder called the Drop Box, in your own Public folder. To share files with Guest users, you have to first copy them into the Drop Box. To do this:

Beware

If another user is having problems accessing the files in your Drop Box, check the permissions settings assigned to the files. See Chapter Eleven, page 186, for further details.

Hot tip

The contents of the Drop Box can be accessed by other users on the same computer, as well as by users on a network.

1 Create a file and select File>Save from the Menu bar

2 Navigate to your own home folder (this is created automatically by OS X and is displayed in the Finder Sidebar)

3 Double-click on the Public folder

4 Double-click on the Drop Box folder

5 Save the file into the Drop Box

Accessing a Drop Box

To access files in a Drop Box:

1 Double-click on a networked computer in the Finder

2 Click on the Connect As button in the Finder window

3 Select the Guest button

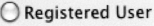

Beware

It is best to copy files into the Drop Box rather than moving them from their current location completely.

4 Click on the Connect button

5 Double-click on the administrator's home folder

nickvandome

Hot tip

Set permissions for how the Drop Box operates by selecting it in the Finder and Ctrl+clicking on it. Select Get Info from the menu and apply the required settings under the Ownership & Permissions heading.

6 Double-click on the Drop Box folder to access the files within it

Drop Box

File Sharing

One of the main reasons for creating a network of two or more computers is to share files between them. On networked Macs, this involves setting them up so that they can share files and then accessing these files.

Setting up file sharing

To set up file sharing on a networked MacBook:

 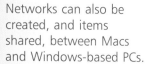
1. Click on the System Preferences icon on the Dock

2. Click on the Sharing icon

    Sharing

3. Check the boxes next to the items you want to share (the most common items to share are files and printers)

    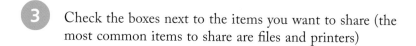

    - ☐ Screen Sharing
    - ☑ File Sharing
    - ☐ Printer Sharing
    - ☐ Scanner Sharing
    - ☐ Web Sharing
    - ☐ Remote Login
    - ☐ Remote Management
    - ☐ Remote Apple Events
    - ☐ Xgrid Sharing
    - ☑ Internet Sharing

4. Click on the padlock to close it and prevent more changes

10 MacBook Mobility

MacBooks are ideal for mobile working, for business or pleasure. This chapter looks at the issues of being mobile with your MacBook, including protecting it, security concerns and making phone calls. It also shows how to use the online MobileMe service.

Transporting your MacBook

When you are going traveling, either for business or pleasure, your MacBook can be a very valuable companion. It can be used to download photographs from a digital camera, download movies from a digital video camera, keep a diary or business notes and keep a record of your itinerary and important documents. Also, in many parts of the world it can access the Internet via wireless hotspots so that you can view the Web and send emails. However, when you are traveling with your MacBook it is sensible to transport this valuable asset in as safe and secure a way as possible. Some of the options include:

MacBook cases and sleeves

There are a range of MacBook cases and sleeves designed specifically for providing protection for the MacBook. They can be bought from the Apple website or Apple stores.

Metal case

If you are concerned that your MacBook may be in danger of physical damage when you are on the road you may want to consider a more robust metal case. These are similar to those used by photographers and, depending on its size and design, you may also be able to include any photographic equipment.

Backpacks

A serious option for transporting your MacBook while you are traveling is a small backpack. This can either be a standard backpack or a backpack specifically designed for a MacBook. The latter is clearly a better option as the MacBook will fit more securely and there are also pockets designed for accessories:

Don't forget

A backpack for carrying a MacBook can be more comfortable than a shoulder bag, as it distributes the weight more evenly.

Keeping your MacBook Safe

By most measures, MacBooks are valuable items. However, in a lot of countries around the world their relative value can be a lot more than it is to their owners: in some countries the value of a MacBook could easily equate to a month's, or even a year's, wages. Even in countries where their relative value is not so high they can still be seen as a lucrative opportunity for thieves. Therefore, it is important to try and keep your MacBook as safe as possible when you are traveling with it, either abroad or at home. Some points to consider in relation to this are:

- If possible, try and keep your MacBook with you at all times, i.e. transport it in a piece of luggage that you can carry rather than having to put it into a large case

- Never hand over your MacBook, or any of your belongings, to any local who promises to look after them

- If you do have to detach yourself from your MacBook, try and put it somewhere secure such as a hotel safe

- When you are traveling, try and keep your MacBook as unobtrusive as possible. This is where a backpack carrying case can prove useful as it is not immediately apparent that you are carrying a MacBook

- Do not use your MacBook in areas where you think it may attract undue interest from the locals, particularly in obviously poor areas. For instance, if you are in a local cafe the appearance of a MacBook may create unwanted attention for you. If in doubt, wait until you get back to your hotel

- If you are accosted by criminals who demand your MacBook, hand it over. No piece of equipment is worth suffering physical injury for

- If you are abroad make sure your MacBook is covered by your travel insurance. If not, get separate insurance for it

- Trust your instincts with your MacBook. If something doesn't feel right, don't do it

Hot tip

Save your important documents onto a pen drive or CD/DVD on a daily basis when you are traveling and keep this away from your MacBook. This way you will still have these items if your MacBook is lost or stolen.

Temperature Extremes

Traveling consists of seeing a lot of different places and cultures but it also invariably involves different extremes of temperature: a visit to the pyramids of Egypt can see the mercury in the upper reaches of the thermometer, while a trip to Alaska would encounter much colder conditions. Whether it is hot or cold, looking after your MacBook is an important consideration in extremes of temperature.

Heat

When traveling in hot countries the best way of avoiding any heat damage to your MacBook is to prevent it from getting too hot in the first place:

- Do not place your MacBook in direct sunlight

- Keep your MacBook insulated from the heat

- Do not leave your MacBook in an enclosed space, such as a car. Not only can this get very hot, but the sun's power can be increased by the vehicle's glass

Cold

Again, it is best to try and avoid your MacBook getting too cold in the first place and this can be done by following similar precautions to those for heat. However, if your MacBook does suffer from extremes of cold, allow it to warm up to normal room temperature again before you try to use it. This may take a couple of hours, but it will be worth the wait, rather than risk damaging the delicate computing elements inside.

Beware

If a MacBook gets too hot it could buckle the plastic casing, making it difficult to close.

Hot tip

Try wrapping your MacBook in something white, such as a T-shirt or a towel, to insulate it against extreme heat.

Dealing with Water

Water is one of the greatest enemies of any electrical device, and MacBooks are no different. This is of particular relevance to anyone who is traveling near water with their MacBook, such as on a boat or ship, or using their MacBook near a swimming pool or a beach. If you are near water with your MacBook then you must bear the following in mind:

- Avoid water. The best way to keep your MacBook dry is to keep it away from water whenever possible. For instance, if you want to update your notes or download some photographs, then it would be best to do this in an indoor environment, rather than sitting near water

- Keeping dry. If you think you will be transporting your MacBook near water then it is a good precaution to protect it with some form of waterproof bag. There are a range of "dry-bags" that are excellent for this type of occasion and they remain waterproof even if fully immersed in water. These can be bought from outdoor suppliers

- Drying out. If the worst does occur and your MacBook does get a good soaking, all is not lost. However, you will have to ensure that it is fully dried out before you try and use it again. Never turn it on if it is still wet

Power Sockets

Different countries and regions around the world use different types of power sockets, and this is an issue when you are traveling with your MacBook. Wherever you are going in the world it is vital to have an adapter that will fit the sockets in the countries you intend to visit. Otherwise you will not be able to charge your MacBook battery.

There are over a dozen different types of plugs and sockets used around the world, with the four most popular being:

North America, Japan
This is a two-point plug and socket.
The pins on the plug are flat and parallel.

Hot tip

Power adapters can be bought for all regions around the world. There are also kits that provide all of the adapters together. These provide connections for anywhere worldwide.

Continental Europe
This is a two-point plug and socket.
The pins are rounded.

Australasia, China, Argentina
This is a three-point socket that can accommodate either a two- or a three-pin plug. In a two-pin plug, the pins are angled in a V shape.

UK
This is a three-point plug. The pins are rectangular.

Airport Security

Because of the increased global security following terrorist attacks, such as those of September 11 2001, the levels of airport security have been greatly increased around the world. This has implications for all travelers, and if you are traveling with a MacBook, this will add to the security scrutiny you will face. When dealing with airport security when traveling with a MacBook, there are some issues you should always keep in mind:

- Keep your MacBook with you at all times. Unguarded baggage at airports immediately raises suspicion and it can make life very easy for thieves

- Carry your MacBook in a small bag so you can take it on board as hand luggage. On no account should it be put in with your luggage that goes in the hold

- X-ray machines at airports will not harm your MacBook. However, if anyone tries to scan it with a metal detector, ask them if they can inspect it by hand instead

- Keep a careful eye on your MacBook when it goes through the X-ray conveyor belt and try to be there at the other side as soon as it emerges. There have been some stories of people causing a commotion at the security gate just after someone has placed their MacBook on the conveyor belt. While everyone's attention (including yours) is distracted, an accomplice takes the MacBook from the conveyor belt. If you are worried about this you can ask for the security guard to hand-check your MacBook rather than putting it on the conveyor belt

- Make sure the battery of your MacBook is fully charged. This is because you may be asked to turn on your MacBook to verify that it is just that, and not some other device disguised as a MacBook. This check has become increasingly common in recent years due to security threats

- When you are on the plane, keep the MacBook in the storage area under your seat, rather than in the overhead locker, so you know where it is at all times. Also, it could cause a serious injury if it fell out of an overhead locker

Beware

If there is any kind of distraction when you are going through airport security it could be because someone is trying to divert your attention in order to steal your MacBook.

Hot tip

When traveling through airport security, leave your MacBook in Sleep mode, so it can be powered up quickly if anyone needs to check that it works properly.

Downloading on the Road

When you are traveling with your MacBook, one of the most common activities that you may also be doing will be taking photographs, particularly if you are on vacation. If you are doing this it is good practice to download your photos onto your MacBook at regular intervals. The reasons for this are:

- You can view and edit your photos before you get back home

- Keeping them in another location lessens the possibility of losing your photos (once they are on your MacBook you can also back them up further by copying them to a disk or a pen drive)

MacBook comes with the photo storage/editing program iPhoto already installed. This is ideal for downloading your photos while you are on the road. To do this:

Hot tip

When travelling with a MacBook and a camera, it is worthwhile taking a card reader for downloading photos. This is an external reader that is attached via a USB cable and can accommodate all standard camera memory cards. It is generally more convenient than attaching the camera.

1 Connect your camera to your MacBook using a USB cable

2 iPhoto should open automatically. If it does not, click on this icon on the Dock

3 The connected camera is listed in the Devices section

▼ DEVICES

NIKON D80

4 The photos on your camera are displayed in the main iPhoto window

5 Enter an Event Name and Description for your photos. This will be added as metadata, enabling you to search and find your photos more easily once they have been downloaded onto your MacBook

Event Name: | Animals

Description: | Wildlife Park

6 Select individual photos and click on the Import Selected button, or click on the Import All button to download all the photos on your camera

Import Selected   **Import All...**

...cont'd

7 Once the photos have been downloaded, you will be asked if you want to delete them from your camera or keep them. Select the option you want

Delete Photos on Your Camera?

12 photos were successfully imported into iPhoto.

Delete Photos   Keep Photos

8 The downloaded images are displayed in the main window, with the Event Name given in Step 5, and with the download date

Don't forget

When photos are first downloaded, they are shown under the Last Import tab in the left-hand navigation panel. To see all of your photos, click on the Photos tab.

9 Drag this slider to increase or decrease the size of the photos in the main window

10 Double-click on a photo to view it at full size in the main window. Click on it once to return to the thumbnails

Don't forget

When you select an individual photo, its details are displayed in the Information box at the bottom left of the iPhoto window.

11 Use these icons to edit a selected photo

12 Use these icons to view photos as a slideshow or to order items, such as prints or photo books

13 Use these icons to post your images on social networking sites or to attach them to an email

MobileMe

Due to the increased coverage of Wi-Fi Internet coverage, computer users on the move now expect access to the same services they have when they are at home. MacBook users are no different in this respect and they are catered for by Apple with the MobileMe online service. This is a subscription based service that offers MacBook users online access to a variety of services:

- Email

- Address book

- Calendars

- Gallery for photos

- iDisk storage

- An option for locating a lost or stolen iPhone

The MobileMe service is accessed from the website of the same name and you can undertake a 60-day free trial to assess the service. To access the MobileMe service:

Don't forget

Once you have an online MobileMe account, you will also be able to access your email directly on your MacBook, using the Mail program.

1 Access the MobileMe website at www.me.com/

2 Click here to access a 60-day free trail of MobileMe

3 The MobileMe sign up page contains information about the service

Don't forget

At the time of writing, the subscription fee for MobileMe was $99/£60 per year. However, there have been rumors of a reduction in this.

4 Click on this button to sign up for the free trial

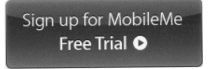

5 Enter your personal details to start the free trial. These are the details that will be used if you decide to sign up for the full subscription service

...cont'd

Using MobileMe

Once you have signed up for the MobileMe free trial (or the full subscription service) you can start using the service. To do this:

1 Access the MobileMe homepage at www.me.com

2 Enter your login details (these will have been created during the sign up process)

3 Click on the Cloud button to view the available MobileMe services

4 Click on an icon to go to that specific service

The MobileMe services are:

● Mail, for email services

● Contacts, taken from your MacBook Address Book

● Calendar, taken from your MacBook iCal application

● Gallery, used to upload photos from iWeb

● iDisk, used as storage space within MobileMe

● Find My iPhone, used to find a lost or stolen iPhone

MobileMe settings

MobileMe is not a standalone service; it can also be synchronized with the items on your MacBook, so you always have the most up to date information, whether you are using the online service or your MacBook. Within System Preferences there are settings that can be applied to determine the operation of MobileMe. To do this:

1. Within System Preferences, click on the MobileMe icon

2. General information about your MobileMe account is displayed under the Account tab. This includes information about the type of account and available email and disk storage. Click on the Account Details button to get more information about your account

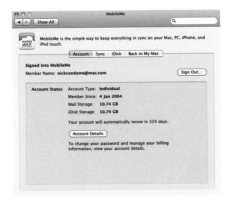

3. Click on the Sync tab to specify which items you want to sync with your MacBook and MobileMe

Hot tip

The Sync function can be used to synchronize the information on MobileMe with a range of Apple devices, such as iMacs, MacBooks, iPhones and iPads.

...cont'd

4 Click on the Sync Now button to synchronize your MobileMe account and the equivalent information on your MacBook

Hot tip

As well as manually synching information between MobileMe and your MacBook, you can also set this to be performed automatically.

5 Click on the iDisk tab to see how much storage space you have on your iDisk within MobileMe. It also has settings for the operation of your public folder within your iDisk

6 Click on the Back to My Mac tab to allow screen sharing with another computer that also has this facility enabled

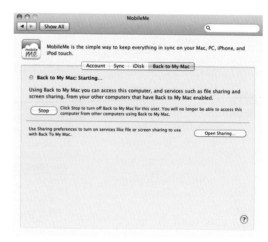

Using iDisk

iDisk is the storage space on MobileMe that can be used for backing up your files or for making files available when you are mobile. To use iDisk:

1 Once you have registered for MobileMe the iDisk icon will appear under the Devices section in the Finder

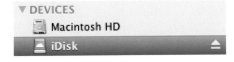

2 The files in the iDisk are displayed in the main Finder window

Don't forget

You have to be connected to the Internet in order to use your iDisk.

3 Files can be added to your iDisk from the Finder. To do this, select a file or folder

4 Drag the selected file or folder onto the iDisk icon

...cont'd

5 To view your online iDisk, login to MobileMe and click on the Cloud button

6 Click on the iDisk icon

7 The folder and file structure is the same as the one viewed on your MacBook via the Finder. Files can then be

accessed and used in the same way as on your MacBook

iDisk Preferences

iDisk preferences can be set within System Preferences on your MacBook. To do this:

1 Open System Preferences and click on this button

2 Specify how you want your Public folder to be accessed within iDisk (this can be useful for making files available to other people)

Making Telephone Calls

Just because you are traveling, it does not mean that you cannot keep in touch with colleagues, family and friends at home. Telephone calls via your MacBook are an ideal way to do this. As long as you have access to the Internet you can make telephone calls around the world, using a program called Skype. Once this has been downloaded, you can make free telephone calls to anyone else who has Skype on their computer, and cheap ones to landlines or cell phones too.

Downloading Skype
To download Skype ready for use on your MacBook:

1 Access the Skype homepage at www.skype.com

Don't forget

Skype is free to download and works with Mac OS X.

2 Click on the Get Skype button to access the page for downloading Skype

Get Skype

Don't forget

Once Skype has been downloaded it is available in the Applications folder.

3 Downloading information is displayed on the page

4 Click on the Get Skype for Mac OS X button to start the downloading process

Get Skype for Mac OS X

...cont'd

Adding contacts

Before you start making telephone calls with Skype, you have to add the contacts whom you want to call. To do this:

1 Click on this icon to launch Skype, or select it from the Applications folder in the Finder

2 In the search box, enter the name of a person you want to find

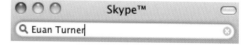

Hot tip

You can also find other Skype users by clicking on this button in the bottom left of the Skype main window.

3 If the person is not in your Contacts List, this message appears. Click on the "Search for Skype Name" button

Euan Turner is not in your Contact List.

(Search for Skype Name)

4 Matching names are listed in the Search results

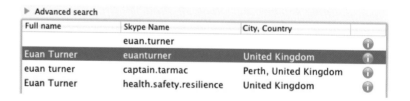

▶ Advanced search

Full name	Skype Name	City, Country	
	euan.turner		ℹ
Euan Turner	euanturner	United Kingdom	ℹ
euan turner	captain.tarmac	Perth, United Kingdom	ℹ
Euan Turner	health.safety.resilience	United Kingdom	ℹ

5 Select an entry and click on the "Add contact" button

(Add contact)

6 The selected person is added as a Skype contact

Don't forget

When you have found a contact, you can call them directly from the Contact Added window.

Making a call

To make a telephone call to another Skype user:

1 In the Skype window, click on the Skype Test Call link to test the connection

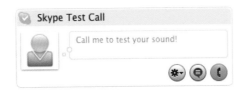

2 The Test Call window enables you to record a message to test your connection

Don't forget

Once you are connected to another user, you will require a microphone attached to your computer in order to make the call and be heard by the other person. Skype can also be used to chat using text messages.

3 Select one of your Skype contacts and click on the green Call button

4 Click on this red button to end the call

...cont'd

Calling other phones or cell phones/mobiles

Skype can also be used to call other landline phones and also cell phones/mobiles. However, there is a charge for this, even if the users have a Skype account. To do this:

1 In the Skype window, click on this button, located in the bottom, left corner

2 Enter a number using the keypad and click on the green call button to start the call

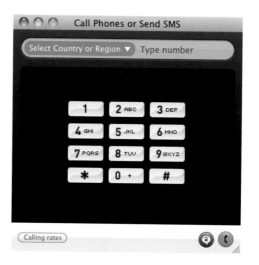

3 Go to the Prices section on the Skype homepage to see different ways to pay for calls to non-Skype phones

Prices

Pre-Pay

Pay Monthly

Skype Credit

SMS rates

Ways to pay

4 Click on this button to see the Skype rate for calling different countries

11 MacBook Maintenance

Despite its stability, OS X still benefits from a robust maintenance regime. This chapter looks at some of the ways to keep OS X in top shape and also at some general troubleshooting.

Time Machine

Time Machine is a feature of OS X that gives you great peace of mind. In conjunction with an external hard drive, it creates a backup of your whole system, including folders, files, programs and even the OS X operating system itself.

Once it has been set up, Time Machine takes a backup every hour and you can then go into Time Machine to restore any files that have been deleted or have become corrupt.

Setting up Time Machine

To use Time Machine it has to be set up first. This involves attaching a hard drive. To set up Time Machine:

1 Click on the Time Machine icon on the Dock or access it in the System Preferences

2 You will be prompted to set up Time Machine

A storage location for Time Machine backups isn't set up.
To choose a location for backups, set up Time Machine.

Cancel   Set Up Time Machine

3 Click on the Set Up Time Machine button

4 In the Time Machine System Preferences window, click on the Choose Backup Disk button

Choose Backup Disk...

5 Connect an external hard drive and select it

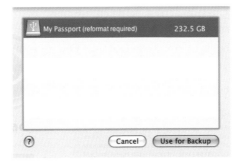

6 Click on the Use for Backup button

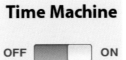

7 In the Time Machine System Preferences window, drag the button to the On position

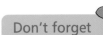

Don't forget

If you stop the initial backup before it has been completed, Time Machine will remember where it has stopped and resume the backup from that point.

8 The backup will begin. The initial backup copies your whole system and can take several hours. Subsequent hourly backups only look at items that have been changed since the previous backup

9 The progress of the backup is displayed in the System Preferences window and also here

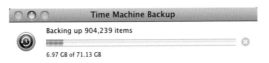

175

...cont'd

Using Time Machine

Once Time Machine has been set up, it can then be used to go back in time to view items in an earlier state. To do this:

If you have deleted items before the initial set up of Time Machine, these will not be recoverable.

1 Access an item on your MacBook. In this example, it is a document folder where the item Folder One has been deleted

2 Click on the Time Machine icon on the Dock

3 Time Machine displays the current item in its current state. Earlier versions are stacked behind it

The active item you were viewing before you launched Time Machine is the one that is active in the Time Machine interface. You can select items from within the active window to view their contents.

4 Click on the arrows to move through the open items, or select a time or date from the scale to the right of the arrows

5 Another way to move through Time Machine is to click on the pages behind the front one. This brings the selected item to the front. In this example, Time Machine has gone back to a date when Folder One was still in place, i.e. before it was deleted

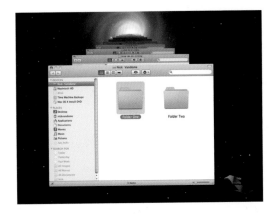

177

6 Click on the Restore button to restore the item that has been deleted

7 Click on the Cancel button to return to your normal environment

8 The deleted item (Folder One) is now restored in its original format

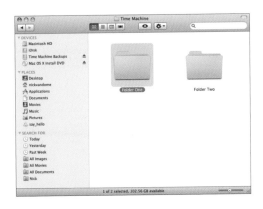

Disk Utility

Disk Utility is a utility program that allows you to perform certain testing and repair functions for OS X. It incorporates a variety of functions, and is a good option for general maintenance and if your computer is not running as it should.

Each of the functions within Disk Utility can be applied to specific drives and volumes. However, it is not possible to use the OS X start-up disk within Disk Utility as this will be in operation to run the program. Disk Utility cannot operate on a disk that has programs already running. To use Disk Utility:

Checking disks

Don't forget

Disk Utility is located within the Applications> Utilities folder.

① Click the First Aid tab to check a disk

② Select a disk and select one of the first aid options

Don't forget

If there is a problem with a disk and OS X can fix it, the Repair button will be available. Click on this to enable Disk Utility to repair the problem.

Erasing a disk
To erase all of the data on a disk or a volume:

① Click on the Erase tab and select a disk or volume

Beware

If you erase data from a removable disk, such as a pen drive, you will not be able to retrieve it.

② Click Erase to erase the data on the selected disk or volume

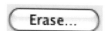

Erase...

System Profiler

This can be used to view how the different hardware and software elements on your MacBook are performing. To do this:

1 Open the Utilities folder and double-click on the System Profiler icon

System Profiler

2 Click on the Hardware link and click on an item of hardware

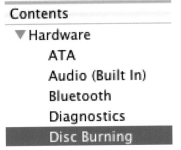

Contents
▼ Hardware
  ATA
  Audio (Built In)
  Bluetooth
  Diagnostics
  Disc Burning

Don't forget

System Profiler is located within the Applications> Utilities folder.

3 Details about the item of hardware, and its performance, is displayed

OPTIARC DVD RW AD-5670S:

Firmware Revision:	2AHF
Interconnect:	ATAPI
Burn Support:	Yes (Apple Shipping Drive)
Cache:	2048 KB
Reads DVD:	Yes
CD-Write:	-R, -RW
DVD-Write:	-R, -R DL, -RW, +R, +R DL, +RW
Write Strategies:	CD-TAO, CD-SAO, CD-Raw, DVD-DAO
Media:	To show the available burn speeds, insert

4 Click on software items to view their details

iTunes	8.2.1
iWeb	3.0

iTunes:

Version:	8.2.1
Last Modified:	13/07/2009 21:46
Kind:	Universal
64-Bit (Intel):	No
Get Info String:	iTunes 8.2.1, © 2000-2009 Apple Inc.
Location:	/Applications/iTunes.app

179

Activity Monitor

Activity Monitor is a utility program that can be used to view information about how much processing power and memory is being used to run programs. This can be useful to know, if certain programs are running slowly or crashing frequently. To use Activity Monitor:

1 Click on the CPU tab to see how much processor memory is being used up

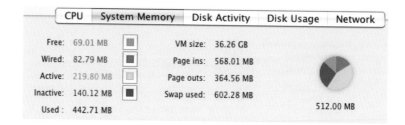

2 Click on the System Memory tab to see how much system memory (RAM) is being used up

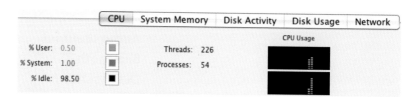

3 Click on the Disk Usage tab to see how much space has been taken up on the hard drive

Updating Software

Apple periodically releases updates for its software: both its programs and the OS X operating system. The latter are probably more important, as they contain security fixes for the system that have come to light. To update software:

1 Click on the System Preferences icon on the Dock

2 Click the Software Update icon

Don't forget

In a lot of cases, software updates will be downloaded and installed automatically.

3 Click the Check Now button to view available updates

OPTIARC DVD RW AD-5670S:

Firmware Revision:	2AHF
Interconnect:	ATAPI
Burn Support:	Yes (Apple Shipping Drive)
Cache:	2048 KB
Reads DVD:	Yes
CD-Write:	-R, -RW
DVD-Write:	-R, -R DL, -RW, +R, +R DL, +RW
Write Strategies:	CD-TAO, CD-SAO, CD-Raw, DVD-DAO
Media:	To show the available burn speeds, insert

4 Check on the boxes next to the updates you want to install

Install	Name	Version	Size
☑	iWeb Update	3.0.1	16.8 MB
☑	iTunes	9.0.1	89.8 MB
☑	GarageBand Update	5.1	145.9 MB
☑	Mac mini EFI Firmware Update	1.2	2.3 MB
☑	Bluetooth Firmware Update	2.0.1	1.7 MB
☑	Remote Desktop Client Update	3.3.1	6 MB
☑	iLife Support	9.0.3	54.9 MB
☑	Mac OS X Update	10.6.1	9.8 MB

Don't forget

For some software updates, such as those to OS X itself, you may have to restart your computer for them to take effect.

5 Click on the Install button

Install 10 Items

6 Check the Check for Updates box to have updates checked for automatically

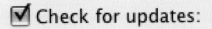
☑ Check for updates: Weekly

Restoring Preferences

One factor that can cause problems with a program is if its Preferences folder becomes corrupted. This was a particular problem with OS 9 and earlier, but it can still occur with OS X. If a program is crashing a lot, you can try removing its Preferences folder and closing down the program. The next time it is opened, OS X will create a new Preferences folder that should be corruption free. To do this:

1 Click on the Finder icon on the Dock and click on your Home folder

Library

2 Double-click on the Library folder

3 Double-click on the Preferences folder

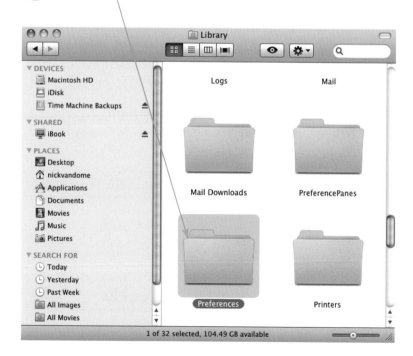

4 Select the Preferences folder of the program that is causing problems

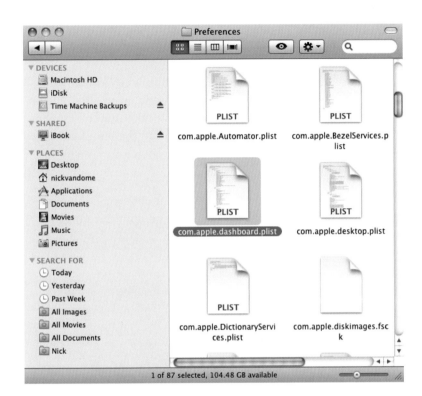

1 of 87 selected, 104.48 GB available

5 Drag the Preferences folder into the Trash. Close the program and then reboot

Hot tip

If you have several programs running when a problem occurs, delete all of the relevant Preferences folders in turn. After deleting each one, open the programs to see if the problem has been resolved. If not, repeat the process with another Preferences folder. In this way, you should be able to isolate the program with the problem. After each Preferences folder has been removed to the Trash, you will have to reboot your computer so that OS X can create a new Preferences folder for that program.

Problems with Programs

The simple answer

OS X is something of a rarity in the world of computing software: it claims to be remarkably stable, and it is. However, this is not to say that things do not go wrong sometimes, although this is considerably less frequent than with older Mac operating systems. Sometimes this will be due to problems within particular programs and, on occasion, the problems may lie with OS X itself. If this does happen, the first course of action is to close down OS X using the Apple menu>Shut Down command. Then restart the computer. If this does not work, or you cannot access the Shut Down command, try turning off the power to the computer and then starting up again.

Force quitting

If a particular program is not responding, it can be closed down separately, without the need to reboot the computer. To do this:

1 Select Apple menu>Force Quit from the Menu bar

2 Select the program you want to close

3 Click Force Quit

General Troubleshooting

It is true that things do go wrong with OS X, although probably with less regularity than with some other operating systems. If something does go wrong, there are a number of items you can check, and also some steps you can take to ensure you do not lose any important data if the worst case scenario occurs and your hard drive packs up completely.

- Backup. If everything does go wrong, it is essential to take preventative action in the form of making sure all of your data is backed up and saved. This can either be done with the Backup program available from the .Mac service or by backing up manually by copying data to a CD or DVD

- Reboot. One traditional reply by IT helpdesks is to reboot, i.e. turn off the computer and turn it back on again and hope that the problem has resolved itself. In a lot of cases, this simple operation does the trick but is not always a viable solution for major problems

- Check cables. If the problem appears to be with a network connection or an externally connected device, check that all cables are connected properly and have not worked loose. If possible, make sure that all cables are tucked away so they cannot be pulled out inadvertently

- Check network settings. If your network or Internet connections are not working, check the network setting in System Preferences. Sometimes, when you make a change to one item, this can have an adverse effect on one of these settings. (If possible, lock the settings once you have applied them by clicking on the padlock icon in the Network preferences window)

- Check for viruses. If your computer is infected with a virus, this could affect the efficient running of the machine. Luckily, this is less of a problem for Macs as virus writers tend to concentrate their efforts towards Windows-based machines. However, there are plenty of Mac viruses out there, so make sure your computer is protected by a program, such as Norton AntiVirus, which is available from www.symantec.com

Don't forget

In extreme cases, you will not be able to reboot your computer normally. If this happens, you will have to pull out the power cable and reattach it. You will then be able to reboot, although the computer may want to check its hard drive to make sure that everything is in working order.

...cont'd

● Check Start-up items. If you have set certain items to start automatically when your computer is turned on, this could cause certain conflicts within your machine. If this is the case, disable the items from launching during the booting up of the computer. This can be done within the Accounts preference of System Preferences by clicking on the Startup Items tab, selecting the relevant item and pressing the minus button

● Check permissions. If you, or other users, are having problems opening items, this could be because of the permissions that are set. To check these, select the item in the Finder, click on the File button on the Finder toolbar and select Get Info. In the Ownership & Permissions section of the Info window, you will be able to set the relevant permissions to allow other users, or yourself, to read, write or have no access

Click here to view permissions settings

● Eject external devices. Sometimes external devices, such as pen drives, can become temperamental and refuse to eject the disks within them, or even show up on the desktop or in the Finder. If this happens, you can eject the disk by pressing the mouse button when the Mac chimes are heard during the booting up process

● Turn-off your screen saver. Screen savers can sometimes cause conflicts within your computer, particularly if they have been downloaded from an unreliable source. If this happens, change the screen saver within the Desktop & Screen Saver preference of the System Preferences, or disable it altogether

Index

W

X

THE WORLD OF
WORLD WAR TWO

THE ALLIES
ALLIED OCCUPIED
THE AXIS POWERS
AXIS POWERS OCCUPIED
NEUTRALS

UNION OF SOVIET SOCIALIST REPUBLICS

CZECHOSLOVAKIA
AUSTRIA
HUNGARY
NIA
ARIA

TURKEY

SYRIA
IRAQ   IRAN   AFGHANISTAN

EGYPT

SAUDI
ARABIA

ANGLO-
EGYPTIAN
SUDAN

BRITISH
SOMALILAND

ITALIAN
E. AFRICA

ITALIAN
SOMALILAND

UGANDA
KENYA

NO

TANGANYIKA

HODESIA

MOZAMBIQUE

S.
RHODESIA

ANA

MADAGASCAR

OUTER
MONGOLIA

MANCHUKUO

KOREA   JAPAN

CHINA

INDIA

BURMA

SIAM

CEYLON

FRENCH
INDO-
CHINA

FORMOSA

PHILIPPINES

SUMATRA

BORNEO

NEW GUINEA

JAVA

AUSTRALIA

NEW ZEALAND

WORLD WAR II

Ronald Heiferman

derbibooks

Planned and directed for
Octopus Books Limited by
Peter Dunbar Associates, London

Designed by David Eldred
Cartography by Arka Graphics
Picture Research by Robert Hunt

First published in paperback in the
United States of America 1975 by
Derbibooks and distributed by
Book Sales Inc., 110 Enterprise Avenue
Secaucus, N.J. 07094

© 1973 Octopus Books Limited

ISBN 0 7064 0485 8

Produced by Mandarin Publishers Limited
Toppan Building, Westlands Road, Quarry Bay,
Hong Kong

Printed in Hong Kong

Contents

Introduction by S. L. Mayer

The Second World War was by no means the second world war ever fought; it was only the second fought in the 20th century. The wars of Spanish Succession, the Seven Years War, the Napoleonic Wars, even the American War of Independence were international wars fought on many continents by European states. The First World War was probably about the eighth war fought in all parts of the world, but it was the first to begin to involve in a substantial way states whose base of power was extra-European, chiefly the United States and, to a lesser extent, Japan. The Second World War, however, was the first of these global conflicts to be fought with equal intensity on both sides of the world. In fact, a major part of the Second World War hardly involved European states at all, except in a peripheral way. In many respects the Second World War was a combination of three quite separate wars which eventually became linked together. The first of these wars was European. It was the German-Polish war of 1939, which involved Britain and France insofar as they supported their Eastern European ally. Russia was involved because Stalin chose to forge an alliance with Hitler on the eve of the war which, in effect, sealed Poland's fate. The Soviet Union, after all, participated in the partition of Poland which concluded this month-long conflict at the end of September 1939. Although war had been declared by Britain and France on Nazi Germany, it was scarcely waged during the period called the 'phoney war' between the fall of Poland and the invasion of Scandanavia in the spring of 1940. The second of these separate wars was a concomitant of the first. The Soviet Union attacked Finland after the fall of Poland in order to secure her northern flank against what was generally considered to be an inevitable double-cross of the Nazi-Soviet pact by Hitler. Both Russia and Germany recognized the alliance as temporary, with each buying time and dividing Eastern Europe in the process. Finland struggled hard and heroically, but when she capitulated in the early spring of 1940 only bits of territory were taken from her, mainly to protect Leningrad against an eventual German attack and to effectively neutralize Finland for the course of the wider war which was expected. The absorption of the three Baltic states, Estonia, Latvia and Lithuania by the Soviet Union in 1940 was an extension of Russia's policy to secure her western flank if a war with Germany was to come.

On the other side of the world, however, a third conflict was already in progress, a war which could be said to have begun years before the Second World War started and which continued after it had begun. This was the Sino-Japanese War, which began in earnest when Japanese troops crossed the Marco Polo Bridge on 7 July, 1937 and moved into China proper. Japan, of course, had already seized part of China in 1931 when she took over Manchuria and later part of Inner Mongolia. But by the time German troops crossed the Polish frontier on the morning of 1 September, 1939, Japan was in control of much of coastal China, and the Nationalist government of Chiang Kai-shek had move to the mountainous interior of China to form a new capital at Chungking. Japan's movements into French Indo-China in 1940 and 1941 were merely an extension of the struggle with China, which by that time had lapsed into an enervating guerrilla war which neither side was capable of winning. Even when Germany overran most of Western Europe in the spring of 1940, there was little connection between these events and the struggle for supremacy in Asia, despite the fact that Germany, Italy and Japan were allies. They were allies on paper, perhaps, but there was little trust and even less cooperation between the Axis and Japan. In the question of possible disposition of French and later British and Dutch colonies in Asia, there was rivalry between Germany and Japan. After all, the Russo-German alliance was forged without the knowledge or approval of Japan. The Germans invaded Russia in June 1941 only just over two months after Japan had signed a non-aggression pact with the Soviet Union. Had the Japanese known of Hitler's plans, it is unlikely that the Japanese would have agreed to a pact with an enemy of their Axis ally. Thus, in 1941 Japan was still at war with China, Britain and Germany were still fighting their air war over the Channel and in Africa, and Germany was preparing to invade Russia. But there was not more than a slender link connecting these conflicts.

The event which turned a series of separate wars into World War Two was the attack on the American naval base at Pearl Harbor. The entry of the United States into the Pacific war changed the character of developments throughout the world. First of all, it transformed the war in Asia from merely a wide-scale local conflict to a struggle for supremacy throughout the whole of East Asia and the Pacific. The Japanese quickly overran the whole of Southeast Asia, swept through the Western Pacific, and within four months were at the gates of India, the doorstep of Australia and were within striking distance of Midway Island and Hawaii. Japan had achieved hegemony over East Asia and much of the Pacific, the Europeans were imprisoned and humiliated, and it was left to the United States to redress the balance of power in the Pacific. But this would have only been an expansion of the East Asia war had it not been for Germany's declaration of war against the United States a few days after Pearl Harbor. It was not beyond the realm of possibility that America might have gone to war against Japan alone if it had not been for the fact that, for once, Hitler honored an alliance and declared war against the principal enemy of Japan. President Roosevelt, who had tried every means short of war to bring the United States into the European war, including the waging of undeclared naval war against Germany for months prior to Pearl Harbor, was relieved that Hitler had once again blundered into war against a great power with seemingly endless material and human resources. Now war could be waged on two fronts, but Roosevelt made certain, even before Pearl Harbor during his talks with Churchill, that the emphasis would be on winning the war in Europe first. Japan would have to come afterwards.

The history of World War Two has tended to follow the lead set by Roosevelt. Although the war became a world war because of the entry of the United States, a great power prepared to fight in earnest in both the Atlantic and the Pacific as well as in Africa and capable of doing so, thereby making the European and Asian wars all part of one cataclysmic struggle, the emphasis of most historians has been placed on the European phase of the war. Much is already known about the rise of Hitler and Nazism, the steps through which the appeasers encouraged Hitler's appetite for territory and power by sacrificing one after another of the agreements made at the Paris Peace Conference of 1919 – the Rhineland, the military and naval buildup of Germany, Austria, and finally the Sudetenland and Czechoslovakia – leading ultimately to the guarantee of Poland by Britain, a country which Britain could not defend, with or without the collusion between Germany and the Soviet Union. Somewhat less is known about the reasons why Mussolini, after almost a generation in power, decided to throw in his lot with Hitler. But still less is generally known about why Japan could not be satisfied with control over Manchuria, Korea and Formosa, and extended her quest for Asian hegemony to China and ultimately the whole of the Western Pacific and Southeast Asia. It is understandable to expect the European colonial powers in Asia – Britain, France and Holland – to oppose the spread of Japanese imperialism into what they had come to consider as their sphere of influence. But how did the United States become involved in a war with Japan? It is ironic to witness the retreat of America from Southeast Asia and Asian commitments in general in favor of Japan when, only a generation ago, the United States did everything in its power to try to prevent exactly what it is presently encouraging to take place.

The wars which became a world war after Pearl Harbor remained one great war because of the presence of the United States in both. If America and her Allies fought Japan alone, there can be little doubt that the war in the Pacific would have ended at least a year to a year and a half before it did. If, on the other hand, the Allies could have fought against the Rome-Berlin Axis, the pressure from both the Soviet Union and Britain and America would have inexorably crushed Hitler even sooner than it did. For example, were it not for the drain of equipment to the Far East, an invasion of the Continent could have taken place

in 1943. Even though the emphasis by the Allies was clearly on Europe and victory over Hitler throughout the war, as General MacArthur bitterly commented, the tools of war had to be forged in the States, and full wartime industrial production was not underway until the end of 1942. This explains the continuing series of setbacks for American arms in the Pacific until the Japanese were stopped at Midway. Although American arms did not stop Germany at Stalingrad or at Alamein, they played some role. In the Second World War it was not merely armies which contended; it was whole economies, the whole of each nation which struggled for national survival. The principle of unconditional surrender made it clear to Germany and Japan that compromise and a negotiated peace would be difficult if not impossible to achieve. In any event, neither Hitler nor Tojo would have been capable of making a deal with the Allies even if such a deal were possible. The plot of July 1944 to assassinate Hitler was the last vain attempt to prevent the destruction of Germany as a nation-state. Even if Hitler had been killed, it is unlikely that the policy of unconditional surrender would have been abandoned.

But this is not to say that although prior to 1941 separate wars were being fought, that one united effort to destroy the Axis took place after Pearl Harbor. Certainly from the American point of view this was the case. But as Churchill himself put it, the war in the Pacific and in Burma took absolutely bottom priority. It was clear to every Briton that Hitler was the principal enemy, and that the ever-present danger to the safety of the British Isles should be eliminated by the destruction of Nazi Germany. The war in the North African desert had to take second place to that aim, and was important only insofar as it affected Britain's natural aim to invade the Continent of Europe and remove the danger to her people. Thus, because of her unwillingness and inability to do much east of Suez after 1941, Britain chose

to concentrate on the enemy across the North Sea. Even the reconquest of Burma came very much as an afterthought once it became clear that victory in Europe was at hand. As for the Soviet Union, the third principal ally, there was no question about identifying the enemy.

In 1942 much of Russia's industrial machine, tens of millions of her people, and roughly a third of her territory was in German hands. Russia was not at war with Japan. If any nation defeated Germany it was Russia. Russia bore the brunt of the fighting in Europe for three years, and Stalin's insistence on the opening of a second front in Europe was genuine as it was necessary. Daladier and Chamberlain had hoped in the dark days of 1938 and 1939 that somehow the West would be spared the destruction of a world war, and as late as May 1939 it was hoped that Russia and Germany could be goaded into war on their own, so that the great dictatorships of Europe would wear each other out in a titanic struggle from which Britain and France would ultimately benefit. Stalin surprised the world when the Molotov-Ribbentrop Pact was signed, but he did not forget the fact that Churchill was no friend of international Communism. By 1943 Stalin was convinced that the US and Britain deliberately put off the day when a real second front in Europe would be opened, and he thought little of Operation Torch which opened a second front in Africa. After all, Rommel's Afrika Korps was fighting a sideshow. The main action was at the gates of Moscow and Leningrad and in the streets of Stalingrad. There Russia fought alone and won. Admittedly, lend-lease support from the US helped the Soviet Union, but it is arguable whether or not this aid was decisive for victory in the east. Only after D-Day in June 1944 could the Russians breathe easily in the knowledge that Germany, for the first time, had to fight all-out war in Europe on two fronts.

Thus, during the period 1941–44 different wars were being fought by different combinations of states and for differing reasons. The US carried the war in the Pacific to the Japanese until Hiroshima. The Soviet Union, true to her word at Yalta, came into the Far Eastern war only during the very last days when victory was inevitable. The only tangible aid coming to the United States in the Pacific war came from Australia and, to a lesser extent, New Zealand. Britain could do little until 1944, and in the last year of the war, held her own in driving the Japanese from Burma, but the airlift to China as well as the whole of the China-Burma-India (CBI) theatre of operations was secondary to the war in the Pacific itself. In Europe Russia fought German armies alone until D-Day, while the British, Americans and groups from defeated allied states fought in North Africa and Italy, thereby diverting German resources from the Eastern Front but not sufficiently to materially affect the outcome of the war until a proper second front was opened in Western Europe. British and American bombing missions over Germany took their toll of civilian lives in 1943, but war production actually increased during the bombing of Germany and did not cease to increase, thanks to the efforts of Albert Speer, until the Allies plunged into the Reich itself at the beginning of 1945.

The course of the war and the irony of its legacy is a complex story which, even a generation after its end, is difficult to assess.

In this book Ronald Heiferman attempts to analyze the causes and course of World War Two in the Pacific as well as in Europe. Professor Heiferman, whose historical interests lie primarily in East Asia, has placed a good deal of his emphasis on the lesser-known aspects of the Second World War in order to cast light on the events and motivations which cast their shadow on the present as never before. It has often been stated that the primary reason why the Allies went to war against Germany and Japan was to prevent Germany from dominating Europe and Japan from dominating East Asia. What do we see today? West Germany, a truncated version of the prewar Reich, has an industrial capacity considerably greater than that of Hitler's Germany, and now stands as the fourth largest industrial power in the world, dominating the Common Market of Western Europe in somewhat the same way as she did in 1940. Japan, reduced to rubble in 1945, is the third largest industrial country in the world

today and may become the second by the end of the decade. Several revaluations later, the Deutsche mark and the Japanese yen are among the strongest in the world, while the American dollar, the French franc and the pound sterling have suffered more than one devaluation in recent years. Japanese travellers cheques are considered perhaps even more valuable than those of American Express in Singapore and Hong Kong, and for a time even American companies preferred to hold German marks than the currency of their own country. If the United States pulls most of its troops out of Western Europe, there is little doubt that it will have to be soldiers of the Bundeswehr which will take their place to defend France, Italy, Britain and Scandanavia. In the light of these developments, one wonders why Britain and America fought Germany and Japan. Nations seldom go to war for reasons of morality and realists would argue that they never go to war for reasons which are purely or even primarily altruistic. The situation was no different at the start of World War Two. Did millions die during the Second World War so that German troops could defend Western Europe and that the German economy would dominate it as well? Did the thousands of Americans and Japanese who died on Iwo Jima and Okinawa fight to make East Asia safe for Japanese commerce? Many would wonder today why Japanese domination of China was opposed so fiercely in the light of the growth in power and prestige of the China of Mao Tse-tung.

The answers to these questions are neither simple nor facile. Many of them lie in the developments which the Second World War helped to engender. Professor Heiferman, realizing that if the center of world power lay in Europe in the 19th century, would contend that increasingly it lies in the Pacific in the 20th century. The rise of Asian nationalism received an incalculable boost during World War Two, and the proliferation of states after the war was a direct cause of it. The course of World War Two was as significant and fascinating in Europe and North Africa as it was in Asia. Ronald Heiferman has chosen to emphasize Asia because events there are less well-known and, to the Western viewer, far more difficult to comprehend. Professor Heiferman traces the course of the war with an eye to present events and makes them meaningful as well as exciting.

History is more than a catalogue of events. If there are lessons to be learned from history, if the mistakes of the past are not to be repeated in the future, recent history in particular must be examined if the horrors of World War Two are not to be repeated. Genocide, the seemingly senseless slaughter of millions in the name of nationalism, atomic warfare and the rise of Communism are all to be found in World War Two. No sensible man could contemplate repeating these disasters of the recent past without sacrificing the humane values both European and East Asian civilization has constructed for thousands of years. Churchill hoped that in future generations men would still say of the British in 1940 that 'this was their finest hour.' But no one could say today that World War Two was anything except one of humanity's most tragic and futile hours.

CHAPTER ONE

Between the Wars

At the end of the Great War the victorious Allies assembled at Versailles to build a new world order. After four years of bloody brutal conflict in which empires perished, more than ten million lost their lives, and the lives of countless additional millions were disrupted, the delegates to the Paris Peace Conference convened to make the world safe, to provide a better future for the young or yet unborn. Never had there been a better opportunity to create a new political equilibrium. Never has such an opportunity been lost so pathetically.

The historian Harold Nicolson, himself a delegate to the Paris Peace Conference, suggested shortly after the conference adjourned that future historians would, with some justifications, conclude that the delegates to the conference were stupid men who had arrived in Paris determined that a wise and just peace should be negotiated, but who left the conference conscious that the treaties imposed on their enemies were neither just nor wise nor workable. The reason for the debacle was more clearly articulated by Charles Seymour, another historian also present at Paris, who explained the failure of the conference in the following terms:

The Peace Conference, representing the democracies, reflected the mind of the age; it could not rise measurably above its source. That mind was dominated by reactionary nostalgia and a traditional nationalism . . . It was not so much the absence of justice from the Paris Peace Conference that caused the ultimate debacle; it was the failure to make the most of what justice there was.

When the Allied delegates assembled in Paris, revenge was in the air, and all their lofty rhetoric could not mask their true intent. The Central Powers had caused the war and they (especially), would pay the price for that calumny. Unlike the deliberations at Vienna after the Napoleonic Wars, a century earlier, the vanquished would have no voice at the peace conference, would not participate in the creation of a new world order, and would not be returned into the family of nations until proper retribution had been made. Indeed, the conference ultimately proved little more than a punitive device to extract a pound of flesh from the defeated, and produced not a lasting peace, but the seeds for a future war.

To be sure, some justice was administered in Paris. As empires toppled, subject nationalities were granted independence and national goals and aspirations were formally recognized. Yet even here the delegates to the conference were

selective, preferring to mete justice out to those people who had lived under the domination of the vanquished while failing to deal with those who sought the same rights and equality, but happened to fall under the hegemony of the victors. The Czechs, Hungarians, and Poles realized their independence; the Burmese, Chinese, and Vietnamese did not. It remained for the next war to settle their fate.

When the conference adjourned, a treaty of peace had been imposed on Germany and a League of Nations had been created. Beyond this, little had been accomplished. The treaty provided reparations for the victors, the League a forum for the idealists among them. The rest of the convention's agenda remained untouched. Wilson's vision of a new world order would never be achieved.

The Rise and fall of the Weimar Republic

For the German people the Paris settlement was a shock from which they never quite recovered. The Weimar Republic was forced to accept an ignominious end to a war which it had not initiated, and to acknowledge a huge indemnity for the destruction brought about by this war; foreign forces would occupy German soil and her armed forces would be dismantled. These were bitter pills to swallow for a people who as late as the summer of 1918 expected that they would win the war, and who had not seen allied forces in Germany at any time. It was no wonder, then, that the Germans reacted with digust to the peace which had been thrust upon them. The Allies had been just, but it was justice without mercy.

The fragile Weimar government attempted to fulfill Germany's obligations under the treaty in good faith, but the combination of revenge abroad and hostility at home was more than it could handle. The Republic had been born in chaos and represented the will of a minority of the German population. From the very beginning, conservatives and monarchists refused to accept its legitimacy while radical socialists and communists rebelled against its authority.

That the Weimar Republic survived at all was due to the genius of its leaders and not its institutions. Thanks to the efforts of Walter Rathenau and Gustav Stresemann, the government lived through the Sparticist revolt and the Kapp Putsch and re-established Germany's position in the world community, while attending to pressing domestic problems such as inflation and economic stabilization. By 1929 many of these problems

Opposite: Inflation almost destroyed Germany in 1923. These banknotes, worth billions of marks, might have been enough to have purchased a loaf of bread.

Above: Unable to maintain any sort of a large standing army, the German General Staff was forced to train with these wooden tanks during the years of the Weimar Republic.
Below: Hitler and Ludendorff join forces in an attempt to overthrow the Weimar Republic in 1923.

had been solved or solutions were near at hand. Then came the economic chaos of the Great Depression.

The depression, which had disastrous effects in America and throughout Western Europe, proved fatal to the Weimar Republic. Just as it appeared to be winning greater support from the public and the press, the floor fell out from under it; ironically, Stresemann, the architect of Ger-

many's economic reconstruction, died in the same month, October 1929, when the New York stock market crashed. This coincidence was most unfortunate for the government since Stresemann was, perhaps, the only moderate political leader capable of holding the Weimar coalition together while attending to the problems posed by the new economic disaster in Germany. With his death the coalition rapidly collapsed.

The impact of the depression in Germany was profound, bringing an immediate end to the renewed prosperity of the late 1920's. In 1930 over three million Germans were out of work; two years later the number of jobless workers was over six million. Payment of reparations, always a sore point in Germany, could not be continued and the Allies responded to this failure by sending troops into the Saar valley in order to punish the German government.

With the nation in economic dislocation and its most able defender dead, the Weimar government struggled to maintain its existence. In September 1930 Chancellor Heinrich Brüning, Stresemann's successor, was forced to call for new elections. By this time the depression had become severe, and the conservative-moderate *bloc* in the Reichstag was replaced by radical delegates from the left and right. The Communist Party increased its share of the vote from 3,263,000 in 1928 to 4,600,000. The National Socialist tally increased even more, from 810,000 in 1928 to 6,410,000 in 1930. As a result the conservatives and moderates no longer constituted a majority.

Rather than permit the creation of a communist government, President Hindenburg permitted Chancellor Brüning to remain in office and the country was governed by presidential decree from 1930 to 1932. So long as Brüning had the support of Hindenburg and the leaders of the army, the system worked well, for however much the leaders of the non-authoritarian parties in the Reichstag disliked the arrangement, they dared not cause the defeat of Brüning's government for fear of a Nazi accession to power or, on the other hand, a communist victory. Brüning was forced to resign in May 1932 only after leaders of the army refused to support him, and even then a moderate government was assured by the appointment of Franz von Papen as chancellor. Papen, who

continued to rule through presidential decree, hoped to factionalize the Nazi party and forge a new conservative coalition in the parliament. To this end, he called for an election in July 1932.

The election resulted in an increase of Nazi strength in the Reichstag, 230 National Socialist delegates being returned as opposed to 108 in 1928. Undaunted, Papen dissolved the new Reichstag and called for yet another election, hoping that the popularity of the Nazis had peaked and that their treasury had been drained by the election campaigns of July. When the new Reichstag convened in November, the Chancellor's predictions proved to have been correct, for the Nazis won two million fewer votes than four months before and lost thirty-four seats in the Reichstag. No sooner had the election been concluded, however, than his resignation was demanded by the very men who had persuaded

Hindenburg to appoint him in the first place. By this time, December 1932, the President was ill, and tired of the schemes of the Nazis' the conservative opponents. After the brief and unsuccessful chancellorship of General Kurt von Schleicher, Hindenburg finally agreed to allow Adolf Hitler to form a new government.

With Hindenburg dying, Hitler quickly moved to consolidate his power. In March 1933 he persuaded the Reichstag to pass an enabling act granting him unfettered power to legislate and conclude treaties for four years. During the following months, opposition parties were dissolved and anti-Nazi officials were dismissed from the bureaucracy. When Hindenburg died on 2 August 1934, Hitler assumed the office of the presidency as a result of a popular plebescite and the Nazi revolution began in earnest.

Having eliminated his political rivals, Hitler

Above: French troops occupied the Ruhr Valley when Germany was unable to pay reparations to the Allies.

Below: Early Nazis who tried to overthrow the State in the Beer Hall Putsch in 1923.

turned his attention to rivals within the National Socialist movement, purging them from the party in a brief reign of terror. Ernst Röhm, leader of the SA, was killed during the night of 29–30 June, and Gregor Strasser, a leading party organizer and leader of the left-wing clique within the movement, met the same fate. How many of Hitler's associates were murdered during the purge remains unknown but when it was completed, he emerged as the unchallenged leader of the Nazi movement.

Hitler was now able to turn his attention to the creation of a Nazi state. Labor unions were abolished, strikes were forbidden, and special courts were established to arbitrate labor-management disputes. Economic development plans and programs were immediately initiated and public works projects on a massive scale commenced to solve the problem of unemployment. In less than three years these plans bore fruit: unemployment declined from over six million in 1932 to less than a million in 1936; salaries and fringe benefits for workers increased; and the average German worker enjoyed a standard of prosperity unknown since the depression. Whatever their political views no one could deny that the Nazis had engineered the economic recovered of their country. As a result, many thinking Germans joined the Nazi band-wagon, and by 1936 Nazism had become a genuine mass movement.

Europe moves toward war

Once established at home, Hitler attended to the revision of foreign policy. His diplomatic object-ives had originally been stated in *Mein Kampf* in 1924, and included union with Austria and other Germanic peoples in central and eastern Europe, and the creation of an area of expansion to include western Russia and the Ukraine. Although he repudiated *Mein Kampf* on occasion for political reasons, Hitler never really wavered from his original goals.

Although he recognized that conflict with the Soviet Union and France was inevitable, Hitler hoped to avoid a confrontation with Great Britain or the United States, since his aspirations did not include the creation of a vast overseas empire for Germany. Thus he was careful to pacify these democracies as much as was possible without sacrificing the attainment of his other goals. During the early years of the Third Reich, he tried to appease France as well; as long as Germany's army and navy remained small, it would be imprudent to risk confrontation with the western allies, even the French alone. It was imperative that Germany's armed forces be increased and re-equipped, and this could never be accomplished if the Allies believed that Germany intended waging another war. This being the case, he was careful to speak only of his interest in peace and to discuss only those aspects of the conditions regarding the disarmament of Germany that reasonable men could not deny needed readjustment.

While the rebuilding of Germany's armed forces went on in secret and in violation of the provisions of the Treaty of Versailles, Hitler was not yet ready to repudiate the treaty unilaterally,

Opposite: Outgoing Chancellor von Papen, General von Blomberg, Hitler and Goebbels at a youth demonstration honoring President von Hindenburg in Berlin. **Above:** Leaders of the New Order enjoy the opera in Berlin. Watching *Die Meistersinger* (left to right): Goering and his wife, Rudolf Hess, Frau Goebbels, Hitler, Frau Hess, Goebbels and von Blomberg. **Left:** The Schützstaffeln (SS) destroyed the SA in the Night of the Long Knives and soon replaced it as Hitler's elite guard and leading para-military force.

Below: Hitler reviews the SS in 1938.

nor was he unwilling to negotiate changes in its provisions. Although the French remained intransigent with regard to any alteration of Germany's military status, the British government was more willing to acknowledge that it was time that the treaty be revised. Anxious about French military supremacy on the continent and sympathetic to the reasonable nature of Hitler's proposals, they agreed that there was justice in Hitler's criticism of the peace settlement and in 1935 entered into bilateral arms agreements with the Third Reich. This provided a sanction for the rearmament of Germany which had already taken place and recognized publically what Hitler had long been stating privately, that since the disarmament provisions applied to all signatories, the failure of the victorious allies to adhere to the spirit and letter of the treaty obviated any German obligation to do the same. The French protested, but it was too late to reverse the course of events. In 1936 German forces re-occupied the Rhineland and, for all effective purposes, the Treaty of Versailles was null and void.

Throughout the mid-30's tensions increased as fascism in Italy, Nazism in Germany and the military dictatorship in Japan grew more aggressive. In October 1935 Mussolini launched a campaign against Ethiopia. His success there encouraged him to send troops, planes and supplies to the Spanish fascists when they rebelled against the Republican government in 1936, a venture in which he was soon joined by Germany. Russia promptly moved to support the Spanish government, and the Spanish Civil War, which lasted until 1939, was to prove a testing ground for new weapons and techniques which would be used to great advantage in the larger conflict to come.

As none of the western democracies saw fit to take any effective action to stop these campaigns, Hitler was encouraged to press for a political union with Austria and territorial concessions from the Czech government. Seizing upon the Wilsonian principle that people of common background, culture, and language should be governed by their peers, the Fuehrer took Austria by force

in March 1938 with hardly a word from the Allies. Chamberlain did nothing to prevent the Anschluss because he thought it reasonable that Germans should be governed by Germans; the assumption was that the Austrians were Germans and their relationship with the Third Reich was an internal matter which should be decided without outside interference. The French did nothing because they had no commitment to come to Austria's rescue and were beset by political chaos at home, and the Americans were still clinging to their isolationist policies. Phase one of the plan to create a greater Germany had been achieved; it was now time for phase two, the annexation of the Sudetenland.

The rationale for demanding that the Czech government code the Sudetenland to Germany was even more convincing than the explanation offered for the seizure of Austria. After all, millions of German-speaking people lived under Czech sovereignty and were demanding union with the Fatherland: in asking that their land be annexed to Germany, Hitler was only speaking for an oppressed minority. The Czechs were in a better position than the Austrians to resist Hitler's demands. Their army was large and well equipped, and the French and the Soviets were pledged to come to their assistance in the event of

an attack. The British, although under no treaty obligations to rescue Czechoslovakia, were known to oppose German military intervention, or so the Czechs believed. Thus, when Hitler began to rattle his sword in May 1938, the Czech army was partially mobilized and the Prague government prepared for war.

Since Hitler's generals were opposed to a military confrontation with the Czechs, the Fuehrer agreed to a suggestion made by Mussolini and convened a four-power summit conference in Munich on 29 September 1938. Again France and Britain remained unprepared to actively oppose a re-armed Germany and accepted his position, agreeing that some ten thousand square miles of Czech territory should be annexed by Germany. In return Hitler disowned any further territorial aims in the country and the British Prime Minister, Neville Chamberlain, returned to London hailing the conference as a harbinger of 'peace in our time'. His optimistic words, however, failed to reassure the Czechs, who had been forced to sit by and watch the great powers dismember their country. Their pessimism proved to be well justified, for in less than a year, in March 1939, Hitler swallowed up the rest of the small country; not to be outdone, Mussolini took Albania three weeks later.

The English people, who had been told repeatedly that Munich was a final settlement, felt that their government had been made fools of, and Chamberlain's own confidence in appeasement was severely shaken. When he heard rumors of German troop movements near the Polish border in March he wrote to that country, promising that if their independence was threatened, 'His Majesty's Government and the French Government would at once lend them all the support in their power'. It was an empty gesture, since Britain had no means of fulfilling her bargain, and was hopefully indended to incline Hitler toward a policy of moderation. In fact Hitler used it as an excuse to repudiate the German non-aggression pact with Poland of 1934 and the Anglo-German naval agreements of 1935; in August 1939 he shocked the world by signing a non-aggression pact with Russia. Britain responded by signing an Anglo-Polish treaty of mutual assistance, but it was too late. With his eastern front secure, Hitler was free to move troops into Poland over the issue of Danzig and the Polish Corridor. Great Britain declared war on Germany at 11 a.m. on 3 September 1939 and the French unhappily followed suit at 5 p.m.; belatedly, the two governments began leisurely to prepare for battle.

Above left: The Nuremberg rallies were often used to demonstrate Germany's new armed might. **Above:** Austrians rejoice in Salzburg when Germany annexed their country in the Anschluss of 1938.

Below left: German troops cross the Ludendorff Bridge to re-occupy the Rhineland in 1936. The Allies could have stopped them if they had tried. They didn't. **Below:** Hitler signs the Munich Pact which sealed the fate of Czechoslovakia. Behind him (from left to right) Chamberlain of Great Britain, Mussolini, and Premier Daladier of France.

Japan's rise to power

Japan, unlike Germany, had attended the Paris
Peace Conference as a member of the victorious
allied coalition. Indeed, the war had been more
profitable for Japan than for the other Allies.
With a minimal commitment of manpower, the
Japanese had annexed German leaseholds in
China early in the war and consolidated their
position during the remainder. When the armistice was signed on 11 November 1918, Japan was
the paramount outside force in China and her
economy was still in high gear, responding to the
economic vacuum created by the pre-occupation
of the European powers in the war against
Germany. It might well be said that no country
was so ill prepared for the coming of peace as
Japan in 1918.

With the war over, Japanese activities in China
would once again come under the jealous scrutiny
of the Western powers whose governments and
businessmen hoped to re-establish the pre-war
equilibrium in China. This boded ill for the
Japanese but well for the Chinese, who hoped to
use the peace conference as a forum in which they
might secure redress of their grievances from
Japan with the aid of the Western powers, particularly the United States. When the conference
convened, the Japanese delegation soon found
itself justifying Japan's position in China and
defending this position from a joint Sino-American
attack. This they did successfully, but not without
cost.

The Japanese, rightly or wrongly, believed that
consideration of their actions at the peace conference was inappropriate and prejudicial, since
the other victors were not asked to justify their
own colonial policies and economic interests. As a
member of the Allied coalition whose annexations
of German leaseholds in China had been approved
by the other allies in 1915, Japan found it difficult
to understand their belated concern with the well
being and sovereignty of the Republic of China in
1919, and attributed this interest to economic
gain and racial prejudice. Although China's
advocates could not force Japan to return her
territory in China to the Chinese government, the
Japanese did not view the outcome of the peace
conference with much favor. On the contrary,
government leaders in Tokyo saw the abortive
challenge to Japan's position in China as an
indication that the honeymoon with the Western
allies would soon end, forcing a re-evaluation of
diplomatic policies and alliances. This new mood
contributed in no small way to the development
of Japan's foreign policy from 1919–1937.

The re-adjustment of Japan's policy in China
was a major topic when the Nine-Power Conference was convened in Washington in the
winter of 1921–1922. Although ostensibly called
to implement naval arms limitations, China was
one of the most important topics at the conference
and, under considerable pressure from the western
powers, the Japanese government finally agreed
to return Tsingtao most of their rights in Shantung
to the Chinese, reluctantly accepting the United
States' 'open door' policy.

From 1921 to 1928 the Japanese pursued a
conciliatory policy toward China and the Western
powers which paralled the advent of democratic
government at home. This policy came to an

Above: Japanese forces enter Tientsin, July 1937.

abrupt end in 1928 when the renaissance of Chinese nationalism threatened to curtail Japanese commercial interests in China. Under the government of Prime Minister Tanaka the Japanese reverted to a tougher policy and even intervened militarily to protect Japanese interests. Nevertheless, the Japanese stopped short of wholesale military intervention in the hope that they might strike an arrangement with Generalissimo Chiang Kai-shek which would guarantee Japan's position in China.

If nothing else, Chiang Kai-shek was pledged to the proposition that special foreign interests and privileges in China would have to end, and in this regard he was no more sympathetic to the Japanese than to the West. While China remained divided and beset by warlordism, the anti-imperialist policy of the Kuomintang threatened no one. But with the establishment of the Nationalists in Nanking in 1928, their anti-imperialist stance could no longer be dismissed. While the Chinese Nationalists were in no position to force a readjustment of the enequal treaties on the Western powers or Japan, it would not be long until Chiang might feel secure enough to force the issue. Furthermore, it appeared likely that if such a readjustment were demanded, at least one of the powers, the United States, would stand behind the Nationalist government, if for no other reason than to insure the sanctity of the open door doctrine. Rather than wait for this to happen, the Japanese chose to act before it was too late.

Failing to extract concessions from the Chinese government, the Japanese resorted to force to insure their position in China. In 1928 officers of the Kwantung army assassinated Chang Tso-lin, the warlord of Manchuria, whom they considered incompetent and uncooperative. Although no friend of the Chinese Nationalists, Chang was a threat to Japanese expansion in Manchuria, a mineral-rich area vital to the development of heavy industry in Japan; although his murder was not ordered by the government in Tokyo, no effort was made to discipline the officers involved for fear that this might damage the prestige of the army. Government leaders were hardly appalled by the deed, for the mood of the nation had changed considerably since 1921, as had the situation in China.

The action of the Kwantung army in Manchuria reflected this change and gave rise to other heavy handed efforts to secure Japanese control in the province, culminating in the Manchurian Incident of 1931.

The Manchurian Incident created a war psychosis in Japan and resulted in the rapid Japanese occupation of China's three northeastern provinces and the creation of the Kingdom of Manchukuo in 1932. Faced with a *fait accompli* and the loss of three provinces, the Chinese government took its case against Japan to the League of Nations which appointed the Lytton Commission to investigate the matter. By the time the commission published its findings and reported to the League in 1933, Japan's presence in Manchuria had been cemented and there was nothing the League could do to extract concessions from the Japanese, who walked out rather than face its condemnation in 1933.

23

Right: Fighting in Shanghai was fierce. Here Japanese marines man a barricade on the steps of the gutted Chapei Church.

The Chinese protested and the League condemned, but the Western powers did nothing to prevent the Japanese from annexing Manchuria. Only the United States responded to Japan's aggression but even this response was limited to a verbal slap on the wrist. Try as he might to throw some weight behind his denunciation of the Japanese, Secretary of State Henry L. Stimson knew full well that Congress and the American people were in no mood to engage in anything more than a verbal debate. His non-recognition policy angered Japanese leaders but it in no way inhibited their policies in China. In fact, it moved Japan further out of the Allied coalition which had survived the Great War.

Rebuffed by the Western powers and the League of Nations, the Japanese developed a new Asian policy based upon the notion of pan-Asianism and the creation of a Japanese sphere of influence throughout Asia. As the only Asian country to successfully industrialize and come to grips with the problem of modernization, the Japanese came to view themselves as benevolent and paternalistic leaders of the Asian world and proposed to lead an anti-colonial coalition against the European powers and the United States. Although a formal program to achieve this end was not articulated until 1938, Japanese interest in the Asian world increased markedly from 1928–1938, and no opportunity was lost to advance Japanese goals and priorities in the decade prior to the war. On the other hand, there is no evidence to suggest that Japan's leaders were unwilling to

Left: Japanese troops advance warily through a town in North China. By early 1939 the forces of the Empire of Japan had swept Chiang Kai-shek's Nationalists from most of coastal China.

consider a rapprochement with the Western powers and the United States if this could be achieved without losses in Manchuria and elsewhere.

Any chance for a rapprochement with the Western powers was all but smashed when Japanese forces invaded China in 1937. More than any other single act, the invasion of China nullified diplomatic efforts to avoid a confrontation. Whatever the original merits of the response to renascent Chinese nationalism, the invasion of China proved costly and futile to the Japanese. The China incident lasted more than seven years, occupied the attention of nearly a million Japanese troops and strained Japanese-American relations almost to a breaking point. The Chinese Nationalists did not collapse in the face of the Japanese invaders but retreated to the interior of China where, together with Chinese Communist forces in northwest China, they resisted Japan until September 1945.

What were the origins of the Second World War? German dissatisfaction with the terms of the Treaty of Versailles, certainly, and the economic disaster brought on by the depression. The Japanese desire for growth in the Far East and subsequent American pressure were other factors, as were expansionist policies by Russia and Italy. But no one could have foreseen that three separate wars caused by these factors, the German-Polish war, the Sino-Japanese war and the Russo-Finnish war, would mushroom, overlap and turn nearly the entire world into a battlefield.

Left: Shanghai burns after Japanese bombers wiped out the northern part of the city.

CHAPTER TWO
Blitzkrieg
(September 1939 - June 1940)

On 1 September 1939 German armies crossed the Polish frontier and launched an attack which immediately shattered the fragile interwar peace. Britain and France had anticipated that Poland would be Hitler's next target; indeed, German forces had hardly sealed the fate of the Czech government in March when Mr Chamberlain, speaking on behalf of the British government, offered Poland his pledge of support. This the Poles were only too ready to accept, despite the fact that there was little the British could do to nullify the effect of Hitler's first blitzkrieg. Both in Warsaw and in London, it was vainly hoped that this new 'tough line' would deter Hitler from using force in Poland if and when diplomatic means failed. The somewhat less enthusiastic French declaration of support for the Poles which followed shortly after Chamberlain's statements simply served to reinforce this view and, unfortunately, gave the Polish government false confidence in its ability to withstand the Nazi onslaught.

While heads of state were making ever more ominous statements, an abortive attempt was made to solve the Polish problem through diplomacy. The Germans, made bold by their triumph at Munich and confident of the unwillingness of the other European powers to go to war on Poland's behalf, lost little time after Munich in presenting their bill of particulars to the Polish government; their demands included the return of Danzig to German control and the right to build a major highway and rail facility across the Polish Corridor to East Prussia. In effect, Hitler and his associates were seeking to nullify one of the most unpopular provisions of the Treaty of Versailles through negotiation and consent. When such consent was not easily forthcoming from the Poles, Hitler turned his attention to their British and French allies.

If Hitler assumed that his solution of the Polish question would be as easily foisted upon the British and French as the dismemberment of Czechoslovakia, he was gravely mistaken. Mr Chamberlain, the architect of appeasement in 1938, had suddenly 'acquired a spine,' a fact which caught both the French and the Germans off guard. Although Chamberlain had chosen not to respond with force over the Czechoslovakian *débâcle*, his almost unqualified support of the Polish government in 1939 marked the end of appeasement. Unfortunately this change was temporarily overlooked by Hitler, who continued to perceive the new situation in old stereotypes until continued rebuffs forced him to look elsewhere for allies in the Polish affair.

With Mr Chamberlain forcefully condemning Germany's appetite for territory with the French following reluctantly behind, Hitler turned toward the Soviet Union for help in solving the Polish question. Such an approach, though compelling because of the seeming intransigence of Chamberlain and Daladier, was nonetheless difficult given the deep and mutual distrust felt by Hitler and Stalin. Thus, although preliminary discussions of a Nazi-Soviet *détente* were initiated in April 1939, no agreement was reached until the end of August. It is quite possible that even after this prolonged period of negotiation an agreement might not have been reached were it not for the Molotov's arrival at the Foreign Ministry in Moscow and, especially, Stalin's frustration over the slow progress of Anglo-Russian deliberations.

Any guarantee of Polish sovereignty was meaningless without Soviet compliance. This point was not altogether lost on the British and French, but neither party was enthusiastic about seeking Russian support. Some of their reluctance to court Stalin reflected the Poles' strong distrust of any arrangement that might permit the Soviets military passage through their territory, and in addition, British and French military leaders tended to underestimate the Red Army's ability to effectively counter German units in the event of an attack on Poland. They preferred, instead, to rely on the ability of the Polish army to withstand a German onslaught until their own forces could be mobilized and sent to Poland's rescue. Thus, there appeared to be little need for bringing the Soviets into a tripartite pact to preserve the sovereignty of Poland, and in fact, the first gesture toward an entente was to be made by the Soviets and not the Anglo-French allies despite the fact that such an agreement was far more in the interest of England and France than of Russia.

The Russians revived the notion of a tripartite anti-Nazi pact shortly after the fall of Czechoslovakia, presenting it formally on 16 April 1939. Though an alliance between Russia, England, and France would have certainly given Hitler reason to pause and might well have avoided the dismemberment of Poland, neither Chamberlain nor his French colleague, Daladier, were particularly enthusiastic. Their lack of response placed the architect of the proposal, M. Litvinov, under great pressure. Litvinov was an outspoken proponent of the western alliance, a staunch anti-fascist, and a Jew, and so long as he remained

Opposite top: Germans cross the Polish frontier: 1 September 1939.
Opposite bottom: German forces streaked through Poland in a week.

27

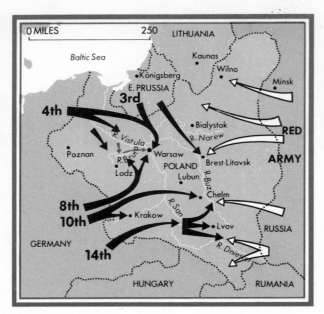

Daladier was as much responsible for the announcement of 23 August 1939 as the assurances Hitler's associates gave to Stalin prior to the signing of the pact.

The Nazi-Soviet Pact provided for the fourth partition of Poland as well as for Soviet annexation of Latvia, Estonia, and Finland. Even more important, it provided time and a temporary breathing space which was advantageous for both countries. That this was its main purpose can be easily demonstrated, both by later events and contemporary evidence. Though Churchill might well say that 'only totalitarian despotism in both countries could have faced the odium of such an unnatural act,' neither Hitler nor Stalin had any illusions about the true nature of the agreement. Indeed, one might well wonder which dictator abhorred the pact the most! Whatever the answer, it is clear that both men were far more pragmatic than their opposite numbers in the west.

The pact between Germany and the Soviet Union made war certain, and there was little the British and French could do except to reaffirm their pledges to Poland and prepare for the inevitable. Though Chamberlain made one last diplomatic move to avert hostilities, it was an empty gesture and was understood to be so by both sides: it was now only a question of when and where the war would begin.

The invasion of Poland

German forces crossed the Polish border early in the morning on 1 September 1939; by the end of the month, Poland had ceased to exist. The speed and ease of the German victory was a monument to the ruthless efficiency of their 'blitz' and the hopelessly inadequate defense offered by Polish forces and their allies. Contrary to popular opinion at the time, the Germans possessed neither numerical superiority nor an absolute technological advantage over their enemies in this first battle of the European war. As Basil Liddell Hart points out, the German army was hardly more ready for war in 1939 than its adversaries; in numbers alone, the Polish army had ample forces (thirty active divisions, ten reserve divisions and twelve cavalry brigades) to contend with the hold, the German strike force (48 active divisions and six reserve divisions) until help arrived from England and France. What the allies lacked was an appreciation of the fact that new developments in mobile equipment had revolutionized modern warfare. Nowhere was this more pathetically manifested than in the defensive deployment of Polish forces.

Russia's Foreign Commissar a Nazi-Soviet agreement was unlikely. Unfortunately, Stalin grew tired of the rebuffs of the British and the French and on 3 May 1939 replaced Litvinov with Vyacheslav Molotov. Molotov was more sympathetic to the fascist regimes in Germany and Italy and lost little time in altering Soviet foreign strategy; under his stewardship, Russo-German negotiations began in earnest, culminating in August 1939 with the Nazi-Soviet pact.

The German Foreign Ministry was not slow to take advantage of the Anglo-French failure to accept the Soviet initiative. Even before Molotov replaced Litvinov, new discussions of German-Russian relations had been initiated in Berlin and Moscow; though the Soviet press still seemed to echo the anti-fascist line so commonly found in England and the United States, German diplomats sensed that Stalin was growing restless and resentful at the way he was being treated in London and Paris and advised the Fuehrer to press for a rapprochement with Moscow. The advent of Molotov gave rise to redoubled efforts toward that end, but the path was still difficult and there is no reason to believe that at this point the conclusion of a Nazi-Soviet pact was inevitable. If such had been the case, it would not have taken so long for Molotov to cement the arrangement. Clearly, the dallying of Chamberlain and

The Polish command was hopelessly antiquated in its military strategy and the pattern of its forces. Though the Polish government might eventually muster as many as 2,500,000 men, its army had few armored and motorized divisions and were very short of anti-aircraft and anti-tank guns. The cavalry, the pride of the Polish forces, could not resist Germany's mechanized units; like many other horse-minded soldiers, Poland's commanders had virtually ignored the lessons of the American Civil War and the First World War and persisted in the illusion that cavalry charges could repel tanks and armored vehicles. They paid heavily for this belief.

In anticipation of a possible German attack, Polish forces were deployed along the long and virtually open frontiers with Germany and Czechoslovakia, a strip approximately 3500 miles long. A third of her forces were located around the Polish Corridor, a smaller number in Silesia, and the rest were thinly scattered along the southern border with the exception of a reserve force in the Lodz-Warsaw area. Although it would have been wiser to avoid this concentration of forces in the forward areas, the economic importance of the Silesian coalfields and patriotic attachments the recently acquired Corridor dictated the deployment of forces in these areas. Had the Poles assembled their forces further to the east they might have been able to resist the German offensive more successfully, but national pride would never have allowed this abandonment of the forward lines. Nor did Poland's military leaders see their deployment of forces as a liability; on the eve of the invasion, they continued to remain confident in their ability to resist until their western allies could mobilize and take counter measures to relieve the pressure.

Poland's topography was perfectly suited for the German assault, the Polish plain providing the invaders with a large area across which their mechanized mobile forces could rapidly advance. The blitzkrieg, based upon the deployment of a highly armored and mobile striking force of tanks, self-propelled guns, and truck transports, rapidly broke through Poland's front lines, wrecking command areas and cutting off supplies. With inadequate means of transportation and supply, Polish forces along the frontier could not offer a coordinated defense against their enemies nor, since railway lines from the front to the interior were savagely and successfully knocked out by the German air force, could they be quickly moved to the rear to engage in delaying action. Marching on foot or riding on horseback, large numbers of Polish troops were almost instantly trapped behind German lines as German mobile units raced toward the east.

The cavalry, upon which Polish leaders had pinned their defense, proved entirely ineffective in stopping German tanks. Despite the heroic Polish cavalry men who rode against German Panzer divisions, the heavy equipment would not be stopped by swords and lances; the use of horsed cavalry in modern warfare was unequivocably proven to be inadequate defense against the new technology of death.

Within two days German forces had sealed off the Polish Corridor and were converging on the cities of Cracow and Lodz. The German attack force, consisting of two army groups (Bock's army group in the north and Runstedt's in the south), might have advanced even further were it not for the somewhat orthodox policy of restraining the mobile forces until infantry units could catch up to them. However, as the German commanders realized how confused and inadequate the Polish defense was, even this restraint was abandoned; by 6 September Cracow, the old imperial capital, had fallen and the Polish army was in retreat. On 8 September, German forces reached the outskirts of Warsaw.

The speed of the German advance (some 140

miles within the first week) caught the Poles off-guard, but it was not until 10 September that Marshal Smigly-Rydz ordered a retreat toward southeast Poland where a more prolonged defense might be prepared. By this time most of the Polish forces had been captured behind enemy lines or were spent in the brave but useless offensive actions that had been ordered prior to the call for retreat. This failure to call for an early retreat and the insistence on launching useless counterattacks extracted a price in men and material which far exceeded any possible benefits. Though Polish forces fought bravely and won the grudging admiration of their enemies on the battlefield, the stubbornness and over-confidence of their leaders was not easily overcome; by the end of the second week of the campaign, the Polish army had ceased to exist as an organized force.

On 17 September, as the Germans pressed their attack on Warsaw and the remnants of Poland's army retreated toward the southeast, Russian forces struck across the eastern border. This attack sealed Poland's fate, although the Warsaw garrison continued to hold out until 28 September. By 5 October organized resistance had collapsed, the fourth partition of Poland had been accom-

Above: On 17 September the Russians moved into Eastern Poland to secure their part of the infamous bargain struck in the Molotov-Ribbentrop Pact.

Right: German infantry during the assault on Warsaw. The Poles stubbornly and vainly defended their capital.
Opposite: A Stuka dive bomber moves in for the kill over Warsaw.

plished, and the terms of the Nazi-Soviet Pact had been fulfilled; as its critics had predicted as early as March, the guarantee of aid from the Western allies had proved virtually meaningless. Churchill declared on 1 October that the heroic defense of Warsaw shows that the soul of Poland is indestructible, and that she will rise again like a rock . . ., but words of praise were of little consolation to the Polish people.

The 'phoney war'

Sitzkrieg followed blitzkrieg. After the dismemberment of Poland the war entered a brief quiescent stage when, except for the 'winter war' in Finland, no new fronts were opened for eight months. The 'phoney war,' as the American press called it, was a time for reflection on both sides. In Berlin, London and Paris statesmen sought to analyse the implications of the German victory in Poland while generals planned future actions and contemplated the strategies of their adversaries.

In Berlin the momentum of the Polish campaign had not excited the German general staff as much as it had fired the imagination of their

Below: Blitzkrieg was followed by 'sitzkrieg'. British children were evacuated to the country during the phoney war.

Fuehrer. Although Hitler had temporarily revived the hope of a new European peace conference to avoid prolonged world conflict, he also hastened to plan for an early offensive in the West, and once his peace bid had been rebuffed (9 October) he presented the plans to his military lieutenants. Almost to a man, they balked at his suggestion of an early offensive against the British and French, but the Fuehrer persisted in his belief that such an action would forestall a longer and more costly campaign in the future. Fearing that the marriage of convenience with the Soviets would evaporate now that both parties had achieved their immediate aims in Poland, Hitler insisted that peace would have to be forced on the English and French before the Russians joined them in a plot against Germany.

Hitler's bold plans for a confrontation with England and France frightened his military advisers. Although the German press had changed the Polish conquest from an event to a legend, the generals knew better than the reading public the difficulties of repeating such a triumph against the Western allies. England and France, after all, were far more formidable foes than Poland; though they had remained virtually paralysed as the Germans swept through Poland, they could hardly be expected to do the same while their own territory was violated. In addition, the revelation of the strategy of blitzkrieg could not have been expected to go unnoticed. The preparations that were surely being made in London and Paris would prove extremely costly in the event of an attack – or so the generals thought.

On paper, the hesitation of the German General Staff appears to have been well founded. Even with the elimination of Polish forces on the east, the Germans would face superior numbers on the western front; the French alone could mobilize a total of 110 divisions to which the British might add four to six divisions at the start of the conflict with more to follow. The German generals, with a potential mobilization of 98 divisions of which as many as 36 were unfit for combat because of insufficient training and/or equipment, were understandably wary, also knowing that the French army was fully their

equal and actually possessed a numerical superiority in tanks, long-range guns, and artillery pieces. Only in the size of her air force did Germany possess an advantage over her enemies.

If the generals doubted their commander-in-chief, their troops and the German people stood behind their leader. Realizing this, Hitler grew increasingly impatient with his military advisers; he chastised them for their lack of confidence and aggressive spirit and ordered the preparation of an offensive plan. Although Brauchitsch, the Commander-in-Chief of the Army, and Halder, the Chief of the General Staff, continued to harbor reservations about the wisdom of the scheme, they finally complied with his command after failing to persuade him to change his mind.

The offensive in the west was supposed to commence in mid-November 1939, but had to be postponed several times due to meteorological conditions. The original plan, drafted by Halder and other of the older generals, was closely reminiscent of the Schlieffen Plan of 1914, calling for the main German attack to proceed through Central Belgium with a secondary and lighter thrust in the area of the Ardennes. This plan, reluctantly drafted at Hitler's insistence, was sharply criticized by some younger officers who feared it was too obvious; fortunately for them and the German army, a German liaison officer carrying a copy of the plan landed in Belgium on 10 January 1940 when his plane went astray on a flight from Münster to Bonn. Fearing that it had fallen into Allied hands, Hitler scrapped the old plan and commissioned a new one.

The architect of the new plan was Erich von Manstein, Chief of Staff of Rundstedt's army and a critic of Halder's original scheme. Collaborating with Guderian, an expert in tank warfare who had participated in the blitz of Poland, Manstein proposed a reversal of the earlier plan. Whereas Halder had called for a primary attack in central Belgium, Manstein proposed a major assault through the Ardennes with diversionary actions in central Belgium, along the Maginot line, and in Holland. Such a move through the 'impenetrable forest' would catch the allies off-guard, thus permitting the main German force to rapidly break through weakly held French lines and head toward the Channel coast, cutting off the Belgians, British, and French in the process.

Manstein's plan was a bold one, and his departure from orthodox strategy was resisted by the General Staff, who not only held that such a scheme was impractical, but also resented the personal manner in which Manstein had pressed his case. Nevertheless, their opposition went unnoticed; Hitler insisted upon its implementation and ordered a spring offensive. So pleased was he with the whole idea that he later claimed credit

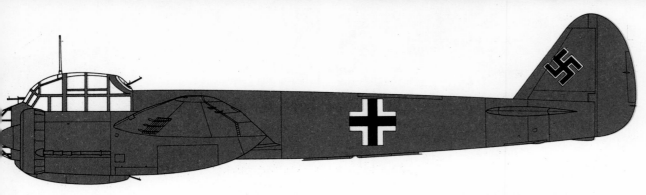

J.U. 88–A4 Length: 47 ft.
1½ in. Span: 65 ft. 10½ in.
Maximum speed: 293
m.p.h. Armament:
2 × 13 mm., 3-4 × 7.9 mm.

for the victory in the west, reducing Manstein to the status of the only general who had understood him when he raised the idea of an attack through the Ardennes.

Norway and Denmark fall

Preparations for the western offensive were temporarily interrupted by the German invasions of Denmark and Norway in April 1940. Unlike the previous Polish campaign, these ventures were ad hoc affairs, hastily improvised in response to the German navy's fear of a British action in Norway; this would preclude Germany's use of the long Norwegian coastline, facilitate the British blockade of Germany, and cut off the flow of iron ore from northern Sweden upon which the German steel industry was dependent.

On 19 February 1940 Hitler reluctantly ordered the completion of plans for seizing Norway; a decision undoubtedly precipitated by the British search and seizure of a German vessel in Norwegian territorial waters on 16 February. The Altmark affair, more than any other argument or incident, convinced the Fuehrer of the validity of Admiral Raeder's arguments for a preventive strike against Norway. Norwegian neutrality would inevitably be violated by the British. Was it not, therefore, wise for Germany to strike first? Hitler could hardly dispute this judgement; the bold action of the Royal Navy and the seeming compliance of the Norwegian government demanded effective countermeasures.

While Chamberlain and Daladier debated possible pre-emptive measures in Scandinavia, the German strike force under the command of General Falkenhorst completed its preparation for the invasion; aided and abetted by traitors such as Vidkun Quisling, the Germans were ready to launch their offensive at the beginning of April. Curiously enough, the Allies also planned

Below: German infantry moves into Norway behind a Panzer.

Far left: Finnish soldiers defend their untenable border when Russia invaded Finland in the Winter War of 1939–40. Russia hoped to secure its northern flank against its ally Germany, but the Red Army received a nasty shock when the Finns refused to roll over and play dead. **Center left:** Grand Admiral Raeder (center) charts the course for the German Navy, which was effectively blockaded almost from the outset of the war. **Left:** German mortars in action against Norwegian mountain troops.

Left: The *Graf Spee* was scuttled in the River Plate in Argentina after having been chased and trapped. The *Graf Spee* wreaked havoc with British shipping in both the Atlantic and the Pacific. Its destruction virtually eliminated German sea power outside the North Atlantic.

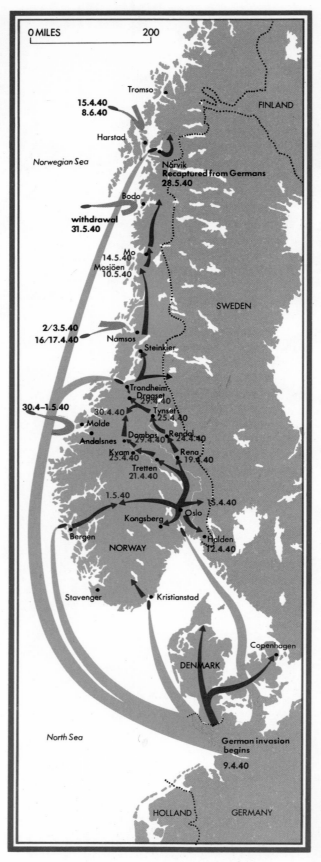

Legend:

German invasion of Denmark and Norway, started 9 April 1940

14.5.40 — German advance and dates of capture

15.4.40 / 8.6.40 — Allied landings, (top date) and later withdrawals, (bottom date)

Map labels:

0 MILES 200

Tromso

15.4.40 / 8.6.40

FINLAND

Harstad

Norwegian Sea

Narvik — Recaptured from Germans 28.5.40

Bodo

withdrawal 31.5.40

Mo 14.5.40

Mosjöen 10.5.40

SWEDEN

2/3.5.40 / 16/17.4.40 — Namsos

Steinkier

Trondheim — Orpaset 29.4.40

Tynset 25.4.40

30.4.40

30.4–1.5.40

Molde

Rendal 24.4.40

Dombas 29.4.40

Andalsnes

Kvam 25.4.40

Rena 19.4.40

Tretten 21.4.40

1.5.40

15.4.40

Kongsberg

Oslo

Bergen

Halden 12.4.40

NORWAY

Stavenger

Kristianstad

Copenhagen

DENMARK

North Sea

German invasion begins 9.4.40

HOLLAND

GERMANY

---

arrival of German bombers over Copenhagen later that morning left little room for doubt as to Hitler's intentions. Shortly after 7:00 a.m. King Christian X accepted the German terms and by the end of the day, Denmark was under German occupation.

The invasion of Norway commenced one hour after German troops had crossed the Danish frontier. The Norwegian government was presented with the same alternative as the Danes – capitulate without resistance or suffer the consequences of a German blitz. Indeed, even as this ultimatum was being delivered by the German minister, forces were being landed at Narvik, Trondheim, Bergen, and Christiansted and had begun moving toward Oslo. Despite these intimidations, the Norwegian government refused to accept Hitler's conditions. Although all major Norwegian cities were in German hands by noon, King Haakon VII and his government successfully escaped from Oslo and resistance to the German occupation began that afternoon.

With the evacuation of the monarchy, Vidkun Quisling was installed as head of the Norwegian government. His designation, contrary to German expectations, did not eliminate resistance but increased it. Meagre Norwegian army forces, buoyed by hastily improvised and somewhat indirect assistance from the British navy, attempted to stand against German units north of the capital. At the same time, frenzied preparations were being made in London to engage the German fleet off the Norwegian coast and launch relief efforts at Narvik and Trondheim. When finally mounted, these operations were ineffective and were rapidly halted by the Germans. Although resistance had not yet ceased when the western offensive was launched on 10 May 1940, the Norwegian affair was settled for all intents and purposes by the end of April.

The invasions of Denmark and Norway were a smashing success for the Germans, insuring their continued access to iron ore from Sweden and the use of air bases from which allied shipping in the North Sea might be attacked. For the British, the affair was a disaster of the first magnitude which could not be easily erased, even by their naval victory over the German fleet. For the people of Denmark and Norway, the long winter of German occupation had begun.

The Western offensive

Germany's western offensive began on 10 May 1940 with simultaneous thrusts into Belgium and Holland. At dawn, while German diplomats informed their Dutch counterparts that an invasion was being launched to preclude a similar Franco-British move, German airborne units were dropped behind Dutch lines and the Luftwaffe attacked military installations and airbases. Four days later (14 May 1940) the Dutch surrendered.

The speed of Germany's conquest of the Netherlands was the direct result of the deployment of large numbers of paratroopers, the first major airborne assault of the war. The Dutch were not unprepared for a German attack, but they had expected that attack to come on the ground and prepared accordingly. The defensive plans devised at the Hague called for the consolidation of the

some action in this area at that very time but the end of the Russo-Finnish War and the fall of the Daladier government forced its postponement. Thus, when the Germans struck, they were barely a step ahead of their adversaries.

On 9 April 1940 at 4:00 a.m. Falkenhorst's army crossed the Danish frontier. Shortly thereafter, the German ambassador presented the Danish foreign minister with his government's case: the Danes might capitulate immediately and accept the German occupation as a 'friendly necessity' or they would be forced to capitulate. If this message was not sufficiently clear, the

Top: German heavy machine-gun on Norway's coast. **Bottom:** Wrecked shipping in Narvik Bay after an attack by British warships in the First Battle of Narvik; 10 April 1940.

Above: German paratroops land in Holland on the first day of the Blitzkrieg in the West: 10 May 1940.
Above right: German troops moved quickly across Dutch canals to successfully trap the Dutch Army. **Opposite top left:** The center of Rotterdam was wiped out on 14 May 1940, ironically after the Dutch had capitulated.
Opposite top right: German forces streak through Flanders and the towns which were so heroically defended by the Allies in the War of 1914–18.

Right: German troops enter the port of Rotterdam even while the city was burning. **Far right:** Belgians welcome British armored vehicles as they pass forward to the front.

Dutch forces behind the Grebbe-Peel line if the Germans crossed the border. Since the Dutch-German border was over 200 miles long, it was useless to consider making a stand there; only the eastern lowlands would be flooded to slow the German advance while 'fortress Holland' was being consolidated. Here, in Amsterdam, Rotterdam and the Hague, the Dutch army proposed to make its stand. Although the possibility of an airborne assault had been considered, it was ruled out as being too impractical and beyond the capability of the German army. Thus, when it was actually launched, the Dutch were caught completely off guard and could do little to defend themselves.

That an airborne assault on Holland might strain German resources was true; when the invasion was launched on 10 May there were only some 4500 trained parachute troops in all of the German army. Of these, 4000 were deployed in Holland. There was little margin for error but the benefits to be derived from such a surprise proved well worth the risk involved. As it happened, only 180 of General Student's **4000 men** were killed or wounded; by seizing important bridges, investing the major urban centres, and capturing enemy airfields intact, they cleared the way for the conventional support troops, who followed to mop up the operation and dispose of the Dutch. Germany's double blow on fortress Holland and the frontier was more than the Dutch could handle; French relief from the south under General Giraud came too late, and in any case could not have turned the tide. There was no alternative but to sue for peace.

After the conquest of Holland the Germans were free to concentrate on the campaign in Belgium and the attack through the Ardennes. In Belgium, things were going according to plan. Fort Eben-Emael had been effectively neutralized by a small contingent of airborne forces while the few other airborne units that were left after the invasion of Holland were landed west of the Albert Canal, securing important bridges to allow German ground forces to advance westward and southward. By the second morning of the invasion (11 May 1940), a general retreat was

ordered by Belgian commanders. At about the same time, British and French reinforcements arrived on the scene.

The German breakthrough across the Albert Canal and the Meuse was of far less import than the rush of British and French forces into Belgium to counter the German advance. By throwing the best and most mobile part of their army into Belgium, the Allies had left the Germans free to launch their attack through the Ardennes, safe in the knowledge that by the time Allied forces could be redeployed against them, their own would be well on the way to the Channel coast.

While German Army Group B pushed rapidly into northern Belgium occupying the attention of 36 Allied divisions in the process, Army Group A traversed the Ardennes, crossing the French frontier on 14 May, the same day that the Dutch surrender was accepted. Meeting little resistance from the weak French units guarding this sector between the end of the Maginot Line and central Belgium, German armored units quickly broke through and headed toward the coast. After some initial hesitation over the implications of too rapid progress, the green light was given to Panzer commanders Guderian, Hoth, and Reinhardt who immediately raced westward. By

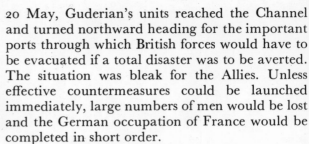

Above: Stukas in a Norwegian fjord. **Right:** A German destroyer in a fjord near Narvik. **Below right:** A German minesweeper in Norwegian waters.

Below: The German attack on Norway was swift and decisive. **Below right:** A dying French soldier is assisted by the man who shot him. **Opposite:** German infantry was not stopped by Holland's river barriers.

20 May, Guderian's units reached the Channel and turned northward heading for the important ports through which British forces would have to be evacuated if a total disaster was to be averted. The situation was bleak for the Allies. Unless effective countermeasures could be launched immediately, large numbers of men would be lost and the German occupation of France would be completed in short order.

There were few alternatives open to Allied forces: the men now isolated by Army Group B in Belgium might strike south in an effort to link up with the remainder of their forces or they could evacuate the continent. The latter course was anethema to the French, and General Gamelin issued an order for a strike to the south on 19 May, one day before German forces reached the Channel coast. But, on that same day, Gamelin was removed as Commander-in-Chief of French forces and replaced by General Weygand who immediately cancelled his predecessor's order pending further consideration. With no directions from command headquarters, the Allied armies were virtually paralysed and lost any chance to salvage the situation.

Fortunately for the British Expeditionary Force, Weygand's vacillation was paralleled by a similar lapse on the German side. Although Guderian's forces were within ten miles of Dunkirk, the only port from which the expeditionary force could possibly be evacuated, the Fuehrer insisted that he pause short of this target. Why this decision was made remains one of the unsolved mysteries of the war, but whatever the reason British commanders lost little time in taking advantage of the situation.

On 25 May, General Lord Gort, Commander-in-Chief of the BEF, decided to pull his forces back to the sea and evacuate the continent. It had become abundantly clear that the situation was deteriorating rapidly and that Weygand's new call for a counter-offensive was little more than wishful thinking. The French could refuse to save their forces through an evacuation, but the British commander would not waste his men in a vain effort to save face for his French colleagues; with German forces only ten miles from Dunkirk, there was no time to lose.

The British War Cabinet cabled its approval of Gort's request to 'retire' his forces on 26 May. One day later, the plan to evacuate the continent

Above: The Germans reach the Channel coast, and the BEF is trapped.
Above right: Weary British Tommies who did not escape from Dunkirk.
Right: British soldiers used their rifles against attacking enemy aircraft during the last days of the siege of Dunkirk.

by sea was approved. This approval came just in time, for on that same day the Belgian government, its forces broken and backed to the wall, sued for peace and a cease-fire was proclaimed. With the Belgians disposed of, the Germans could turn their full attention on the Franco-British forces; any further delay in issuing the evacuation order would have doomed the British force, and even as it was, the retirement to Dunkirk was more a race than an orderly retreat. Only Hitler's temporary hesitation saved the day.

The 'miracle of Dunkirk' was facilitated by earlier plans to evacuate British forces from the continent if necessary. Operation Dynamo, the preparation of a flotilla of British ships both large and small to rescue stranded units of the BEF, was initiated on 20 May, a week before the actual evacuation was authorized. Although it was originally conceived as a modest action to rescue small groups who had been cut off as the army pushed south, the early preparations made it possible to rescue the entire expeditionary force when it became clear that an Allied counterstroke could not succeed.

When the operation began, not even the most optimistic officer was ready to believe that over 300,000 men could be successfully evacuated from the continent. If one-fifth of this number could be carried across the Channel before the Germans took vigorous measures to stop the exodus, the Admiralty would count itself fortunate. But the period of grace was to last considerably longer than had been anticipated. Although the pace of evacuation remained slow for the first two days due to confusion and lack of sufficient vessels to ferry forces across the Channel, the Germans did not strike at Dunkirk until 29 May. This first air strike failed to destroy the port and evacuation

German artillery mops up, attacking the Maginot Line from the rear. The French gun emplacements could not turn around, and the long fortress wall was captured intact.

Below: The infantry
played a vital part
supporting the Panzers in
the Battle of France.
Right: A Panzer moves
swiftly through open
country after the break-
through at Sedan.
Far right: A brave
proclamation by General
de Gaulle: 'France has lost
the battle. But France has
not lost the war!' **Below
right:** De Gaulle alone
refused to co-operate with
the Germans.

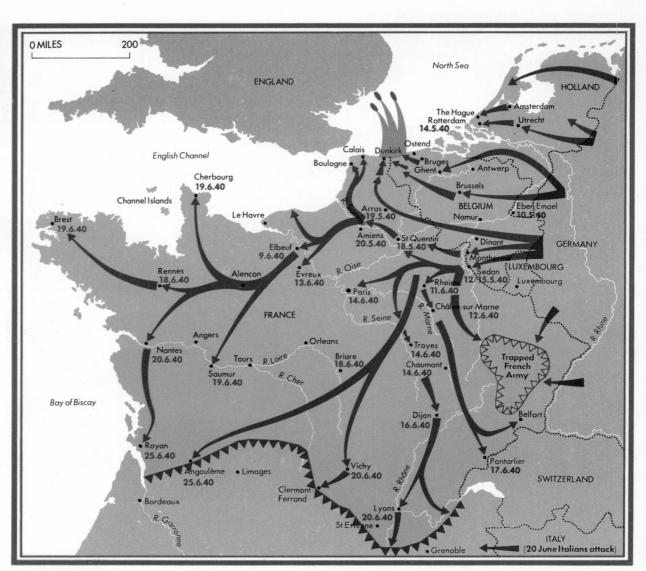

45

Right: 'What General Weygand called the Battle of France is over. The Battle of Britain is about to begin.'

continued until 2 June when daylight movement out of Dunkirk harbor had to be suspended due to heavy German raids. By this time, thanks to the efforts of the men who manned the ships of the motley naval task force and the Royal Air Force, some 224,000 British forces and 95,000 French forces had been evacuated when the operation was ended. Many of these men were to see action against Germany again, when their good luck would contribute to Germany's downfall, but for the moment Hitler had triumphed.

The departure of the British Expeditionary Force sealed the fate of the remaining French forces. Weygand had already lost some 30 divisions apart from the units evacuated to England and could count on only 49 divisions; the Germans, who had more than 130 divisions, quickly overran French resistance. Weygand was proposing the negotiation of a cease-fire even before the French government left Paris on 9 June, but the Reynaud cabinet would not hear it. From their retreat in Tours they ordered Weygand to stand fast, while the Prime Minister urgently appealed to the United States for aid. This was

Left: Hitler ecstatically celebrates the fall of France near the railway carriage in which Germany was forced to sign the surrender in 1918. Hitler saw to it that the French surrender in 1940 took place in exactly the same spot.

not forthcoming and when Paris fell on 14 June a cabinet crisis was precipitated, resulting in Reynaud's resignation on 16 June. By this time, Italy had joined Germany, having declared war on 10 June, and the situation looked absolutely hopeless. Not even Churchill's profound rhetoric and emotional appeals could persuade French leaders to hold fast. On 16 June a new cabinet was formed by Marshal Pétain who immediately begged Hitler for an armistice and cease-fire; his request was granted four days later.

The battle for France ended on 25 June 1940 at 1:35 a.m. when the armistice agreements with Germany and Italy became effective. Six weeks after the beginning of the western offensive, Hitler had realized most of his goals. It remained only to arrange a compromise with the British or, failing that, to force them into submission. It was indeed a dark hour for England, left alone to champion the cause of democracy. Although Churchill would state that 'We shall defend our island home . . . until the curse of Hitler is lifted from the brows of mankind . . .,' he could not be sure that they would triumph in the end.

Left: Marshal Pétain, hero of Verdun, formed a new cabinet to conclude an armistice with Hitler.

Right: Germans sunbathe on the Channel coast.
Opposite top left: The advance through the Low Countries met little effective opposition.
Top right: A triumphal German parade down the Avenue Foch in June 1940.
Opposite left: French aircraft destroyed on the ground. The Germans quickly established their supremacy in the air.
Opposite right: After the last ship had left, the Germans broke into Dunkirk at last.

CHAPTER THREE
The Battle of Britain

Above: Hermann Goering, who was chosen to mastermind Operation Sealion.

Below: Winston Churchill atop the White Cliffs of Dover speaking to infantry manning it: July 1940. **Below right:** Germans practice landing on beaches in preparation for Operation Sealion. **Opposite:** Spitfires cruise in formation at 300 mph between cloud layers at 6000 ft.

The fall of France would have opened the way for an immediate invasion of England had it not been for two facts. First, adequate preparations for an aerial and seaborne invasion of the British Isles had not been made prior to the launching of the western offensive. Second, Hitler hesitated to order the preparation of such an offensive, hoping that a peaceful settlement of Anglo-German differences might be reached despite the events of September 1939–June 1940.

The mounting of an assault on England involved an effort for which the German army and navy had made little preparation. The army had few if any troops trained for seaborne landing operations and the navy had few if any transports to carry the men across the Channel. Neither the General Staff nor the Admiralty had seriously considered plans for such an operation before the fall of France, nor had they been prodded to do so by Hitler; more important still, there was little enthusiasm for such a venture. The military leaders of the Reich had prepared only for continental war. In their minds, a crossing of the Channel could only be undertaken as a last resort and even then they were not willing to guarantee the result. Only the Luftwaffe seemed anxious to initiate the conflict, but Goering could not persuade his peers or the Fuehrer to take immediate action.

Hitler continued to cling to the notion that he could reach a compromise with Churchill. Even after the British Prime Minister refused to accept his proposal that England recognize German hegemony on the continent in return for German recognition of the sanctity of the Empire, Hitler appears to have been reluctant to force an invasion of England. His military advisers were only too happy to follow his lead in the matter, hoping that Churchill's stubborness would give way and a rapprochment could be reached; they dallied for almost a month after the fall of France before ordering the preparation of a comprehensive scheme to invade England, and even then discussed the operation with little enthusiasm.

The German plan, 'Operation Sealion,' was finally commissioned on 16 July 1940, but was not ready for consideration until the end of the month. As presented to the chiefs of staff, it called for a hurried accumulation of shipping from Belgian, French, and Dutch ports to transport Rundstedt's Army Group A across the Channel for landings near the Thames estuary along the southeast coast. Following the initial landing of some 10 divisions plus one airborne unit in this area, the second and main force would be ferried across the Channel. This would be the major part of the operation, necessitating the requisition of thousands of ships both large and small to transport several hundred tanks and other armoured vehicles plus an additional 17 infantry divisions. Once landed, these forces would join up with the first wave, isolate London, and cripple British resistance. If carried out, the operation would be by far the most complex and difficult the Germans had undertaken.

The original target date for launching Operation Sealion was set for mid-August 1940 at the insistence of the Fuehrer, who was growing increasingly angry at Churchill's intransigence. However, since actual preparations for the maneuver were not begun until the last week in July, sheer magnitude of the task of assembling hundreds of thousands of men and thousands of transports for the venture defied Hitler's time-table and the military and naval commanders involved were forced to ask for a postponement until September. Reluctantly, Hitler acceeded to their appeals and the invasion was pushed back some two weeks; in the meantime the Luftwaffe was told to go ahead and soften the British for the eventual kill.

Goering's anxiety to annihilate the Royal Air Force as soon as possible delighted his peers in the other services; they continued to be sceptical about the whole affair and were only too happy to have the Luftwaffe prepare their way. Admiral Raeder was frightened enough at the possibility of having to engage the British fleet while ferrying thousands across the Channel, and if Goering could neutralize the RAF in advance of the effort, his task would be much easier. If, on the other

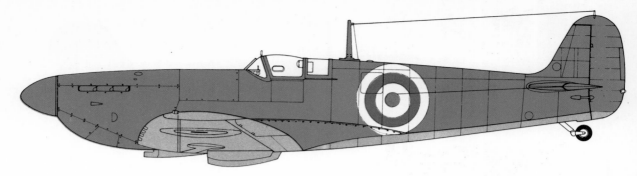

Spitfire II. Length: 29 ft.
11 in. Span: 36 ft. 10 in.
Maximum speed: 370
m.p.h. Armament:
8 × .303 machine guns.

hand, the Luftwaffe failed to carry out Goering's mission, the Fuehrer might think twice and cancel or drastically alter the operation. In any event, by encouraging the Luftwaffe to 'carry the ball,' the resources of the army and navy remained intact, at least for the moment.

When Hitler issued his order on 5 August authorizing massive air strikes against England, Goering was more than ready to respond; by the beginning of August, he had already gathered a force of nearly 2700 aircraft for this purpose. Like his colleagues in the Admiralty and on the General Staff, Goering placed little faith in Operation Sealion but was anxious to employ his aircraft not simply in support of the objections of the operation, but in a total effort to prove the supremacy of air power in modern warfare. During the months of the Luftwaffe attack on England this was to cause considerable friction between the Air Marshal and the heads of the other services who feared that Hitler might continue to insist on the execution of Operation Sealion whether Goering had correctly followed his orders and prepared the ground for them or not. The bickering and confusion continued until the operation was superseded by the invasion of the Soviet Union and proved to be of indirect but immense aid to the British, who were spared the worst consequences of the attacks by Goering's frequent changes of tactics and targets.

At the start of the Battle of Britain, the Luftwaffe possessed a numerical superiority over the Royal Air Force. Numbers, however, proved to be somewhat misleading; although the Germans had more bombers and dive bombers, the two sides were nearly equal in numbers of fighter aircraft. Germany's slight edge at the outset was more than compensated for by the superior output of British aircraft plants which were eventually able to build planes faster than they were destroyed. It was the fighter and not the bomber which held the key to victory or defeat in this encounter, and here the British had one great advantage: their nimble Spitfires and Hurricanes did not have so far to fly. The German Bf 109, like its British counterparts, only had a radius of action of about 125 miles, and thus, after leaving

a fuel margin for combat, could barely cover the distance from Calais to London and back. Even to do this much required a fairly inflexible routing plan, which greatly aided the British defenders. What the RAF did lack as the battle progressed was not aircraft so much as trained pilots. Had RAF training schools been producing more pilots, or had there been a larger reservoir of trained men available at the beginning of the battle, the situation would have been far less critical for the British.

The first phase

Although German aircraft had appeared over England in July, the Battle of Britain was not begun in earnest until 13 August 1940, when the Luftwaffe launched the first in a series of concentrated attacks on British fighter bases and radar installations. Such attacks were to last until the middle of September when tactics and targets were changed and a second phase of the battle began.

The raid on 13 August was the largest aerial attack to that date; over 1400 aircraft were sent aloft over England and German pilots were instructed to destroy the forward bases of the Royal Air Force southeast of London. This was to be the first in a series of four raids, to be launched on consecutive days, with which Goering hoped to destroy the aerial defense in the greater London area, thus opening the way for uncontested German bombardment of British naval and merchant marine targets. The success of Operation Sealion would depend upon the accuracy of the Air Marshal's predictions.

Adlertag, or 'Eagle Day' proved to be somewhat disappointing for the Luftwaffe and its commanding officer. The weather co-operated with the British defenders and this plus the early warning radar system allowed them to 'scramble' into the air and meet the attacking German fleet before that armada could successfully unload its cargo of bombs and explosives. By the end of the afternoon the Luftwaffe had managed to seriously damage only two of the forward bases at a cost of 45 of their aircraft. The RAF lost only 13 planes, managed to prevent the destruction of all but two

Lancaster IB. Length:
69 ft. 6 in. Span: 102 ft.
Maximum speed: 287
m.p.h. Armament:
8 × .303 machine guns
Weight: 35,500 lbs. empty.

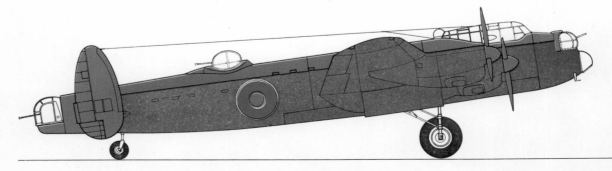

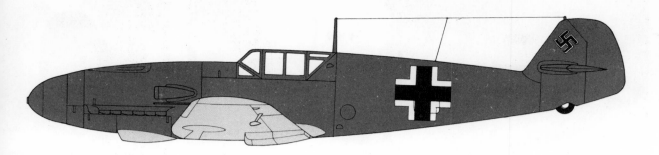

M.E. 109 F.I. Length:
29 ft. 8 in. Span: 31 ft.
6½ in. Maximum speed:
369 m.p.h. Armament:
2 × 7.92 machine guns,
1 × 20 mm. cannon.
Weight: 4440 lbs. empty.

Hitler will send
no warning –
so always carry
your gas mask

ISSUED BY THE MINISTRY OF HOME SECURITY

'SPOT AT SIGHT' CHART Nº 1
ENEMY UNIFORMS

GERMAN PARACHUTIST

GERMAN SOLDIER

Below: At first the Luftwaffe concentrated on bombing airfields. The outskirts of major cities, however, did not escape.

Right: Bombing continued throughout the day and night. Here a mobile YMCA canteen gives tea to men on a gun site.
Far right: WAAF's plot the Battle of Britain at radar control.

Right: "Never in the field of human conflict have so many owed so much to so few". **Right center:** The other side. German pilots plan another bombing raid on Britain. **Far right:** Members of the Luftwaffe relax before take-off.

Right: Hawker Hurricanes of the RAF. **Far right:** Me-110 sinks slowly into the Channel.

fighter bases and, most important, kept the Germans from destroying the radar installations that dotted the coastline. That night, however, the Luftwaffe returned and succeeded in attacking several aircraft plants, thereby exposing the RAF's inability to combat night attacks as efficiently as those flown during daylight hours. Such night flights, therefore, were to become increasingly common and devastating.

The Luftwaffe launched another massive attack on 15 August, the largest raid to be mounted by Goering during the battle for Britain. Over 1800 aircraft, including Scandinavian based units, took part in this effort to destroy RAF fighter bases in southeast England, but these bases were not the Luftwaffe's only target. Goering and his subordinates also hoped to destroy installations in the Midlands and Yorkshire while RAF units from these bases were sent south to aid Fighter Groups 10 and 11, who were protecting the southern approach to London and the Channel coast. If the plan was successful, England's fighter defense would be incapacitated in one stroke and the Luftwaffe would be able to bomb military and naval targets with impunity.

The sheer number of aircraft in the German armada dwarfed the resources of the British defenders and Germany might well have scored a dramatic victory were it not for the early warning provided by British radar installations and aircraft spotters, and the superb co-ordination of RAF units by Air Vice-Marshal Keith Park, the commander of Fighter Group 11 and his counterpart in the north, Air Vice-Marshal Leigh-Mallory, commander of Fighter Group 12. By the time German task forces arrived over the Channel coast, British units were already in the air and what they lacked in numbers was more than compensated for by their spirit, and the information they had received from flight headquarters.

In the north the Luftwaffe was badly mauled. There a fleet of over 100 bombers accompanied by 35 fighters attempted to attack airfields near Newcastle and in Yorkshire, but met with little success. Savage fighter resistance and effective anti-aircraft fire cost the invaders over 15 aircraft while little damage was done to British bases. A second attack by some 50 bombers met with better luck later in the day and managed to circumvent RAF defenses in the north, destroying at least one

not adequately coordinated their efforts. Thus, although confusion at the radar stations caused by the sheer number of German planes threatened to deprive the RAF of the time they needed to prepare their defense, the Luftwaffe's inability to deliver a single well coordinated attack insured that the RAF could at least hold its own. By the end of the day the Luftwaffe had not succeeded in its major goal of eliminating England's southern aerial defence. Thirty-nine British planes had been lost and several bases were badly damaged, but the RAF still flew. Churchill might well say of this encounter that: 'Never in the field of human conflict was so much owed by so many to so few.' Unfortunately, however, there was still more to come.

The loss of 75 planes on 15 August did not stop Goering's campaign against British bases. On 16 August yet another attack was launched and almost 1700 planes were sent over England. Based upon intelligence reports which estimated current British strength at no more than 300 planes, Goering remained confident that the end of the RAF was near. He was so confident, in fact, that he suspended attack on British radar sites on the grounds that the few aircraft left to the RAF could hardly benefit by such installations, and that by using all of his aircraft against the bases instead of diverting some to the radar sites, he could hasten the collapse of England's aerial defense, guaranteeing absolute German air supremacy within a matter of weeks. Neither of these assumptions proved to be correct.

Although British losses had been heavy during the first days of the Battle of Britain, they were not nearly as high as German leaders believed; thus, the German raiders suffered heavier losses than were necessary in their raids of 16 August and later because they were not prepared for the stiff resistance they encountered. During the first three weeks of August alone, Germany lost over 450

Previous page: Bombs being loaded into a Stirling. **Top:** Night raids on London began to intensify by September 1940. **Above:** This bus fell into a bomb crater. **Opposite: top:** Damage from air raids became increasingly severe. This is the City looking down from St. Paul's.

Right: Kesselring and Goering watch from the cliffs near Calais as a thousand German planes were sent against England. **Opposite bottom:** Field Marshal Albert Kesselring wasn't smiling so broadly after 15 September.

base in the process; on the run back to Denmark, however, RAF pilots downed at least 10 of the 50 with no loss to themselves. Such losses proved the vulnerability of bombers without adequate fighter cover, a fact which the Luftwaffe was slow in comprehending. In any case, 15 August marked the first and last major attempt to destroy British bases north of London.

In the south, the RAF was less successful in turning back the German attackers. Faced with far greater numbers of enemy aircraft than their colleagues in the north and with more bases to defend, about the best that Fighter Groups 10 and 11 could do was to soften the German blow by engaging the enemy wherever and whenever possible; even this might not have sufficed were it not for the fact that the two German airforces sent over southern England, Luftflotten 2 and 3, had

planes, an average of about 150 per week. During the weeks to come, this number was to increase considerably.

Despite the heavy losses suffered by the Luftwaffe, Goering still pressed the attacks on British fighter installations, and by the beginning of September they were beginning to bear fruit. Although British morale was buoyed up by exaggerated reports of RAF successes, the almost daily pouding of their facilities by Goering's air force was not without grave consequences. During the month of August the RAF had lost 359 planes while many more were damaged on the ground, and the loss per week had increased rather than decreased by the beginning of September. Since the aircraft production schemes introduced by Lord Beaverbrook had not yet reached the point where replacements exceeded losses, the situation

looked bleak as summer drew to a close. Had Goering not been diverted to another course of action early in September, the RAF might well have been destroyed.

The campaign against the forward bases of the RAF was brought to an abrupt end by the British bombing attack on Berlin on 25 August. This attack, itself precipitated by the accidental bombing of London the night before, had a stunning effect on the people of Berlin and their leader, as did renewed bombings of the German capital during the last days of that month. An infuriated Hitler, speaking before the German people on 4 September, vowed to repay the British in kind. 'The British,' he said, 'drop their bombs indiscriminately on civilian residential communities and farms and villages. . . . If they attack our cities, we will rub out their cities from

Above: The Dornier "Flying Pencil", used to raze Rotterdam, was turned on British cities.

the map. . . . The hour will come when one of us two will break and it will not be Nazi Germany.' Three days later, on 7 September 1940, Goering was ordered to begin the blitz on London. Although countless thousands would suffer in England's largest city, the RAF would be spared.

The attack on London

Hitler's order initiating the Blitz on London was welcomed by Goering's lieutenants in the Luftwaffe who did not share the Air Marshal's enthusiasm for the campaign against RAF installations. Ironically, their attitude was even beginning to affect Goering who appeared to be wavering just as the effort was on the brink of success. When he and his commanders met at the Hague on 3 September, it did not take them long to persuade him to abandon the first phase of the offensive in favor of a new course of action. The main advocate was Field Marshal Albert Kesselring whose Luftflotte 2 had borne the brunt of the original attack plan; having sustained extremely heavy losses, his advocacy of the bombing of London was not difficult to understand, as it afforded the Luftwaffe an easier target and promised the collapse of British resistance at an early date. With his own commanders clamoring for a change of tactics and Hitler demanding revenge for the British raids over Berlin, Goering had little choice but to accept their suggestions.

Once the new plan was agreed, the Germans lost little time in beginning raids on London; on

Below: Grey Tube Shelter: by Henry Moore.
Opposite: Old Bailey in ruins during the Blitz.

7 September, the same day that Hitler had ordered Goering to seek reprisals, the first was launched; while Goering and Kesselring watched from the cliffs at Blanc Nez a thousand planes (almost 400 bombers and slightly more than 600 fighters) were sent against England. Arriving over the Channel coast in the late afternoon, the German fleet met little opposition and was able to unload its cargo of bombs over the docks, central London, and the East End. By the end of the afternoon, much of the city was in smoke and over 1600 Londoners were either killed or injured.

As if the daylight attack of London was not enough, the Luftwaffe returned that evening to continue its devastating work. Over 250 bombers maintained 'a slow and agonizing procession over the capital' which lasted from early in the evening until 4 a.m. the following morning. With inadequate numbers of anti-aircraft guns to protect the capital and few if any aircraft equipped for night fighting, there was little that could be done to resist the attack; only one plane was shot down and much of the city was aglow with flames.

From 7 September to 3 November, the Luftwaffe attacked London nightly. At first there was little that the British could do to protect themselves, but as they grew accustomed to the raids more adequate precautions were taken. People took to the underground railway stations, evacuation was stepped up, anti-aircraft installations were increased, and the RAF began to master the technique of night fighting. Soon after the start of the blitz the Luftwaffe was forced to discontinue daylight bombing runs, and even the nightly raids over the capital became increasingly costly as anti-aircraft gunners became more and more accurate with their weapons. Most important, the abandonment of daylight raids prevented the Luftwaffe attacking military and naval targets whose destruction was absolutely necessary if Operation Sealion was to be launched before winter. That possibility, however, seemed increasingly remote as the campaign over London was obviously not succeeding.

Fourteen September was Operation Sealion's target date, and on the French side of the Channel, all was ready. British reconnaissance aircraft confirmed the presence of thousands of barges and other seagoing vessels. It remained only for Goering to destroy London and the RAF and the invasion of England could begin, but since neither of these tasks had been accomplished the operation had to be postponed yet again. Although Hitler remained confident that the attacks

on London would succeed, Goering and his associates were under pressure to produce signs of progress. If more time was lost, weather would indefinitely postpone the venture; if the RAF was not quickly neutralized, they would inevitably strike back. There was little time to lose.

Goering and Kesselring decided to make an overwhelming effort to destroy London, and that effort, launched on 15 September 1940, proved to be a major turning point in the Battle of Britain. On that day 1000 aircraft were sent over the British capital. The weather was good, the time was right, the Luftwaffe was ready. But so too was the RAF: this was to be their finest hour.

The fact that the raid took place in daylight nullified the Luftwaffe's numerical advantage over the Royal Air Force, and German bombers, even though accompanied by five fighter air-craft per bomber, did not succeed in breaking through the British defenses. Luftwaffe formations were broken up, scattered, and doggedly pursued by RAF pilots. The battle raged all day and took every plane the British could muster; the sky above London was a 'bedlam of machines,' but by day's end the attack had been repulsed. The Germans lost 60 planes, most of them bombers, at a cost of 26 aircraft to the RAF, once again, proving the value of the early warning system. Had it not been for this and the skilful coordin-ation of the defense by Air Chief Marshal Sir Hugh Dowding, the Luftwaffe raid might indeed have been successful. As it was, not only was the RAF still intact, but it was soon able to take the offensive, hitting the landing craft that the German navy had assembled for Operation Sealion.

destroy British morale and humble Mr Churchill.

Night time raids had become almost commonplace and by the beginning of October the residents of London were dug in and resigned to suffer more of the same. The Germans however, had a new surprise in store for them; on 15 October and every night thereafter, incendiary bombs were added to the Luftwaffe's manifesto. Londoners had become accustomed to seeking shelter when the Luftwaffe approached, but now they were forced to leave their basements and take to the roofs. The incendiary bombs were far more destructive than the more conventional high explosive bombs, as they set fire to the structures they hit instead of just pulverizing them. Fires were difficult to control in the midst of an attack and even the organization of civilian fire brigades and spotters could not contain the destruction wrought by these weapons. By the end of October, fire bombings were extracting a greater and greater toll. Each night the Luftwaffe destroyed the homes of thousands, hundreds were maimed, and business and government were disrupted. Despite these and other horrors the people of London stood fast, and with them stood their government and their monarch.

On 3 November, for the first time in nearly two months, no air raid alarms sounded in the British capital. After nightly ritual of Luftwaffe attacks the silence must have seemed strange indeed, giving rise to conjecture as to what the Germans might be up to next. Did this mark the end of the Battle of Britain or was there more to come? Would the Germans return to London or

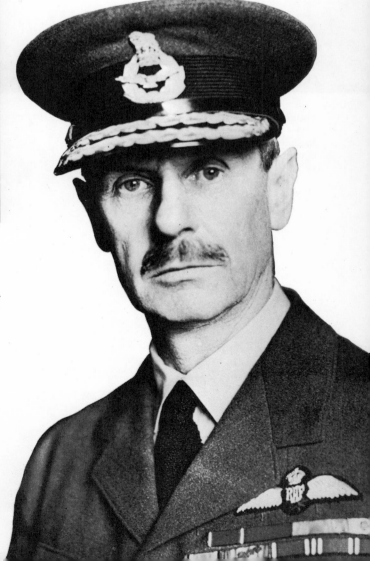

Raids spread to the provinces

The Luftwaffe's failure on 15 September sealed the fate of Hitler's plans for invasion. The weather had already begun to turn cold, turbulent conditions in the Channel were predicted for the rest of the month, and most important of all, the Luftwaffe had failed to destroy the RAF or significantly devastate other military and naval targets. On 18 September, the craft assembled in French coastal ports were dispersed lest additional losses be suffered from RAF attacks and on 12 October the campaign was officially postponed until the spring of 1941.

The death of Operation Sealion effectively eliminated the threat of invasion but the aerial harassment of England was to continue for another three months. If Goering could not succeed in defeating the RAF, Hitler would still attempt to

Above: The center of Coventry was obliterated.
Right: Sir Hugh "Stuffy" Dowding, whose RAF was able to take the offensive by mid-September. His quiet, even taciturn manner camouflaged an intensity and stubbornness which Goering discovered at his cost.

Above: Barrage balloons were extensively used.
Right: Battle of Britain 1940: by Paul Nash.

"..... but of course it _mustn't_ go _any_ further!"

CARELESS TALK COSTS LIVES

were other cities to be subjected to the blitz? The answers to these questions came soon.

A new phase in the air war over England was initiated on 14 November when German bombers attacked Coventry. Failing to obliterate London, Goering and his lieutenants had decided to change policy and refocus the German attack on provincial cities and industrial installations. The capital had been too large and 'vague' a target to destroy, but the provincial cities might be more efficiently devastated. Also, attacks on munitions facilities, especially aircraft plants, would decrease or destroy their capacity to provide replacements and new equipment for the RAF which was daily becoming bolder in its defense.

The attack on Coventry destroyed much of the center of the city and took the lives of over 400 of its residents. Other cities were also to be attacked during this phase of the battle. Birmingham was struck from 19–22 November, and Bristol, Liverpool, and Southampton were attacked the following week. Glasgow, Leeds, Manchester, Plymouth, and Sheffield were added to the list during the

first weeks of December and, of course, London was not forgotten. Thousands lost their lives as a result of these attacks; tens of thousands were made homeless; commerce and industry were disrupted. But British resistance was not destroyed.

The end of the Blitz

At the start of the new year (1941), there was no sign that England had been humbled by the Luftwaffe. The program of raids over provincial cities and munitions works had been no more successful than previous attacks on London and RAF installations. The German offensives had, perhaps, caused more damage than was publically admitted at the time but the Luftwaffe had failed in achieving its main objectives, the destruction of the RAF and the breaking of British morale. Although attacks over England would continue for several months, the major blitz was over. Bad weather and faltering enthusiasm would soon abort the entire venture and, having failed to defeat England, the Fuehrer would look to the east for new satisfaction.

Above: Stirlings over Britain. These were among the first RAF bombers to be used against German targets.

Left: Spitfire, symbol of the Battle of Britain.

CHAPTER FOUR
The Invasion of Russia

The cancellation of Operation Sealion opened the door to a German invasion of the Soviet Union, a prospect which Hitler had viewed with increasing enthusiasm as the Battle of Britain dragged on with no victory in sight. The notion could not be considered seriously as long as there was any chance that Goering might succeed in his mission of humbling England, but when it became apparent that the Luftwaffe's efforts were in vain, the Fuehrer was quick to revive the scheme to refocus the thrust of Germany's offensive posture from England to Russia.

As had been the case so often in the past, Hitler's enthusiasm for a new military venture was not shared by his military advisers who remembered only too well the difficulties imposed by fighting a two front war from 1914–1918. That experience had been a sobering one which none of the senior officers wished to repeat. There was hardly an officer of any consequence willing to take the risks involved in an invasion of the Soviet Union, and members of the General Staff were agreed almost to a man that such a scheme would result in a disaster which would dwarf the fate suffered by Napoleon's armies a century earlier. Their personal pleas might not suffice to dissuade the Fuehrer from such a venture, but he could hardly refute cold facts – or so they thought.

The generals argued against an invasion of Russia with candor and vigor but their position, unfortunately, did not prevail. Hitler had long been critical of his senior officers' conservation and bitter over their past opposition to his plans. Had they not opposed the invasions of Poland, the Low Countries, and France? Had they not privately predicted that these ventures would bring only disaster? The success of these operations despite the opposition of the older generals had convinced Hitler that his judgement on military matters was superior to that of his advisers, who were tied to the past and fearful of initiating bold new programs. Arguments against an invasion of Russia were dismissed as militarily and politically naive: Hitler would once again have his way.

To those who predicted doom and disaster should Germany invade the Soviet Union, Hitler issued a stern rebuke. The generals were reminded that the Nazi-Soviet *détente* was never meant to be permanent; it was a temporary expedient, designed to buy time while Germany disposed of the Western powers. Once this was accomplished, it was only a question of which partner acted first to annul the agreement. The Soviets had already indicated their intentions vis-à-vis Germany by their occupation and annexation of Lithuania, and their territorial demands in Rumania. If Germany did not act quickly, Stalin's forces would be well entrenched on the eastern border

Opposite: Russians parade on Red Square before moving up to the front. **Left:** Nazi troops paddle across the Russian border. This is one of the first pictures of the invasion of Russia, 22 June 1941.

67

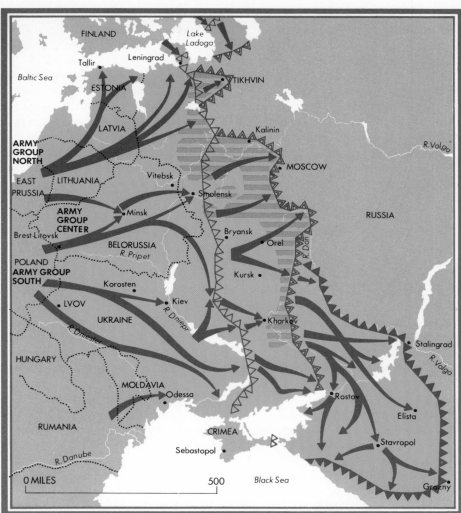

within easy striking distance of the heartland of the country. Those who refused to recognize this were blind to reality; their blindness could not and would not be tolerated. In the end, the generals were left with no alternative but to follow Hitler's direction.

Preparation for the invasion

Having failed to deter the Fuehrer from invading Russia, it became the unhappy lot of the General Staff to prepare plans for such an invasion; the assignment was given to General Paulus in October 1940. Although details of German operations in the Soviet Union were to be worked out by the general, the Fuehrer insisted on three things. First, the Wehrmacht was to destroy Russian forces in the western part of the Soviet Union. Second, following its success, German armies were to push eastward, establishing a defensive line stretching from Archangel to the Volga to provide territorial insurance against a Russian counterattack. Third, preparations for the invasion were to be made in a manner that would not excite Soviet suspicions. This dictated the most discreet movement of men and munitions as well as close cooperation with the Foreign Ministry, which was to maintain the facade of *détente* while military preparations were completed.

An outline for the attack on the Soviet Union was ready at the end of November, tested in a series of war games, and presented to Hitler on 5 December. The plan called for a three-pronged attack aimed at capturing production centers in the Ukraine, the Donetz basin, and the cities of

Axis Powers advance into Russia

22 June–1 Sept 1941

1 Sept–5 Dec 1941

Reoccupied by Russians during counterattack, 6 Dec 1941– April 1942

Further advance in the South 28 June–18 Nov 1942 (Regaining some of the ground lost in 41/42 winter campaign)

Opposite top: Stukas on a Luftwaffe base in Bulgaria. **Bottom:** Hitler's Panzers met with success after success in the first weeks of Operation Barbarossa. **Left:** German progress towards Moscow was as swift as the infantry could march.

69

Leningrad and Moscow. By dividing their forces and sweeping rapidly into European Russia, the Germans would overcome the Red Army before adequate defenses could be prepared. Since the number of men available for the invasion was small compared to the resources of the Red Army, speed and surprise were essential if the Soviets were to be overwhelmed before they could mobilize. Quality would make up for quantity. What the Wehrmacht lacked in numbers would be more than compensated for in the efficient and fast execution of the plan. By such daring action Germany would win her greatest victory of the war, taking hundreds of thousands of prisoners, and capturing Russia's agricultural and industrial resources intact. If all went well, a German victory would be a *fait accompli* by December 1941. Hitler, needless to say, was excited by the prospect of presiding over the dismemberment of the Soviet Union and quickly gave his approval to the plan prepared by Paulus and the General Staff, ordering all necessary preparations to commence on 18 December 1940. It was now up to the diplomats to do their part while the preparations were completed. This was no simple task.

Soviet leaders were not blind to the possibility of a German attack but preferred, for the time being, to preserve the Nazi-Soviet pact, for Russia needed time to prepare for war; while the diplomats dallied, Russian factories could continue to produce guns, tanks, and planes. Since it was unlikely that Hitler would strike before the successful conclusion of the Battle of Britain, there was no reason not to respond to German diplomatic feelers. When Molotov was invited to Berlin in November 1940, Stalin was only too happy to accept the invitation. Little did he realize that his willingness to extend the *détente* with Germany played right into Hitler's hands.

While men and munitions were readied for the invasion of Russia, Soviet diplomats were lulled into thinking that Hitler wished to preserve the status quo with Stalin. German-Russian discussions were pursued in an atmosphere of 'mutual trust and mutual understanding' while the Wehrmacht was preparing for war. Diplomats might gloat over the atmosphere of the summit but it was the German military which had won a victory in this matter. Never had deception been more brilliantly practiced.

A new German-Russian treaty was signed on 10 January 1941 embodying the results of the Berlin negotiations, and to the world, and many in Germany, all seemed well between Hitler and Stalin. Nothing could have been further from the truth; convinced that Stalin did not expect the Germans to attack Russia, Hitler reached the point of no return on the invasion of Russia.

Operation Barbarossa begins

Operation Barbarossa was launched on 22 June 1941. At 0400 that Sunday morning German forces crossed the Russian frontier. In the north an army group under the command of General Leeb crossed from East Prussia into Lithuania. In the south a second army group under the command of General Rundstedt moved from Lwow toward Galicia. In the center, a third group under the command of General Bock moved across northern Poland toward the Russian border. The long awaited invasion of the Soviet Union had begun.

As Hitler had expected, the Russians were unprepared for the German attack. Although units of the Red Army had been moved into the Baltic states and the western provinces just weeks before the attack, they were not deployed systematically. Such forces as there were on the German frontier were thinly spread over a large area. When the three German army groups initiated action, these forward units were easily overrun and could not be rescued, due to the distance between them and the rest of the Russian forces, scattered anywhere from 60 to 380 miles away in the hinterland. With little effective resistance from the Red Army, German forces were able to race eastward at a pace never dreamt of by Hitler and Paulus. Even the most whole-hearted advocates of the operation were stunned at the speed and facility of the Wehrmacht's advance.

Germany's military leaders had reason to be impressed by the results of the first day's activities against the Soviets. Within twenty-four hours, 10,000 prisoners had been taken, the Luftwaffe had destroyed or disabled 1200 Russian aircraft, and German mechanized units had moved fifty miles into Russian controlled areas of Poland. It was an unmitigated triumph for the Germans and in succeeding days they were able to press on further, repeating the feat of the first day. By the beginning of July few in Berlin doubted that Hitler would feast in Moscow at Christmas.

Success posed certain problems for Hitler's lieutenants, who were divided over whether to alter the original plan of invasion and race toward Moscow and other interior points, or maintain the original program which called for a slower eastward advance and the encirclement of Russian armies in the western part of the Soviet Union. Tank experts, like Guderian, wanted to take advantage of the momentum to rush eastward, driving as deep as space and time would permit, thus repeating in Russia the program which had been so successful in France. More conservative strategists urged restraint. They advised Hitler to use tank forces in support of infantry action until the bulk of Russia's western armies were defeated, promising the capture of tens of thousands of prisoners when the encirclement of Soviet forces was completed. To the chagrin of the tank experts, Hitler chose to accept the more orthodox approach.

The decision to abide by the original plan of invasion proved to be of greater benefit to the Red Army than to the Wehrmacht because it allowed the Russians to finally respond to the invasion while German forces were still tied up on the fringe of the Soviet Union, far removed from the important urban centers and rear grouping areas of the Russian army. Although the Germans would extract a heavy price in men and material from Russian forces, Stalin could rally the nation while forward units of the Red Army tenaciously held out against overwhelming odds. Losses would be heavy by orthodox standards, but in the end Germany's resources be strained long before Russia's were depleted.

On 3 July, after a silence of nearly two weeks, Stalin spoke to his nation. All Soviet citizens were called upon to defend their motherland and make whatever sacrifice was necessary to defeat fascist aggression. If the Red Army was forced to retreat, nothing of value would be left for the Germans; the Soviet citizenry would pursue the same scorched earth policy against the invader as their forefathers had used a century before. Hitler would reap no easy victory in Russia.

Stalin's refusal to succumb in the face of adversity led him to risk losses that other men would never have considered. If Soviet citizens were prepared to sacrifice themselves in the defense of mother Russia, members of the Red Army could be asked to do no less. Field commanders were instructed to hold positions regardless of cost, so that even when surrounded and clearly defeated, Russian forces continued to fight on, their stubborn resistance slowly blunting the German advance. The proverbial doggedness of the Slav was well illustrated by the Russian conscripts, who seemed to have 'an illimitable capacity for obedience and endurance'; the Germans might outflank and outmaneuver their adversaries, but they would not outfight them.

This stiff opposition, and the changing weather, began to have a serious effect on the morale of the German troops; although the Wehrmacht had made great headway during the first two weeks of the Russian campaign, the pace and progress of the invasion were gradually slowed down. In the north Leeb's army group had raced through the Baltic states but was stalled before Leningrad. In the south Rundstedt was encountering particularly heavy resistance from the Soviet Fifth Army and had to call on Bock's central army group for reinforcement. The diversion of elements of Bock's army to the south crippled the advance on Moscow by depriving it of armored and mechanized units. This was most unfortunate, since it was Bock's group which had the greatest chance for an early victory. The capture of the Soviet capital would have paralyzed Russian communications and severely affected Russian morale, but for the Fuehrer, the most important task of the Wehrmacht was to conquer the

Left top: German troops hit the dirt as a Russian shell explodes in front of them. **Left center:** The first raids of the Luftwaffe on Russian territory went almost unopposed.
Left: Wounded members of Russia's suicide squads. They were purposely left behind when the Russians withdrew in order to hamper the Nazi advance. Few came out alive.
Right: When winter set in suffering for civilians and soldiers alike was severe. This child was among the many evacuated from Leningrad prior to the siege.

Crimea and the Donetz basin, thereby severing Russia's pipelines from the Caucasus. Only after this was accomplished could the assault on Moscow be resumed with full force.

Hitler's diversion of resources to the southern sector proved even more fortuitous to the Russians than his refusal to alter the original invasion plan. Had Bock pressed on toward Moscow, there is little doubt that the city would have fallen into German hands by the end of the summer, but with the movement of armored units south to aid Rundstedt, it was doubtful whether the offensive in the central area could be resumed before the onset of autumn; by that time weather conditions would make such a drive increasingly difficult and Russian reserves from the far eastern provinces would be mobilized and ready to defend the Soviet capital. The specter of being trapped in front of Moscow at the onset of winter was not a pleasant one for the German field commanders and their superiors on the General Staff, and it is not surprising, therefore, that most senior German officers favored disregarding the situation on the southern front and pressing on toward Moscow at full speed and with full strength. If Hitler viewed Moscow as 'a geographical expression only,' his commanding officers were of another mind. So serious was the breach over this matter that Brauchitsch and Halder were prepared to tender their resignations if the advance on Moscow was not continued, but even this threat was not sufficient to change Hitler's mind. In the end, Brauchitsch and Halder chose not to resign, apparently concluding that such a move would serve no useful purpose.

The argument over Rundstedt's reinforcement wasted five weeks; it was not until 21 August that the matter was finally resolved, and by then conditions were considerably more unsatisfactory for a German advance than they had been at the beginning of the summer. Rains had washed out many secondary roads and primary roads were clogged with men and equipment. The advent of cold weather was near and the movement of supplies was becoming increasingly more difficult. Resistance was stiff and victory was still far from sight. Although a triumph of sorts would be achieved in the south, its cost would be far more than the net gain it yielded.

The attack is deflected

Hitler's order of 21 August was unequivocal. The major part of Bock's armored forces were sent south under General Guderian; they joined forces with General Kleist's mechanized units 150 miles east of Kiev, completing the encirclement of Russian forces in that city by 16 September. How many Russians were killed or captured in the Kiev pocket remains unknown. The Wehrmacht claimed to have captured over 600,000 men, while the Soviets acknowledged the loss of 527,000. Whichever figure one chooses to believe, Russian losses were staggering, but if Stalin paid heavily for his determination to hold Kiev, the Germans paid even more.

Rundstedt's double envelopment of the Kiev pocket was a smashing tactical success but it did not prove decisive. Despite an unparalleled loss of men and equipment, the Red Army showed no sign of succumbing to the Wehrmacht. Four Soviet armies may have been lost at Kiev but they would quickly be replaced by fresh units from the east, while the Germans enjoyed no equal availability of manpower reserves. Although they might extract casualties from the Soviets at the rate of 10:1 or higher, the Germans could ill afford the losses they were suffering to say nothing of the time wasted in the south. The Kiev encirclement was not completed until the end of September; winter was fast approaching and there was little time to resume the offensive in the north. The 'brightness of the Germany victory' was overshadowed by his somber prospect.

With the defeat of the Soviet Fifth Army, Guderian's armored forces were returned to Bock, and the northern offensive was resumed at the beginning of October. Although tanks, trucks and other heavy equipment were in poor condition as a result of Guderian's rapid movements south and back again to the northern front, Bock's reunited forces were able to repeat Rundstedt's triumph in the north. Moving rapidly along the Minsk-Moscow road, German forces once again enveloped a huge Russian force, this time around Vyasma some 150 miles west of Moscow. The Vyasma encirclement netted another 600,000 Russian captives and was even a greater tactical success than Kiev, but it was not completed until the end of October. By

this time the weather was rapidly worsening and Russian reinforcements had arrived from the far eastern provinces to defend Moscow.

The German command was divided as to what to do following the Vyasma encirclement. Bock, Brauchitsch and Halder pressed for continuing the German offensive. Bock believed that Russian morale would collapse in the face of an assault on the capital while Brauchitsch and Halder were fearful of the repercussions of a failure to take that city. Thus, for personal and quite varied reasons, the three men urged Hitler to move on, knowing that he would not forfeit his chance to capture Moscow if there was the slightest possibility that this could be accomplished before hard winter forced an end to the fighting. There was little hope, therefore, for the advocates of strategic withdrawal, particularly when the commander of the army in the field wished to press on. At a command meeting early in November, it was decided to continue the campaign. Whatever the price, the Wehrmacht would make one last effort to take Moscow.

Hitler might order his armies to advance on Moscow but he could not alter weather con-

Above: Winter turned the German offensive into retreat.

Below: German troops await the onslaught at Smolensk. **Below right:** The Waffen-SS served as a formidable spearhead in Operation Barbarossa.

ditions which continued to remain poor. The offensive could only be resumed after a break in the weather in mid-November, and even then the going was slow. Communications and supply lines were overextended, mechanized vehicles were short of gasoline and lubricants, and troops lacked adequate clothing and rations. Although efforts were made to alleviate these problems by airlifting clothing and supplies, the shortages remained a hard fact of life and every mile that the Wehrmacht advanced became more difficult to endure.

While German forces trudged on toward Moscow plagued by heavy snows and below-freezing temperatures, the Red Army was digging in in front of the city. The defense of the capital was coordinated by General Georgi Zhukov, one of the most capable officers in the Red Army. Recognizing the precarious position of the Germans, Zhukov carefully husbanded his resources, planning to hold his men back until the Wehrmacht reached the suburbs of Moscow, when he would launch a counter-offensive. Short of arms and ammunition, the exhausted German forces would

be easy prey for the Russians who would then surround them and inflict heavy casualties on their ranks. The encirclement of German forces near Moscow would dwarf German victories at Kiev and Vyasma, forcing Hitler to abandon the entire Russian campaign. It was with cautious optimism, therefore, that Zhukov awaited the arrival of the Wehrmacht. He did not have long to wait.

Advance units of the German army reached the suburbs of Moscow on 2 December. Two days later Zhukov launched his counter-attack. Exhausted and half starving, German troops were too spent to retaliate, but Hitler refused to allow an immediate and general withdrawal. He preferred, instead, to replace his field commanders and assume personal command of the entire operation. Bock and Brauchitsch were dismissed, Leeb resigned, and Guderian was transferred. Having eliminated those officers responsible for the disaster in Russia, he himself would try to salvage the situation.

In the fear that a general retreat would quickly degenerate into an unadulterated rout, the Fuehrer would only permit short local withdrawals; troops were to fall back on their supply dumps, turning these into fortified 'hedgehogs'; proper clothing and supplies were to be rushed to the eastern front by the Luftwaffe so that the survivors of the battle could hold their positions until they were reinforced the following spring. Until then, when another campaign would be launched to pacify the Soviet Union, the men of the Wehrmacht would have to endure hardship and heroic sacrifice without question.

Although those who survived the winter of 1941 suffered greatly, Hitler's decision to stand fast rather than withdraw from Russia was a correct one. No disorderly retreat took place, the Wehrmacht was spared the fate of Napoleon's Grand Army of 1812, and the Germans were in a strong position for launching another attack the following spring. Nevertheless, there was little cause for celebration in Berlin. About 750,000 German troops had been captured, killed or wounded in the Soviet Union by the end of 1941, many of them in the effort to take Moscow. Hitler's goals, the capture of the Caucasus, Leningrad and Moscow, had not been achieved. Victory was as far from sight at the beginning of the new year as it had been in June when the invasion was originally launched. Operation Barbarossa had failed.

Failure of the operation

Hitler blamed the failure of Operation Barbarossa on the weakness and vacillation of his generals, but it was he who was responsible for the Russian debacle. Although his military advisers had understimated Russia's resources and the quality of the Red Army, they still foresaw possible disaster; Hitler had forced the invasion on them despite their vigorous objections. Once the attack was initiated, he refused to abide by their suggestions, preferring to rely on his own judgement. When field commanders suggested a rapid push on Moscow in August, Hitler disregarded their opinion and ordered the transfer of forces from the central zone to the south. When some officers

suggested withdrawing to a winter-line at the end of October, Hitler ordered the advance on Moscow to continue regardless of the cost in men. The conflict between the generals and the Fuehrer not only contributed to the near disaster in Russia, but tainted the relationship between Hitler and the General Staff in future campaigns. Hitler's strategy may have been correct in 1940 but his judgement had tragic consequences for the fate of the Russian campaign.

Above: Men of Hoth's relief force who fought to within 50 miles of the Stalingrad pocket. They were hurled back by a Soviet counter-offensive.

Below: Hitler's thrusts into Russia pushed the endurance of his troops to the limit.

CHAPTER FIVE

America Moves Towards War

Events in Europe and the Far East did not go unnoticed in the United States. Americans roundly condemned Japanese agression in Manchuria and China, viewed with disfavor the advent of the Third Reich and the remilitarization of Germany, and watched with disgust as the Czech crisis was resolved at Munich. Thinking Americans agreed that these and other incidents in the interwar period boded ill for the future but there was less agreement over the appropriate response to such crises. Some, perhaps a majority, believed that strict neutrality and non-interference in the affairs of other nations was the best course for their government to pursue. Others, a vocal

Below: The Great Depression was the primary concern of Roosevelt's first Administration. Here unemployed demonstrators run through Union Square in New York pursued by police.

minority, strongly urged greater American participation in the world community, hoping to thwart aggression by lending the military might and moral support of the United States to those governments which supported democracy. Still others were too deeply caught up in the throes of the Depression to worry about events abroad. Such was the state of public opinion in the United States on the eve of war.

President Roosevelt was an internationalist by virtue of his education, family background, and personal convictions. He was also a shrewd politician, and as such he sensed that most Americans were primarily concerned with setting their own house in order. His election in 1932 and re-election in 1936 were based upon domestic issues and programs; he had received no mandate from the American people to cure the world's ills, nor had Congress prompted him to play the role of mediator between the forces of good and evil. Whatever his own views, the President had to accept these realities and act accordingly.

During Roosevelt's first term (1933–1937) the United States did little to alter the course of world affairs beyond participating in several abortive disarmament conferences. During his second term (1937–1941) even less was done to exert a positive influence in the world community. As the mood grew more somber in Europe and the Far East, the United States seemed to retreat deeper and deeper into its isolationist cocoon. When Italy attacked Ethiopia in 1935, the Congress of the United States responded by passing a neutrality act calling upon the President to refrain from taking any action which might offend either of the belligerents. When civil war broke out in Spain in 1936, Congress restated its commitment to neutrality and expressly forbade the shipping of arms to the republican government in Madrid or its fascist rivals. A third and more comprehensive neutrality act was passed in 1937. It retained previous bans on shipments of munitions and advances of cash to belligerent nations and added additional restrictions which prohibited American nationals from travelling on belligerents' vessels or selling non-military supplies to such nations except on a cash and carry basis.

At first, given the mood of Congress and a majority of the American people, Roosevelt had little choice but to accept the limitations imposed upon him by the legislature, but as tensions increased in Europe and China the President grew increasingly restive and impatient with his colleagues. If Congress could not be persuaded to abandon or modify its isolationist stand, the executive might still articulate America's moral outrage over the misdeeds of the dictators. If the United States could not lend its physical support to sister democracies, the least she could do was to lend them moral support. It was clearly time for the United States to adopt a more constructive policy and Roosevelt felt ready to define it.

Speaking to an audience in Chicago on 5 October 1937, Roosevelt pleaded for a more affirmative foreign policy. Peace-loving nations, the president stated, would have to stand together if law and order were to prevail in the world. Isolation or neutrality would not provide immunity from a disease of the mind and soul.

The Italian invasion of Ethiopia evoked little concern in the United States.

Likening the world situation to an effort to combat a deadly epidemic, Roosevelt called for strong measures, suggesting a political quarantine of those who threatened world peace lest their cancer spread to all members of the family of nations. Those who lived in peace and in accordance with international law must find a way to make their will prevail else they would soon fall prey to the forces of evil. Although the American people wanted to keep out of war, Roosevelt warned that non-involvement would not insure peace. There was no guarantee the United States could remain aloof from war indefinitely.

Reaction to Roosevelt's 'quarantine speech' was less than enthusiastic. Isolationists called the President a warmonger. Critics of his domestic policies and programs charged that he was using the international crisis as a smoke screen to draw attention away from the failure of his political programs at home. The rest of the people remained apathetic, failing to see the relevance of the President's message. Try as he might, Roosevelt could not change the temper of the times. So strong had the partisans of isolation become that even his forceful personality could not effectively counter their influence. As crisis followed crisis, the American people seemed supremely confident that they would escape the conflagration. The President did not succumb to this illusion.

Isolationism remains paramount

By 1938 Roosevelt was convinced that a European war was imminent. Unlike many others, he placed little faith in the appeasement of dictators as a means of preserving the peace. 'Peace by fear', the President stated, 'has no higher or more enduring quality than peace by the sword'. This remark proved to be prophetic; the Munich conference provided no solution to Europe's ills, for no sooner had Hitler been placated by Chamberlain and Daladier than he escalated his demands, taking the rest of Czechoslovakia by force and threatening Poland. Could there by any doubt that war was inevitable? For Mr Roosevelt it was only a matter of when and where.

Germany's invasion of Poland in September 1939 hardly took the President by surprise. As England and France declared war on Germany, Roosevelt delivered his strongest condemnation of fascist aggression to that date. Speaking to the American public in one of his radio 'fireside chats', he promised to maintain American neutrality as long as was possible, but told his audience that neutrality was a political policy which ought not to affect their state of mind. Free men could not applaud aggression. If government could not act, the citizen was free to articulate his moral outrage; in fact, it was his obligation to do so.

While Roosevelt implored Americans to speak out against what he considered international banditry, he assiduously abided by the neutrality legislation then in effect, hoping that mounting public reaction to events in Europe would force the Congress to modify the statutes. Unfortunately the advent of war in Europe did not result in a coalescence of public opinion in the United States. On the contrary, the differences between the isolationists and internationalists seemed to widen; those who opposed intervention in world affairs saw the war as further proof of the need to stand aloof from the quarrels of others, and while the President tried to rally the nation to action, they redoubled their efforts to maintain her isolation.

The America First Committee was the isolationists' response to the war in Europe. A

Below: Ethiopian troops, often armed with little more than spears, fought bravely when the Italians invaded. **Below right:** The Italian army enters Addis Ababa – 1936. It took almost a year to subdue Ethiopia.

A column of Italian tanks
moves towards the
Ethiopian capital.

coalition of diverse groups and individuals, the
organization sought to prevent Congress from
altering neutrality legislation through a nation-
wide propaganda campaign of immense proportions. Led by public figures such as Charles
Lindbergh, the Committee succeeded in rallying
to its banner almost all isolationist groups. Until
the Japanese attack on Pearl Harbor, members
of the organization spread their gospel with zeal,
idealism, and energy but met with only partial
success.

Roosevelt did not adequately anticipate the
strength of isolationist sentiment and was at a loss
as to how to respond to it. Had Hitler immediately
followed the invasion of Poland with subsequent
moves into France and the Low Countries, the
issue of German aggression would have been
clearer and the threat to international order
would have been more universally understood by
Americans. As it happened, however, there was a
lengthy pause between the rush into Poland and
the resumption of the blitz in April 1940; although
the 'phoney war' was only a lull before the storm,
at the time many Americans believed that the
deadlock might become permanent. If this were
the case, a world conflict was hardly inevitable.
As long as the situation remained static, there was
little the President could do, and he was forced to
accept the need to proceed cautiously.

Support for the Allies

The fall of France ended America's complacency,
for even the isolationists could not deny that
Hitler's victory in France and the pending battle
for Britain posed a threat to the United States. If
England suffered the same fate as France, the
United States would stand alone. For most
Americans, the fall of France was a catastrophe
of the first magnitude, and they prepared to

follow the President's lead; only the most un-
restrained isolationists remained sceptical.

Roosevelt quickly pressed for changes in
neutrality legislation and subsequent aid to Great
Britain. Speaking at the University of Virginia in
June 1940, he outlined his view of America's new
responsibilities and how he proposed to prepare
for them:

'In our American unity we will pursue two obvious
and simultaneous courses; we will extend to the
opponents of force the material resources of this nation,
and, at the same time, we will harness and speed up
the use of those resources in order that we ourselves in
the Americas may have equipment and training equal
to the task of any emergency and every defense.'

Soon after his speech in Virginia, Roosevelt
submitted a series of special messages to Congress
outling his plans to strengthen the defenses of the
United States and aid Great Britain. At a time
when the world was 'threatened by the forces of
destruction', the president proposed an immediate
mobilization of America's resources and a major
revision of the neutrality laws so that she could
commence aid to her British allies with no delay.
This time Congress was willing to follow Roosevelt's lead and passed enabling legislation with a
speed and vigor reminiscent of the first days of
the New Deal. By summer's end, huge sums had
been appropriated to modernize America's armed
forces and one by one provisions of previous
neutrality acts were amended or altered to permit
her to become the 'arsenal for the world's
democracies.'

To insure that his program would not assume a
partisan character, Roosevelt appointed leading
Republicans to cabinet and sub-cabinet positions.
1940 was an election year and having decided to

Below left: A patriotic
ceremony in honor of
Mussolini in Addis Ababa
– 1937. **Below:** Japanese
invasion of China Proper
in 1937 aroused little initial
sympathy in the US.

run for an unprecedented third term, the President did not wish to see his foreign policy become a campaign issue. Although he realized that diehard isolationists would keep the issue alive, Roosevelt believed that the majority of the American people supported his policies regardless of their party affiliation. By bringing into his administration such nationally prominent Republicans as Henry L. Stimson, Secretary of State during the Hoover Administration, and Frank Knox, Republican vice-presidential nominee in 1936, Roosevelt hoped to build a coalition which would survive the election.

The plan succeeded, and the election of 1940 did not become a referendum on foreign policy. The Republican presidential candidate, Wendell Willkie, shared many of Mr Roosevelt's convictions on foreign policy matters; he was a strong advocate of military preparedness and aid for the Allies, and his criticism of Roosevelt's administration was almost entirely limited to its domestic programs. For his part, the President did not campaign energetically, making few speeches and remaining in Washington D.C. during most of the campaign period. When the votes were tallied, Roosevelt had won a third term by a comfortable majority; the isolationists had lost their last chance of effectively checking America's movement toward intervention.

With four more years in the White House ahead of him, Roosevelt could now concentrate on implementing his programs. Among his first items of business was arranging aid for the British who, at the very moment the election was concluded, were under daily attack from the Luftwaffe. The United States had already made arrangements to send England surplus stocks of guns and ammunition left over from the First World War, and in addition Mr Roosevelt had concluded an Anglo-American agreement, which permitted the exchange of some fifty old destroyers for leases on naval bases in Britain's American colonies. Now, with his election victory fresh behind him, the President proposed a far more ambitious program to make munitions and supplies available to the Allies.

Speaking to the Congress in January 1941, Roosevelt outlined his proposal:

'I ask this Congress for authority and funds sufficient to manufacture additional munitions and war supplies of many kinds, to be turned over to those nations which are now in actual war with aggressor nations.

Our most useful and immediate role is to act as an arsenal for them as well as for ourselves. They do not need manpower. They do need billions of dollars worth of the weapons of defense.'

In return, Roosevelt proposed to receive compensation in kind, or property, or any other manner deemed satisfactory by the President.

A Lend-Lease bill was submitted to the Congress shortly after the President's address. Needless to say, it was the subject of considerable controversy, but its opponents could not muster sufficient votes to defeat it; on 11 March 1941, it became law and immediately thereafter over seven billion dollars was appropriated for its implementation. According to the provisions of the legislation, military equipment could be

Left: Japanese soldiers pause for a meal on their way southward. **Above:** Charles A. Lindbergh, hero in the 1920's for having flown the Atlantic single-handed, was one of the leaders of the America First Committee.

Far left: The US industrial machine began to gear up for war. **Left:** Roosevelt could not stop the Japanese conquest of China by speeches alone. **Below:** Lindbergh visited Germany in 1936. Although he was not a fascist himself, Lindbergh and others like him honestly felt that the war in Europe was none of America's business.

shipped with a minimum of red-tape to those who opposed fascist aggression. Although most of the funds were initially committed to Great Britain, aid was also extended to the Soviet Union, Nationalist China and some 35 other nations.

The passage of the Lend-Lease Act moved the United States one step closer to war, for although the bill by no means called upon the American government to sever diplomatic ties with Germany, Italy, or Japan, the coordination of vast amounts of aid to those who opposed these powers forced the United States to enter into planning arrangements with them. Such discussions laid the foundation for the grand alliance which emerged after the attack on Pearl Harbor.

An outline of the alliance mentioned above was first worked out in August 1941 when President Roosevelt met Prime Minister Winston Churchill at sea off the Newfoundland coast in what might well be called the first of the wartime summit conferences. As a result of this meeting, Roosevelt's concept of an 'Atlantic Charter' was embraced by Churchill and the two men committed themselves to creating a world order in which democratic nations would unite to quash aggression and maintain the peace. Though not technically a declaration of war, the Newfoundland communiqué was a clear statement of America's intent to aid the Allies which strained beyond belief the veneer of American neutrality. This message was not lost on Hitler.

America becomes a de facto belligerent
Having arranged to send supplies to Great Britain and other nations, the United States was soon involved in an effort to insure that such equipment reached its destination. German submarine attacks on allied shipping extracted a heavier and heavier toll in the months following the passage of the lend-lease program; the Soviets were not equipped to wage anti-submarine warfare; and England's navy was already committed to other operations. If the goods were to arrive safely, the United States would have to assume some of the burden of organizing and protecting convoys.

Although Roosevelt was quick to accept the challenge of supporting allied shipping, he and his advisers realized full well that participation in the convoy system would move America closer to war and thus invite the wrath of the isolationists. Nevertheless, the need to move supplies across the Atlantic was far more critical than the political consequences of a further American commitment and the President did not hesitate to take all

Far left: Henry L. Stimson, a Republican once in Hoover's Cabinet, became Roosevelt's Secretary of War. **Above:** Roosevelt's closest adviser, Harry Hopkins. **Right:** President Roosevelt declared American neutrality and promising the American people that their boys "would not be sent to any foreign war", he won an unprecedented third term in 1940.

Below far left: Lord Beaverbrook (center) stated Britain's needs to administrators of the Land-Lease Act. Left of Beaverbrook, Lord O'Brien and Edward R. Stettinius, later Secretary of State; to his right William S. Knudsen and W. Averill Harriman, Lend-Lease Administrator in London. **Below left:** Churchill aboard HMS *Prince of Wales* on his way to Newfoundland. **Below:** Roosevelt and Churchill conceived the Atlantic Charter in August 1941. **Below right:** The destroyer-base deal brought much-needed support to Britain when she stood alone against the Axis. **Below far right:** Churchill watches the President's ship depart.

Krupp's submarine
production kept Allied
shipping busy.

appropriate measures to achieve this end. In
April 1941 American forces were stationed in
Greenland with the agreement of the Danish
government. From air bases in this northern
wilderness, American pilots patrolled the north
Atlantic tracking the movement of German submarines and providing aerial cover for allied
convoys. Three months later American forces
were stationed in Iceland and assumed similar
assignments.

Of course, America's protection of allied
shipping was bitterly denounced by the Axis
powers as an act of war. Although Roosevelt
might distinguish between patrol and convoy
activities, Hitler did not. By escorting allied
merchantmen across the Atlantic, the United
States Navy was directly contributing to the war
against Germany, and this could not be tolerated.

German U-boats began to attack American
ships in May 1941 but attacks remained sporadic
until the end of August when American naval
vessels were more regularly engaged while 'on
patrol'. The President reacted strongly to these
attacks, warning that if German or Italian vessels
of war entered waters whose protection was
deemed vital to America's security, they would do
so at their own peril. American commanders were
instructed to attack any and all German U-boats
in the north Atlantic security zone. By these
actions, Roosevelt attempted to place the burden
of responsibility on German's shoulders and alert
the American public to what lay ahead.

With Roosevelt's decision to attack Axis warships in the north Atlantic if they fired upon
American vessels, the last pretence of American
neutrality was abandoned. It remained only for

the President to ask Congress to repeal remaining neutrality legislation to make this official and this he did at the end of October, declaring that: 'We Americans have cleared our decks and taken our battle stations standing ready in the defense of our nation that only the thinnest of lines separated the United States from war with the Axis.

Roosevelt's proposal was vigorously discussed in the Congress and might have stalled there were it not for renewed German attacks on American ships early in November. With American vessels and men under attack, Congress could hardly dally over the administration's legislation, and despite a valiant effort by the isolationist lobby, the last of the neutrality statutes was repealed in November, permitting the President to order armed American merchantmen to participate in the convoys and trade with nations already at war.

The Undeclared War

With the repeal of the neutrality statutes, the United States entered into an undeclared war with the Axis powers in Europe, a situation which satisfied neither the isolationists nor the inter-ventionists. Although the President had moved the United States closer to his own foreign policy goals, the nation remained divided. Isolationists demanded an immediate reversal of the policies which had carried the nation to the brink of war while interventionists called for a declaration of war so that American support of Allied forces in Europe could be more efficiently achieved. The situation remained static until 7 December 1941 when Japan decided the matter with her attack on Pearl Harbor.

CHAPTER SIX
The Road to Pearl Harbor

While Germany and the United States moved closer to war, Japanese-American relations were also rapidly deteriorating. For thirty years, the two nations had pursued contradictory policies in Asia but had somehow managed to avoid an armed conflict. As Roosevelt began his third term as president, however, the crisis in China was rapidly undermining this state of peaceful co-existence.

Japan's effort in China seemed as far from completion in 1941 as it had in 1937 when the Sino-Japanese war was initiated; yet the Japanese remained steadfast in their determination to humble the Chinese. This was a policy which Mr Roosevelt could not and would not accept. Since 1899, the United States had consistently supported an 'open door' policy which called upon all nations to recognize and insure the political and territorial integrity of China; Japan's policies violated this dictum and threatened to disrupt the balance of power in Asia, but how to go about changing them remained a problem.

For several decades, the United States had responded to Japanese aggression in China with verbal reprimands. When the Japanese presented the Twenty-One Demands to the government of Yuan Shih-k'ai in 1915, William Jennings Bryan, Mr Wilson's Secretary of State, condemned this action. When the Japanese invaded and annexed Manchuria in 1931, Henry L. Stimson, Mr Hoover's Secretary of State, denounced Japan's

aggression and announced that the United States would refuse to recognize the state of Manchukuo which the Japanese had created out of China's three northeast provinces. When the Sino-Japanese War was launched in 1937, Cordell Hull, Mr Roosevelt's Secretary of State, deplored Japanese brutality and lawlessness. These verbal attacks had little or no effect except to exacerbate the enmity between the two countries; force was the only language that the Japanese might have understood, and this the American government was not prepared to use.

As a result of their previous experience with American leaders, Japanese officials had come to expect a weak response to their activities in Asia. They could hardly feel threatened by the pious platitudes of American administrators, however humiliating their verbal harangues might be. Still, America's readiness to condemn Japan's policies remained irritating; Japanese leaders found it difficult to understand American moral outrage over the attempt to found a new order in Asia when the United States had been doing the same thing for decades in the Americas. If other nations were asked to recognize America's 'special interest' in Latin America and the Caribbean, was it illogical to expect recognition for Japan's 'paramount interest' in China?

Had America's interest in China been simply economic, the United States and Japan might have reached a reasonable understanding, but

Above: Japanese atrocities were commonplace in their war with China.

Opposite: Japan's march through China in 1937–38 was relentless. **Left:** China, 1938 – some effects of the bombardment of Wuchang.

America's commitment to the Chinese was emotional as well as pragmatic. To be sure, the 'open door' policy had originally been designed to secure a fair share of the China market for American merchants. But over fifty years, Americans had come to see this policy as a moral commitment as opposed to an economic expedient. For many, China appeared to be America's special responsibility in the world, and the American people built up a genuine, if patronizing fondness for the country, finding contact with the Chinese adventurous, exhilarating and rewarding in material and spiritual terms. Unfortunately, the Japanese did not share this enthusiasm, nor did they view America's role in China as one of a benign ally. To their mind, the United States was merely another Western power seeking to exploit the people and resources of Asia without regard for the needs of the area, while Japan represented a different, truly 'Asian' ideal which her neighbors would fully accept once their initial reluctance had been overcome.

As long as America's response to Japan was limited to verbal chastisement, the danger of a Japanese-American confrontation remained minimal. However, after Japanese forces escalated their activities in 1937, many Americans demanded stronger action to curb Japan's aggressive appetite; a suggestion which, if followed, would markedly increase tension between the two countries. For the Japanese there could be no turning back if their new order in Asia, the 'Greater East Asia Co-Prosperity Sphere', was to be achieved. For the United States, there was no way to stop the war in China short of forcefully intervening or initiating economic sanctions, neither of which was an attractive alternative for the Roosevelt administration. Nevertheless some action had to be taken.

Economic sanctions against Japan

Although the United States viewed Japanese activities in China with contempt, the Roosevelt administration reacted cautiously, hoping to restrain Japan without inviting retaliation. Some of China's friends had already mounted a boycott of Japanese goods and hoped to persuade the government to follow their lead by embargoing shipments of scrap iron and gasoline to Japan. Although the President made it quite clear that he was sympathetic to the idea of the boycott, the only action that was taken in 1937 was to hint to the Japanese that a boycott might follow if they did not alter their course.

The State Department attempted to articulate the stand of the administration and convey the feeling of the American people to the leaders of Japan. Joseph Grew, United States Ambassador to Japan, bluntly told his Japanese counterpart of the hardening attitude in the States in 1937. In 1938 the Department of State suggested a 'moral embargo' on the sale of aircraft and other munitions to the Japanese. In 1939 this suggestion was broadened to include the shipment of gasoline and other petroleum products. Still, at the time of the outbreak of war in Europe, the embargo was not official nor was any effort made to enforce it. Its effectiveness, such as it was, depended on

Above left: Japanese troops scale the walls of Kaifeng. **Above:** By 1939 the Japanese found great difficulty in pushing westward to the new Chinese capital of Chungking. **Left:** The Cabinet of Prince Konoye (third from left). War Minister Tojo (left of Konoye, in uniform) discouraged Konoye's attempts to avoid war with America.

personal moral judgement and commitment rather than a government regulation. This being the case, it could not succeed, and it was only after the advent of war in Europe that the administration would commit itself to more positive policies.

On 26 January 1940 the Japanese-American Treaty of Commerce lapsed and was not renewed. This allowed the Roosevelt administration to prohibit, except under licence, the export of certain materials to Japan; in July the President used his discretionary power to prohibit the export of certain crucial materials including petroleum products, steel, and scrap metals, except as directed by the White House. Although his proclamation did not specifically limit such action to Japan, it was clearly intended to bring pressure on the Japanese government and was supplemented by additional restrictions in the months that followed. Slowly but surely, the screws were being tightened around the Japanese in an effort to alter their policies in Asia.

The imposition of economic sanctions on Japan posed a fundamental problem for her leaders. Japan's military and civilian industries were dependent upon the importation of large quantities of raw materials from the United States and other Western powers. Without American petroleum it would be difficult to pursue the Sino-Japanese war, to say nothing of projects elsewhere in Asia. Japan's petroleum reserves were limited, and as the war in China was as far from solution in 1940 as it had been in 1937, it would have to cease if the United States put a complete embargo on the export of petroleum products or alternative sources of this vital product were not found.

If the American government had not unrealistically insisted that Japan relinquish the fruits of her aggression, the Japanese might have chosen to extricate themselves from China and modify if not forsake their plan to create a new order in Asia. Since there was no possibility that the Roosevelt administration would seriously consider a compromise, there was no way for the Japanese to get out of China and still maintain face. Humiliation was not a palatable alternative for Japan's leaders who, in their rejection of American demands, were then forced to find new sources of raw materials.

Japan's alternative to a retreat from China was to accelerate the creation of the Greater East Asia Co-Prosperity Sphere. The Japanese had already taken advantage of the European war to occupy the northern part of Vietnam with the reluctant permission of the Vichy government. It was a relatively simple step to extend this occupation to the rest of that country and arrange for similar concessions from other hard pressed colonial powers, namely the Dutch and the British. If the Japanese gained access to the resources of the Indies and Malaya, the effect of America's embargo would be greatly reduced if not nullified.

The Japanese had attempted to obtain larger quantities of petroleum products from the Dutch East Indies even before the United States levied embargos on such products, but it was not until after the German occupation of Holland that the issue was forcefully pressed. By this time, shortages of gasoline and lubricants had become acute and the Japanese government faced the unhappy prospect of having to use reserve stocks for daily needs if another source for these products could not be found. Luckily for the Japanese, the German blitz against the Netherlands succeeded at precisely the moment when their dilemma was greatest, providing an opportunity to reopen negotiations from a position of strength.

During the autumn and winter of 1940–41, several Japanese missions visited the Indies in an attempt to come to new arrangements with Dutch colonial authorities. The Japanese proposed, in essence, that the Dutch supply petroleum products to Japan without restriction and allow Japanese interests to explore and develop as yet untapped oil fields. This the Dutch were unwilling to do, despite the fact that they were hardly in a strong bargaining position and so the authorities in Batavia made only minimal concessions to the Japanese, giving them as little as possible in order to delay a confrontation until assurances of assistance were received from England and the United States. As negotiations were pursued with the Japanese parallel discussions were held by British, Dutch, and American officials; the Dutch were quite willing to follow Washington's lead in limiting the export of petroleum products to Japan, but could only do so if the United States and Great Britain were willing to come to the colonial governments' assistance in the event that the Japanese decided to press their demands by force instead of at the conference table.

But although the United States was not eager to see Japan supplied with high octane aviation fuel and other petroleum products, the Roosevelt administration was unwilling to commit itself to the defense of the Indies in the wake of a Japanese attack. The British, for their part, were somewhat more inclined to support the Dutch, but preoccupation with the defense of their own colonial empire prevented them from committing themselves in the absence of a similar American pledge. Thus, although both powers agreed that Dutch participation in the petroleum embargo was useful and necessary, neither government would make the promises which were absolutely prerequisite for such an agreement as far as the Dutch were concerned. In the end, whatever policy the colonial authorities in Batavia chose to adopt, they would face the Japanese alone.

In the absence of guarantees of assistance from the United States and Great Britain, Dutch leaders agonized over their response to the Japanese. After careful deliberation, it was decided that some oil and low octane fuel would continue to be sent to Japan but that the colonial government would not meet Japan's demands for high octane aviation fuels. Although the Dutch hoped that such a compromise would not overly provoke the Japanese, they could not be sure what Japan's response would be.

The tough attitude of Holland's colonial officials surprised the Japanese, who returned from Batavia to Tokyo almost empty-handed. Japan's leaders felt certain that the Dutch refusal to accede to their demands indicated a secret agreement with England and the United States to expand the embargo of petroleum products in

Far left: While she continued to negotiate, Japan's military buildup went on unabated. **Left:** T. V. Soong, China's Minister of Foreign Affairs, and Cordell Hull, American Secretary of State. The US sent considerable amounts of lend-lease aid to Chungking before Pearl Harbor. **Above:** Major-General Jonathan Wainwright with MacArthur in the Philippines. They faced the Japanese onslaught of 7 December 1941. **Below far left:** Japanese troops march through Osaka on their way to the front in China. **Below left:** General Douglas MacArthur was appointed by FDR to assist the Philippine army.

return for Anglo-American protection of the Indies. This, however, was not the case at all; the Indies government had chosen to confront its fate with no external pledges of support.

The failure of Japanese diplomacy

Having failed to gain their ends through diplomacy, Japanese leaders faced an agonizing decision. They could force the issue by invading the Indies or shift their diplomatic efforts to break the embargo from the Dutch to the Americans. Neither alternative was attractive. An invasion of the Indies would be acceptable only if there was a reasonable chance that the oil wells and refineries in the islands could be captured intact; if they were destroyed as a result of a scorched earth policy before the conquest of the Indies was completed, that conquest would be in vain. A new diplomatic offensive, on the other hand, would be far less costly than taking military action but there was no indication that the American government would be more pliable than it had been in the past. This was the dilemma facing the Japanese government at the beginning of the summer of 1941.

For the moment, it was decided to try diplomacy again. In an effort to appease the United States, Admiral Nomura Kichisaburo, a well known proponent of Japanese-American rapprochement, was appointed the new Japanese Ambassador to the United States. It was hoped that his presence in Washington would reassure the American government and people of Japan's sincere desire to avoid war and facilitate the initiation of new discussions of the situation in Asia. Nomura was instructed to inform the Roosevelt Administration that Japan would not employ force in the Pacific if the United States moved toward reestablishing normal economic relations and helped the Japanese to settle the China incident by pressing the Chinese Nationalists to make peace.

Nomura lost little time in articulating the position of his government and reopening conversations with the Department of State. For his part, Secretary of State Cordell Hull responded to Nomura's suggestions with several counter-proposals. Hull suggested that no progress could be made toward solving Japanese-American differences unless both powers recognized four basic principles: respect for the political sovereignty and territorial integrity of all nations in Asia; an agreement that neither party would interfere in the internal affairs of the nations of the area; an acceptance of the 'open door' principle which provided that all nations have an equal opportunity to develop their commerce in the area; and a renunciation of the use of force in altering the status quo. Only after both powers pledged themselves to abide by these guidelines could substantive discussions begin.

This response was hardly satisfactory, at least in so far as Nomura's superiors in Tokyo were concerned. The Japanese government wanted an end to restrictions on American trade with Japan, not a lecture on morality and international law. Once again, diplomacy seemed to fail. The Roosevelt administration still refused to consider the normalization of economic relations between

Far left: Japanese soldiers leave Tokyo on their way to the Pacific. Left: Admiral Nomura Kichisaburo became the new Japanese Ambassador to the United States in 1941.

the two countries unless the Japanese agreed to accept the principles which Hull advanced, a position which was totally unacceptable as the Japanese had no intention of retreating from China or anywhere else in the Far East.

Japan prepares to fight

Japanese-American relations reached a low point at the end of July, following Japan's occupation of southern Indochina, when in response to new crisis, President Roosevelt issued an executive order freezing Japanese assets in the United States and bringing all trade between the United States and Japan to a virtual halt. After months of vacillation, the administration had determined that no further Japanese aggression would be tolerated. It was at this point that the last diplomatic effort was made to avert hostilities.

Early in August, Premier Konoye Fuminaro proposed a meeting with Roosevelt in a final attempt to avoid war. The president rejected this proposal, informing Japan's Ambassador to the United States that Japan would have to stop her military advances before any such meeting could take place. With this rejection the Hull-Nomura discussions were doomed and war became in-

Left: Kurusa and Nomura, Japan's peace envoys to the US. Right: General Tojo Hideki, who replaced Konoye as Japan's Premier on 18 October 1941.

evitable; although Japanese-American negotiations continued in Washington, they were little more than a facade designed to buy time while both sides prepared for war.

In Japan, operational plans were drawn for an invasion of the Dutch East Indies, Malaya, and the Philippines, and a general mobilization was commenced. At the same time, the Japanese navy began to practice for an attack against American military installations in Hawaii, a plan which had been discussed as early as January 1941 but which now was being most seriously considered. In the United States, preparations for war were also being made. Factories were being rapidly retooled to produce munitions and other necessities of war and the Conscription Act of 1940 was being implemented for the first time. Slowly but surely, both sides were reaching the point of no return.

As it became apparent that Ambassador Nomura was getting nowhere in his discussions with the State Department, the Japanese high command pressed the government for a decision on the matter of war with the United States. After weeks of indecision, an Imperial Conference on 6 September decided to face the issue squarely. Diplomacy was to be given one more month to find a solution to the Japanese-American crisis; if by the beginning of October a solution had not been found, Japan would use force.

On 18 October the Konoye government was forced to resign and General Tojo Hideki became Prime Minister. Now the die was cast; Tojo's government was committed to war, and its plans were approved at a second Imperial Conference on 5 November. It was agreed that one last proposal would be submitted to the United States which would have to be accepted by 25 November. Should the Americans reject it, which seemed probable as it was simply a restatement of Japan's old position, war would follow almost immediately with simultaneous attacks on Pearl Harbor, Manila, and Singapore.

A special Japanese envoy, Kurusu Saburo, arrived in Washington on 17 November. His instructions were simple: he was to present Japan's last offer to Secretary of State Hull and keep the negotiations going until such time as he was ordered to return home. Unknown to him, this would give the Japanese navy time to prepare the attack on Pearl Harbor while maintaining the ruse of diplomacy until the very last moment. No one believed that the Americans would seriously entertain this 'new' proposal, but discussion of it would buy a little more precious time.

The Tojo government were correct in assuming that the United States would not accept this last proposal for settling Japanese-American conflicts through diplomacy. Responding to Kurusu's bid, Hull offered a counter-proposal which, although not an ultimatum, was a denial of everything the Japanese had attempted since 1915. As such, it was completely unacceptable and so, on 1 December 1941, an Imperial Conference made the final decision for war with the United States. The discussions in Washington, however, were to be continued until the attack was ready to be launched.

The War in the Far East Begins

Japan's decision to go to war was hardly a secret to the Roosevelt administration. Thanks to the deciphering of Japanese diplomatic codes, it had long been known in the United States that the hour of confrontation was drawing near. What was not known, however, was when and where the attack might take place. Although American military installations in Hawaii appeared to be a possible target, Roosevelt's advisers believed that the Japanese would strike first against British and Dutch bases or, if they chose to hit the United States, would attack the Philippine Islands rather than Hawaii. In any case, the United States needed more time to prepare for war, and thus it was just as vital for her as for Japan that the Hull-Nomura conversations be continued as long as possible.

The State Department washed its hands of the negotiations at the end of November but kept the discussions formally alive so that the army and navy would have more time to prepare for the imminent clash with Japan. They did not have long to wait. On 6 December Nomura and Kurusu were alerted to expect a lengthy message from Japan, severing diplomatic relations with the United States, which was to be presented to the Department of State the following day. By late evening, the message was received and was being decoded and translated. Unknown to the Japanese, it had also been intercepted by American intelligence authorities.

Thirteen of the fourteen points in Tojo's cable had been received and sent to Roosevelt before midnight on the 6th. Upon reading the despatch, there was little doubt in his mind that war would soon follow, but there was still no indication as to when or where. Neither the President nor his advisers expected the attack to follow the very next day nor did they anticipate that Pearl Harbor would be the Japanese target. But the next morning Roosevelt learned that the decision to terminate diplomatic relations was to be presented to the State Department at 1:00 p.m. that afternoon; thinking that the hour of this presentation might be significant, a cable was sent to American commanders in Hawaii warning of the danger of possible attack. It arrived in Hawaii at 7:33 a.m. and was being delivered to military authorities when the attack on Pearl Harbor began Japan's envoys were received at the State Department shortly after 2:00 p.m., by which time Hull had already received reports confirming the Japanese attack. After a bitter denunciation of Japan's duplicity, they were abruptly dismissed; the time for discussion was over.

Right: Nomura and Kurusu (with hat) leave the White House after conferring with Roosevelt on 27 November. By this time Japan had already sent her fleet steaming toward Pearl Harbor.

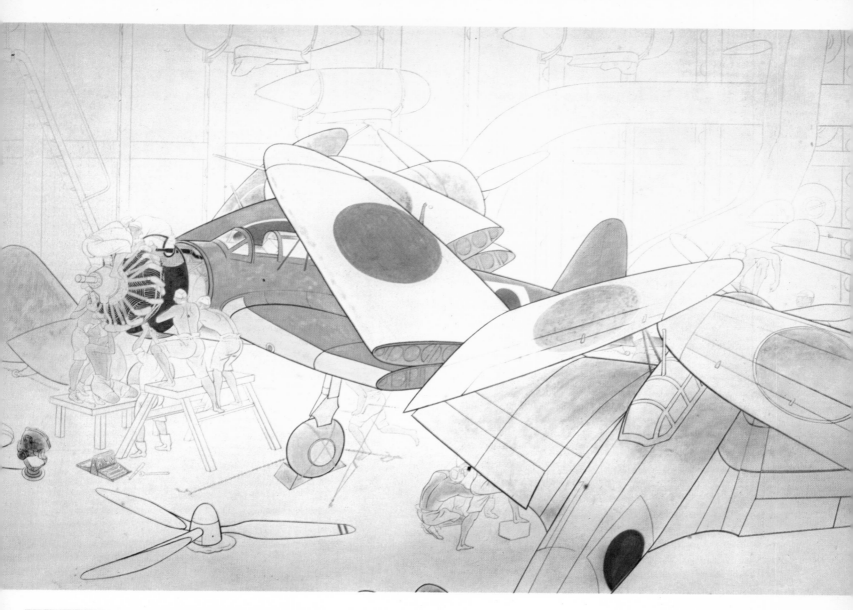

Above: *Aircraft Maintenance
Aboard a Carrier* by the
Japanese artist S. Arai.
Left: Japanese planes on
their way to "a rendezvous
with destiny".

CHAPTER SEVEN

Days of Infamy: Pearl Harbor, the Philippines, and Singapore

As Japan's military leaders prepared for war with the United States and the other colonial powers in Asia, they realized that they could never defeat the United States, Great Britain, and the Netherlands decisively; about the best they could hope for was a temporary victory based upon the neutralization of Allied naval forces in the Pacific and the seizure of certain territories, especially the mineral rich colonies of Malaya and the Dutch East Indies. Beyond this, a permanent solution to the Asian crisis would have to be reached through diplomacy.

Plans for an attack against the colonial powers had been prepared months before 7 December 1941 but it was not until 6 September that the proposal was formally presented to the Supreme War Council in Tokyo. This plan, conceived and articulated by Admiral Yamamoto, called for Japanese forces to launch a four phase attack against the Western allies immediately following the collapse of diplomatic efforts to settle the China tangle. During the first and second stages of the offensive, some six divisions would invade Malaya, Siam, and Burma while another three and one-half divisions would overrun Hongkong and the Philippine Islands. Phase three would see Japanese forces seize American bases in the Pacific, and in the final stage of the operation land forces would complete the occupation of British Malaya and the Dutch East Indies.

To achieve these goals, it was essential that Japanese naval superiority in the Pacific remain

Below: Japanese pilots warm up the engines of their Zero's on the flight deck of the aircraft carrier *Akagi*. Their objective – Pearl Harbor. **Opposite top:** Wheeler Field, Pearl Harbor. 0800 hours, 7 December 1941. **Opposite bottom:** The US fleet around Ford Island in Pearl Harbor was like a flock of sitting ducks.

unchallenged. This, in turn, meant that the American fleet at Pearl Harbor had to be neutralized before it could offer an effective counter-stroke to the Japanese offensive; the Japanese would have to launch a surprise attack on fleet headquarters similar to the British raid against the Italian fleet at Taranto in 1940. Japan's leaders understood this and accepted the risks involved, ordering preparations for the pre-emptive strike to be set in motion.

Anticipating the collapse of negotiations with the United States, a vast armada was gathered and committed to 'war games' off the coast of Japan late in September. The strike force, consisting of four fleet carriers, two light carriers, two fast battleships, three cruisers, a flotilla of destroyers, eight tankers, and a number of submarines, was ready for action against the United States when the Hull-Nomura conversations collapsed at the end of November. In fact, it was under way before Hull had replied to Japan's ultimatum of 25 November, though had the negotiations succeeded at this point the fleet could still have been recalled.

The Attack on Pearl Harbor

Little was done by American authorities to bolster the defenses of military installations at or near the naval base at Pearl Harbor, for although intelligence reports indicated that some form of attack was imminent, the time and place remained unknown. Most senior officers expected

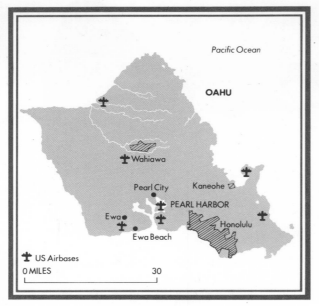

OAHU

Pacific Ocean

Wahiawa
Pearl City
Kaneohe
PEARL HARBOR
Ewa
Honolulu
Ewa Beach

✝ US Airbases
0 MILES   30

in all, reached Oahu shortly before 0800, where-upon the strike force divided into several attack groups. Fighters were deployed to destroy parked aircraft at Wheeler Field and Kanaohe, high-level bombers were sent over Hickam Field, and torpedo planes and dive-bombers flew over Battleship Row at Pearl Harbor. At 0750 Japanese pilots were ordered to attack, and shortly thereafter, all hell broke loose.

Thanks to last minute intelligence reports from Japanese operatives in Honolulu the night before the attack, the Japanese pilots knew precisely where to find their prey and lost little time in carrying out their mission of destruction. Within ten minutes two American battlewagons had been sunk and hundreds of sailors killed or injured; by 0830 90% of the damage of the attack had already been inflicted. American servicemen scrambled out of bed, away from the breakfast

the Japanese to attack the Philippine Islands rather than headquarters of the Pacific Fleet, and the only preparations against a surprise attack that were taken at all were initiated by Admiral Thomas C. Hart, commander of the Asiatic Fleet in Manila. The Hawaiian command remained unprepared for an attack until the very morning of 7 December 1941.

The Pacific Fleet had good reason to remain unprepared for a surprise attack, for the movement of Japan's strike force offered no clue as to its ultimate destination. In charting the course to Hawaii, great care had been taken to avoid normal shipping routes and land-based reconnaissance aircraft. Although this dictated passage through the northern Pacific with its foul weather, and necessitated refuelling at sea, Japan's fleet moved unmolested and undetected toward its target, arriving some 490 miles north off Oahu on the evening of 6 December 1941.

By 0600, on 7 December, the fleet had reached its flying-off position 275 miles north of Pearl Harbor at 0600 7 December 1941. Although it was still dark and the ships of the task force pitched badly in the swell, the first planes were aloft and on their way to Pearl Harbor before 0700. As Japan had anticipated, the entire American fleet, less four carriers, was in port and there were no indications that the command was expecting any action that day. However disappointed they might have been at the absence of the aircraft carriers, the commanders of the Japanese task force could hardly have asked for a more fortuitous situation.

The first wave of Japanese aircraft, some 190

Mitsubishi A6M5 Zero
Length: 29 ft. 8$\frac{11}{16}$ in.
Span: 39 ft. 4$\frac{7}{16}$ in.
Maximum speed: 331.5
m.p.h. at 14,930 ft. Range:
1675 miles. Armament:
2 × 7.7 mm., 2 × 20 mm.,
2 × 60 kg. bombs. Weight:
6164 lbs. max.

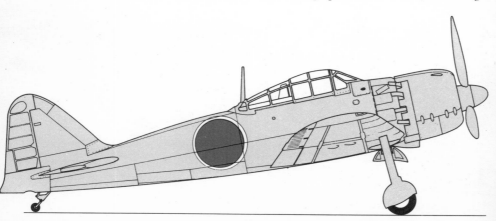

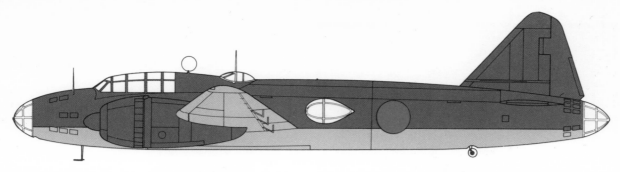

Mitsubishi G4MI. Length: 65 ft. 7$\frac{13}{32}$ in. Span: 82 ft. $\frac{1}{4}$ in. Maximum speed: 266 m.p.h. Armament: 4 × 7.7 mm., 1 × 20 mm. Crew: 7. Weight: 14,991 lbs. empty.

table, or out of church, but it was already too late to save the fleet.

Battleship Row was an easy target for Japanese bombardiers; the eight battlewagons of the fleet were moored to massive quays a short distance from the shore, completely unprotected against torpedo attack. The *Arizona* was attacked first and was torn apart by torpedo and bomb explosions within several minutes. Next, the *Oklahoma* was attacked and before 0800 a call to abandon ship was sounded. Within the next twenty-five minutes, five of the remaining battleships, *California*, *Maryland*, *Pennsylvania*, *Tennessee*, and *West Virginia*, were badly damaged or destroyed; only the *Nevada* managed to get under way before the end of the attack, and even she was hit by bombs and torpedoes. The Japanese attack force had accomplished its most important mission, the neutralization of the Pacific Fleet, in only thirty minutes, and had also inflicted heavy

Below: Most American planes were never able to take off.

Previous page: A small boat rescues seamen from the 31,800-ton USS *West Virginia*.

Right: From left to right: USS *West Virginia*, severely damaged; USS *Tennessee*, damaged; USS *Arizona*, sunk. **Far right:** The USS *California* settles slowly into the mud. **Below:** The battleship *Arizona* was the first to be attacked.

losses on American air units and installations. In short, the attack was a tactical success.

As morning wore on, the Japanese armada retreated and American officials surveyed the destruction wrought by their savage attack. In a little more than two hours, Japan had mauled the fleet, destroyed American air strength, and killed over two thousand men.

The Philippines Fall

News of the Japanese attack at Pearl Harbor reached the Philippines eight hours before Japanese forces invaded the Islands. Realizing that an attack was probably imminent, the senior military commanders, General Douglas Mac-Arthur and Admiral Thomas Hart, immediately alerted all units to prepare for action. Defensive preparations had already begun, thanks to a warning from the War Department on 27 November, but were still incomplete when news of the disaster at Pearl Harbor reached Manila at 0230 on 8 December (0880, 7 December, Hawaiian time); however one may feel about the abilities of MacArthur and Hart, there was nothing they could do to successfully defend the Philippines. For decades, critics of American colonial policy in Southeast Asia had warned of the difficulties of defending the Islands in the event of attack, but even as war approached Congress refused to appropriate enough money to allow for the establishment of an adequate insular force. The eight-hour notice of possible attack might just as well have come eight minutes before the strike; the battle for the archipelago was lost even before it was begun.

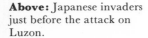
Above: Japanese invaders just before the attack on Luzon.

Japanese planes began their attack in the Philippines at 0530, 8 December 1941, sinking a sea plane tender off the coast of Mindanao. Six hours later, Formosa-based bombers attacked American bases on Luzon, destroying dozens of fighters and several B-17 bombers at Clark, Nichols, Iba, and other air fields near Manila. Although warnings were received at Army Air Force headquarters at least forty-five minutes before the attack, nothing was done to evacuate the aircraft before the Japanese reached Manila; Japanese pilots found their targets parked like sitting ducks on the runways and, with no anti-aircraft fire to distract them, proceeded to annihilate America's air force in the Philippines. Not only had the Far Eastern Air Force been destroyed just as the Pacific Fleet had been neutralized at Pearl Harbor, but the Asiatic Fleet, such as it was, was badly mauled and important dock and repair facilities in the port of Manila were destroyed.

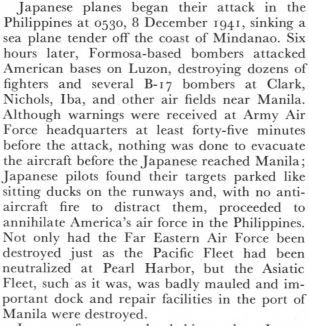

Japanese forces were landed in northern Luzon (Aparri) on 10 December and in the following weeks additional forces were carried into other ports on the island. Without aerial or naval strength Admiral Hart could no nothing to stop these amphibious operations; the fleet at his disposal was too small even to harass them. With absolute control of the air over Luzon and complete superiority at sea, Japanese forces made rapid headway as the new year approached.

This hopeless situation gave American commanders little choice but to withdraw from Manila to safer quarters. On 21 December Navy command moved to Corregidor and on Christmas Eve General MacArthur was forced to withdraw his forces to the Bataan Peninsula under heavy bombardment. What remained of the Asiatic Fleet was sent to Java and preparations were made to evacuate the leaders of the Philippine Commonwealth to the United States.

By withdrawing to the Bataan Peninsula and Corregidor, MacArthur hoped to be able to hold out against Japan until reinforcements could be brought to Luzon. This proved impossible and although American forces and their Filipino comrades fought bravely, it was soon necessary to abandon even these fortresses. On 11 March 1942, MacArthur reluctantly left the Islands for

Below: Admiral Thomas Hart.

Above left: Back to Bataan – the 4th Marines retreat to the peninsular redoubt.
Above: Japanese tanks enter Manila after the American withdrawal.
Far left: The Japanese close in on the beleaguered American perimeter.
Center left: An anti-tank company holds the line at Bataan. **Left:** Thousands of American and Philippine troops were captured only to face the "Death March" to prison camp or death.
Far left: The men on Corregidor resisted to the last. **Center left:** The Japanese breakthrough at Bataan forced the Americans back to the island of Corregidor.

Left: The Japanese land on Corregidor.

Right: Americans cover their retreat on Panay.

Australia, leaving General Jonathan Wainwright in command of army forces on Bataan. Wainwright held Bataan until 8 April when he finally had to evacuate to Corregidor. There the remnants of MacArthur's army and a few Marine units held out for another month but finally, on 6 May 1942, Wainwright surrendered Corregidor and all armed forces in the archipelago to the Japanese. America's inability to hold the Philippines had cost tens of thousands of lives and untold billions of dollars and was a disaster. Although MacArthur had vowed to return and liberate the Islands, it would take him nearly three years to do so.

Malaya and Singapore are Occupied

On 8 December 1941 Japanese forces invaded British Malaya, crossing the Siamese frontier and landing at Kota Bahru. Unlike the Americans who were completely unprepared for the attack on Pearl Harbor, the British actually traced the movement of Japanese forces from Indochina to the Malay peninsula. Nevertheless, despite the fact that they had at least two days notice of the movement of men and ships from Saigon and Camranh Bay, they chose to wait and see what the Japanese would do before implementing their plans to defend Malaya and Singapore. This delay proved to be a tragic mistake.

Below. The Japanese push through Malaya was devastating. **Below right:** The Japanese moved swiftly down the Malay Peninsula by bicycle.

Left: British surrender at Singapore. **Below:** British retreat through the jungles of Malaya.

Plans for the defense of Malaya and Singapore had been prepared years before, and relied on the ability of the Royal Navy and Air Force to repel any amphibious landings or assaults from the Siamese border. On paper and in the minds of those who prepared the plan, there was no doubt that the British could defend their colony if the fleet was reinforced and adequate numbers of aircraft were despatched to bases in the colony. Unfortunately, when Japanese forces struck, British air strength was barely half that required by the plan and the fleet was hardly on a par with Japanese naval forces in the Pacific. Whether or not the British would have been able to hold the

line against Japan with their forces at full strength will never be known; as it was, the Navy and the RAF could not hope to deter Japan's advance through Southeast Asia.

When the Japanese launched their attack, British forces in Malaya were commanded by Air Marshal Sir Robert Brooke-Popham. He based his defense of the colony on the assumption that the Japanese would make their main thrust across the Siamese frontier and, with this in mind, hoped to deploy British forces in a defensive line across the Kra Isthmus. With proper advance notice (at least thirty-six hours), additional forces could be sent across the border to capture the port towns of Singora and Patani before the enemy could land; at the very least, British forces could close the roads and railway lines between Singora and Jitra in Malaya, thus slowing if not stopping the Japanese advance. In any case, however, the British commander refused to close the Siamese ports or to implement the Jitra alternative until the Japanese first violated Siam's neutrality.

While one may sympathize with British unwillingness to be branded an aggressor, waiting for the Japanese to make the first move cost precious time which allowed them to gather too much momentum. By the time Brooke-Popham was ready to respond to Japanese violation of the frontier on 8 December it was already too late to close the ports or to employ the Jitra alternative effectively. British forces made a valiant attempt to hold the line in northern Malaya, but the

Below: The British C-in-C in Malaya, Sir Robert Brooke-Popham.

Far left: Emergency footbridges were constructed by the Japanese. **Left:** British seamen scramble over the side of the doomed *Repulse*.

Far left: Japanese troops mop up in Kuala Lumpur. **Left:** General Sir Archibald Wavell (left) took over command of the Allied Forces in the Southwest Pacific. Rear Admiral Thomas C. Hart (center) and Major-General George Brett, Deputy Supreme Commander (right) confer with Wavell.

Far left: HM ships *Prince of Wales* and *Repulse* after being hit by Japanese torpedos. A British destroyer moves off in the foreground. **Left:** The abject surrender of Singapore was a stain on British honor and a death blow to the Allied defense of Southeast Asia.

Left: Japanese troops march toward the Raffles statue in Singapore.

Japanese were able to break through their line within four days of the initial attack, forcing them into hasty retreat.

Even more important than Brooke-Popham's failure to seize the initiative in northern Malaya was the destruction of the *Prince of Wales* and the *Repulse* on 10 December. Both battleships had joined the fleet 2 December and were being deployed under the command of Admiral Sir T. S. V. Phillips, Commander-in-Chief of the Eastern Fleet, when they were sunk after a two-hour bombardment by Japanese planes. The loss of these mainstays of the fleet sealed the fate of Malaya and Singapore as, without effective naval resistance, Japanese forces were moved ashore in large numbers where they quickly solidified Japan's hold on the peninsula and pushed south toward Singapore.

By mid-January 1942 the Japanese had reached the State of Johore and were preparing to attack Singapore. By this time command of British forces had been transferred to General Sir Archibald Wavell who hoped to be able to hold Johore until he was strong enough to launch a counterattack, for unless Johore was successfully defended, Singapore would fall, and it would not be long before Japan invaded the Dutch East Indies. This decision to make a stand in Johore and Singapore necessitated the rapid withdrawal of all British forces north of Kuala Lumpur, thus leaving the Japanese free to travel on the roads leading south. The latter were able to move much faster than their adversaries, and as a result were poised to attack Wavell's forces in Johore before the reinforcement from the north was complete.

On 8 February 1942 two Japanese divisions attempted to cross the straits from the mainland to Singapore in the dark of night. By the next morning, 13,000 Japanese troops were ashore, and there was little that could be done to save the city Unlike Bataan and Corregidor, Singapore did not offer its defenders a position of natural strength or a fortress from which to resist the invaders; even the naval base could not be held since its defenses were useless against an attack from the mainland. Although British forces fought on for a week following the first Japanese crossing, their effort was in vain, and Singapore fell on 15 February 1942.

The Sun Sets on the British Empire

In less than three months the Japanese had occupied Malaya and were ready to complete their conquest of what remained of the colonial empires in Southeast Asia. Like the Americans, the British had underestimated the capability of Japanese forces and had based their defense on obsolete principles and strategy. Assuming that Japan would be deterred by the presence of a strong American fleet in the Pacific, the British government did little to provide for an adequate defense of Malaya by bringing the fleet at Singapore up to full strength; thus, when the United States Pacific Fleet was destroyed at Pearl Harbor, all chances of successfully defending the empire were lost. The loss of Singapore shattered British prestige in Asia and, although she would avenge this loss some years later, Britain would never be able to re-establish her prewar position.

The Battle for Burma

The Japanese attack on Pearl Harbor shattered the illusion of neutrality which had characterized the diplomatic situation between Great Britain, the United States and Japan before 7 December 1941. With Japanese forces attacking the Philippines and Malaya, it would only be a matter of time before they crossed the Burmese border and preparations for defense were hastily begun. General Wavell, commander of British forces in Burma, believed that the colony could be defended with a minimum of outside aid, asking only that the Chinese commit one and one-half divisions to its defense and that lend-lease supplies destined for China be used in Burma if necessary.

For the Chinese, even more than for the British, the defense of Burma was absolutely vital. The closing of the Haiphong-Yunnan railroad soon after the Japanese occupation of Indochina in 1940–1 left the Burma Road as China's only link with the outside world. This road which wound its way some 750 miles from Lashio in Burma to Kunming in China, was literally China's jugular vein; if the Japanese succeeded in closing it, her ability to resist would be greatly diminished. Chiang Kai-shek, therefore, was willing to do anything that might facilitate the defense of Burma, though for the moment, the British did not call for his assistance.

Rangoon Falls to Japan

The Japanese launched their first raid on Rangoon on 23 December 1941, expecting no resistance over the city, and retreated quickly when units of the Royal Air Force and the American Volunteer Group (Flying Tigers) attempted to block their path. Nevertheless, the raid was costly to the combined British-American force for, although they managed to wreck at least ten Japanese aircraft, the defenders lost nine of their own planes; this was a loss of major proportions since the British and their American allies only had fifty-seven planes at their disposal, thirty-six of which were antiquated and hardly suitable for combat against modern Japanese fighters.

More important, perhaps, than the loss of nine planes was the effect of the bombing on the people of Rangoon. Fires raged throughout the city, thousands were killed or wounded, and many shorefront warehouses were damaged or destroyed. Although British volunteers cleaned up efficiently and attended to the needs of the injured, they could not prevent the exodus of Burmese and Indian coolies to the countryside; by Christmas 1941, all activities in the city had ground to a halt, resulting in shortages of fuels and other essentials, and martial law had to be imposed to prevent looting and rioting. As Japanese raids continued the main railroad station was knocked out, lend-lease equipment was destroyed in warehouses along the waterfront, and thousands more Burmese and Indians fled the city. By 1 January 1942, the devastation of Rangoon was virtually complete.

On 20 January 1942, after almost a month of bombing raids against Rangoon and other sites, Japanese forces crossed the Thai border into southern Burma, their purpose being to cut the link between Rangoon and Kunming. Moving straight across country they easily defeated the

Left: The Japanese move swiftly through Burma. **Right:** Japanese bombs and the British scorched earth policy reduced most of Rangoon to rubble.

Top: A living bridge in the Burmese jungle. **Far left above:** Japanese armor met little effective Allied resistance. **Far left:** Banzai! Japanese victory in Burma was complete. **Left:** Burmese women give water to their new masters.

British, Burmese and Indian troops in their path; on 23 February, Japanese forces ambushed Indian forces near the Sittang Bridge, crossed the Sittang River, moved past Pegu, and turned south toward Rangoon. The city was now seriously threatened and AMMISCA personnel prepared to move lend-lease supplies northward or destroy them at the docks and warehouses so that they would not fall into Japanese hands. As the Japanese moved toward the city, goods were moved out at a rate of a thousand tons per day, but even at this accelerated rate of shipment there was not enough time to move all the lend-lease supplies north to China. Much of the equipment was either given to British forces or destroyed, but when the Japanese captured Rangoon on 6 March 1942, they still found almost 20,000 tons of lend-lease supplies intact in warehouses.

The fury and rapidity of the Japanese advance into Burma far exceeded anything that its defenders had anticipated. As the Japanese drew near to Rangoon, Wavell hastily requested the additional aid from China that he had refused at the beginning of February. Despite the ill will between the Chinese and the British which had resulted from Wavell's original rebuff, Chiang Kai-shek responded to his later request and Chinese forces began to move across the Sino-Burmese border on 28 February.

Shortly after the Japanese captured Rangoon, Chinese forces were massed in Toungoo and points north while British and Indian units were concentrated in Mandalay, Prome, and Yenangyaung. Wavell hoped to hold those cities and cut the road from Rangoon to Mandalay; if the Japanese could be held south of Prome and Toungoo, the oil fields at Yenangyaung which were China's major source of crude oil would be protected and a new road could be built from Assam to Burma linking the Indian ports of Calcutta and Chittaging to Yunnan province. Once the new road was completed, lend-lease supplies would once again be funnelled into China.

The Allies Retreat

After taking Rangoon, Japanese forces moved northward along the Sittang and Irrawaddy rivers toward Prome and Toungoo. As they moved north, they were harassed by RAF and AVG pilots flying out of a base at Magwe, some 200 miles north of Rangoon, but a series of massive raids against the installation on 27 March by some 200 bombers forced its abandonment. The RAF retreated into India while the AVG moved north into China; Allied air strength in Burma had been almost totally destroyed, leaving the Japanese in complete control of the skies over southern Burma. The loss of air cover and the absence of adequate aerial reconnaissance left the British and Chinese easy prey for the Japanese who had secured information about Allied troop movements from Burmese nationalists.

The Japanese began their attack at Toungoo on 19 March and took the city within a week. As they prepared to march north from their new stronghold, General Joseph Stilwell, Commander-in-Chief of American forces in the China-Burma-India theatre and Wavell's lieutenant in the defense of Burma, sought to persuade the Chinese forces in the area to mount a counterattack. Failing in this, he persuaded British commanders to take up the idea, with disastrous results. The Japanese easily routed the few forces the British has mustered in the area, and moved on immediately to take the city of Prome.

Japanese victories at Toungoo and Prome checked the Allied plan to cut the Rangoon-Mandalay road, and soon they were advancing northward, threatening Yenangyaung, Mandalay and Lashio. As total victory became an increasing reality, steps were taken to evacuate these important centres; the British prepared to destroy all stores, equipment and supplies which might be of use, including the oil rigs and depots at Yenangyaung.

Lashio, the southern terminus of the Burma Road, fell to the Japanese on 29 April 1942 along with 44,000 tons of lend-lease supplies destined for China. With the closing of the Burma Road, the only land routes open to China were the old silk highway across Sinkiang province from Russia and the ancient caravan trails across the Himalayas and through Tibet from India, neither of which were much use for transporting large quantities of goods and supplies. To reach the borders of Sinkiang, American and British supplies would have to be moved through crowded Russian ports and over the inadequate and overburdened Russian railroads for thousands of miles, after which they would have to be transferred to trucks and pack animals and moved thousands of miles more to the war front in China. The caravan trails through Tibet offered a much shorter route but only pack animals could negotiate the mountain trails; the trip was slow, and heavy equipment could not be carried. Thus, the fall of Lashio represented a crushing blow to the Chinese from which they might never have recovered were it not for the establishment of the air lift over the Hump. At the time the loss of the Burma Road seriously hampered all Allied operations in China and Burma.

The 'Flying Tigers'
With the fall of Lashio, Allied forces retreated rapidly toward China. During this retreat, the American Volunteer Group played an important role. AVG planes flying from bases in China were the allies' only source of reconnaissance and intelligence and its pilots provided valuable air cover for the retreating Chinese and British armies. The men of the AVG also prevented a Japanese advance from Burma into Yunnan by destroying the northern portion of the Burma Road and many of the bridges across the Salween River.

AVG reconnaissance missions were inaugurated in March 1942. Although the pilots in the group disliked such missions, considering them a waste of resources, the switch from combat missions to patrol and reconnaissance was dictated by shortages of fuel and equipment; since Chennault's mercenaries had no bombers at their disposal, they could not undertake offensive raids against Japanese bases in Thailand or Indochina. In the lull between battles AVG pilots were assigned to patrol missions, but as the retreat of Allied forces

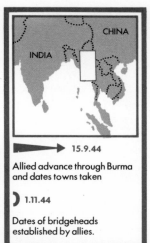

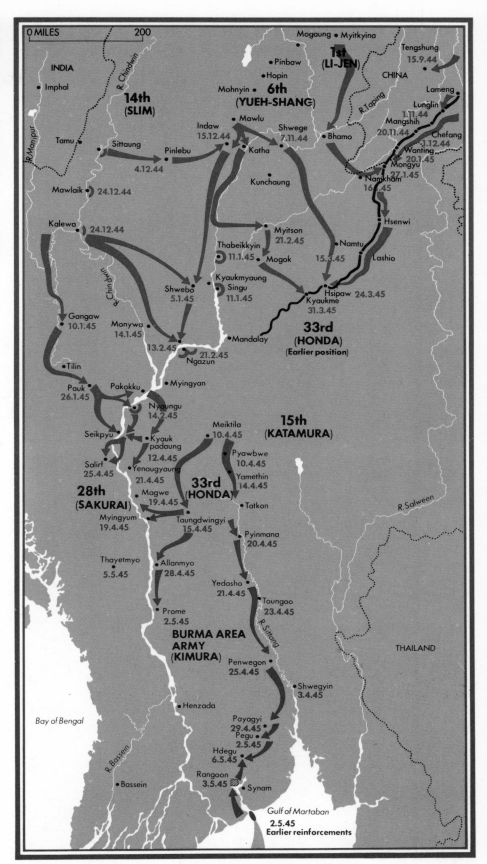

INDIA   CHINA

15.9.44

Allied advance through Burma
and dates towns taken

1.11.44

Dates of bridgeheads
established by allies.

Left: The Japanese
advance stopped at the
Indian border. This
Japanese fighter met its
end at Chittagong, East
Bengal. **Below left:** HMS
Cornwall was sunk in the
Indian Ocean, 5 April
1942. **Below right:** A
Flying Tiger.

Map labels:

0 MILES   200

INDIA
CHINA
THAILAND
Bay of Bengal
Gulf of Martaban

1st (LI-JEN)
6th (YUEH-SHANG)
14th (SLIM)
15th (KATAMURA)
33rd (HONDA) (Earlier position)
33rd (HONDA)
28th (SAKURAI)
BURMA AREA ARMY (KIMURA)

R. Chindwin
R. Manipur
R. Taping
R. Salween
R. Sittang
R. Bassein

Mogaung   Myitkyina
Tengshung 15.9.44
Pinbaw
Hopin
Imphal
Mohnyin
Lameng
Tamu
Mawlu
Lunglin
Sittaung
Indaw 15.12.44
Shwege 7.11.44
Bhamo
1.11.44
Mangshih 20.11.44
Chefang
Pinlebu 4.12.44
Katha
Wanting 1.12.44
Mongyu 20.1.45
Mawlaik 24.12.44
Kunchaung
Namkham 16.1.45
27.1.45
Kalewa 24.12.44
Myitson 21.2.45
Hsenwi
Thabeikkyin 11.1.45
Namtu 15.3.45
Lashio
Kyaukmyaung Singu 11.1.45
Mogok
Shwebo 5.1.45
Hsipaw 24.3.45
Gangaw 10.1.45
Kyaukme 31.3.45
Monywa 14.1.45
Mandalay
Tilin
13.2.45
Ngazun 21.2.45
Pauk 26.1.45
Pakokku
Myingyan
Nyaungu 14.2.45
Meiktila 10.4.45
Seikpyu
Kyauk padaung 12.4.45
Pyawbwe 10.4.45
Salin 25.4.45
Yenaugyaung 21.4.45
Yamethin 14.4.45
Magwe 19.4.45
Myingyum 19.4.45
Taungdwingyi 15.4.45
Tatkon
Thayetmyo 5.5.45
Allanmyo 28.4.45
Pyinmana 20.4.45
Yedasho 21.4.45
Toungoo 23.4.45
Prome 2.5.45
Penwegon 25.4.45
Shwegyin 3.4.45
Henzada
Payagyi 29.4.45
Pegu 2.5.45
Hdegu 6.5.45
Bassein
Rangoon 3.5.45
Synam

2.5.45
Earlier reinforcements

toward the Chinese border was stepped up, AVG pilots resumed limited combat activities.

The Allied evacuation to China necessitated the destruction of bases and supplies in Burma; in order to prevent the Japanese from crossing the Salween into China, the bridges across the river and roads leading to these crossings had also to be destroyed. Strafing and bombing raids carried out against the advancing Japanese armies were equally important, and optimum use was made of the limited number of planes left in the AVG.

To maximize the use of available aircraft and minimize equipment losses, AVG units were scattered over several bases in China; strikes against the Japanese were launched from many bases and planes were never immediately returned to the base from which they had taken off. Thus the Japanese were kept off balance by the group's total mobility and consistently overestimated the numbers of planes available to their enemies. Undoubtedly, had they realized the real strength of the AVG, they would have taken even bolder steps in the Burma campaign.

In retrospect, the performance of the American Volunteer Group in Burma was impressive. Despite shortages in supplies and equipment, failing morale, and the deteriorating situation of the allies in Burma, the men of the group performed bravely and as effectively as circumstances permitted. Nevertheless, by the end of April, Japanese forces reached the Salween River, completing their occupation of Burma.

The rôle of Burmese nationalism

The speed of the Japanese conquest in Burma and the ease with which they rallied to their banners indicated the weakness of the British colonial system. British efforts to persuade nationalist leaders to resist Japan failed dismally because these men saw little profit in remaining true to their colonial masters; the failure of the British to promise independence in return for active Burmese participation against Japan insured that such cooperation would not be forthcoming. In contrast, the Japanese held out the prospect of independence and participation as equal members in the Greater East Asia Co-Prosperity Sphere, and these promises of a better tomorrow were enough to win the support of most Burmese leaders.

Left: US forces unload supplies in India for the flight over the "Hump".
Right: Airdrop to guerrilla teams in Southeast China.

The successful occupation of Burma was the result of a period of several decades during which the Japanese assiduously cultivated their interest and image in the country. Capitalizing on their victory over Russia in 1905, Japan attempted to make a psychological impact on all the peoples of Asia including the Burmese and, although such efforts were subdued until the 1930's, there can be little doubt that pro-Japanese sympathizers had increased markedly in the area. In Burma, interest in things Japanese grew steadily until by 1930, when the Japanese government consciously sought to increase its influence in Burma, there was already a small but influential group of Burmese Japanophiles.

To facilitate expanded Japanese activities in Burma, particularly contacts with the nationalist movement, several Japanese military and civilian officials were dispatched to the colony. Among them was Colonel Suzuki Keiji, a man who soon became the chief of Japanese cadres operating in Burma. He was to establish contacts with anti-colonial elements and help them to equip and train a nationalist army which might later support Japanese action in Burma. As a result of his efforts, several dozen young nationalist leaders were sent to Japan where they were trained in the art of warfare; upon their return to Burma, these men formed the nucleus of the Burma Independence Army which fought with the Japanese against Britain from December 1941–May 1942.

Participation of the Burma Independence Army in the Japanese invasion and occupation of Burma transformed what might have simply been an exchange of one colonial master for another into a liberation campaign, and Burma welcomed the Japanese, seriously believing in their willingness to die for her freedom. Swept off their feet by the speed of Japanese victories, all segments of Burmese society welcomed the Japanese invaders.

This enthusiasm also benefited the nationalist movement, which was able to mobilize a large segment of the population as a result of Japan's victories against the colonial regime. Operating under the protective umbrella of the Japanese army, the leaders of the Burma Independence Army established their authority in the villages and hamlets. For the first time in fifty years,

119

foreigners did not rule the country, though the period in which the BIA operated independently was to be very short.

Despite the eagerness of Burmese nationalists to declare the establishment of independence and self-rule, Japanese military authorities refused to sanction any such move. Independence was to be postponed for at least a year; a military administration would govern the country, reestablish law and order, and define the new administrative apparatus which would govern the country until independence was granted. Japan did not pledge independence until 1 August 1943, and even after this formality Burmese independence was more imaginary than real.

Realities of life Under the Occupation

Japanese influence and prestige, at its high point during the first days of the occupation, declined steadily thereafter, for the reality of Japanese rule proved to be far different from the benefits Burma had expected to derive from their presence. Although most Burmese had refused to see Japanese shortcomings prior to the invasion, the severity and brutality of their conduct was soon manifestly clear to all. Understanding little about the character and traditions of the Burman majority and other ethnic groups, the Japanese tried to remold them in their image, under-taking a moral conversion that was doomed to failure. Pan-Asianism could not bridge the important differences between their cultures and habits; the Japanese, with little regard for Burmese traditional values, mistakenly assumed that Burma was ready to adopt Japanese culture, and when it did not, responded with brutality.

Burmese hopes for equality within the Great East Asia Co-Prosperity Sphere were never realized. Having come to expect inferior treatment and racist attitudes from the British, the Burmese nationalists looked for better treatment from the Japanese, especially since much of their propaganda in the prewar period had been based on the promise that they would treat other Asian peoples with dignity and equality. The reality proved altogether different and soon, repelled by the frequently boorish, patronizing and uncivil attitude of Japanese officers in Burma, even the most ardent Japanophiles recognized the ill treatment they were receiving from the occupiers. Ultimately the Japanese lost considerable support in Burma as a result of their lack of sensitivity and appreciation of the indigenous culture. Their expectation of 'filial piety' from other Asians was never realized because these people soon learned that Japanese interests and their own did not coincide. The Japanese conquest began the drive forward to independence in Burma.

Headquarters, 14th Air Force, China. Chinese and Americans load bombs.

Left: American aid to the British in Burma came late and in insufficient quantities to materially help the British until 1945.
Below: An American mechanic introduces Chinese recruits to the P-40.

CHAPTER NINE
Crisis in Southeast Asia

On 1 March 1942, Japanese forces landed on Java. Seven days later Dutch authorities surrendered, and the colonial period came to an abrupt end. There was little resistance to the Japanese invasion, for Javanese natives did not rally to the Dutch; some were passive, but others enthusiastically welcomed the Japanese as liberators. After centuries of colonial rule, Dutch prestige was suddenly destroyed.

The Japanese conquest of the Netherlands East Indies marked the achievement of a long cherished goal: the control of the rich natural resources of the area and its incorporation into the Greater East Asia Co-Prosperity Sphere. Japanese military men, diplomats, and industrialists had long been sensitive to the lack of strategic raw material available within their own borders. They had looked longingly toward the Indies as a source for such materials for decades, but it was not until the end of the 1930's that this interest was intensified as a result of menacing changes in American foreign policy. Under the growing realization that vital supplies and dollar assets could be frozen at any moment, the cautious policy of Japanese diplomats gave way to a more militant approach. The decision to invade the Dutch East Indies was not arrived at precipitously however, and there were several attempts to secure sufficient quantities of important materials through negotiation.

The Japanese realized that they could not seize the Netherlands East Indies without risking almost certain war with the United Kingdom and the United States. Therefore, in an attempt to use 'peaceful persuasion', the Japanese minister at the Hague presented a note to the Dutch Foreign Ministry on 2 February 1940 which requested the Dutch to end their restrictions on imports and exports between Japan and the Netherlands East Indies. It also asked that Japan be permitted to play a greater role in the development of resources in the area. No Dutch response was immediately forthcoming, but events in the months that followed caused the Japanese to renew their bid.

German forces invaded Holland on 10 May 1940, and their rapid occupation of the country and the flight of the Dutch government to London had an immediate effect on the situation in the Far East. On 12 May, the Japanese Ambassador at the Hague issued a statement expressing concern and demanding assurances that the Netherlands Indies would continue to supply Japan with vital materials; he also asked whether Holland's allies planned any intervention in the Indies similar to the landing of British and French forces on the Dutch held islands of Aruba and Curaçao in the Caribbean. The Dutch replied that no such intervention had been requested nor was one anticipated, but their assurances did not satisfy the Tokyo government.

On 18 May 1940, three days after the government of the Netherlands capitulated to the Germans, the Japanese consul in Batavia presented a note to colonial officials expressing anxiety over the meaning of events in Europe. Several days later, the Dutch Ambassador was summoned before the Foreign Minister in Tokyo and handed a list of thirteen vital materials normally obtained from the Indies and the minimum quantities of each required by the

Japanese. In addition, Japan demanded assurances that these materials would be shipped under 'any circumstances'.

The Dutch response was cautious, avoiding direct rebuff for fear of what the Japanese might do if turned down. The Dutch government announced its willingness to provide certain materials, but refused to guarantee delivery or to permit the Japanese to develop resources in the colony. Japan found this answer was unacceptable and continued to press for a substantial adjustment of the export quotas of oil and other petroleum products and guaranteed delivery of such goods.

Throughout the period of preliminary negotiations with the Dutch, Japanese diplomats tried to sound out the German government on its policy toward the Indies and sought to obtain a pledge that Germany would not interfere with Japan's sphere of influence in East Asia, nor in particular with Japanese plans to tap the resources of the Netherlands Indies. On 22 May 1940, the German government formally informed Japan that it was not interested in the problems of the Indies and that Japan was free to exploit and develop the riches of the area. In fact, the German government encouraged the occupation of the Indies in the hope that such a move would precipitate a confrontation between Japan and the United States and divert America's attention from Europe to Asia. The Japanese, however, were anxious to secure concessions without force if at all possible.

With pledges of German non-intervention and support in hand, Japan continued to press for concessions, and on 16 July, the Dutch minister in Tokyo was informed that the Japanese government wished to send a delegation to Batavia to discuss Japan's increased needs for products from the Indies. It is interesting to note that no effort was made to send an emissary to the Dutch government-in-exile to discuss the matter; clearly the Japanese were hoping to develop and exploit cleavages between the home government and the colonial administration.

The Dutch reluctantly accepted the delegation, but clearly specified that discussion would be limited to economic and other non-political matters. In preparation for the discussions, the Japanese Foreign Ministry prepared a draft statement of Japan's aims and goals. This document, dated 14 August 1940, suggested the scope of the concessions to be demanded of the Dutch at Batavia: the colonial government was expected to recognize Japan's predominant political and economic interest in the area; the Japanese were to press for the inclusion of the Dutch East Indies in the Greater East Asia Co-Prosperity Sphere and encourage the Indies government to sever all relations with the Western powers. If possible, these goals were to be accomplished by the use of diplomacy and the display of power rather than by the actual use of power and warfare.

The Japanese mission arrived in Indonesia on 12 September 1940. Although it was headed by a cabinet minister, the delegation also included several highranking military and naval officers. Despite the fact that Japan had sent such a high level delegation, the Governor-General, Tjarda van Starkenborgh Stachouwer, refused to head the Dutch negotiating team, delegating the responsibility to the colony's Director of Economic Affairs. Since the discussions were to be non-political, it was deemed improper for the chief official in the colony to be distracted from more important work. The Japanese were not pleased, but accepted the Dutch decision without protest.

Negotiations began on 16 September 1940, but on 27 September Japan signed the Tripartite Pact with Germany and Italy, and the fact that Japan was now allied with Holland's enemies presented substantial difficulties for the delegation. Their explanation, that the main purpose of the pact was to prevent the spread of war to the Pacific, did not satisfy officials of the colonial government who requested clarification of Japan's intentions in the Indies. Were the Japanese going to force the Netherlands Indies into the Greater East Asia Co-Prosperity Sphere? If not, what would they do? The Japanese were irritated that the Dutch should challenge their 'good will' and retaliated by charging that the colonial government was not negotiating in good faith, but had orders from Washington DC to thwart all progress. Although the talks were not broken off as a result of these charges and counter-charges, the chill atmosphere of the discussions never quite thawed.

A tentative agreement was reached on 18 October, wherein Dutch authorities agreed to supply Japan with commodities equal to approximately one-half of her original demands. The agreement was to be limited to a period of six months and contained no guarantee of delivery; more important, the Japanese would not be permitted to explore and exploit untapped resources in the islands. In short, the mission had failed to realize its goals, and so the Tokyo government immediately announced its intention of entering into a second round of negotiations. Although the Dutch believed that little would be gained by continuing the discussions, they acceded to the request lest their failure to do so provoke the Japanese to the use of force.

The second Japanese mission arrived in Batavia on 28 December and negotiations were resumed in January 1941. On 16 January the delegation presented a memorandum to the Dutch which contained a number of sweeping demands aimed at forcing the Netherlands Indies into the Co-Prosperity Sphere. Needless to say, this was totally unacceptable and the conference ended in failure. Although requests for increased shipments of petroleum products to Japan were forwarded to officials of oil companies operating in the colony, the colonial government rejected the notion that the Japanese should be accorded special status and/or privileges in the islands. Despite considerable pressure from Tokyo, the Dutch stood firm.

The failure of the Dutch-Japanese talks ended the latter's attempts to bring the Netherlands Indies into the Greater East Asia Co-Prosperity Sphere by peaceful means. When the Japanese delegation returned from Batavia on 25 June 1941, a conference was held at the Imperial Palace where it was decided that the plans for an invasion of the Indies should be effected.

Japanese forces left for the Indies in January

Opposite top: The Battle of the Java Sea in late February 1942 was the last heroic and futile stand by the Dutch and Allied fleet to defend the Indies.
Opposite: bottom: A Japanese parade of triumph in the Celebes.

1942. Seven weeks after their first landing, Dutch colonial authorities surrendered. The rapidity of the Japanese advance stunned Indonesians, and pro-Japanese feelings, strong even before the invasion, became even stronger as Dutch resistance collapsed. Japanese propagandists had been working with Muslim groups and the secular nationalists for years, but there was still considerable anti-Axis sentiment which might have been exploited by colonial authorities had they chosen to do so. In fact, many nationalist leaders openly expressed a desire to cooperate with the Dutch against the Japanese but were refused. The Dutch authorities never really tried to exploit the anti-Japanese sentiment of some segments of the nationalist movement even during the critical weeks of the invasion, but they did count on the support and affection of the Indonesian masses. In this they were mistaken. Colonial administrators had naively believed that their wards accepted their rule affectionately or willingly, and were too easily convinced of the loyalty of their charges. As a result, they treated nationalist leaders with cruelty and disdain, and after the completion of the Japanese occupation, the anti-Dutch sentiment of the Indonesian masses surfaced in a series of violent attacks on Dutch residents, property, and government offices. The Japanese had to use considerable force to stop the destruction.

Japanese military administration of the Indies was inaugurated on 8 March 1942, with an occupation regime patterned after the government of Japan. Representative institutions were abolished and centralization of administrative functions replaced a decentralized administration. All important positions in the occupation regime were held by Japanese from the home islands, Korea and Formosa, and lower level posts were given to natives who replaced Dutch officials interned in detention centres. Although the Japanese military command in Batavia held the reins of power tightly, the status of Indonesians rose considerably as a result of their employment in the civil service, thus lending credence to the Japanese attempt to portray themselves as liberators.

Indonesian nationalist leaders were released from prisons and returned from exile soon after the occupation, for the Japanese, encouraged by the enthusiastic reception they had received, saw little to fear from the nationalists and were anxious to recruit them in their propaganda efforts. Many of the leading nationalist leaders chose to take advantage of the situation and collaborated, but it is clear that their cooperation was used to further the goals of the nationalist movement and to facilitate the transition from occupation to independence.

Occupation of Indochina

The Japanese occupation of Indochina was not the result of a sudden military thrust, but of blunt diplomatic measures geared to the satisfaction of her strategic needs. This area was most important to the Japanese as a source of essential raw materials and as a base for their activities in other parts of Southeast Asia. In addition, they were also interested in closing the Haiphong-Yunnan railway, a vital link between China and the outside world which would prolong the China Incident as long as it remained open.

Japanese attempts to secure the closing of the Haiphong-Yunnan railway began almost immediately after their invasion of China in 1937. Japanese diplomats diligently sought to secure French concessions on this matter, first by persuasion and later by threats, but they made little headway until war broke out in Europe. After their defeat by Germany in 1940, French authorities were in no position to resist Japan's advances; they could either accede to Japanese demands or face the loss of their Indochinese colonies.

French officials were under no illusions about their ability to resist a Japanese attack, and colonial officials pragmatically decided that cooperation was their only alternative if French sovereignty in the colonies was to be preserved. So, isolated from France and with no pledges of support from Great Britain or the United States, they agreed to close the Haiphong-Yunnan railway and to see that no war materials were shipped through the colony to China. Thus began a movement toward ending French sovereignty in Indochina which culminated in the Japanese *coup de force* of 9 March 1945.

For his pragmatism and acceptance of the Japanese demands, General Catroux, the chief French colonial officer in Indochina, was rewarded with public censure from the newly established Vichy regime, transferred to another post, and replaced by Admiral Jean Decoux, a more 'reliable' public figure. Decoux arrived at his new post in July 1940 and soon found that the Japanese were not yet satisfied. Twelve days after his arrival in Indochina he was presented with a second ultimatum, demanding the freedom to move troops in and out of the colonies as well as free access to and use of air bases and naval facilities. Although his personal inclination was to reject the Japanese ultimatum, Decoux waited for

General Catroux (below left) was soon replaced by Admiral Decoux (below) after the fall of France. **Right:** Japanese troops swiftly moved south to occupy the whole of Indo-China.

instructions from the Vichy régime; when they
arrived, he followed precedent and bowed to
Japan's demands. The result was the Franco-
Japanese Treaty of 30 August 1940 in which the
Vichy government recognized Japan's 'pre-
eminent position in the Far East,' granted the
Japanese full use of aerial and naval facilities in the
colonies, and pledged France's aid in ending the
China Incident. In return for all this, the Japanese
formally recognized French sovereignty in Indochina.

The occupation begins

The Franco-Japanese agreement was beneficial
to both countries. The Japanese were able to
close another gap in their blockage of China and
gained free access to military facilities in the
colonies without incurring the heavy responsibility of conducting a colonial administration and
providing services to millions of Indochinese. The
cost of their presence was borne by the French
regime which also provided them with badly
needed food and war supplies. In return, the
French were permitted to conduct business as
usual; armed French troops moved freely throughout the colonies as did French civilians – the only
Europeans to do so in Asia during the war. The
Japanese had little to do with the Indochinese
population, and as a result, the people of the
colonies continued to look to the French for
direction, not realizing the extent to which the
French colonial administration was controlled by
Japanese military authorities.

The facade of French sovereignty not only
fooled the people of Indochina but apparently
convinced French colonial officials that the
Japanese had not occupied the colonies but were
merely stationed there. Writing several years after
the war, Admiral Decoux summarized this
attitude:

'A country is not occupied if it keeps its own army free
in its movements, if its government and all the wheels
of its administration function freely and without
impediment, if its general services and particularly its
police and security forces remain firmly in the hands
of the sovereign authority and outside of all foreign
interference.'

Although some of Decoux's observations were
technically correct, later events proved the real
nature of French sovereignty and authority.

The French, it is true, wished to avoid total
compliance with Japanese demands. Although
forced to accept their presence and powerless to
curtail their propaganda, French officials judici-
ously sought to evade the Japanese whenever
possible and countered Japanese propaganda
with an expanded propaganda program of their
own. In making the most of limited opportunities,
the slightest opposition to Japan was expanded by
French minds into resistance of epic proportions.
This may have satisfied their need to feel some
sense of independence but it did not influence
nationalist leaders in their favor; on the contrary, the plight of the French authorities called
forth little sympathy or support from most
nationalists. One might even go so far as to say
that Indochinese nationalists felt more sympathy
for the Japanese than for the French.

Above: A Japanese landing in Cochin-China. Although Japan occupied the country, the French remained nominally in charge.

French authority undermined

The Japanese presence in Indochina encouraged anti-French nationalist groups to challenge French authority, but their insurrections, like the Bac Son rebellion of 1940, failed. The Sureté Fédérale, permitted by the Japanese to continue its normal activities, ruthlessly stalked nationalist leaders, forcing them to leave the colonies or to go underground. The cessation of open resistance did not, however, mark the end of opposition to the French colonial presence; some nationalist groups secretly established networks of cadres in and outside the colony while others threw in their lot with the Japanese.

French fortunes during the early occupation were also challenged by the Thai government who, taking advantage of France's weakness and encouraged by their Japanese allies, pursued an irredentist policy designed to recover the lost provinces of Laos and Cambodia. A Franco-Thai conflict broke out soon after the Franco-Japanese agreements of August 1940 and proved to be a true barometer of French freedom of action, for it was brought to a speedy end under pressure

from Japan. The settlement, signed in Tokyo on 8 May 1941, favored the Thai position and resulted in a temporary but important revision of Thai-Indochinese borders.

Faced with the loss of territory in Laos and Cambodia and a barrage of hostile Japanese propaganda, the French colonial administration took measures to bolster its sagging prestige. To counter Japanese Pan-Asianism the French launched a propaganda offensive of their own. As an alternative to independence or alliance with Japan, they projected the idea of an 'Indochinese Mystique' which they thought would be based on pride in Indochina and gratitude for being part of greater France. These assumptions were erroneous; cultural and political uniformity meant little to the people and disgusted the intellectuals, for whom the collection of non-political concessions offered by the French was meaningless. The French authorities, however, interpreted the lack of open insurrection as a sign of declining popular support for the nationalists, and happily embarked on their program of social, political, and economic 'reform.'

Pro-Japanese movements

The Japanese, despite their cooperation with French colonial officials, used all available means of undermining French prestige among the peoples of Indochina. With the ultimate aim of replacing France as the paramount influence in Indochina, the Japanese carefully but systematically destroyed French authority while, at the same time, maintaining the fiction of French sovereignty. To this end, they vigorously pursued the essentially rascist Pan-Asia line by means of campaigns calculated to impress the Indochinese with Japan's achievements and virtues. Of particular significance was the effort to impress the peoples of Indochina with Japan's military power; victories over Great Britain, Holland and the United States were described in glowing terms as triumphs over the white man, a statement clearly designed to exploit decades of pent-up anti-colonial feelings.

Japanese contacts with anti-French groups and infiltration of certain nationalist organizations preceded their occupation of the colonies. Contacts with the Cao Dai and Hoa Hao religious organizations had been established in 1939, and liaisons with secular organizations went back as far as the beginning of the twentieth century when Prince Cuong De and Phan Boi Chao fled to Japan after unsuccessfully attempting to lead an insurrection against the French in 1906. Indeed, Cuong De remained in Japan until the outbreak of the war, and his Vietnam Restoration League (*Viet Nam Phuc Quoc Dong Minh Hoi*), like so many other Asian revolutionary groups, remained the beneficiary of Japanese support and political asylum for years.

In addition to their sponsorship of the Restoration League and similar groups, Japan's wartime leaders sought to exploit powerful religious communities like the Cao Dai and Hoa Hao. This policy was consistent with their manipulation of religious movements elsewhere in Southeast Asia, such as the Moslems in Indonesia and the Buddhists in Burma. The Cao Dai and Hoa Hao sects were logical targets in Indochina, for they were already anti-French; indeed, leaders of the sects soon became the champions of Japan's new order in Asia, a fact which was not lost on French colonial authorities.

In response to Japan's efforts to infiltrate nationalist organizations and religious sects, the Sureté Fédérale attempted to suppress the activities of these groups by exiling or interning their leaders. The Japanese could do little to stop this persecution beyond providing political asylum for those who escaped the French. The fact that the Japanese could not or would not do anything to effectively aid the nationalist groups no doubt contributed to the decline of pro-Japanese sympathy in Indochina.

Nationalist resistance groups

As a result of Sureté activities, nationalist organizations were splintered and divided. Some, like the Hoa Hao and Cao Dai, adopted a pro-Japanese policy. Other groups resisted the Japanese as they had the French. These organizations did not present a united front, although many found sanctuary and support in Nationalist China.

Chinese leaders made every effort to unite non-communist nationalist organizations into an effective alliance against Japan. In October 1942, they sponsored a congress of Vietnamese nationalist leaders in south China which resulted in the creation of the Vietnam Revolutionary League (*Viet Nam Cach Menh Dong Minh Hoi*). A union of ten nationalist groups modeled after the Kuomintang, the Revolutionary League was subsidized by the Chungking government in return for information about the activities of the Japanese in Indochina and other unspecified assistance. Although it originally excluded members of the Indochinese Communist Party and the Viet Minh, the League later accepted Viet Minh participation after it had become clear that the anti-communist nationalist front could not achieve the cooperation of its members or efficiently collect vital information in Indochina.

The communists had the best organization and largest following of all the nationalist groups in Indochina, particularly in Vietnam. Organized under the facade of a united front of anti-Japanese nationalist groups known as the Viet Minh, the

Above: Ho Chi Minh founded the Viet Minh in in May 1941, the first nationalist group to effectively resist Japan in Indo-China.

communists succeeded in building a network of cadres and bases during the war years. The Viet Minh itself was founded in May 1941, led by Ho Chi Minh, and called for the rejection of the French and Japanese and the establishment of a Vietnamese republic. Aware that independence was the only issue which could rally Vietnamese of all social classes, leaders of the Viet Minh set up the organization as a basically anti-French, anti-Japanese resistance group and did not stress their Marxist inclinations. Nevertheless, despite all attempts to provide the appearance of a political coalition, the Viet Minh remained a communist-dominated organization, and few of the other nationalist movements sought to join or cooperate in its activities. This was especially true of the Chinese-sponsored nationalist groups.

Of all the nationalist groups in Indochina, only the Viet Minh had a network of cells throughout the colonies that was large enough to gather much needed information. Even the Nationalist Chinese were forced to recognize this; although the Chungking regime had sponsored the anti-communist Revolutionary League, they were soon forced to cooperate with the communists. Ho Chi Minh was released from Chinese custody and the resources of the Viet Minh were mobilized to aid the Chinese as early as December 1942. But though the Chinese planned to use the Viet Minh, they also prepared for the emergence communist threat in the postwar era, planning to use Chinese occupation forces in Tonkin to crush any communist insurrection. For the moment, however, Ho Chi Minh and his associates were presented to the world as nationalists first and Marxists second. American intelligence officers also established contact with the Viet Minh. Only the French refused to collaborate with them.

Viet Minh activities during the war were limited to the organization of an underground anti-Japanese resistance movement, and the conduct of a clandestine propaganda program aimed at both the French and Japanese. Until the Japanese coup of 9 March 1945, there were few if any overt actions against the French or Japanese. The leaders of the Viet Minh staked everything on their ability to outmaneuver their adversaries in the nationalist movement and equate the aims and goals of the Viet Minh with those of the allies; anti-fascism was the fulcrum of their program, and discussions of social and economic policies were avoided in order to attract the widest possible following. As the impossibility of a Japanese victory became increasingly apparent, leaders of the Viet Minh stressed their connection with the allies in order to discredit pro-Japanese nationalist groups, stressing that such, collaborators could expect little from the returning allies. Independence, according to Viet Minh propaganda, could only be gained by participation in their united front.

French resistance and its results
The carelessness of Free French agents and their supporters gave the Japanese full knowledge of their activities; the Kempeitai monitored their movements and even infiltrated their ranks. When Japanese authorities realized that the French might actually succeed, they moved against the colonial administration with speed and vigor. On 9 March 1945 the Japanese demanded that all French forces in the colonies be placed under their command, having previously prepared their troops for a confrontation. As soon as Decoux announced his refusal to comply with the request, the Japanese moved to disarm French forces and, except for a few pockets of resistance, the disarmament of the colonial garrisons was carried out with little difficulty. Disarmament was accompanied by the abolition of French sovereignty in Indochina and declarations of independence for the constituent units in the empire.

The bold Japanese attack marked the final humiliation of the French and completely shattered colonial authority in the colonies. For the first time in almost a century, French sovereignty was disrupted and as in other countries in Southeast Asia, the spectacle of the Japanese defeating and disarming their former colonial masters left an indelible impression on the natives. Their compliance and passivity, so long the foundation of French rule, could not be restored.

Stalemate in China
By the time of the German invasion of Poland in September 1939, the Sino-Japanese War had become a stalemate. Although the Nationalist armies had been depleted in the first months of the war, the Japanese were unable to force Chiang Kai-shek and his lieutenants to surrender. Ensconced in their southwest retreat, the Chinese Nationalists stubbornly resisted all Japanese offers of appeasement and negotiation, and it seemed that neither diplomacy nor warfare could settle the China Incident.

With the advent of war in Europe, the situation worsened for Chiang Kai-shek. What little aid had been forthcoming from the Soviet Union ceased while the British and French, fearful of Japanese retaliation against their colonial empires in Asia, went out of their way to avoid provoking a conflict. Translated into specific terms, both colonial powers agreed, under threat of force, to close the lifelines from Free China to the outside world, namely the Haiphong-Yunnan railroad and the Burma Road. Although the British later re-opened the Burma Road, the situation after 1939 was far more critical for the Chinese than it had been in the two preceding years. Were it not for belated assistance from the United States in 1941, the Chinese Nationalist regime might have succumbed to Japan; even this aid was of a marginal nature, limited to surplus weaponry and equipment and tacit American support from Claire Chennault's Flying Tigers, a unit of American volunteer airmen and mechanics.

The Japanese attack on Pearl Harbor changed the nature of the war in China. For the first time in four years, China had allies. Within days after the Japanese attacks on Pearl Harbor, Malaya, and the Philippines, the Allied powers, of which China was now one, established the China-Burma-India theater of war and designated Chiang Kai-shek as supreme commander of the war effort in China. Optimism replaced pessimism in Chungking as the Chinese Nationalists looked forward to extracting revenge.

Left: Once the Chinese coast had been conquered by Japan, attention was turned to the West in an attempt to seize the new Nationalist capital in Chungking.

The Allies enter the war in China

At first the creation of the China-Burma-India theater and the designation of Chiang Kai-shek as the commander of Allied forces in China solved few problems and actually created additional headaches for the Chinese and their American allies. From the beginning in January 1942, the two sides pursued contradictory courses which resulted in hostility, recriminations, and a legacy of bitterness and frustration. The Chinese wished China to be the major theater of war against Japan, while the United States and Great Britain had other ideas, seeing China only as a holding action, a second priority sideshow. To complicate matters further, personalities in the CBI clashed even more than policies, contributing to the near collapse of the alliance. Nowhere was this more clearly illustrated than in the relationship between Chiang, the commander of Allied forces in China, and his lieutenant and chief-of-staff, General Joseph Stilwell, United States Army.

General Stilwell was despatched to China on 5 January 1942, charged with the command of American forces in the CBI and the reorganization of Chinese forces. A one-time military attache in Peking and fluent in Chinese, General Stilwell could have been an effective liaison between China and the United States. Although his superiors knew that he was not a diplomat, they hoped that his knowledge of China and the Chinese might enable him to rally dissident political factions and increase the capability and efficiency of the Chinese army. Unfortunately, this was not to be the case.

His experience in China had made Stilwell distrustful of the leadership of the Kuomintang, and he insisted that Chiang give him *carte blanche* as his chief-of-staff to reorganize Chinese forces. This the Generalissimo refused to do for, although he appreciated the need for a strong, effective army, he feared the political repercussions that a reorganization was likely to yield. Above all, Chiang wished to preserve his command intact and hold his forces in reserve for the postwar battle with the Chinese communists which he believed was inevitable. Thus it was necessary to negate Stilwell's schemes, particularly the re-organization of the army and its commitment in a second Burma compaign.

Had it not been for the presence of another American officer in China, General Claire Chennault, Chiang might have been forced to accommodate his chief of staff. Chennault, however, provided him with an alternative by his very presence and strong advocacy of an aerial strategy, which required little commitment of Chinese manpower and promised fast and cheap results. The Chennault plan, needless to say, was far more attractive than Stilwell's proposals; more important Chennault, who shared the Generalissimo's dislike of Stilwell, was successful in winning Chiang's personal approval.

The substance of Chennault's proposal, which was advanced by Chiang to President Roosevelt later in the war, was outlined in a series of memoranda from Chennault to Stilwell in the fall of 1942. Shortly after assuming command of the China Air Task Force, on 16 September, Chennault submitted a statement outlining his views on the potential of China-based air power. His objectives for the CATF were sixfold: (1) to protect the air supply route over the Hump; (2) to destroy Japanese aircraft in China in large numbers; (3) to damage and destroy Japanese military and naval bases in China and encourage Chinese resistance; (4) to disrupt Japanese shipping along the Yangtze and Yellow rivers and the China coast; (5) to damage Japanese bases in Thailand, Indochina, Burma, and Formosa and to interest Japanese air concentrations being ferried from Chinese bases across Indochina and Thailand to Burma; (6) to destroy the efficacy and morale of the Japanese air force by destroying rear depots and aircraft production facilities in Japan.

To accomplish these ends, Chennault requested additional aircraft, operational independence, and an increased share of supplies flown over the

Vinegar Joe's Response

Stilwell responded less than enthusiastically to Chennault's proposals. Although he was not opposed to the aggressive spirit of Chennault's memo, Stilwell urged moderation in light of shortages of equipment and problems of supply. Chennault's plan, according to Stilwell, went well beyond the capability of his tiny force; to bring it within the realm of possibility would require equipment and supplies which could not be obtained at the time, given priorities in the CBI and the capacity of the air lift from India to China. Stilwell refused to release the supplies necessary for the scheme and rejected Chennault's proposal to separate the CATF from the 10th Army Air Force Command in Delhi.

Chennault never accepted Stilwell's reservations about the potential of air power in China and lost no opportunity to criticize his military judgement. In a letter to Roosevelt, dated 8 October 1942, Chennault presented his case against Stilwell directly to the commander-in-chief, maintaining that Japan could be defeated by effective use of air power and requesting

Below: Lieutenant-General Hap Arnold inspects P-40's with Chennault.

authority to build and command an enlarged and independent air force in China. This, Chennault predicted, would bring about an early victory.

If his objectives were to be reached, Chennault deemed it essential that he have complete freedom of action and direct access to Chiang Kai-shek and the Chinese government. The military task of defeating Japan was a simple one which had been complicated by an unwieldy and illogical military organization and men who did not understand aerial warfare and its potential. At the end of his note, Chennault summed up his plan:

'Japan must hold Hongkong, Shanghai, and the Yangtze valley. They are essential to hold Japan itself. I can force the Japanese to fight in the defense of these objectives and I am confident that I can destroy Japanese aircraft at the rate of between ten and twenty to one. . . . My air force can burn up Japan's main industrial areas and Japan will be unable to supply her armies in her newly conquered empire in China, Malaya, and the Dutch East Indies with the munitions of war. The road then is open for the Chinese army in China, for the American navy in the Pacific, and for MacArthur to advance from his Australian stronghold all with comparatively slight cost.

My entire above plan is simple, it has been long thought out. I have spent five years developing an air warning network and radio command service to fight this way. I have no doubt of my success.'

Disagreement in Chungking and Washington

Roosevelt received Chennault's proposal enthusiastically and passed it along to the Department of War for consideration. The circulation of the letter at the Pentagon caused a major military scandal. It was already well known that Chennault and Stilwell disagreed over questions of strategy in the CBI, particularly regarding Stilwell's plan for a land invasion of Burma, but Chennault's note revealed the depth of their differences and forced Stilwell's supporters to respond immediately to Chennault's scheme lest the President agree.

In general, military leaders at the Pentagon reacted cooly to Chennault's air plan. General Arnold, head of the Army Air Force, informed General Marshall, Chief of Staff of the United States Army, that he was opposed to seeing the China Air Task Force turned into an independent air force under Chennault and dismissed the plan as unrealistic because of the logistical problem of supplying such an operation. Although Arnold was willing to concede that Chennault was an excellent tactician, he agreed with Stilwell that Chennault did not understand the logistics of supply and recommended, therefore, that the CATF be kept under the command of the 10th Air Force in India.

Marshall shared Arnold's view and discussed his reservations about the plan with Roosevelt in December 1942. By that time, however, Roosevelt was leaning increasingly toward Chennault's position and informed Marshall that he believed that Chennault should receive an independent command in China and that he should be immediately given a force of one hundred planes with which to begin the bombing of Japanese military bases and shipping in China.

If for no other reason than for its psychological effect on the Japanese, the President favored Chennault's aerial strategy.

Roosevelt's increasing tendency toward implementation of Chennault's plan reflected the tremendous influence of the China Lobby in Washington. This group, which included in its inner circle such presidential intimates as Harry Hopkins, Henry Wallace, and Lauchlin Curry, consistently promoted the scheme and presented Roosevelt with regular appreciative evaluations of the man himself. Although Stilwell had considerable support from General Marshall and other military leaders, his stock at the White House steadily declined and he and his supporters were placed on the defensive, attempting to justify their policies in the face of increasing criticism from Chennault's proponents and the press.

In part, Stilwell's problem reflected the difficulty of his mission, for his assignment was undoubtedly the most delicate diplomatic mission thrust on a professional soldier during the war. Stilwell served in several roles in China, being at one and the same time commanding general of American forces in the CBI theater, Chief-of-Staff of the Chinese army, director of the lend-lease program in China, and American representative to the Southeast Asia Command. Such a multiplicity of duties doomed Stilwell from the outset but most disastrous of all was his position as Chiang Kai-shek's Chief-of-Staff.

Stilwell was not the sort of man the Chinese situation required. He had difficulty in handling other nationalities tactfully and could not cope with the overwhelming political problems he faced in China. Had his been solely a military command, he might have been successful, but he was not as much a strategist as a diplomat, and his temperament was not suited to the role.

Arguments over strategy

When Chennault proposed his air plan in September 1942, Chiang Kai-shek quickly became its principle adherent. In a cable to Roosevelt on 9 January 1943, the Generalissimo expressed his support in the following manner:

'The remarkable potentialities of an air offensive in China have already been demonstrated by a small and ill-supported force. I believe that an early air offensive is feasible, since, owing to the peculiar tactical conditions which prevail here, neither the supply, material, and personnel requirements are such as to embarrass the United Nations air efforts elsewhere. The return, I predict, will be out of proportion to the investment, and by further weakening the Japanese air arm and striking at the seaborne communications with their new conquests, an air offensive in China will directly prepare for the ultimate offensive we are looking for.'

Left: General George C. Marshall, US Army Chief of Staff, disagreed with both Stilwell and Chennault about the conduct of the war in China.

In the same cable, Chiang expressed his reservations about Stilwell's plan for an invasion of Burma to reopen the Burma Road and announced his unwillingness, at that time, to commit large numbers of Chinese troops to the effort.

As might have been expected, Stilwell did not accept Chiang's position without protest, but mounted a propaganda campaign of his own through his associates at the Pentagon. He suggested to Marshall that if Chiang did not accede to his demands voluntarily, a *quid pro quo* policy toward the Generalissimo should be adopted and military aid to the Chinese withheld until Chiang agreed to cooperate. It was Stilwell's belief that China's total dependence on the United States gave the latter sufficient leverage to force the Kuomintang into accepting his views, views which were shared by most high ranking officers at the Pentagon.

Stilwell firmly believed that strong-arm tactics were the only way of dealing with the Chinese, and in his notes to Marshall, he repeated this view many times. Logic, reason, and persuasion would do no good. Pressure was the only effective technique in dealing with the Generalissimo. 'In dealing with him,' said Stilwell, 'we should exact a commitment for everything we do.' This view was shared by other American officers in China but, unfortunately for Stilwell, not by the president's intimates in the White House.

Stilwell's *quid pro quo* policy was pursued with a tactlessness which eventually cost him his position. His acid comments on Chiang Kai-shek and his government, which were as well known in Chungking as at the Pentagon, aroused an emotional reaction from the Kuomintang which destroyed any remaining influence Stilwell had at the White House where Roosevelt's advisors were openly critical of him and suggested his recall. Whatever good will existed between him and the generalissimo evaporated in the debate over Chennault's plan. Chiang had little trouble in making Stilwell position untenable, particularly in so far as Roosevelt had refused to agree to the *quid pro quo* formula. Turning his nearly total dependence on the United States into a position of political strength by taking advantage of the important role that Roosevelt had assigned to China in the defeat of Japan, Chiang Kai-shek used his diplomatic talents to persuade Roosevelt to support Chennault's proposal and increase aid.

The arguments continue

President Roosevelt ultimately accepted Chiang Kai-shek's suggestion that Chennault be given an augmented force and an independent command in China. In March 1943, he decided to overrule his military advisors and prepared a cable to the generalissimo announcing his intention to place Chennault in command of a new air unit in China. In explaining his decision to General Marshall, Roosevelt pointed out that Stilwell did not fully appreciate the potential of air power in China or Chiang's commitment to the Chennault plan. Moreover, in so far as the maintenance of good Sino-American relations was involved,

Opposite: The Burma Road was the lifeline of the Nationalist China until 1942, when Japan seized Lashio. **Above:** After the Burma Road was cut, the only link between India and China was by air. Here British and Indian troops load supplies to be carried "over the Hump".

Roosevelt felt that he had no choice but to submit to Chiang's request. At the same time, he warned Marshall that Stilwell was using the wrong approach in dealing with the generalissimo and might have to be removed if he continued to treat Chiang as one might the Sultan of Morocco.

Chennault was promoted to the rank of major-general on 3 March 1943 and placed in command of the newly created 14th Army Air Force, formerly the CATF, on 11 March. According to the President's instructions, he was to be given complete control over all aerial operations in China; Stilwell was informed that he was not to interfere with Chennault in any manner that was likely to anger Chiang Kai-shek. Although Stilwell was to continue to direct the air ferry over the Hump, he was to allocate sufficient tonnage to Chennault to facilitate his operations while, at the same time, leaving enough free for land operations in China and Burma.

At the request of Chiang Kai-shek and General Marshall, Chennault and Stilwell were summoned to Washington in April 1943 to present their proposals to the Allied leaders assembled for the Trident Conference. Chennault presented his case on 30 April, Stilwell on 1 May. Roosevelt reacted positively to Chennault but postponed a final decision until he had heard Stilwell's objections. At this meeting, Stilwell outlined his objections to Chennault's plan, his methods of operation, and Chiang Kai-shek's failure to honor his commitments.

Stilwell did not deny that opportunities for aerial attacks on Japanese bases and shipping were real nor that the results of such attacks would be impressive. He did fear, however, that once Chennault's attacks proved sufficiently damaging, the Japanese would launch a major attack against the bases of the 14th Air Force. Unlike Chennault, Stilwell was not optomistic about the ability of the Chinese army to stop this advance. Should Chinese resistance falter, the Japanese would surely push on to Kunming and Chungking would be left virtually defenseless. Only a well trained and equipped land force cold hold these centers; the Chinese did not constitute such a force. This being the case, Stilwell suggested that the first priority in China should be the reorganization of the Chinese army followed by an offensive to reopen the Burma Road. Only after these two goals were achieved would Chennault's plan become feasible.

Stilwell then told Roosevelt that reorganization of the Chinese army could not be completed until Chiang Kai-shek agreed to cooperate. He suggested that the president remind Chiang of the

reason for the American presence in China and of his agreement to furnish manpower and accept assistance in training these men. He also suggested that Chiang be requested to use regular military channels in dealing with American forces in China; this would mean that in dealing with Chennault, Chiang could not bypass Stilwell's command, nor would Chennault be allowed to willfully bypass his superiors and disobey orders. Above all, Stilwell believed, as he had consistently stated in the past, that Roosevelt must use a strong hand in dealing with the Generalissimo. As he put it to the President:

'The only short-cut to Japan is through China. The Chinese know this and are disposed to extract from the situation every possible advantage. Unless we are prepared to accept infinite delay, they must be held to their commitments as fully as we are holding ourselves to ours.'

The President makes his decision

Having listened to the arguments, Roosevelt decided in favor of Chennault's proposal for an aerial offensive against Japan. In making this decision, the President was influenced by both political and military factors, overruling the objections of his military advisers because he believed it promised a quick victory over Japan. Stilwell's plan to reoccupy Burma, on the other hand, would require a major commitment of American, British, and Chinese manpower and take considerably longer to execute. Since the British did not view the liberation of Burma as a matter of high priority and Chiang Kai-shek was unwilling to commit his forces to such a campaign unless the other allies did the same, Roosevelt dismissed Stilwell's plan as impractical.

Politically, the President felt bound to support Chiang Kai-shek, and placated the Generalissimo by supporting Chennault. Once again, fear that the Chinese might pull out of the war and make a separate peace with Japan prevailed over reason and logic. Since the War Department wished, above all, to keep China in the war, even Chennault's critics at the Pentagon recognized that Roosevelt had little alternative other than to accept the Chennault plan if only to bolster the morale of the Chungking regime.

As might have been expected, Chennault and the Chinese hailed Roosevelt's decision while Stilwell and Marshall decried it. Unfortunately the promises made so freely could not be fulfilled, resulting in increased tension between Chennault and Stilwell, Chiang and Roosevelt. As Stilwell put it, 'it was fatal to promise anything.'

CHAPTER TEN

Chess in the Desert: The Desert War 1940-1943

The Italian government entered the war on 10 June 1940. Although Mussolini's belated decision to join Hitler presented no additional danger to the Allied position in Europe, which had already collapsed, it did pose an immediate threat to Britain's position in Africa and the Mediterranean. The British garrison in Egypt was small and there was little possibility that reinforcements could be sent, given the disaster that had recently befallen British forces in France. With an Italian force of half a million men facing them across the Libyan frontier, the British garrison of 50,000 in Egypt hardly appeared capable of defending Suez against the Axis. In addition, Italy's participation in the war closed the sea route through the Mediterranean to Alexandria; supplies and reinforcements had to be sent via the Cape of Good Hope into the Red Sea, a long and circuitous route which added to the difficulty of maintaining an efficient supply operation.

British forces in the Middle East were commanded by General Sir Archibald Wavell. Rather than wait for the Italians to strike the first blow, he was determined to take the offensive and waited only four days after Italy's entry into the war to move against Italian border positions in Cyrenaica. On 14 June 1940 British forces struck at Fort Capuzzo, capturing this border post in one day but abandoning it the next. Thus began a series of raids across the border which lasted for over a month and netted some 3500 Italian casualties at a cost of only slightly more than 150 men to the British.

After a month of successful raids against their installations, the Italians moved cautiously across the western desert toward the British position at Mersa Matruh. On 13 September they captured Sidi Barrani where they established a chain of fortified camps; in the following weeks, however, they made no effort to push on to Mersa Matruh, allowing Wavell to bring in reinforcements which had been rushed to North Africa on Churchill's orders. Strengthened by the arrival of these reinforcements, which included three armored regiments, Wavell again decided to take the offensive.

Wavell's offensive was an unmitigated triumph and almost led to the destruction of the Italian army and the collapse of Italy's position in North Africa. Although British forces were outnumbered by more than two to one, and by three to one in tank power, they succeeded in thoroughly mauling their adversaries and inflicting heavy losses in manpower and equipment. The speed and ease with which the Italians were pushed back

Opposite: Italian troops move forward into the fray.
Above and overleaf: Masses of Italian prisoners march back, in some cases guarded by only one soldier.
Right: Benito Mussolini commanded over a half million troops in Libya.

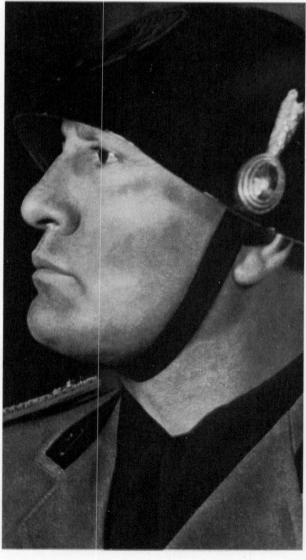

surprised the British command which, unfortunately, had made no provisions for a sustained offensive and lost the opportunity to obtain an overwhelming victory. Nevertheless, they did succeed in pushing as far west as Tobruk, capturing that port city on 21 January 1941. By the end of the month, the British had taken over 125,000 prisoners and paused to regroup before pursuing the offensive into Tripolitania.

British forces resumed their push westward early in February, hoping to capture the city of Benghazi and complete their conquest of Cyrenaica. Aerial intelligence reported that the Italians were preparing to abandon Benghazi in favour of a stronger position at the Agheila bottleneck, and the British field commander, General Richard O'Connor, quickly altered his plan to proceed along the coast road and diverted part of his force across the desert in an effort to beat the retreating Italians to El Agheila. On 5 February, this force established a blocking position at Beda Fomm and waited for the Italian army, which reached the cross-road on the following day. The retreating Italian force was considerably larger than the British garrison, but the British were comfortably dug in and were able to destroy most of the Italian armor as it tried to pass through the bottleneck. At the end of the day, 120 tanks were disabled and 20,000 prisoners of war were taken. This was nothing short of amazing considering that the British force at Beda Fomm numbered only 3000 men. As Anthony Eden had said of an earlier battle, 'never has so much been surrendered by so many to so few'.

After the victory at Beda Fomm, O'Connor prepared to complete the destruction of the Italian army in North Africa. Much to his horror and the regret of his superiors in Egypt, the offensive was not permitted to go any further. On 12 February Churchill cabled Wavell and instructed him to withdraw most of the British forces in Cyrenaica so that an offensive in Greece could be mounted. O'Connor was confident that he could go on to capture Tripoli but his appeals were of no avail. The Prime Minister was committed to the Balkan offensive and there was no changing his mind. Accordingly, 50,000 British troops were landed in Greece in March and the North African campaign came to an abrupt end.

The Greek diversion was a disaster. On 6 April German forces invaded Greece and shortly thereafter the British had to evacuate their forces in a move reminiscent of Dunkirk. Twelve thousand

Above left: The Italian retreat in the desert was even swifter than their advance.
Above: General Sir Archibald Wavell chatting with the Commander of the Desert Forces, Lieutenant-General Richard O'Connor.

Opposite: British forces moved swiftly through Cyrenaica. **Left:** The Italian invasion of Greece met with initial success.

143

Right: The Italian invaders were soon slowed by Greek partisans and the Greek Army. **Below:** A storm trooper barks his orders during the Greek campaign. **Below right:** The Wehrmacht was forced to move into Macedonia to save the Italians from humiliation. **Opposite: center:** A Panzer column enters Salonika. **Opposite bottom:** Fortified by German support in Greece, the Italians moved to the attack once again. **Overleaf:** The Luftwaffe over Athens.

men were lost and, more important, the opportunity to annihilate the Italian army in Cyrenaica was lost as well. By the time that the withdrawal of British forces to North Africa was completed in late April, the Italians had regrouped in Tripolitania and were reinforced by the arrival of additional units, including a small German force under the command of General Erwin Rommel.

Rommel had distinguished himself as commander of the 7th Panzer Division in the French campaign; on 6 February 1941 he was summoned by Hitler to lead a small German force to the rescue of the Italians in North Africa. He flew to Tripoli on 12 September and immediately took charge of the defense of Axis forces in the desert. Although technically the inferior of several of the Italian officers and immediately responsible to the Italian command, Rommel was the architect of Axis participation in the desert war from his arrival until 1943 when the Axis position in Africa collapsed. His career in Africa was to become legendary.

It would be several months before Rommel's men and equipment arrived in Tripoli. However, finding that the British had depleted their strength in Cyrenaica and showed little inclination

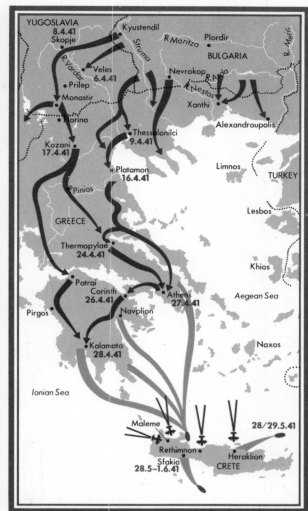

German Invasion and dates of capture

German parachute and airborne landings in Crete 20 May, 1941

British evacuation

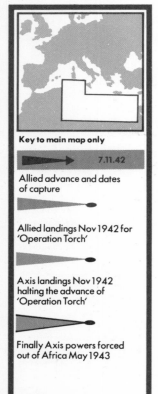

to revive the offensive against the Italians in Tripolitania, Rommel decided to assume the offensive himself. Massing what forces were available and constructing a fleet of dummy tanks mounted on Volkswagen chassis in order to confuse the British as to his actual strength, Rommel disregarded his orders to wait until May and began his first offensive on 2 April.

Rommel's ruse worked. With only fifty tanks and two divisions of Italian infantry, he crossed into Cyrenaica and quickly overwhelmed British forces there. Benghazi fell on 3 April, Michili on the fourth. By 11 April, all British forces except the garrison at Tobruk were evacuated to Egypt. In nine days, Britain's fortunes in North Africa had been reversed. As the late Sir Basil Liddell Hart so aptly observed, the British paid a heavy price for forfeiting the golden opportunity of February 1941.

On 11 April 1941 Rommel ordered the investment of Tobruk, the last British garrison in Cyrenaica, and the siege began on the following Monday, 14 April. Although their forces had been routed in Cyrenaica, the British command was determined to hold Tobruk at all costs; this decision was reinforced by Churchill's insistence

that the defense of the port was absolutely vital if Rommel's advance toward Egypt was to be halted. Accordingly, General Leslie Morshead, commander of the 9th Australian Division which held the city, was instructed to hold out as long as was humanly possible or until reinforcements could be brought in by sea.

The Axis army repeatedly failed to pierce Tobruk's defenses. This undoubtedly reflected the weakness of Rommel's forces rather than the strength of the defenders but was sufficiently disheartening to his superiors in the Italian command, who insisted that the campaign be halted. When Rommel refused to listen, the Italians pressed their case with General Halder in Berlin. Halder was sympathetic, for he feared that to push the offensive in North Africa further might require reinforcement of Rommel's forces; this he could not think of doing in light of the anticipated invasion of Russia. General Paulus was despatched to Africa to 'head off this soldier gone stark mad', but Paulus sanctioned Rommel's scheme and persuaded Halder to do likewise.

The attack on Tobruk was resumed on 30 April but proved no more successful than the first assaults. Although Rommel's forces were able

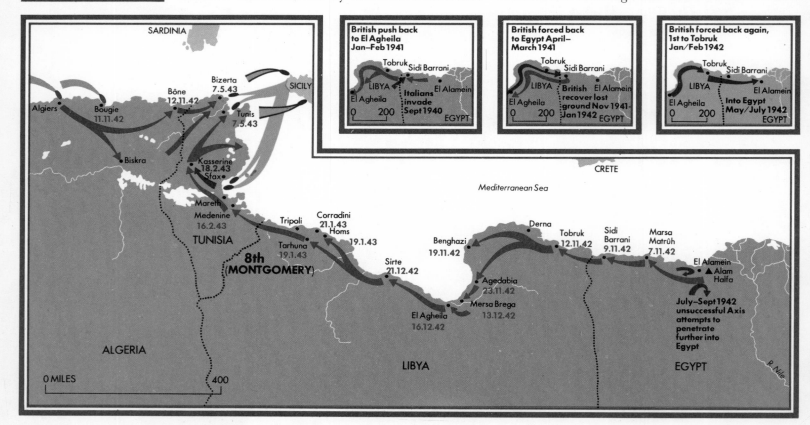

SARDINIA

Algiers

Bougie
11.11.42

Bône
12.11.42

Bizerta
7.5.43

SICILY

Tunis
7.5.43

Biskra

Kasserine
18.2.43
Sfax

Mareth

Medenine
16.2.43

TUNISIA

Tripoli

Tarhuna
19.1.43

Corradini
21.1.43
Homs
19.1.43

**8th
(MONTGOMERY)**

Sirte
21.12.42

El Agheila
16.12.42

Mersa Brega
13.12.42

Agedabia
23.11.42

Benghazi
19.11.42

Derna

CRETE

Mediterranean Sea

Tobruk
12.11.42

Sidi
Barrani
9.11.42

Marsa
Matrûh
7.11.42

El Alamein   ▲ Alam
                          Halfa

July–Sept 1942
unsuccessful Axis
attempts to
penetrate
further into
Egypt

ALGERIA

LIBYA

EGYPT

R.Nile

0 MILES   400

**British push back
to El Agheila
Jan–Feb 1941**

Tobruk   Sidi Barrani

LIBYA   Italians
                invade
El Agheila   Sept 1940

El Alamein

0   200   EGYPT

**British forced back
to Egypt April–
March 1941**

Tobruk   Sidi Barrani

LIBYA   British
              recover lost
El Agheila   ground Nov 1941–
Jan 1942   El Alamein

0   200   EGYPT

**British forced back again,
1st to Tobruk
Jan/Feb 1942**

Tobruk   Sidi Barrani

LIBYA   Into Egypt
El Agheila   May/July 1942

El Alamein

0   200   EGYPT

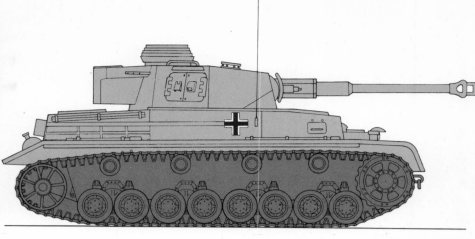

to breach the outer defenses of the city, they were not strong enough to break through the intense artillery barrage coming from inside the port. After four days the attack was broken off; although German and Italian forces continued to lay siege to the city, for the moment, it remained in British hands.

The failure to take Tobruk did not dent Rommel's determination to push on toward Egypt; on the contrary, it seemed to reinforce it. To do so, however, would require more men and equipment than the general could muster, and he therefore requested that the General Staff send him an additional four Panzer divisions as soon as possible. Unfortunately, the invasion of the Soviet Union was still occupying the minds of the Nazi command in Berlin; even had Hitler and Halder been willing to send such a force to North Africa, it is doubtful whether the Italians would have accepted a large German presence in their African empire. Rommel's requests were refused, and in so doing the General Staff forfeited the chance for a German victory in North Africa. Although this might not have seemed obvious in June and July 1941 when Rommel's request was first made, it proved fateful the following year

when German fortunes in the desert war were gradually reversed.

If the German command was hesitant to comply with Rommel's requests, the British government had no reservations about the need to reinforce Wavell's forces in Egypt. After the abortive Greek campaign, Churchill and his advisors badly wanted a victory in North Africa, and the British, despite critical shortages of arms and equipment, quickly assembled a large convoy in April and sent it to Egypt by the end of the month. Rather than waste time sending the convoy around the Cape of Good Hope, Churchill ordered the Navy to run the ships through the Mediterranean, a risky but considerably shorter route. The mission was successfully concluded on 12 May; one ship carrying some sixty tanks was sunk by a mine near the coast of Sicily, but all the others delivered their cargo of 238 tanks intact.

Wavell took the offensive in May. Knowing that Rommel's forces were short of supplies and gasoline, Wavell ordered Brigadier W. H. E. Gott into Cyrenaica with orders to overrun the enemy's border positions and push on to relieve Tobruk. The attack began on 13 May and might have been successful had not Rommel reversed the initial

Above: P2KW IV. Length: 21 ft. 9 in. Width: 9 ft. 5½ in. Maximum road speed: 24.9 m.p.h. Range: 130 miles. Armament: 1 × 75 cm. L/43, 2 × 7.92 mm. MG34 machine guns. Crew: 5 Weight: 23.2 tons.
Opposite far left: After the conquest of Greece, Crete was next. German paratroops prepare for the initial attack. **Opposite center:** Masses of German parachutists descend upon Crete. **Opposite right:** By mid-June 1941 the Germans made it impossible for the Allies to unload supplies in Crete. **Above left:** After the German conquest of Crete the RAF continued their challenge.
Below left: Rommel enjoyed initial success as the Afrika Korps raced toward Egypt. **Below:** General Erwin Rommel flew to Tripoli in September 1941 to take command.

German-Italian retreat and called for a counter-attack against Gott's positions. At the end of the month, the British retreated to Egypt and the Germans occupied the Halfaya pass and other positions near the border.

The Defense of Suez

Having chased the British back into Egypt, Rommel fortified his border positions so that they would have to break through strong anti-tank batteries before gaining access to the coast road leading to Tobruk. With his tanks outnumbered by four to one, this was his only chance to stop Wavell, for he knew that once the British reached the coast road it would be impossible to halt their advance. He therefore deployed his limited forces in order to create a bottleneck which would stall the British until reserves could be brought up from the west.

Rommel did not have to wait long to test his defenses. Undaunted by the failure of 'Operation Brevity' in May, Wavell mounted an even larger attack in June. The new plan, 'Operation Battleaxe', was even more ambitious than the first offensive and aimed to destroy Rommel's forces in North Africa by means of a three-stage assault on German-Italian positions in Cyrenaica. During the first phase of the attack, British forces would assault enemy strongholds at Halfaya, Sollum, and Capuzzo. During phase two, an additional force would lunge toward Tobruk, taking the city and clearing German forces from the area. In the last phase, the British forces joined by the garrison at Tobruk would push toward Tripolitania, eventually driving German and Italian forces from the continent. The plan was a bold one upon which Churchill was staking his political fortune. There could be no defeat if Wavell wished to continue his command of England's forces in the Middle East.

The British attack was launched on 14 June 1941. As Rommel had hoped, the enemy's armored units were unable to pass through Halfaya without sustaining heavy losses. Of the tanks that attacked the German position, only one was able to pass through the bottleneck without being destroyed. The British had better luck, however, at Fort Capuzzo where they encountered no anti-tank batteries and captured the stronghold in short order. This might have given Wavell cause for optimism were it not for the destruction of a second British armored column at Hafid ridge where Rommel had established another battery of anti-tank guns. British losses at Hafid were even greater than at Halfaya; by the end of the first day almost half of Wavell's tanks had been lost.

Never one to wait for his opponent's next move, Rommel, whose strength remained undiminished, took the offensive on 15 June and attempted to recapture Fort Capuzzo. To facilitate his counter-attack, Rommel called upon the German-Italian force laying siege to Tobruk to send an armored column to his assistance. Although he failed to recapture Capuzzo, the presence of an enlarged German force seizing the offensive was enough to disrupt the momentum of the British who were forced to switch to the defensive if they were to escape Rommel's flanking moves. After four days,

Above: The British moved forward to defend Tobruk. **Left:** The British took Tobruk easily in January 1941. **Left center:** Italian prisoners captured before Tobruk. **Bottom left:** British tanks negotiated some rough country in the defense of Tobruk. **Right:** South African troops, one poised with a hand grenade, search for the enemy. **Far right:** Tobruk remained in British hands and by June 1941 they moved to the attack. **Bottom right:** A British convoy risks the dangers of the Mediterranean.

Previous page: German personnel carriers in the desert.

Right: British infantry disperse and take whatever cover there is as they approach the enemy in the Western Desert.

the British scrapped their offensive. Once again, the desert fox had outwitted his adversaries.

Following the collapse of 'Operation Battleaxe', Churchill removed General Wavell from command of England's African forces replacing him with General Sir Claude Auchinleck. The Prime Minister refused to accept Rommel's victory and remained convinced that with a properly aggressive commander, British forces would succeed in destroying the Afrika Korps. In Auchinleck, Churchill believed he had found his man.

Auchinleck shared Churchill's view that a victory over the Axis allies was possible but he did not share the Prime Minister's impatient wish for a victory before the end of the year. In fact, he insisted that the men and equipment lost in June be replaced before a new offensive was launched; otherwise he would resign his commission. Churchill could hardly argue with such an ultimatum nor could he afford another defeat since his prestige at home had reached a low ebb. He was forced to bide his time and provide the men and supplies necessary for launching the next offensive, 'Operation Crusader'.

Operation Crusader

Preparations for Operation Crusader took the better part of four months during which time a vast muster of planes, tanks, and artillery pieces were sent to North Africa. When Auchinleck opened the campaign in November 1941 he possessed an unprecedented numerical superiority in men and equipment. British air strength was nearly three times that of the Axis, tank strength was over two times greater, and in manpower British forces outnumbered their German and Italian adversaries by tens of thousands. According to all indices, the British had an easy victory in sight.

The plan for Operation Crusader, however, had one fatal flaw: it called for the division of British forces into several attack groups, reasoning that the dangers involved in spacing out the troops were a small price to pay for the element of speed and surprise that such a deployment would allow. Auchinleck hoped to pin the Germans and Italians down in their fortified positions near the coast while simultaneously racing toward Tobruk and destroying Rommel's armored divisions. Britain's absolute numerical superiority seemed to ensure the plan's success as long as communication between the various fronts could be maintained, but as Rommel himself recorded in his diary, that superiority was neutralized by the deployment of troops which enabled him to play havoc with one unit at a time.

British forces crossed the Egyptian frontier on 18 November and, catching Rommel by surprise, penetrated rapidly into Cyrenaica. By the morning of the 19th Auchinleck's forces had reached Trigh el Abd and were pushing west to Tobruk; By night fall they were at Sidi Resegh, twelve miles southwest of Tobruk's defense perimeter. Hastily, Rommel rushed forces between the port and the airfield and, in the absence of reinforcements to Sidi Resegh, were able to keep the British from linking up with the garrison in Tobruk. Hampered by lack of reconnaisance aircraft and shortages of fuel, however, he was able to do little more than hold while Britain continued to advance on other fronts.

Rommel did not have a clear picture of British positions until 21 November; even then he continued the encirclement at Sidi Resegh, bringing up men and tanks to supplement German units in the area. When the British garrison in Tobruk tried to break out of the port and link up with the force at Sidi Resegh he effectively prevented the maneuver and immediately struck Sidi Resegh itself, taking the stronghold on 23 November. Three thousand British troops were killed or captured, but 70 tanks were lost as well. Although the victory at Sidi Resegh was a tactical triumph it proved to be a strategic error for which the Germans would pay heavily in the months that followed.

Encouraged by his victory, Rommel once again assumed the offensive. In a bold effort to outflank his opponents he sent his mobile forces on a race toward the border, intending to relieve the German-Italian border garrisons and mop up isolated British pockets in the process. His break for the frontier upset the equilibrium of the British attack and threw their command into a panic.

Before the British knew what had happened, German forces had advanced perilously close to the Egyptian frontier. By 25 November Rommel's army was poised to cross the border.

On 26 November the British recovered their composure and launched a counter-attack across the frontier. Italian forces failed to break through and reinforce his meagre army and Rommel had no choice but to order a fast retreat lest his men be caught between two British forces, one advancing west across the frontier, the other moving eastward from Tobruk. By the evening of 27 November, Rommel's forces had fallen back to a position south of Tobruk. Both the German counter-attack and Operation Crusader had failed, at least for the moment.

As Rommel and the Afrika Korps retreated, the British pursued them relentlessly. Commonwealth forces broke through to Tobruk on 27 November; on the following day they continued their drive, but could not manage to annihilate the Afrika Korps before it joined the rest of Rommel's forces on 29 November. Even then, the British far outnumbered the Germans and might have completed their destruction had they continued to press their drive. They did not, and as a result Rommel was once again able to take offensive action, isolating a unit of New Zealanders between Tobruk and Belhamed. By 1 December they were overrun. Rommel had triumphed again.

Rommel's ability to turn defeat into victory discouraged British field commanders, but General Auchinleck refused to give up the offensive. Sensing that Rommel could ill afford the loss of men and equipment however stunning his victories, Auchinleck determined to turn the desert war into a campaign of attrition. Therefore, he refused to abandon Operation Crusader and persisted in his design to carry the war to the Germans. Tired and demoralized men would be replaced by fresh troops. Battered and worn out equipment would be replaced as well. Time and patience would prevail.

While the British command pondered over its position, Rommel was also taking stock of his situation. He had succeeded in blunting Operation Crusader but only at substantial cost to himself. Since he could not expect reinforcements until the new year (1942), he had no choice but to withdraw German and Italian forces to Tripolitania where they would be safe from British attack. Accordingly, the siege of Tobruk was abandoned on 7 December and all Axis forces

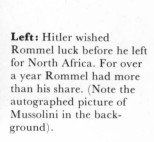

Left: Hitler wished Rommel luck before he left for North Africa. For over a year Rommel had more than his share. (Note the autographed picture of Mussolini in the background).

were ordered to retreat to the Mersa Brega bottleneck. The retreat was completed in January 1942, not without heavy losses inflicted on slow moving infantry forces, largely Italian, by British units.

Scarcely had Rommel retreated to Tripolitania when fresh supplies and reinforcements arrived. On 5 January 1942, a task force of six ships landed several dozen tanks and other equipment which enabled Rommel to consider resuming offensive action against the British later that month. It did not take much to persuade him of the necessity to reestablish the Axis position in Cyrenaica; on 21 January he moved eastward.

Rommel's newest offensive irritated the Italians, but by the time Italy's Minister of War arrived at Rommel's desert headquarters to protest, the campaign was under way and the Axis forces had pushed well into Cyrenaica. The offensive was a *fait accompli* and showed every sign of being successful. Nothing could be done to abort the drive and whatever objections the Italians held evaporated in the face of the promising situation in the desert. In any case, Rommel was not about to court the Italian command. He had better things to do.

By 25 January Rommel's forces had taken the port of Benghazi and British forces had been withdrawn to Derna and Michili. The capture of Benghazi was significant because of the large stock of weapons and ammunition left behind by

Left: As the Afrika Korps swept into Egypt they seemed to be invincible.

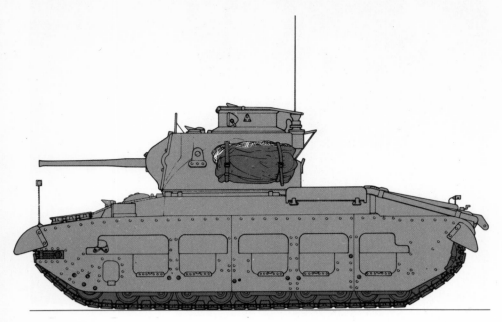

Above: Matilda 3. Length: 18 ft. 5 in. Width: 8 ft. 6 in. Maximum road speed: 15 m.p.h. Armament: 1 × 2 pdr. or 1 × machine gun. Crew: 4 Weight: 26.5 tons.
Opposite top: German barrage in the desert.
Opposite center: The British surrender after the fall of Tobruk. Their retreat was cut off when Rommel encircled their garrison.
Opposite lower center: The Commander of the British 8th Army, Montgomery, decided to defend Suez at El Alamein.

the retreating British. With these and the new equipment that reached Tripoli at the beginning of the month, Rommel was able to press on with his offensive and soon his troops were astride the Gazala line less than fifty miles west of Tobruk. There the offensive stopped momentarily to await the arrival of additional Italian forces.

Rommel did not outflank the Gazala line until 26 May, feigning an attack on the stronghold while moving his forces around the position in an attempt to move back to the coast road just before Tobruk. This maneuver failed when the Germans encountered British armored units equipped with the Grant tanks. Rommel's forces were trapped for two days, cut off from their supply caravan which was stuck just west of the British position at Gazala. Had the British moved swiftly, they might have trapped Rommel then and there but, rather than move mechanized units in to tighten the noose around Rommel's neck, the British chose to soften the German force by aerial bombardment before they moved in for the kill. This gave Rommel time to take stock of the situation and make one last effort to break out of 'the cauldron' before it was too late. Typically, he turned near defeat into victory when his forces broke the back of the British position at Gaza on 13 June and captured the stronghold on the following day.

With Gazala neutralized, the Axis army moved quickly toward Tobruk. The city, its garrison of 35,000 men, and a vast stock of supplies were taken on 21 June with little difficulty and surely consistuted one of the worst disasters to befall the British during the entire war. Rommel had tried

to take Tobruk for two years, with little success. In less than a fortnight in June, he succeeded.

After the fall of Tobruk British forces retreated rapidly into Egypt. Had the Desert Fox had his way, he would have moved after them immediately, but his superiors hesitated to carry the offensive into Egypt. In fact, the day after Tobruk fell, Rommel was ordered to suspend the offensive, and it was only as a result of his direct appeals to Hitler and Mussolini that these orders were countermanded. Rommel, who had been promoted to the rank of Field Marshal as a reward for his triumphs in the desert, was a favourite of the Fuehrer who used his good offices with Mussolini to have Marshal Bastico's orders annulled, but he did not receive permission to march into Egypt until 24 June. By this time the panic in the British command had subsided.

Rommel crossed the frontier into Egypt immediately. There was little resistance along the coast road, as the British had wisely decided to regroup east of Mersa Matruh; Rommel's forces were able to move within less than one hundred miles of Alexandria by 30 June, reaching El Alamein by the end of that day.

Rommel's rapid thrust made it necessary for the British to prepare to evacuate Alexandria lest the fleet and government offices in the port fall into German hands. Accordingly, the fleet left the city on 2 July with orders to withdraw through the Suez Canal into the Red Sea. Government offices were abandoned in the expectation that Rommel would reach the outskirts of the port on the following day. Fortunately for the British, these precautions proved unnecessary.

Despite the initial success of the thrust into Egypt, Rommel's forces were tired and their equipment and supplies were almost exhausted. Repeated attempts to pass the Alamein line failed, and on 7 July the Germans were no better off than they had been on the 2nd while the British were preparing to launch a counter-offensive. This attack was initiated on 8 July and within a week Rommel's army was on the verge of collapse. By 20 July, the situation had become so critical that Rommel was forced to consider a retreat; in fact, with no ammunition and only a small number of operating tanks, disengagement was a foregone conclusion.

Rommel opted to disengage but not to retreat. He hoped to remain west of the Alamein line until reinforcements could be sent so that he could resume his offensive. Since the British had broken off their counter-attack, there was little reason to withdraw to safer positions. His reinforcements

Right: One of the deadly 88-mm's of the Halfaya garrison, which Rommel found particularly effective in the Western Desert.
Far right: Erwin Rommel – the Desert Fox.

arrived early in August, and by the end of the month the Afrika Korps was again ready to attack.

Rommel launched his second attack against Alamein on 30 August, hoping to catch the British by surprise by moving out under cover of darkness. Thanks to aerial reconnaisance and the artful positioning of mines in the desert, however, the British were prepared. On 31 August Allied aircraft made a debilitating raid on the Afrikan Korps, inflicting heavy losses. Rommel refused to call off the offensive; instead he ordered the main body of attack to concentrate on the British position at the Alam Halfa ridge where they could take the enemy by surprise. This attack could not be completed, however, for the Afrika Korps ran out of fuel. With only a day's ration of gasoline left, Rommel reluctantly abandoned his position on 3 September and withdrew toward the frontier.

No effort was made to block Rommel's retreat, for Montgomery refused to move until his forces regrouped and new supplies and equipment arrived. Thus, despite heavy pressure from Churchill, it was seven weeks before the British began their pursuit of the Afrika Korps. Montgomery and Alexander were determined to wait until the odds were overwhelming in their favor before launching 'Operation Lightfoot'.

Operation Lightfoot began on 23 October 1942, by which time British forces had been increased until they represented a numerical superiority of men and equipment hitherto unprecedented in the desert war. With these odds in their favor, capable leaders in Montgomery and Alexander, absolute command of the air and an increasingly more efficient intelligence operation, it seemed only a matter of time before Rommel was forced off the continent.

On the other hand Rommel's armies, short of fuel, food, and supplies, were anything but ready for battle. Moreover, Rommel himself was desperately ill and had to leave the front to seek medical treatment in Germany shortly before the offensive began. His replacements, Generals Stumme and von Thoma, were able men but neither had any experience in desert warfare, both having arrived in Africa via the Russian front. Earnestness proved to be no substitute for experience and ability and, as the British pressed

Below: German 88 Gun.
Length: 20 ft. 3 in.
Width: 7 ft. 10½ in.
Maximum speed: 31 m.p.h.
Crew: 12 Weight 9.6 tons
unladen, 11.4 tons laden.

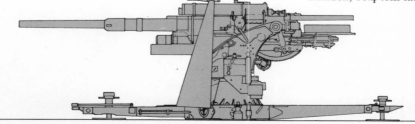

the offensive, Rommel, was ordered from his sick bed back to the desert.

When he arrived near the Alamein line on 25 October, the situation was already critical. British aircraft, flying almost uncontested missions, had bombed and strafed German positions for several days, inflicting reasonably large losses on the Axis army and demoralizing the men. The Germans were short of ammunition and shells, and could do little to stop the advance of British infantry units. Only the carefully laid minefields, planted before the attack on Rommel's orders, slowed the British advance, and even these could be navigated.

For four days the Axis forces stalled Montgomery's offensive, but not without sustaining heavy losses, especially of tanks. By 28 October Rommel had only ninety tanks left on the front line while Montgomery possessed nearly eleven times that number. Even the perpetually optimistic Rommel could not deny that this was a bad omen. Sick and downhearted, he prepared himself for the worst. Although he refused to give one inch of unnecessary ground to his adversaries, he realized that once the British pierced his defenses. there would be no stopping them. Preparations were made for a strategic retreat, and when, by the end of the last week in October, it appeared that further resistance was useless, the Germans fell back to more easily defended positions.

Rommel had never encountered the wrath of Hitler nor had the Fuehrer ever intervened to countermand his orders. But when the German and Italian forces prepared to abandon their positions near the Alamein line, Hitler ordered the Desert Fox to hold them at any cost. Always the Fuehrer's obedient servant, Rommel temporarily suspended the order to retreat, but this did not stop him trying to change Hitler's mind. He did not succeed, unfortunately, until 4 November, by which time the Afrika Korps had been further decimated. Had the British moved less cautiously, they might have finished their enemies then and there.

Once retreat was ordered, the Afrika Korps quickly evacuated their forward positions, outrunning British efforts to cut them off. When Allied forces reached Fuka on the coast road, the Germans had already passed through the city and only those tanks which had run out of fuel, largely older Italian vehicles, were captured. The bulk of Rommel's mobile force was well on the way to Mersa Matruh and passed through that bottleneck a day before British forces arrived. By 7 November, Rommel's forces had arrived at the Halfaya pass; they were almost destroyed by British aircraft, but thanks to excellent traffic management most units had escaped by the time night stopped the RAF attacks.

Rommel's forces reached Fort Capuzzo in Cyrenaica on 11 November but were in no condition to take up a defensive position; instead they were ordered to continue the flight westward. Although Rommel had managed to elude Montgomery and a final encounter was still some weeks away, the retreat had taken a heavy toll. Tens of thousands of German and Italian forces were captured along with many of the weapons of those

Top right: The Afrika Korps bombarded British positions at El Alamein. **Center right:** The Luftwaffe made a supreme effort to break the British lines of defense. **Right:** Rommel and von Thoma ponder their fate at El Alamein. **Below:** The Commander of the Afrika Korps, General Ritter von Thoma, surrenders to Montgomery: 7 November 1942. **Opposite:** Australians break out from El Alamein.

who had managed to escape. The fact that British losses had also been high, some 13,000 men wounded or killed, was little consolation, as Rommel could ill afford the loss of even one able bodied man or piece of equipment.

As the end of November neared, Rommel's army reached Mersa Brega and passed through the Agheila bottleneck where, for the first time in the campaign, defensive positions were prepared. When British forces arrived on 26 November, they encountered heavier resistance than they had since the first weeks of the campaign and were held for two weeks by Rommel's forces supplemented by three Italian infantry divisions newly arrived from Tripolitania. They finally broke through on 14 December, but even so, the British army did not enter Tripolitania until after the beginning of the new year.

As 1943 dawned, the Axis powers faced an unprecedented crisis in North Africa. Montgomery's forces threatened Rommel from the east and the Anglo-American expedition in Algeria and Tunisia threatened the Axis position from the west. Rommel's forces could not possibly

be sufficiently increased to meet these demands and he begged his superiors to allow him to evacuate the continent before his forces were completely destroyed.

Once again his appeal was temporarily rebuffed; Mussolini hesitated to give up Italy's African empire while Hitler, for his part, was unwilling to admit that he had been defeated in the desert. When Marshal Bastico refused to assist him in evacuating the troops, Rommel personally appealed to the Fuehrer in Berlin flying there after his unsuccessful discussions with the Italian commander. Hitler refused to compromise, flying into a rage when Rommel suggested that the situation was lost in Africa, but Mussolini proved somewhat more pliable. Rommel had a long conference with Il Duce on his way back to Tripolitania; although the Italian dictator would not hear of a retreat from Africa, he did agree that the German-Italian army should be moved nearer to the Tunisian frontier. Upon his return to Tripoli, Rommel hastily carried out his plan, and the game of chess in the desert was moved to Tunisia.

Above: Me-109 in the desert.

Left: Weary members of the Afrika Korps pause during their retreat.
Below: The 1st Household Cavalry round up thousands of prisoners.

CHAPTER ELEVEN

Operation Torch: Defeat of the Axis Powers in North Africa

Soon after the United States entered the war, Allied leaders met in Washington to consider coordination of the effort against the Axis powers. Although it was the Japanese attack on Pearl Harbor which occasioned America's entry, Roosevelt agreed with Churchill that the first task of the Allies was the defeat of Germany. What remained to be determined was just how the United States might contribute to the Allied effort in 1942. Here, the two statesmen disagreed.

Churchill proposed that the United States commit its forces to a campaign in North Africa, nicknamed Operation Gymnast by British military planners. According to this proposal, first presented to the Americans at the Arcadia Conference in December 1941, the United States would start an offensive in North Africa, landing forces in Algeria and coming to the relief of the British Eighth Army in Cyrenaica. Together, the British and American armies would crush Rommel's forces and drive the Axis powers off the African continent. Having accomplished this, the Anglo-American allies would move on to Sicily, from Sicily to the Italian boot and from there to Germany, eventually forcing Hitler to capitulate.

Roosevelt did not share Churchill's enthusiasm for a venture in North Africa. To begin with, American officers did not favor a war in the desert and criticized the plan for Operation Gymnast as being both too risky and relatively ineffective. Marshall and other senior American officers proposed instead a landing along the French channel coast. Such a plan would have the virtue of stunning the Germans and stimulating French resistance and the eventual defection of the Vichy regime. It would also satisfy Stalin's demand that the Allies open a second front in Europe to reduce Nazi pressure on the Soviets. For the moment this latter plan prevailed, and it occupied the attention of Allied planners until the summer of 1942 when the situation in Cyrenaica dictated a return to Churchill's original proposal.

By the beginning of July 1942 Rommel's forces had carried their offensive into Egypt and were attacking El Alamein. Had it fallen, the road to Alexandria would have been open to the Germans and it would only have been a matter of time before the Suez Canal was threatened. In this critical situation Churchill could not possibly consider going ahead with the preparations for Operation Sledgehammer, the cross-channel crossing, and advised Roosevelt to this effect on 8 July, suggesting in the same cable that the

United States carefully reconsider the now-abandoned Gymnast scheme. His argument failed to convert Marshall and the other American chiefs of staff but the President, sensing Churchill's desperation, found it impossible to refuse his comrade and overruled his military advisers, ordering them to prepare an acceptable version of the Gymnast plan.

Since there was no changing Roosevelt's mind, Marshall and his lieutenants set to work on a new plan for the invasion of North Africa by American forces, presenting their proposal to the President on 24 July. The new plan, codenamed Operation Super-Gymnast, was reminiscent of the original British proposal, but sought to restrict the area of operations in which the American army would be involved and maintain the integrity of the American command as opposed to integrating the forces of the Anglo-American allies under a joint command. Although precise details of the operations were yet to be worked out, Roosevelt quickly endorsed the proposal and forwarded it to Churchill who did the same, requesting only that the offensive be renamed Operation Torch.

With the approval of the President and Prime Minister in hand, British and American officers met to finalize plans for the operation. It was generally agreed that the offensive could not be launched before October 1942 with the Americans preferring a date in November. A greater problem was the definition of the scope of the landings and where they should take place. Marshall and his

Left: Lieutenant-General Dwight D. Eisenhower, who helped lead Operation Torch. **Below:** Major-General Charles Ryder commanded the forces which were to land at Algiers. **Below right:** Lieutenant-General George S. Patton and Ike plan the landing at Casablanca.

associates wished to proceed cautiously, limiting American landings to Casablanca and points west of this city in Morocco. The British, however, wished to have American forces landed on the Mediterranean as well as the Atlantic coast of North Africa and pushed for simultaneous American landings in Morocco and Algeria. They argued that if the Americans did not move boldly, German and Italian forces would be rushed into Tunisia, giving the Allies little if any chance of seizing this area before the Axis powers cemented their position there. Equally important, British commanders felt that once the Germans understood the scope of Allied operations, they would lose no time in overrunning French-controlled Algeria and Morocco, having little faith that the Vichy forces in North Africa would stand fast with the Third Reich. Thus, if the Allies did not seize Algeria before the Germans, there would be no chance of pinning Axis forces between the converging Americans in the west and British in the east.

Eisenhower's Compromise

In August General Eisenhower proposed a compromise. According to his proposal, which was submitted to Allied leaders on 9 August, American forces would be landed in Algeria as requested by the British, but would not be landed east of Algiers where they would be exposed to attack from German-Italian aerodromes and installations. As in the original American proposal, there would also be a landing near Casablanca.

Eisenhower's proposal represented a concession to the British but they continued to balk at the idea of wasting American forces at Casablanca when they could be used to take more important points east of Algiers and closer to Tunisia. Vigorously pressing their case, the British persuaded Roosevelt of the soundness of their scheme and he, in turn, ordered General Marshall to proceed with plans for an expanded venture in North Africa. Marshall told Eisenhower to reconsider his proposal and continue his conversations with British planners until a satisfactory agreement could be reached. This he did, but it took until the middle of August to come to an agreeable arrangement, and even then there was still disagreement over a landing along the Atlantic coast of Morocco.

On 21 August Eisenhower proposed that the landing at Casablanca be eliminated, as the only way to placate the British. His superiors, however, refused to sanction the change, pointing out to Eisenhower and Roosevelt that if the United States placed all of its eggs in one basket by restricting the operation to Algeria, there was a very real danger that the Germans would close the supply line through the Straits of Gibraltar either by forcing General Franco to seize Gibraltar or by shelling the Straits. If, on the other hand, a bridgehead was established at Casablanca, supplies would be moved overland if necessary.

Marshall's argument was hard to refute and Roosevelt was inclined to support his chief-of-staff on this matter. Although he continued to disagree, there was little Churchill could do but accept the American plan lest more time be wasted. He gave his tentative approval on 5 September, and on the 15th, after agreement had been reached on the locations of the Allied landings and the approximate numbers to be landed at each spot, the plan was finally approved by both sides.

The final Allied plan for Operation Torch called for a three-pronged landing in North Africa. An American force under the command of Major General George S. Patton would land near Casablanca. A second American group under the command of Major General Lloyd Fredendall would land at Oran. The third landing party, a joint Anglo-American force under the command of Rear Admiral Harold Burroughs and General Charles Ryder would be set down near Algiers. The target date for the operation was set for 8 November.

The transport of the Allied armies presented a major problem for the British and American navies and called for the closest cooperation and coordination. Patton's army, some 25,000 men, would be ferried across the Atlantic by an armada under the command of Rear-Admiral H. Kent Hewitt. The other landing parties were to be dispatched from England, but would have to pass through the Straits of Gibraltar in order to reach their targets. This would be no simple feat since the Italian navy had the potential to contest the passage if it took too long. There was also the matter of several hundred slow-moving and relatively unprotected supply vessels which were vital to the success of the effort.

To coordinate this herculean naval effort, Eisenhower chose the commander of the British Mediterranean Fleet, Admiral Sir Andrew Cunningham. It would be his responsibility to move ships quickly through the Straits while keeping the Italian fleet at bay. This was a difficult assignment, but one which Cunningham was perfectly capable of carrying out.

The Allied convoys left England on 22 October and rendezvoused just west of Gibraltar on 5 November, passing through the Straits during that night without incident, since the Italian navy did not dare challenge Cunningham's Mediterranean Fleet. Altogether, over 250 merchant ships and transports had arrived safely in the Mediterranean by the morning of 6 November, all according to plan. By 7 November, all Allied units were in position and ready for the landing the following morning.

The Allies were partially dependent upon the cooperation and good will of Vichy French authorities in North Africa for the success of Operation Torch. With their cooperation, the landings would occur incident; without it, they might be a disaster. It was imperative, therefore, that an effort be made to discover the sentiments of French officials in the colonies before plans for the landings were finalized. This mission fell to Robert Murphy and General Mark Clark.

Murphy was the top-ranking American diplomat in North Africa, tactful, trustworthy, and a friend of many of the Vichy leaders. In short, he was the perfect man to inform the French of the Allies' intention without, at the same time, revealing the full details of their plan of operation. As Roosevelt had anticipated, he fulfilled his mission

brilliantly. While the Anglo-American attack was being prepared, Murphy met secretly with military leaders of the Vichy colonial governments in North Africa, seeking out those who were sympathetic to the Allies and soliciting their blessing for the venture. When he was convinced that a sufficient number of these men would support the Allied landings, Murphy suggested that a ranking Allied officer be sent to join the underground discussions. General Mark Clark, Eisenhower's deputy commander, was chosen for this mission and was carried to Algeria aboard a British submarine, to join Murphy and the French leaders on 21 October, the day before the first British convoy left for Gibraltar.

After a series of mishaps trying to land, Clark met Murphy and General C. E. Mast on 22 October. Mast was the commander of French forces in Algiers and a subordinate of General Juin, commander of French forces in Algeria. According to Murphy, Mast was one of the most reliable of the Vichy generals and was sympathetic to the Allied cause; indeed, it was he who suggested to Murphy that Clark be sent to North Africa in the first place. Clark found Mast a decent fellow and generally agreed with Murphy's estimate of the man, but he refused to tell the French general anything more than was necessary

to prepare him for the landing; Murphy was authorized to fill in details of the size and scope of the operation once the offensive had been launched. Such caution was understandable, but proved unfortunate in the long run since Mast, ill informed of the mechanics of the landings, was caught off guard when they finally began, which caused him no small amount of embarrassment and seriously jeopardized his position.

In their conversations, Clark, Murphy and Mast spent much time discussing the question of leadership among the Vichy community in North Africa. While it was known that many Vichy officials and officers were secretly ready to support the Allies, particularly the Americans, an endorsement of Allied effort by a prominent French leader would help convert some of the more cautious colonials, who this man might be, however, was difficult to determine. Mast's superior, General Juin, might have been chosen to lead the French defection from the Axis camp, but he was considered rather bland and given to vacillation. General de Gaulle might have been considered for the 'assignment', but he would never have been accepted by the senior French officers or Roosevelt. This left only two alternatives, General Giraud or Admiral Darlan.

Since Admiral Darlan had been a sympathetic

Right: American troops disembark from assault boats and land on a North African beach.

out immediate incident in the early hours of the morning of 8 November 1942. Despite problems with the weather and the general's pessimism about the navy's ability to deliver his forces safely, all went well. The landings were made at several points along the Moroccan coast with the main group coming ashore at Fedala, fifteen miles north of Casablanca. Thanks to the confusion of French authorities as to the time, place, and scope of the attack, there was little resistance along the beaches; Patton's men and equipment were unloaded and a beach-head was easily established. Some confusion did result, not from hostile action by the French, but rather from the difficulty of moving heavy equipment along the beach and onto the main coast roads. Nevertheless, Patton's forces were ready to roll toward Casablanca the following morning.

The landing at Oran was considerably more difficult than at Casablanca, Arzeu, Les Andalouses and Mersa Bou Zedjar. Eventually the assault party was repulsed at great loss of life for the invaders. Nevertheless, it was only a matter of days before General Fredendall's forces reached the port and the French officially surrendered the city on 10 November.

The landings near Algiers proved the most difficult of all. Although there was no initial resistance, thanks to the orders of General Mast, he was relieved of his command when news of the operation reached his superiors, and forces collaborating with the allies were replaced by loyal troops. It was necessary, therefore, to negotiate with Vichy authorities if the city was to be taken without bloodshed and once again the task fell to Robert Murphy. Since General Giraud's appeal for cooperation had fallen on deaf ears, Murphy had no choice but to seek the support of General Juin, hoping that he in turn would convey the hopelessness of resistance to Admiral Darlan,

supporter of Hitler and the Third Reich, Churchill and Roosevelt had little faith in him, and public opinion in England and the United States would not have tolerated an alliance with such a man. By process of elimination, General Giraud was the only viable candidate to lead the defection; whatever his vices, at least he had not been an enthusiastic Nazi supporter and in fact he was known to be plotting a revolt against German rule in France.

Having decided to seek Giraud's assistance, it was necessary to bring the general to North Africa for consultation with French leaders and Allied diplomats. This was no easy task since the general's political activities were being closely monitored and he was under regular surveillance by French and German authorities. Nevertheless, on 7 November he was carried by submarine and sea plane to a rendezvous with General Eisenhower on Gibraltar; he was to be dropped in Algeria when the landings began the next morning.

Patton's army landed near Casablanca with-

commander-in-chief of Vichy's armed forces. Fortunately, Darlan happened to be in Algiers and Juin was able to hastily arrange a meeting between the two men.

When Murphy informed the admiral of the size and scope of the Allied landings he was furious, but agreed to send a radio message to Marshal Petain seeking permission to negotiate. At approximately 0800, Petain answered Darlan's message, authorising the admiral to make whatever arrangements were necessary to preserve the French position in Algeria. Darlan, always a realist, swallowed his pride and entered into serious discussions with Murphy which quickly resulted in an order for French forces to quit their resistance in Algiers pending a final agreement for a ceasefire throughout French North Africa.

Giraud reached Algiers on 9 November and joined the discussions between Murphy and Darlan that afternoon. Murphy, who was also joined by General Mark Clark, pushed hard for an early ceasefire agreement, but the two French officers seemed more interested in quibbling over which one of them was authorized to lead French forces in Africa. Darlan contended that Giraud's very presence in Algeria would excite the German-Italian command, inviting their intervention in Algeria and leading to a rapid build up of Axis forces in Tunisia. Although the Allies preferred to deal with Giraud, Clark and Murphy could hardly refute Darlan's argument and did not wish to risk his prediction coming true if Giraud called for the ceasefire. Giraud was scuttled and Darlan became the Allies' chief compatriot in North Africa.

Darlan issued an order for a ceasefire throughout French North Africa on 10 November and cabled a message to this effect to Pétain. Pétain privately approved of the action but could not publicly sanction it lest the Germans take

Top left: Eisenhower was apparently in no mood to take orders from Admiral Darlan (center); Major-General Mark Clark stands to the right of Darlan.
Center left: The American occupation of North Africa was not always as easy as this picture would indicate.
Left: The landings at Oran met considerable opposition. Here an American sniper is looking for trouble.

Left: Operation Torch: personnel and equipment unload near Oran.
Below: General Giraud proved to be far more acceptable to the Allies than Darlan.

Right: American tanks move in to Tunisia to close the circle around Rommel.

punitive action against the Vichy régime; to placate the Germans, therefore, he countermanded Darlan's order and transferred command of French forces in North Africa to General Noguès, a 'more reliable officer'. In reality, however, Darlan's order stood and a ceasefire was achieved in Algeria; in other parts of French North Africa, the situation remained confused.

Pétain's charade may have been designed to quiet the Germans but they were not fooled by the masquerade. When Pétain refused Hitler's request to allow German and Italian forces to move into Tunisia to forestall an allied thrust into that colony, the Fuehrer ordered German forces to occupy the area by force if necessary. German commanders lost little time in carrying out the order; on 9 November, they had crossed the Libyan border and by the end of the month almost 24,000 Axis troops occupied the area. They arrived just in time, for the Allies were ready to launch their drive into Tunisia in the middle of the month.

Had the French cooperated wholeheartedly, the Allies would have been able to push into Tunisia two days after the first landings in Algeria. Except for a small commando force landed at Bone on 12 November, however, the Anglo-American attack force did not commence operations in Tunisia until 15 November when British and American paratroops were dropped west of Tunis to gain control of forward air bases and military installations. On succeeding days, Allied forces were dropped east of Tunis in an effort to trap the Axis garrison in the city and prevent its further reinforcement.

Rather than wait for additional troops, Axis forces in Tunis were placed on the offensive immediately and sent out along the Tunis-Algiers road to clear French troops from the highway before they defected to the Allies. By striking quickly and feigning strength, the German-Italian forces surprised their new enemies and made remarkable headway considering their actual numbers. Parallel assaults were launched east of Tunis, resulting in the occupation of the strongholds of Sousse, Sfax, and Gabès and guaranteeing the Axis a safe passage from Tripolitania to Tunisia. By the end of the month, General Nehring's army controlled most of northern Tunisia and was in an excellent position to defend it against Allied assaults from the east or west.

Above: A Gurkha detachment faces the enemy on the Tunisian Front.
Left: President Roosevelt was escorted through Casablanca by Eisenhower when Morocco and Algeria had been secured.

For their part, the Allies preferred to proceed cautiously in Tunisia. The original timetable had already been modified and Eisenhower agreed with General Anderson, commander of Allied forces in the Algiers area, that there was no reason to rush into Tunisia until they were at full strength and the Royal Air Force was fully prepared to support British and American ground units. Although the push had begun on 15 November, they did not feel ready to make a major effort to dislodge the Germans until the end of December. By that time, however, Axis forces in Tunisia were estimated at over 35,000 and a new commander, General von Arnim, had been sent to Tunis. This increase in the enemy's strength and the onset of bad weather forced yet another postponement. For the moment, Tunisia would remain in Axis hands.

The Fall of Tunisia

The Allied push into Tunisia was resumed in February 1943. In actual numbers, the Axis army in Tunisia, which included the remnants of Rommel's Afrika Korps, was five times the size it had been at the beginning of November 1942, but many of the soldiers in this army had been exhausted in the desert war in the east and tank strength in the mechanized units was well under par. Although equipment and supplies were once again being received, Axis commanders had little to be happy about; they were faced on two sides

by hostile forces and had nowhere to retreat. Tunisia was the last Axis beachhead on the continent.

Although he was tired and ill after managing the retreat from Cyrenaica, Rommel understood that if the Axis command waited until Allied armies converged on Tunis, it would be too late to salvage a position in North Africa. There was no choice but to strike again before the Allies could mount their final assault; Rommel contended that the best place was west of Tunis where Allies forces were most vulnerable. However, his own forces were preparing to bar Montgomery's entrance from the east. General von Arnim controlled the western sector, and it would be up to him to launch the pre-emptive strike.

Von Arnim was less than enthusiastic about launching an offensive but he could not deny that it was necessary. Consequently, although he ordered an attack in the west, he did so half-heartedly, holding a good part of his tank strength in reserve for future encounters. The result was predictable. The Anglo-American advance was slowed but not stopped, and it soon became clear that the Allies might turn von Arnim's drive into a rout. Rommel, who was already fuming at his colleague's reluctance to engage the Anglo-American forces, was forced to join the fray in order to preserve the Axis position in northern Tunisia.

By 17 February Rommel's forces, except for a

This plane was among the hundreds destroyed by the Allies when the Desert Campaign neared its conclusion in Tunisia. **Below left:** British infantry move through a wired position on the Mareth Line. **Opposite above:** Rugged terrain did not prove insuperable for these American Rangers. **Opposite below:** German artillery digs in to defend Tunis after Rommel's departure. **Bottom:** Breakthrough on the Mareth Line sealed the fate of the Axis in North Africa.

few small garrisons adjacent to the Libyan frontier, were being moved westward. It was the Desert Fox's intention to push through the Kasserine Pass and break through to the coast road near Bone before the Allied army captured that position and moved on Bizerta. To succeed, however, he needed the cooperation of von Arnim and the Italian command, neither of whom looked upon such a bold venture with pleasure. In fact, von Arnim was absolutely opposed to the plan. Since there seemed little hope in discussing the matter with him, Rommel appealed directly to Mussolini in the hope that Il Duce would accept the risks involved in order to salvage a victory in North Africa. As he had hoped, Mussolini gave him the 'green light' on 18 February, placing him in command of all Axis forces in Tunisia.

Rommel wasted no time; on 19 February, Axis forces were ordered to the Kasserine Pass, taking it two days later. As the Axis drive continued, Thala was taken from American forces 22 February. But Rommel had no time to rejoice over these triumphs, for Montgomery's forces were threatening German positions near the Tunisian border. The western offensive had to be broken off so that he could rush back to stop the Eighth Army. Rommel's forces reached the Mareth Line at the end of February, but it was already too late to prevent Montgomery entering Tunisia. Realizing that the situation was hopeless, Rommel begged his superiors to prepare for an evacuation. When they refused to consider it, he took a long overdue sick leave, leaving Tunisia on 9 March 1943. Although he could not have salvaged the Axis position in Africa by his

Previous page: German bombers and fighters never had a chance to take to the air when the Allies closed in on Tunis.
Above: General von Arnim is taken into custody: 14 May 1943. Opposite: French and Tunisians cheer the Allied victory in North Africa: Tunis, May 1943.

Below: Allied troops in action during the street fighting in Tunis: 7 May 1943.

continued presence, there seems little doubt that Rommel might have been able to engineer a German Dunkirk had he chosen to remain. Without him, although Axis forces fought bravely to hold their positions, they were decimated when Tunisia finally fell to the Allies.

After Rommel's departure, the defeat of Axis forces was swift. On 20 March Montgomery's forces attacked the Mareth Line, forcing the enemy to withdraw to the west. On 10 April the Eighth Army captured Sfax. On 12 April Sousse was taken and the southern defenses in Tunisia were abandoned as the Axis army retreated to the north where they attempted to maintain a blocking position near Enfidaville. Here they held Montgomery for awhile but in the west, the situation was rapidly deteriorating.

By the end of April, American forces under the command of General Omar Bradley were ready to deliver the *coup de grace* to the remnants of Rommel's once-proud African army. Pushing across rear areas to the north of the front, Bradley's II Corps had captured Bizerta and Tunis by 7 May. Within days after the fall of these ports, German forces in northern Tunisia surrendered. Only the Cape Bon Peninsula remained in Axis hands. Had Hitler and Mussolini followed Rommel's advice, this area might have been the staging point for a retreat to Sicily. Instead, the remaining 250,000 troops were ordered to hold their ground and fight to the death. Actually, German and Italian units surrendered in large numbers until, by the end of the war in the desert, a quarter of a million men had surrendered to the Allies. On 12 May 1943 the Axis empire in North Africa came to an end.

CHAPTER TWELVE

The Allies Return to Europe: Sicily and the Italian Campaign

As the North African campaign drew to a close, Allied leaders met at Casablanca from 14–24 January 1943 to decide upon the next steps to be taken in the war against the Axis powers. It would only be a matter of months before converging Anglo-American forces trapped the Germans and Italians in Tunisia, forcing the Axis partners to abandon the continent. The Allies could then either pursue the enemy across the Mediterranean or discontinue further action in that area and launch a cross-Channel attack. Both options were attractive and each had its supporters, but after considerable discussion it was decided to opt for the former plan and invade Sicily.

The decision to attack Sicily before attempting a cross-Channel invasion of France was based upon the assumption that if pressure was taken off Axis forces in the Mediterranean, they could be withdrawn from the Italian peninsula and sent to France where they would make the Channel crossing that much more difficult. If by a small investment of manpower the Allies could tie up these units in Italy, the risks of failure in France would be greatly diminished. Thus, the Sicilian campaign was not merely a continuation of the North African conflict, but a diversion which would permit the Allies to build up their strength for the Channel crossing in 1944. As such, it had the unanimous support of Churchill, Roosevelt, and their military advisors.

General Eisenhower, as Supreme Commander of Allied forces in North Africa, was chosen to coordinate the Italian campaign, but the actual planning and execution of the operation was to be the joint responsibility of Generals Montgomery and Patton. The date for 'Operation Husky' was not set immediately but all agreed that it could not possibly take place until the summer. As it happened, the North African campaign ended on 12 May and the Allies did not launch the invasion of Sicily until 10 July, a delay of two months.

The final plan for Operation Husky was largely the work of General Montgomery and called for a joint Anglo-American assault. The Eighth Army was to land along the southeast coast of Sicily, take the port of Syracuse, and push on toward Messina. Patton's newly activated Seventh Army was to land at Gela, Licata, and Scoglitti, where they could protect Montgomery's flank and push toward Palermo.

To carry the Allied armies across the Mediterranean to Sicily, a vast armada of ships and landing craft gathered off the coast of North Africa. Operation Husky was to be the first major Allied amphibious assault of the war; in fact, it was the largest operation of its kind in the entire conflict, including the Normandy landings. All told, 478,000 men (250,000 British troops and 228,000 Americans) were moved from North Africa to Sicily during the first weeks of the campaign. They were carried on troop transports but put ashore in new landing craft, including LST's (landing ship-tank), LCT's (landing craft-tank) which carried equipment, LCI's (landing craft-infantry) and (LCVP's (landing craft-personnel and vehicles). Over 2500 vessels were employed in the operation and the Allied armies were landed in an area less than 100 miles wide.

Allied commanders prepared for stiff resistance to the landings, knowing that there were 230,000 Germans and Italians on the island. But in fact, except for some difficulty encountered at Gela where the Hermann Goering division supported by two Italian units put up a fight, the landings were made without incident. By 12 July all Allied beachheads were secured and the two armies were ready to proceed toward their targets.

To reach Messina, the Eighth Army had to pass through Catania or move around Mount Etna, an active volcano which dominated the valley below. It was here, at Catania, that the Axis forces offered their heaviest resistance, attempting to block the road to Messina until the rest of their army could be evacuated to the Italian peninsula.

Opposite: Domination of the central Mediterranean was crucial to a successful Allied invasion of Italy.

Allied troops landing by sea

22.7.43

Allied advance and dates of capture

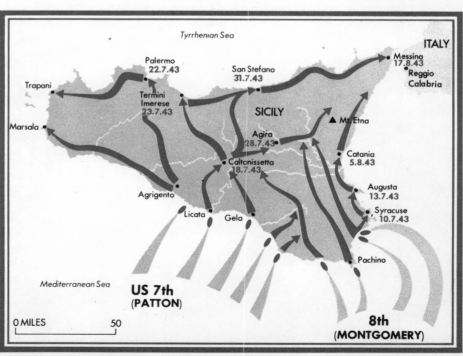

Frustrated, Montgomery tried to send some of his
men around Mount Etna, hoping to outflank the
enemy and break through to the coast behind their
rear lines. This was both wise and necessary, but
by using his own forces to make the run, Montgomery was usurping Patton's position. Never one
to play second fiddle without protest, Patton was
not going to allow the British to upstage his army.
If Montgomery did not need the Second Army's
assistance, it would be used for other purposes like
the capture of Palermo. Accordingly, Patton's
forces and General Bradley's II Corps drove north
and west respectively, capturing Palermo on
22 July and Marsala the following day. These
were the first American victories of the war and
Patton, ready to take advantage of the high morale
of his men, eagerly pressed on toward Messina,
hoping that he could beat Montgomery there.

Patton encountered heavy resistance in his drive
along the northern coast road from Palermo to
Messina, and Montgomery also met stiff opposition. Catania did not fall to the Eighth Army until
8 August, almost a month after the landings, and
heavy casualties were inflicted on both sides.
Nevertheless, once Catania fell, the end was in
sight. With Patton's armies rushing eastward along
the northern coast road and Montgomery's
forces pushing northward along the eastern coast
road, the Axis command had no choice but to
evacuate their forces. This was accomplished by
the morning of 17 August; later that day, Patton's
forces entered Messina.

In many ways, the Allies had won a pyhrric
victory in Sicily. To begin with, a good part of the
Axis garrison, some 100,000 men, were safely
ferried to Italy along with their equipment and
tanks. Although an almost equal number of
forces were left behind and were taken as prisoners
of war, these were freshly conscripted Sicilian units
and not the hard core veterans of the German or
Italian army. Although Axis losses (dead and
wounded) were estimated at 24,000, the Allies lost
a similar number so that the campaign could
hardly be called an unmitigated triumph. Nevertheless, the tide of war seemed to be definitely
turning. If the Axis had achieved a moral victory,
the Allies had a physical victory and the stage was
now set for carrying the war across the Straits of
Messina into Italy proper.

As Allied forces pushed toward Messina, a
political crisis brewed in Rome. The loss of North
Africa and the impending defeat in Sicily forced
Italian leaders to reconsider their position before
Allied forces reached the Italian mainland and
occupied their country as conquerors. Accordingly, the Fascist Grand Council was convened on
24 July to consider what was to be done, and
arrived at a swift answer. On 25 July King
Victor Emmanuel was restored to full power, the
Parliament was reconvened, and Mussolini was
forced to resign, to be replaced as Prime Minister
by the aging Marshal Pietro Badoglio.

Needless to say, the Germans viewed the palace
revolution in Rome with alarm. Despite Badoglio's
assurances that Italy would continue to participate
in the war, Hitler believed that if the Allies
offered the Italian government peace with some
honor, Badoglio would not hesitate to abandon
the Axis. He was quite correct; immediately after
Mussolini was deposed, the Italians entered into
secret negotiation with the Allies in the hope of
arranging a surrender on favorable terms.
Badoglio even let it be known that he would be
willing to join the Allies against the Germans if
participation would give Italy the status of a
co-belligerent and a position of influence at the
peace conference after the war.

Hitler did not intend to tolerate this defection;
Rommel and a German army were ordered to

occupy northern Italy in anticipation of the surrender, and an attempt was made to rescue Mussolini and establish him at the head of a rival Italian government loyal to the Axis. Both of these measures were completed in August 1943, weeks before the Badoglio government signed its military armistice with the Allies on 3 September. When the Allied invasion of Italy was launched in earnest six days later, the Germans were ready to seize Rome and push south to prevent the rapid movement of Allied forces toward the Austrian border. Badoglio took no effective measures to resist this incursion, and as a consequence, the Allies paid a heavy price for Italy.

Across to Italy

Units of the Eighth Army were ferried across the Straits of Messina on the evening of 3 September 1943, landing near Reggio on the toe of the Italian peninsula. Resistance was light and although retreating German forces attempted to destroy bridges, highways, and tunnels in the path of the advancing Allies, they made rapid headway. Taranto, site of a major Italian naval base, was taken on 9 September. Bari, an important harbor on the Adriatic, was seized several days later. By 17 September the Eighth Army had secured a firm hold on southern Italy. In the north, however, the Allies were not faring nearly as well.

The operation in southern Italy and along the Adriatic coast had been designed as a primarily diversionary maneuver. The major thrust of the invasion was to take place on the west coast near the port of Salerno, from which point Allied armies would seize control of air fields in the area and proceed north along the coast road in an effort to break through to Rome. After the signing of the armistice with the Badoglio regime, Allied commanders did not anticipate much resistance and hoped to attain their goal in a matter of weeks.

When General Clark's Fifth Army landed at Salerno on 9 September, however, they immediately encountered fierce resistance from German units and gun positions located in or near the port. The Germans had not been fooled by the activities of the Eighth Army in southern Italy. They fully expected a major Allied assault along the west coast; the obvious advantages of such a landing site were as clear to the Germans as to the Anglo-American command, and the Nazis had lost no time in preparing their defense.

By 10 September the Allied landings had been completed, but not without sustaining heavy casualties along the beaches and in the push for the coast road. Although Salerno was taken by the evening of 10 September, the Germans had done an efficient job of destroying useful installations and gutting the air fields surrounding the city so that they could not be used to launch aerial attacks on retreating German forces which were preparing a new line of defense near Naples.

In pushing inland and north from the beaches, American forces encountered even stiffer resistance than they had in attempting to land. German artillery positions were well placed in the hills above the coastal plain and helped to pin down the invading forces near the beaches. German ground forces had also encircled the Salerno area and

179

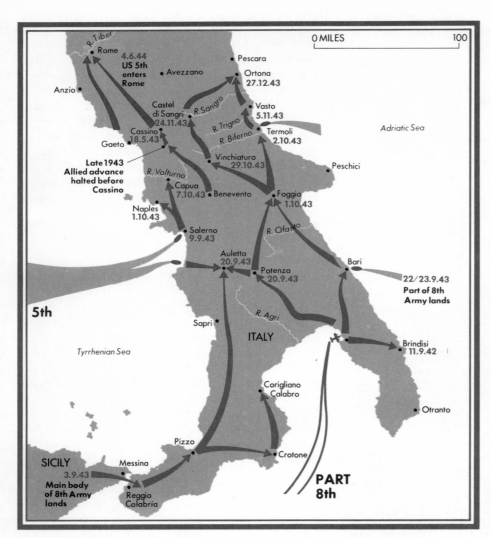

Allied troops landing by sea

Allied troops landing by air

Allied advance and dates
of capture

counter-attacked wherever Allied lines were most vulnerable. With the sea at their backs, American forces had to fight very hard to preserve their beachhead and the breakthrough to the coast road and the interior was considerably delayed, allowing the Germans to prepare their next defensive position before the Fifth Army was able to break through the ring around Salerno.

Allied forces did not reach the Volturno River north of Naples until the first week in October. By this time, the Eighth Army had seized the Axis air field at Foggia and was moving west to the aid of the Americans, in the hope that through a joint assault the Allies could break through the German line on the Volturno and speed on toward Rome, some 100 miles to the north. The capture of Rome with its air fields and communications facilities would be a genuine triumph and a great morale booster, and hence every effort would be made to take the Eternal City as quickly as possible. But the Allies were also sure that Hitler would spare no effort to deprive them of this victory and that the march toward Rome would be difficult. Even so, they did not realize just how difficult it would be.

The distance from the Volturno to Rome was relatively short but the path was difficult to traverse and easy to defend. Aside from the narrow marshy coastal plain, the area west of the coast road was mountainous and impossible for heavily mechanized units to pass through. On the other hand, such terrain provided unlimited opportunities for defensive positions and permitted the enemy to harrass advancing Allied forces with a minimum investment of manpower and equipment. This allowed the Germans to use their

resources to prepare additional defensive positions in the north. Dislodging the Germans required such a tremendous expenditure of manpower and was so frustratingly slow, that Allied leaders began to wonder whether they would reach Rome by the end of the year as planned.

When the Allies crossed the Volturno in mid-October the Germans retreated to the Gustav line, a defensive position astride the Liri, Sangro, Rapido, and Garigliano rivers, and here they held the Allies at bay until the spring of 1944. For every inch the Allies advanced, they sustained heavy losses. Something drastic had to be done to break this stalemate, or the contest might go on indefinitely and endanger the long awaited cross-Channel offensive.

At Churchill's insistence, Allied commanders prepared an amphibious assault around the end of the German position at the Gustav line. General Patton had employed similar techniques on a smaller scale in the Sicilian campaign with good result, and the Prime Minister and some of his military advisors hoped that the same results could be achieved in Italy, despite the fact that a similar proposal had been introduced earlier but had been dismissed as too risky.

'Operation Shingle', as the plan was known, called for the landing of two divisions at Anzio, sixty miles north of the German's main defensive positions. Once landed, these divisions would push south, attacking the Germans' rear along the Winter line while the Fifth and Eighth armies pushed through the front. If all went well, a breakthrough would be achieved, German units would be trapped between two advancing Allied armies, and the long delayed push toward Rome could be resumed with all speed. If the attempt failed, two divisions might well be lost on the beaches, but this was a risk that had to be taken. Preparations for the landings began in January 1944.

As preparations for the Anzio assault were completed, General Clark ordered the Fifth Army to attack the enemy stronghold of Cassino in order to divert their attention. Reinforced by units of the Eighth Army and the Free French Expeditionary Force, commanded by General Juin, the battle for Cassino started on 12 January 1944 with simultaneous attacks on German positions along the Gustav line. Clark wanted Allied forces to be ready to break through Cassino when the VI Corps landed at Anzio on 22 January so that he could link up with the landing force before the Germans had time to patch the hole in their defensive wall. Had the scheme worked, the Allies would have soon been on their way to Rome.

During the first three days, the attack on enemy positions near Cassino went relatively smoothly; by 15 January French forces had taken Sant' Elia and the American II Corps was ready to cross the Rapido river. The X Corps had already crossed the Garigliano and established a beachhead on the other side of the river. At this point, however, the Allies suffered reverses. First, the Americans were not able to cross the Rapido. The Germans who had laid mine fields on the northern bank of the river and had pill boxes constructed in the hills overlooking it forced the Americans to abandon the crossing after sustaining heavy casualties.

Second, the beachhead on the northern bank of Garigliano could not be expanded due to heavy German counter-attacks. It was only through sheer luck and dogged resistance that the Americans managed to hold on to this position at all.

Given these unexpected reverses, General Clark ordered his forces to move north of Cassino and try once again to cross the Rapido while the French assaulted Monte Cassino. The crossing was completed at the end of January but the attempt to move beyond the river failed after two weeks of intensive fighting. It proved impossible to dislodge the Germans from their hilltop bunkers and machine gun emplacements and

Above: Mussolini, captured by Skorzeny, was flown back to Germany. **Below left:** Italian anti-US poster. **Below:** Partisans and Americans talk with captured German officers near Milan.

I DELITTI INUMANI DEI "GANGSTERS PILOTI" RADIANO PER SEMPRE GLI STATI UNITI DAL CONSORZIO CIVILE

Victory in Italy was dearly bought. This tank was knocked out by a 75-mm gun and its crew paid the supreme penalty.

Allied prisoners captured near Anzio are marched through the Piazza Venezia in Rome.

American forces were withdrawn from the area on 12 February, to be replaced by fresh troops from the New Zealand Corps.

The New Zealanders had no better luck than the Americans or the French. Although Allied aircraft bombed German positions atop Monte Cassino, completely destroying the old and famous monastery, Commonwealth forces failed to break through and capture Highway 6 which would lead the Allies to Rome. In fact, the bombing strikes helped the Germans hold the area, since the rubble provided an additional obstacle course for the Allies to overcome. When it became obvious that there was little point in continuing

what was essentially an impossible mission, the effort was broken off and the attempt to take Monte Cassino was postponed until March. As February drew to a close, Germany's defensive positions remained intact.

The Allies' failure at Cassino had grave consequences for the landing party that had been put ashore at Anzio on 22 January. The landing had been conceived as an outflanking maneuver which would permit the Allies to break through German defenses in a simultaneous assault on rear and frontal enemy positions. But when the attack at Cassino failed, the invaders found themselves trapped along the coast with no place to retreat but the sea. What had started out as a relief expedition was now in need of relief.

Ironically, the actual landing had been carried out without incident, but it was not long before the Germans isolated VI Corps near Anzio and counter-attacked. Although the Americans were only forty miles south of Rome and might well have seized the Eternal City by surprise, this was not within the scope of their operation. Failing to receive orders to the contrary, General Lucas kept his forces in place where they were soon surrounded by German units rushed in from northern Italy and Yugoslavia at the order of Marshal Kesselring. Here the Americans were contained until May.

Hitler was infuriated by the audacity of the Anzio landing and was determined that the Allies

be given no quarter. Referring to the Allied offensive as an 'abcess', the Fuehrer told Kesselring that the situation should be treated as if it were a medical crisis, through radical surgery. This Kesselring was only partially successful in achieving. The Allied landing party was driven back to the beaches, but there they stubbornly held out until late in May when a breakthrough was finally achieved at Monte Cassino. Operation Shingle may have failed, but no thought was given to evacuating Anzio if the position could be held.

In the long run, Hitler's obsession with turning back the Allied landing party at Anzio proved fortuitous, for while German forces were concentrated in this area no effort was made to reinforce their position along the Gustav line. When the Allies resumed their attack the lack of an adequate reserve force hampered German efforts to keep them at bay. In launching the new attack, Allied commanders were careful to avoid concentrating their forces at Cassino. General Alexander preferred, instead, to deploy his troops along a broader front; units of the Eighth Army were withdrawn from positions along the Adriatic coast and despatched to assist the Fifth Army. Together, they were to attack German defensive positions over a thirteen mile front stretching from the sea to the Liri valley. If all went well, a hole would be punched in the German position somewhere along the line, the American garrison at Anzio would be relieved, and the Allies would gain coastal Highway 7 which led to Rome.

The Fifth Army concentrated its attack in the hills since previous attacks along the coast had proved costly and unproductive. At the same time, the Eighth Army resumed the attack on German defenses near Cassino, hoping to ford the Rapido

below the city. A third effort, an attempt to scale Monte Cassino, would be undertaken by the newly arrived Polish Corps. The battle was to begin on 11 May.

The Germans had not thought that the Allies would renew their offensive nor had they prepared for an action along such a wide front. As a result, although the early action was heavy and not immediately successful for the Allies, they were finally able to break through the German line. By 17 May French forces, which had supplemented the Poles in the attempt to take Monte Cassino, had succeeded in dislodging the Germans from positions near the base and in the foothills of the mountains, and on the following day Polish forces reached the summit. For the Poles, this was a significant breakthrough and one which was frought with poetic justice. Like their French compatriots, they found that revenge was sweet.

With Monte Cassino and the surrounding area in Allied hands, the Germans were forced to abandon the Gustav line on 23 May. They withdrew to Rome where a brief but unsuccessful attempt was made to establish another defensive position in front of the city. To his credit Marshal Kesselring refused to destroy the city in order to block the Americans' advance. On 4 June the capital was declared an open city and American forces entered it later that day. The capture of Rome was an achievement of tremendous importance and symbolized more graphically than any other victory to that date the collapse of the Axis. Although the sequel to the march into Rome was slow and frustrating, with the Germans grimly holding on in northern Italy for six more months, Hitler was unmistakenly on the defensive, retreating from Italy and trying to defend France.

When the tables turned, Italians cheered the Allied entry into Rome after it was declared an open city.

CHAPTER THIRTEEN
Operation Overlord

In January 1944 General Dwight D. Eisenhower returned to London to take charge of the mightiest fighting force in Western history. The directive from the Allied Combined Chiefs of Staff was simple. The principal paragraph read, 'You will enter the continent of Europe and, in conjunction with the other Allied Nations, undertake operations aimed at the heart of Germany and the destruction of her Armed Forces.' The destruction of the German forces was the paramount principle; the occupation of land was important only in so far as it would help to achieve this goal.

Even before the United States entered the war American planners had concluded that, in the event of war with the Axis powers, Germany would have to be defeated first. Not only was she industrially far more powerful than Japan, but the Allies would find it easier to mass forces for a concentrated attack against her. Any offensive mounted against the Japanese would have to be conducted almost solely by the United States.

The 'Japan First' viewpoint, however, was not without its advocates and, especially after the attack on Pearl Harbor on 7 December 1941, found increasingly vocal support. But the black days immediately after the attack found Allied forces reeling backward, trying desperately to slow the Japanese advance. Meanwhile, the Germans had been stopped short of Moscow and, with the winter of 1942 setting in, Russian partisans were strangling German communications and supply lines. Thus while in the Pacific Allied

forces were steadily being driven out of Asia, in the West the Germans appeared to be an easier target, wedged in between British and Russian threats.

Keeping Russia in the war was imperative, but it was necessary to assure her that, contrary to appearances in those last days of 1941, she was not carrying on the war with Germany alone. To the Russians, anything other than a direct attack on Germany would be unpalatable, but especially a front in the Pacific where the Soviet Union was not even a belligerent. Thus from 1941 to 1943, the goal of defeating Germany first became more urgent.

Although British and American planners were in agreement over the need to defeat Germany before Japan, they could not decide where and when the offensive should take place. As early as 1942 General George C. Marshall had planned a cross-channel invasion (code name 'Roundup') but the British had balked. In 1942 the British would have had to bear the brunt of the responsibility and provide most of the manpower, which they could not afford to do at a time when their forces were hard-pressed in North Africa.

The Russians, desperately holding off the Germans, were not favorably impressed with Allied gains in the Mediterranean, for they failed to see how it would materially relieve the pressure on their front. Winston Churchill, however, continued to advocate the 'soft underbelly' of Europe approach, arguing that these operations would knock Italy out of the war and stop the attacks upon British convoys that were trying to continue the lifeline through the Mediterranean to the Suez Canal. Control of the Italian bases would undermine if not completely remove the Luftwaffe as a threat to Allied shipping in the Mediterranean, and German forces might have to be diverted from other fronts to replace the Italian troops that would be lost.

American thinkers, however, felt that the application of Allied resources to what was essentially a side show would mean diverting badly needed and meager supplies to a painfully slow, grinding war that would not yield immediate dividends either in the early defeat of Germany or the relief of the Russian front. As a compromise, the invasion of Sicily and the subsequent Italian campaign were launched.

The slow but steady progress in Italy permitted the Combined Chiefs of Staff to turn once again to the planning of a cross-channel invasion. Such an operation had in the meantime attained a new

Below: Planning Operation Overlord – left to right: Eisenhower, Air Chief-Marshal Leigh-Mallory, Air Chief-Marshal Tedder and Montgomery.
Opposite top: A German Kampfgruppe marching to take up their positions along the Atlantic Wall.
Opposite center: American Flying Fortresses, newly arrived in Britain, soon to be used against the factories of the Ruhr.
Opposite bottom: American airmen shortly before D-Day.

sense of urgency. The Russians had smashed the Germans at Stalingrad and were on the offensive for the first time. Their demands for a coordinated attack on two fronts would not be satisfied by the diversionary Italian front.

On the German side, since the failure to capture Moscow in the fall of 1941, the unpleasant prospect of having to fight a two-front war had become a reality by 1942, first with the Allied North African invasion and then with the Italian campaign. Allied progress in Italy pointed out their vulnerability in the West and now, for the first time since Dunkirk, Adolf Hitler set about defending that flank.

The task of defending land which had already been conquered in the West appeared to be far more difficult than the original *blitzkrieg*. Since the invasion coastline, which stretched in a mighty arc from Norway to Greece, had been penetrated by the Allies in Italy, Allied superiority in air and naval forces could assure a safe cover for landings anywhere. The coasts of Denmark and Norway appeared especially vulnerable; landings via the North Sea south into Germany was also a possibility. As a matter of fact, German intelligence agents flooded higher headquarters with reports of prospective landings in the vicinity of the Franco-Spanish border as well as in southern France.

Logic, however, dictated that a direct invasion across the English Channel could be best supported from England and this possibility came to receive the most urgent attention in Germany. The strengthening of fixed fortifications along the Channel coast and the reinforcing of the garrisons manning these structures claimed the highest priority; responsibility for the project was given to Field Marshal von Runstedt.

The Atlantic Wall

The nucleus of the coastal defense system was the Atlantic Wall, built under the auspices of a Nazi labor organization called Todt. The quality and quantity of the fortifications was hardly uniform, being strongest in Holland and the Pas de Calais area, reasonably strong in Normandy and Brittany, with the stronger areas connected by structures which were little more than field earthworks.

The acerbic von Runstedt was appalled by the concepts and quality of the fortifications, and even more bitter about the men that were assigned to hold them. The Russian front had drained most of the divisions of their best fighting men, and many were under strength, woefully under-equipped and demoralized. Large numbers of the troops consisted either of older men, convalescents from the Russian front, or captured foreign prisoners of war (most notably Russians) from earlier campaigns. According to von Runstedt, of the sixty nominal divisions assigned to defend the West, no more than fifteen could be considered to be first-line units.

It is always difficult to take a hostile shore by direct assault and the task is increased tenfold when the enemy has long anticipated such an attack and is doing his utmost to strengthen his defenses. Though Allied bombing raids had taken their toll of German aircraft the enemy had

British women serve tea to American servicemen during the build-up before D-Day.

General von Rundstedt was appalled by the quality of the coastal fortifications.

responded to the growing threat in the West by increasing fighter aircraft production. Most of the factories were beyond the reach of Allied fighter escort range in 1943 and early 1944 and Allied bombers were being lost at an alarming rate.

The effectiveness of strategic bombing in World War II has been the center of much controversy; it is sufficient to state that its results were overrated. The role of enemy fighter interdiction against a landing operation was the cause for great anxiety, and the choice of a landing site depended in part upon the ability of Allied airpower to maintain its superiority until the beachhead could be successfully established.

Another consideration in choosing a landing site was the need to establish supply lines to the assault troops once they had gained a foothold. It was known that the major ports would be destroyed in the event of Allied attack and thus the attacking forces would have to depend on protected beaches for reinforcement and supply.

The coast of western Europe offered a number of prospective landing areas from Holland to Bordeaux. The limited range of fighter air cover precluded Denmark or the German coastline on the North Sea, and other considerations such as restricted exits from beach areas, the ease of German counterattack and supply problems gradually reduced the number of areas to Pas de Calais and the Normandy coast between Caen and Cherbourg. The Pas de Calais area offered

the shortest distance across the English Channel, being only some 20 miles from Dover, but intelligence reports indicated that the Germans were rushing reinforcements into this area as fast as they could and were rapidly improving the fortifications. The Caen area, though farther away, appeared to be less well-fortified and more removed from enemy supply and troop concentrations. Moreover, it was within range for most of the fighter cover that the Allies considered vital to the success of the operation.

Thus it was decided that the landing operation (now given the code name 'Overlord') be conducted in Normandy. Plans called for an initial assault wave of five divisions with two more in reserve. Once the landing had been successfully concluded, the five-division force should be strong enough to pick a soft spot on the wide beach for a breakout toward Paris.

The initial responsibility for planning such an invasion in the early days of 1943 had been British, but as American manpower had begun to predominate, an American, General Dwight D. Eisenhower was appointed Supreme Commander with a British deputy, Air Chief Marshal Sir Arthur Tedder. The field commander of the entire assault was Lt. Gen. Omar Bradley. The assault forces would be composed of American, British and Canadian forces.

One major restriction placed upon selecting a date for the operation was the shortage of landing craft. Though priority was given to Overlord and landing craft were gathered in from all over the world to the protests of their commanders, the original plan to invade in May 1944 had to be postponed until June so that more vessels could be produced. In the meantime, the Allied command had to contend with an increasingly impatient Soviet Union on the need to open a second front.

Plans called for an airborne assault to precede the actual landing; this required a moonlit night for parachute and glider landings. At the same time, the Allied command needed a period of relatively low tides so that landing craft could avoid the thousands of steel barricades on the beaches. Furthermore, the navy wanted to approach the shore under cover of darkness, yet have at least an hour of daylight to bombard shore defenses. This combination of requirements fixed the alternate dates to a period between 5 and 7 June, or about the 20th of the month. The latter date was discarded since it meant further delay. Thus, 5 June was picked as the date and 0630 as the time.

Ironically, the Germans had also guessed that the attack would take place either at Pas de Calais or in Normandy. Pas de Calais was considered more likely since it was the closest point to Britain and also because it was near the launching sites of the V-1 and V-2 rockets that would soon be creating havoc in England. With the erratic intuition that he sometimes seemed to possess, Adolf Hitler had personally picked Normandy as a likely place. This was transmitted to von Runstedt, but while the Field Marshal agreed that Normandy offered a possible site, he persisted in the belief that it would afford only a feint designed to draw German forces away from the main assault at Pas de Calais.

The possibility of a secondary or diversionary attack in support of the main attack did, of course, exist. The Allied Combined Chiefs of Staff had formulated an operational plan called 'Anvil' to be launched simultaneously against the southern French coast. But though it was to be a supporting attack, the landing craft it required would take equipment away from Overlord. Eisenhower hung on to the idea for weeks, but finally, when he realized that Overlord would be seriously undermined, the Supreme Commander reluctantly decided to postpone Anvil.

The German high command in the west at this time suffered from a difference in opinion between von Runstedt and his chief subordinate, Field Marshal Erwin Rommel, who commanded Army Group 'B', the organization charged with the defence of the coastline itself. The controversy centered around the commitment of the mobile reserve of some ten tank divisions which constituted the chief hope of shattering any Allied landing.

Rommel was convinced that the only time to smash the Allied effort was at the beach areas and therefore he argued for placing the tanks as near the coast as possible. Though von Runstedt agreed with the need to shake the Allies loose from whatever toehold they could gain as soon as possible, he was afraid of using his reserves prematurely, before the actual size and disposition of the Allied attack could be discerned.

Above: Artillery being loaded into LCTs for the attack on Normandy.
Left: Ike gives final instructions to US paratroopers, just before they board their airplanes in the first assault of the invasion of Europe.
Below left: "Synchronize your watches".

Below: Scharnhorst
Length: 741½ ft. Beam:
98½ ft. Draught: 24½ ft.
Maximum speed: 31½
knots. Armament:
9 × 11 in., 12 × 5.9 in.,
14 × 4 in., 16 × 37 mm.,
38 × 20 mm., 6 × 21 in.

torpedo tubes, 4 aircraft
Crew: 1800. Displacement:
32,000 tons.

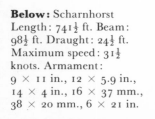

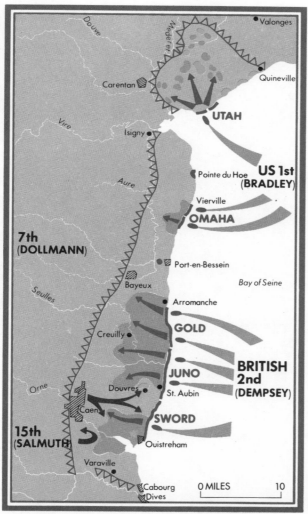

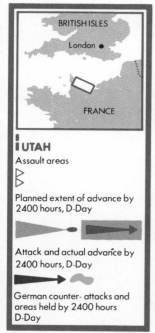

Top left: US paratroops practice for a training drop.
Top right: RAF base jammed with Dakotas.
Above left: A German warning which almost came true for the Americans.

The relations between the aging and haughty von Runstedt and the Fuehrer had never been cordial, whereas Rommel was the hero of the African campaign. Due to his direct influence with Hitler, he was able to inject his personal view into von Runstedt's overall plan. The result was a rather fatal compromise; the tanks were placed neither close enough to have an immediate effect upon the landing nor far enough away to be able to respond flexibly to changing situations. Furthermore, four of the ten divisions were scattered in the general reserve for south and southwest France. Control of the divisions was divided between the two commanders. When the Allied attack began, there was neither sufficient power to push the Allies into the sea, nor enough to form a significant counterattack.

The German analysis of the situation was confused by the Allies' efforts at deception. Throughout southern England phoney camps were assembled with false unit designations; radio traffic simulated an army commanded by General George S. Patton, and as the invasion date drew near – movement in and out of the staging area became increasingly restricted. British agents deliberately sought to confuse German commanders by planting false information, aided in their task by disagreement between German intelligence and the Nazi political command Postwar reports show that when the all-Nazi secret service under Himmler tried to assess invasion data, they made over two hundred guesses, all of which proved incorrect.

Actually the German side was not alone in being deceived. Nazi efforts to build up the 'invincibility' of the Atlantic Wall were at least partially effective in creating the impression that the Pas de Calais area was heavily fortified. This was true, but the extent of fortification was greatly exag-

Previous page: Thousands of reinforcements and pieces of equipment poured into Normandy when the beachhead was secured.
Left: British Commandos attack Sword Beach.

Bottom: Caen was the crucible of Normandy. Its seizure insured Allied victory in France.
Below: MA–A2 Sherman
Length: 19 ft. 5$\frac{7}{16}$ in.
Width: 8 ft. 7 in. Maximum road speed: 29 m.p.h.
Armament: 1 × 75 mm., 1 × .30 machine gun, 1 × .50 machine gun. Crew: 5. Weight 31.8 tons.

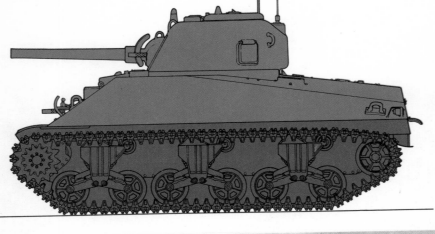

gerated. This in turn helped influence the Allied decision to invade Normandy instead.

An operation involving such vast numbers of men in a wide area created many security problems, and there were a number of incidents that could have compromised the plans. Loose-mouthed officers and freak accidents gave the planners nightmares. One hot day in May, copies of a top-secret document were actually blown into the streets of London. Frantic staff officers recovered all except one, and a few agonizing hours passed before it was discovered that a passerby had picked it up and given it to a Horse Guard.

The crucial factor upon which the entire operation depended was the weather, since men and ships would have to move at least three days before the actual D-Day. Should a sudden change occur prohibiting landing operations, the lead elements would have gone too far to be recalled. On 1 June, to the horror of the high command, the skies turned ominously grey. The next day, weather forecasts predicted high winds and low visibility for June 5, 6 and 7. At a meeting on 3 June, the chief meterologist advised the Supreme Commander to postpone the operation. For Eisenhower, those were heavy hours. A postponement of this sort was sure to undermine the physical status and morale of the troops at sea. Furthermore, there would be no way to avoid letting the troops out on leave, and the chances of secrecy would be practically impossible. In practical terms, postponing the invasion meant almost 30 days of keeping a secret that was

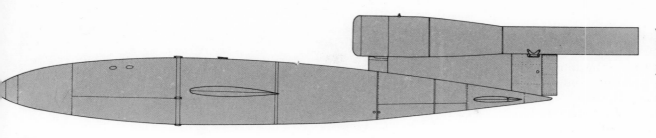

Vergeltungswaffe Ens (V.I.)
Length: 26 ft. Span:
17 ft. 6 in. Maximum speed:
410 m.p.h. Range: 150
miles. Armament: 1870 lbs.
warhead. Weight: 4800 lbs.

The British landing on Juno Beach. Some men never made it and their bodies had to be carried out of the water.

no secret to almost 150,000 men. The effect of a delay were not limited to immediate problems. It would also mean reducing the time available for a summer campaign in France and would restrict the use of the channel ports before stormy weather arrived.

The Germans relaxed during the bad weather, realizing that the chances of invasion were considerably less promising. Rommel made plans to return to Germany to celebrate his wife's birthday on 6 June. Most of the senior commanders were scheduled to attend a paper war exercise to test out anti-invasion plans. But at a meeting on 4 June, Eisenhower was told that a

temporary break in the weather might occur on the 6th. It was at best a fifty-fifty chance, but the next definite break would not be toward the end of the month, and besides, there was the commitment to the Russians to consider. Reluctantly, Eisenhower gave the order to proceed.

In the dark, British and American paratroops preceded by special Pathfinder teams and followed by glider troops dropped into Normandy. Their mission was to seize and secure bridges and other vital points behind the coastal defenses to delay German attempts to reinforce the shore garrisons. Due to errors in judgment and wind conditions, many were dropped a considerable distance from

Below: Normandy prisoners pour into Britain.

their intended zones, but these highly trained men exploited local situations wherever they could, disrupting communications, ambushing German couriers and generally creating confusion. Cut off from each other, the Germans could not effectively assess the extent of the penetration.

Some 2700 vessels loaded with men and equipment crossed the English Channel. At dawn German coastal watchers saw the armada deploy with fascinated horror; shortly afterward, the heaviest bombardment of the war commenced. Overhead, Allied aircraft flew a total of 25,000 sorties. There were almost no German aircraft in operation on 6 June over the beaches while in England, on average, an aircraft took off every 3.5 seconds.

The landing zone was divided into five main areas. Two on the west flank, code named Utah and Omaha, were American responsibilities. The remaining three, named Gold, Juno and Sword, were to be occupied by British and Canadian troops. The first assault wave at Omaha numbered 34,000 troops with 3300 vehicles; a second wave of 25,000 men and 4400 vehicles followed: Behind Omaha, the brush covered ground rose steeply to about 150 feet, and here the Germans concentrated their heaviest forces; soon the landing was considerably behind schedule, creating a serious follow-up problem due to the anticipated change in the weather. The beach was littered with wrecked landing craft and disabled tanks, and the congestion of men and equipment created problems in evacuating casualties.

The landing at Utah Beach went 2000 yards beyond the landing point, but it was a disguised blessing, for the obstacles at that point were far less formidable. Quick thinking exploited the situation and men were fed into the area, thereby avoiding the heavier losses that might have been suffered at the original point of landing.

Despite such difficulties, however, by mid-morning over 18,000 Americans were on Omaha alone, and the Germans had failed to mount a single serious counterattack. By late afternoon Omaha and Utah beaches were linked by a thin sliver of American troops who had made their way through German defenses via a narrow country road.

The British assault began a half-hour after that of the Americans. The landing procedure was similar, but the British had improvised a number of devices to penetrate minefields and bridge shell craters. A number of tanks were equipped with revolving drums attached with short lengths of chain. Acting as a flail, they cleared a path through German minefields for the infantry. The British later were subjected to the only two major German attempts at armour attacks, both of which failed, thus depriving the enemy of their last tank reserves.

The Germans first suspected that a major operation was about to develop after intercepting a large number of coded BBC messages to the French underground. Based on these reports, German forces near Paris went on conditional alert but the men in Normandy were not warned at all.

The first overt signs of invasion activity occurred when reports arrived at von Runstedt's head-

quarters of parachute landings. Attempts to get a clear picture of the situation were negated by the disruptive tactics of the paratroops, and at least in the beginning, much of the activity was dismissed as nuisance tactics.

Once the front-line troops on the coast were hit, the paratroops saw to it that, in effect, the coastal area was isolated from the rest of France and thus from reinforcement. Feeble armor attacks failed because the von Runstedt-Rommel compromise had deprived them of sufficient striking power; without sufficient armor, little could be done about reinforcing the coast until more troops arrived, but Allied air superiority saw to it that few would. The Luftwaffe was effectively shot out of the air in the preparatory air strikes before the invasion. Then, without any enemy to contend with, Allied fighters strafed and bombed every bridge, railway line, marshaling yard and road within range so that nothing could move on the surface.

The Germans had only one other source of troops and that was the Fifteenth Army in northern France, Belgium and Holland. But the notion that Pas de Calais was the main site of an invasion and that Normandy was a diversion died hard. The Allied tactics of deception had done their work, and the Germans continued to believe that there was another army under Patton still in England awaiting embarkation.

After two weeks von Runstedt finally became convinced that Normandy was the main attack but Berlin continued to believe that Pas de Calais would be attacked and refused to release the troops in northern France. Hitler did not change his mind until August, and by then it was too late. With no troops to reinforce the Normandy area, there was little that could be done to patch the break other than to cling desperately to the ground still occupied. Cherbourg and other ports held and inflicted casualties upon Allied forces, but the end was inevitable.

Top left: American Liberty ships were deliberately scuttled off the beaches to provide makeshift breakwaters during the first days of the invasion.
Top center: Not every American made it to the cliffs overlooking Omaha Beach. **Above:** Once the beaches were secured, the Allies clambered over the chalk cliffs to penetrate the interior. **Left:** Two days after D-Day; the beaches were well under control, and an unceasing flow of troops and supplies reinforced combat units.

CHAPTER FOURTEEN
The Russian Front: 1942-1944

Operation Barbarossa ground to a halt in December 1941 and for three months the Russian front remained calm. Although Hitler had failed to achieve a quick victory over the Soviet Union, he remained committed to continuing the struggle against the Russians, using the winter interlude to prepare for a new offensive in the spring of 1942. The Soviets also took advantage of the lull to prepare an offensive of their own.

As it happened, the Soviets struck first. Underestimating the strength of the Germans and overestimating their own capacity, the Russians launched a three-pronged offensive in March 1942: in the Crimea, an effort was made to relieve the siege of Sevastapol; in the north, an effort was made to restore communication and transportation links between Moscow and Leningrad; and in the south, a major campaign was undertaken to recapture Kharkov and reestablish Soviet control of the Donetz basin. All three efforts failed.

The Russian campaign in the Crimea was quickly turned back by German forces and as many as 100,000 Soviet troops were taken prisoner. Far from relieving the siege of Sevastopol, the collapse of the Russian offensive insured that the city would fall, and fall it did on 1 July after a long and bitter confrontation in the suburbs. With the loss of Sevastopol, Russian hopes to reestablish a strong position in the Crimea faded.

The Soviets met with no better luck in their effort to reopen lines of communication between Moscow and Leningrad and relieve the siege of the latter. In fact, the battle for Leningrad proved an even greater disaster than the Crimean offensive. Leningrad had been isolated by German forces during the winter months in an effort to starve the city into submission; though Russian efforts to break the siege had failed repeatedly, a whole army being lost in January 1942 in an effort to cut through German lines, the Soviet commander in the city would not surrender. Except for those who endured the Battle of Stalingrad, few have ever sustained more hardship or suffering than the defenders of Leningrad. During the winter months of 1941 the death rate soared to several thousand per day for want of food, shelter, and proper clothing, while the Germans continued their unmerciful shelling of the city. Unless the siege was soon lifted, the city would surely be destroyed.

Stalin could not permit the slaughter in Leningrad to continue without making one last effort, and Russian forces massed near Moscow in preparation for a march to the west. The offensive was to begin in May with General Andrei Vlasov

Above: Marshal Timoshenko hoped to push the Wehrmacht back into the Ukraine.
Opposite top: The Russian campaign in Crimea was quickly turned back, these three were among almost 100,000 Soviet troops taken prisoner.
Opposite bottom: German soldiers examine a T-34 captured when the Soviet Crimean front collapsed.

Russian T34–76. Length: 21 ft. 7 in. Width: 9 ft. 10 in. Maximum road speed: 32 m.p.h. Armament: 1 × 76 mm., 2 × 7.62 mm. machine guns. Crew: 4 Weight: 27 tons 16 cwt.

commanding the relief army. He fared no better than his colleagues in the Crimea. After an initial breakthrough, Vlasov's army was encircled and, without adequate reinforcements and supplies, was destroyed in front of Leningrad. Residents of the former Russian capital, however, continued to hold fast, refusing to surrender to the Germans. They paid dearly for their bravery; by year's end the population had been reduced to less than a million, one-third the prewar population of the city.

After the failures in the Crimea and Leningrad, the southern offensive remained the Soviet's only hope, and here they mounted their largest effort, massing an army of hundreds of thousands of men and the best equipment available. The Russian army in this area was under the command of Marshal Semen Timoshenko, who hoped to crush German positions south of Kharkov and push the Wehrmacht back into the Ukraine and from there into Poland. The campaign started on 12 May 1942 with a successful dash through German positions south of the city. It was five days before the Germans could recover their equilibrium and counter-attack, but by then Soviet lines were overstretched, forming a corridor seventy miles long which the Germans attacked on 18 May. By 23 May what had appeared to be a Russian victory was turned into a disaster; German forces surrounded Timoshenko's army, capturing over 240,000 men and most of their equipment, and inflicting a defeat even greater than that suffered in front of Leningrad.

Having disposed of the Russian offensives, the Germans were ready to launch one of their own. Hitler intended bringing the Caucasus under German control. To achieve this, German forces were redistributed so as to permit the continuation of the 1941 campaign in the southern sector. Forces in Leningrad and Moscow were placed on the defensive so that Army Group South could be reinforced prior to the new campaign.

Army Group South was divided into two com-

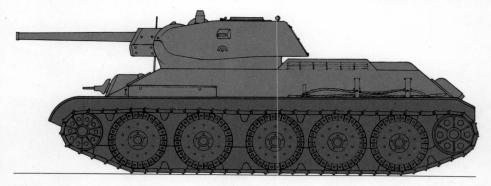

General von Kleist's Fourth Army took the Maikops oilfields by 9 August 1942.

Chuikov was determined to hold the bridgeheads along the Volga.

ponents, Army Group A, under the command of General List, and Army Group B, under the command of General von Bock; Army Group A was to strike for the Caucasus while Army Group B secured its left flank. To bolster these forces, additional troops from the satellite countries (Hungary, Italy, and Rumania) would be despatched to the Russian front where they would assist Army Group B in maintaining the long and vulnerable line stretching from Voronezh to Stalingrad. The scheme was a bold one and perhaps beyond the capacity of the Wehrmacht to fulfill, but Hitler would hear of nothing less than a total seizure of the southern region. Rather than argue with their leader, the German generals once again fell in with his plans.

The German offensive was to begin in June and Russian forces, still retreating after their defeat in May, were not able to offer effective resistance to the Wehrmacht's advance. Army Group B moved easily toward the Donetz and Don basins, and it was only when von Bock's forces reached Veronezh at the beginning of July that the Soviets mounted a counter-attack.

The Stalingrad Slaughter

The Soviet commander at Veronezh, General Vatutin, was under orders from Stalin to prevent the Germans from marching north to Moscow at any cost. Had Hitler permitted von Bock to engage Vatutin, as he originally wished to do, the battle would have undoubtedly been one of the bloodiest and most costly of the war in the Soviet Union. Fortunately Hitler would not permit such

a diversion because he realized only too well that this would delay the race for the Caucasus; since he had no immediate intention of pressing an attack on the Soviet capital, a confrontation with Vatutin's forces be of little value. Von Bock was overruled and later dismissed, and the original plan proceeded apace.

While Army Group B raced toward the Don north of Stalingrad, mechanized units from Army Group A pressed an attack on Rostov, further south. Assisted by units from von Bock's command which had been ordered south at the insistence of the Fuehrer, General von Kleist's Fourth Panzer Army took Rostov on 28 July and proceeded toward the Maikops oil fields; these were taken by 9 August, although the Soviets destroyed much of the equipment in the fields as they retreated to the east. By 22 August German forces reached Mount Elbrus and continued their march east, heading toward the oil fields at Grozny and Baku. It appeared at the beginning of September that Hitler's goals might well be achieved, but the momentum of the offensive was soon slowed as problems of supply increasingly plagued List's army. Dismissing List and replacing him with General von Kleist did not improve the situation. Ironically, although the Germans had struck deep into the heartland of the Caucasus and captured the oil fields so important to their war effort, they were short of petroleum products and could not continue their rapid advance due to the scorched earth policy of the retreating Soviets. Until the rigs and equipment in the Maikops fields could be repaired and replaced, all gasoline and oil for Army Group A had to be carried overland from the west, a difficult if not impossible task. By the end of September they were forced to stop the offensive several hundred miles short of their objective.

The diversion of General Hoth's tank corps to the Caucasus delayed the movement of Army Group B south to Stalingrad, and von Kleist was not able to swing south from Veronezh until the beginning of August. By this time the Soviets had recovered from their earlier defeats and were preparing to defend Stalin's namesake against the invaders. When the Germans reached the outskirts of the city at the end of the month, the stage was set for the greatest contest of the war in Russia.

General Paulus's Sixth Army reached the suburbs of Stalingrad on 23 August and succeeded in penetrating the outer defenses of the city, establishing a bridgehead to the north, on the

Volga. That evening the Luftwaffe launched a massive raid on Stalingrad, killing thousands of people and destroying most of the wooden buildings in the city. Paulus predicted the imminent capture of the city on the morning of 24 August, but far from creating a mentality of surrender, the Luftwaffe raid strengthened Russian resistance. The citizens of Stalingrad refused to bow before the German invaders; rather than have a foreign army occupy their city, they took to the streets, constructing barracades at every intersection from the rubble left by the air raid of the night before. For an army used to rapid movement across an unobstructed plain, the makeshift defense of Stalingrad proved an insurmountable obstacle, with each block a fortress, each house an enemy camp. In Stalingrad Germany's arsenal was neutralized as mechanized warfare gave way to house to house fighting.

Stalled outside the city center, Paulus called for reinforcements, leaving the protection of his flank to troops from the satellite countries, the most unreliable under the German command. For the moment, this seemed the wisest thing to do, but it was to have profound consequences in November when the Russians launched their counter-attack. For the moment, however, even this extra strength did not permit the capture of the city.

Paulus renewed his attack toward the end of September. By this time, German air raids had further reduced the city to rubble; there was hardly a major building which had not suffered some damage and what the bombers failed to destroy, artillery barrages wrecked. By all standards resistance should have been destroyed, but the people of Stalingrad continued to struggle on, manning their barricades and the factories which continued to produce the materials necessary to keep the effort alive.

Paulus succeeded in driving a corridor across the city to the Volga by the end of September, cutting the defending garrison in two as a result. Nevertheless, the fighting remained intense, with gains being measured in inches. Although a good part of the city was in German hands by the middle of November, the Russians continued to hold on, General Chuikov's forces stubbornly clinging to their bridgeheads along the Volga with their backs to the river.

Paulus hoped to deliver Stalingrad to Hitler as a Christmas present, but unknown to him, the Russians were preparing to launch a counter-attack. While Chuikov's forces tenaciously clung

Top: General von Manstein was ordered to relieve the German front. **Above:** Rokossovsky commanded one of Zhukov's three armies defending Stalingrad.

Paulus could not retreat, but the Italians could, and did in December 1942.

to their positions, keeping awake by taking alcohol and benzedrine, General Zhukov was quietly massing a huge force north of the city along the Don. By mid-November he was ready to launch his counter-attack.

Zhukov's forces were divided into three armies under the command of Generals Golikov, Vatutin, and Rokossovsky. A fourth army under the command of General Yeremenko waited south of the city. On 19 November the Russians struck, surrounding the Sixth Army in a classic trap and catching Paulus completely by surprise. He hastily cabled Hitler for permission to withdraw from the city, but the Fuehrer refused to sanction a retreat, commanding Paulus to take Stalingrad or perish in the attempt.

Although he was adamant about refusing to allow a retreat from Stalingrad, Hitler recognized that General Paulus would have little chance of salvaging the situation if German forces did not relieve Zhukov's siege of the Wehrmacht garrison. Accordingly, he commissioned General von Manstein to gather a relief force, Army Group Don, to break through to the city and restore the German front. At the same time, Goering was ordered to supply Paulus's forces by air until ground contact could be reestablished by von Manstein.

Despite his optimistic prattling, Goering could hardly supply the minimum daily needs of Paulus's forces in Stalingrad let alone do more. This failure made it even more essential that von Manstein break through to the city, but he could not begin his mission until rail and road communications were repaired; this was not done until the middle of December, by which time winter was setting in and the relief effort was threatened by the cold weather. Despite these obstacles, von Manstein moved toward Stalingrad on 12 December, getting to within 25–30 miles of the city by the end of the month. There his army was stalled and prevented from linking up with the rest of the Sixth Army by Russian forces which had had time to dig in around the city.

Ever the loyal soldier, Paulus made no attempt to break out of the Russian encirclement. To do so would have meant disobeying Hitler's order. Since the Fuehrer showed no sign of reconsidering his previous order to stand fast, Paulus kept the Sixth Army in the city until the new year. When General Rokossovsky offered him a chance to surrender on 8 January 1943, he refused. A second offer was similarly dismissed on 24 January after Paulus failed to persuade Hitler to

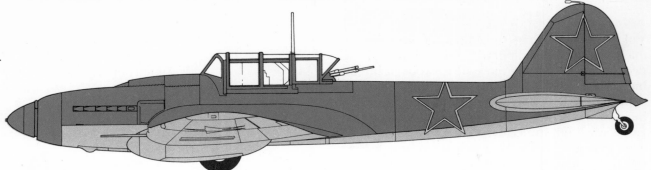

Il-2 Shturmovik. Length:
38 ft. ½ in. Span 48 ft. ½ in.
Maximum speed: 251
m.p.h. Armament:
2 × N-37 or 2 × P37
Anti-tank cannon.

Limit of Axis Powers advance
by Nov 1942

Ground reoccupied:

By 24 Aug 1943

25 Aug–23 Dec 1943

24 Dec 1943–29 Aug 1944

Advances made:

29 Aug 1944–20 Dec 1944

By May 1945

Below: Haggard and
exhausted, the Germans
fought on. **Bottom:**
General von Paulus after
his capture.

save his army. Although he warned the Fuehrer that further resistance was useless, Hitler remained adamant, replying: 'Surrender is forbidden. The Sixth Army will hold their positions to the last man and the last round . . .'.

The Sixth Army held on in Stalingrad until 31 January when Paulus, who had just been rewarded for his obedience by being promoted to the rank of Field Marshal, surrendered to the Russians when they captured his bunker. After more than four months, the battle for Stalingrad was over. In the effort to hold the city, the Germans sustained 72,000 deaths, 42,000 wounded, and 107,000 taken as prisoners of war. Rarely have so many been sacrificed for the whim of one man; rarely have a people fought so bravely for their city and their homes.

Stalingrad was one of the most decisive battles of the war. Before the battle, Germany's fortunes had reached a high point, but after the surrender, 'the paths for Hitler and his legions led only to the grave'. Churchill expressed the significance of the battle most succinctly:

This crushing disaster to the Germans ended Hitler's prodigious effort to conquer Russia by force of arms and destroy Communism by an equally odious form of totalitarian tyranny.

With the surrender of the Sixth Army in Stalingrad, the German offensive collapsed. Army Group A was pulled out of the Caucasus and the remnants of Army Group B and von Manstein's Army Group Don were regrouped in order to prevent the Russians from turning the retreat into a rout. In the north, the tide had also turned. A Russian offensive had succeeded in reopening part of the rail line between Moscow and Leningrad, and it was only a matter of time before the siege of Leningrad would be lifted. Only in the Crimea were the Germans able to hold their positions.

The victory at Stalingrad seemed to inspire the Red Army, which lost no time in pursuing the Germans to the west. By 7 February Soviet forces had captured Kursk, the original starting point of the German offensive in the Caucasus; two weeks later, they captured Kharkov. Although von Manstein managed to rally German forces and

Far left: Deployment of German armor near Kursk, the biggest tank battle in history. **Left:** German Pzkw-111 Specials advance through steppe grass set on fire by Russian shells.

Manstein was faced with an immediate Russian counter-offensive after Kursk.

German troops at Stalingrad, November 1942.

The Soviet triumph at Stalingrad was the most decisive battle of the war in Europe.

retake the latter, the German position was much diminished when the spring thaw made it impossible to continue the confrontation.

During the lull in the battle (April-July 1943), both sides reinforced their armies. Russian forces were strung along a long front stretching from Orel to Stalingrad with a bulge in the Kursk area. German forces occupied a smaller area along the Donetz river. For once, the Russian position was more exposed than the Wehrmacht's, inviting a German attack when the war was renewed in July. Zhukov and his associates expected the Germans to attack at Kursk and made preparations accordingly.

Struggle at Kursk

Von Manstein's Kursk offensive was the last German initiative of the war in Russia. The Germans amassed a large force equipped with the newest tanks and supported by a Luftwaffe armada of almost one thousand planes. The battle

began on 4 July 1943 with an assault on Russian positions near the Kursk bulge. Although the German Porsche and Panther tanks were far superior to Soviet armored vehicles, Russian tank reserves far outnumbered von Manstein's vehicles; even though the Germans inflicted losses on the Soviets at a rate approaching 2:1 tanks, the Red Army could still afford to sustain losses at this rate better than the Wehrmacht. After a week of direct confrontation, which involved as many as 3000 tanks at the height of the battle, the Germans were forced to call off the battle lest Zhukov's forces destroy what was left of the German army. On 13 July von Manstein was forced to sound the call to retreat. This time, even Hitler was forced to accept the inevitable and concur with his field commander. With the crisis brewing on the western front, he could ill afford to sacrifice what remained of Germany's armies in the Soviet Union.

After their defeat at Kursk, German forces were

The Big Three of the Teheran Conference: Stalin, Roosevelt and Churchill.

pushed back to the Russian border, but not before a last ditch attempt to hold strongpoints in the Soviet Union east of the Dnieper line. Hitler stubbornly clung to the belief that something might be salvaged from the Russian debacle. Although he recognized the need to withdraw German forces from the Kursk area, he would not accept von Manstein's advice to retreat rapidly to the Dnieper River, preferring to replace him with a 'more aggressive' commander, General Walter Model. However, by the time von Manstein was removed in February 1944, the situation was hopeless.

Had Hitler followed von Manstein's advice, it might have still been possible to prepare adequate defensive positions along the Dnieper, but by waiting till November to authorise a retreat to the river, he forfeited whatever chance the Germans might have had to establish a strong position. On 6 November, the Russians took Kiev and were pressed west toward Zhitomir, an important rail junction and German communication center. As winter approached, the Germans were still retreating; in January von Manstein was fighting in the Pripet marshes while further south, the Soviets pushed toward the Black Sea. On February 7, Nikopol fell to the Russians. The following week, they took Krivoy Rog. By the end of February, the Germans had been chased back to the Bug River, and when Model arrived to take command of what was left of the German army in the south, the Wehrmacht had been pushed back across the Pruth River into Rumania.

On the northern front, in January 1944, Russian forces crossed Lake Ilmen and moved north across

The Russian sacrifice equalled the German challenge.

Below left: General Model took command of a shattered German army in the South. **Below:** Silent testimony to the Soviet victory.

the adjacent swamps. while other Russian units established a beachhead just west of Leningrad at Oranienburg. By the end of the month, both groups converged on Leningrad forcing the Germans to abandon their 900-day siege of that city. The Germans were chased from Leningrad to the Luga River, from the Luga to Lake Peipus, and from Lake Peipus to Lake Pskov where they maintained a defensive position until May 1944.

With the Caucasus lost and the northern front deteriorating, it was only a matter of time before the Germans were forced to retreat from the Crimea. The Seventeenth Army had successfully withstood Soviet assaults on the Crimea but soon even this force had to be withdrawn, in April 1944.

At the Teheran Conference (November 1943), Stalin agreed to launch an offensive against Germany in 1944 that would coincide with the long awaited invasion of France. He kept his word; as Anglo-American forces were ferried across the Channel and established their beachheads along the Normandy coast, the Red Army prepared to carry its drive against the Germans into eastern Europe and Germany's satellite states. Two and a half weeks after D-Day in France, the Soviets struck in Belorussia.

For this new offensive Stalin's commanders massed more than 100 divisions. The Germans, with a line of defense stretching from the Gulf of Finland to the Black Sea, were ill prepared to contain such a force, and when the Soviets struck the Wehrmacht caved in and collapsed. By the

ВОИНЫ КРАСНОЙ АРМИИ!
КРЕПЧЕ УДАРЫ ПО ВРАГУ! ИЗГОНИМ НЕМЕЦКО-
ФАШИСТСКИХ МЕРЗАВЦЕВ С НАШЕЙ РОДНОЙ ЗЕМЛИ!

Right: Russian poster encourages Soviet troops to drive out the German invader. **Opposite top:** A German soldier crushed by tanks during retreat. **Opposite left:** Russian soldiers dance in the streets of Lvov in the first days of its liberation. **Opposite bottom:** German Panzer forces lost their numerical superiority to the Russians in the southern sector of the front.

end of June the Germans were pushed back to a line stretching from Riga to Rumania but even this was too wide a front to defend. When Zhukov moved against General Busch's Army Group Centre in Belorussia, Hitler ordered Busch to stand fast at all costs, defending German positions to the last man. This policy was to have disastrous consequences.

The Soviets punched a 250-mile hole through Busch's line, moved forces through the hole and trapped Army Group Center. Busch could not escape from the encirclement and when the battle was over on 28 June the Germans had lost 350,000 men, an even greater number than were lost in the Battle of Stalingrad. They could ill afford to sustain such a defeat, for their forces were already spread paper thin. With the loss of Army Group Center, there was little chance of stopping the Russians; it could only be a matter of time before they reached the German border.

By the end of July the Soviets had taken Brest and Lublin, and were poised on the outskirts of Warsaw; Army Group North had been isolated in Estonia and Russian forces were ready to take Riga, while to the south, Lvov had been taken by General Koniev on 27 July, his forces marching north toward Warsaw during the last days of the month. The Russians could have taken Warsaw at the beginning of August but preferred instead to wait until the beginning of September, by which time the Germans themselves had dealt with Polish underground forces and razed the city.

Stalin's failure to relieve the Poles in the liberation of their capital excited the anger of the other Allied leaders but served Soviet interests; by the time Russian forces entered the city, the Germans had done their dirty work for them. There was little love lost between the Russians and the Poles and Stalin's refusal to press the attack against the Wehrmacht did nothing to improve this relationship. His explanation that the strength of the German counter-attack precluded an early move into the capital pleased few and satisfied no one. Nevertheless, Stalin was quite willing to postpone the defeat of Germany in order to extract a pound of flesh from the Poles; there would be time enough to tighten the noose around Hitler's neck.

CHAPTER FIFTEEN
The Tide Turns in the Pacific

Within six months after their attack on Pearl Harbor, the Japanese had succeeded in creating a Greater East Asia Co-Prosperity Sphere through force. Their original plans called for a defensive strategy, to cement their gains and protect against an eventual Allied counterattack. Understandably, however, Japanese leaders (especially in the navy) were reluctant to give up the initiative they had grasped so boldly and so successfully achieved.

Although the attack on Pearl Harbor had been a success in many ways, the American carrier force had not been incapacitated. It was entirely possible for the United States Navy to use these ships in an attempt to block further Japanese efforts and to eventually augment them for a strike against Japan itself. Unless and until this remnant of the American navy was destroyed, Japan's position in the Pacific would not be secure. Consequently, the ranking officers of the Japanese Navy proposed to expand the Pacific naval offensive in a final effort to neutralize the United States fleet. Specifically they proposed to extend Japan's defense perimeter through a campaign in

the area of the Coral Sea and a second attack on Midway Island, and lure the United States Navy into a battle in the Aleutians where it could be destroyed once and for all. After considerable debate, the Imperial Government approved the plan in April 1942.

The Battle of the Coral Sea was to be a combined aerial, land, and naval effort. Japanese ground and aerial units were assembled at Rabaul in New Britain while the fleet gathered off the island of Truk in the Caroline Island chain. On 3 May 1942 Japanese forces were landed on Tulagi, a small island in the Solomon chain, taking the island with no difficulty as its Australian garrison had already been withdrawn. Thanks to intelligence reports, the Allies were prepared for the attack; having deceived the Japanese at Tulagi into assuming that they would have an easy victory, what remained of America's Pacific Fleet prepared to do battle.

Admiral Nimitz had ordered his forces southward from Pearl Harbor as soon as he discovered that the Japanese were up to something. His fleet,

Admiral Chester W. Nimitz, US Commander-in-Chief, Pacific (CINCPAC).

Task Force 16 as seen from the flight deck of the USS *Enterprise* in the Coral Sea.

B.17.F. Length: 74 ft. 8.9 in.
Span: 103 ft. 9.38 in.
Maximum speed: 325
m.p.h. Armament:
7 × .30 machine guns,
9 × .50 machine guns.
Weight: 35,728 lbs. empty.

limited to two aircraft carriers (*Lexington* and *Yorktown*) and several cruisers, was steaming toward the Solomons when the Japanese landed at Tulagi but was still far from the area. *Yorktown* did not get near enough to the Coral Sea to launch an attack on Japanese ships until the following day, 4 May, and even this effort failed; planes from the *Yorktown* sank only one Japanese destroyer. Indeed, *Yorktown* was lucky to escape Japanese retaliation after having revealed its presence.

By 7 May the two fleets were converging and Japanese search planes spotted the Americans. They immediately opened fire, sinking a tanker and its destroyer escort. On the mistaken belief that a carrier and a cruiser had been sunk, the Japanese commander, Admiral Takagi, continued to stalk the Americans, sending several dozen planes aloft from his flagship. Of the twenty-seven planes that were sent, twenty did not return. Meanwhile, the Americans were also searching in the dark for their Japanese counterparts.

Planes from the *Yorktown* went out on the evening of the 7th to attack Japanese forces in the Port Moresby area. Although Admiral Fletcher was mistaken in believing that he would find the major part of the Japanese fleet in this area, the raid was not a complete loss since the light carrier *Shoho* was sunk in the fray.

Battle of the Coral Sea

On 8 May the two sides met in strength, and the Battle of the Coral Sea was decided in a contest which lasted the whole day. When they met that morning, both sides were more or less evenly matched. The Japanese task force consisted of two carriers, *Zuikaku* and *Shokaku*, four heavy cruisers, and six destroyers. The American fleet consisted of two carriers *Lexington* and *Yorktown,* five cruisers, and seven destroyers. Japan's carriers housed 121 aircraft, the American's 122.

The Battle of the Coral Sea was decided by aircraft, not by artillery barrages or naval man-

euvers; as such, it was the first major naval encounter in history in which air power played the major role. Neither fleet saw the other; neither fleet fired upon the other. Guns were aimed at enemy aircraft not enemy ships. Still, the toll in ships lost was heavy: when the battle was over, two American aircraft carriers were disabled, one beyond repair (*Lexington*) while the Japanese lost the *Shokaku*, which was disabled after several direct bomb hits. More important, perhaps, was the loss of aircraft. Here the Americans fared better than the Japanese, destroying almost all of the planes on the *Shokaku* and *Zuikaku* while losing only seventy-six of their own.

After the battle both sides limped away, nursing their wounds. Although neither had won a clear-cut victory, the Americans had some consolation in the fact that they had been able to thwart Japan's efforts to capture Port Moresby and cut the supply line from Hawaii to Australia. This was no small accomplishment, since they were still reeling from the earlier Japanese strike against Pearl Harbor. If nothing else, the experience in the Coral Sea was a leavening one for the United States, giving the commanders and men of the Pacific Fleet new confidence to pursue their enemy. In that sense, along with the Battle for Midway, the Battle of the Coral Sea marked a turning point in the Pacific War.

While the Battle of the Coral Sea was still in progress, the Japanese prepared to take Midway Island. According to the plan for this venture, approved by the Imperial Military Headquarters on 5 May, a huge armada was to be assembled off the coast of Japan and converge on Midway early in June. The Japanese task force consisted of almost two hundred ships, including eight carriers, eleven battleships, twenty-two cruisers, sixty-five destroyers, and twenty-one submarines plus twelve troop transports and 600 planes. Another task force of eleven ships (three troop transports, two light carriers, two heavy cruisers, and four

P.51.D. Length: 32 ft. 2⅝ in.
Span 37.03 ft. Maximum
speed: 401 m.p.h.
Armament: 6 × .50
machine guns.

battleships) was to be dispatched to the Aleutians where the Japanese hoped to divert and trap the American fleet.

American intelligence reports, however, saved the day once again; Admiral Nimitz received decoded communications between Tokyo and the Japanese fleet, learned of Japan's plan to seize Midway and took appropriate measures to prevent it. No effort was made to engage the Japanese off the Aleutians. Nimitz husbanded his resources and prepared to send the Pacific Fleet to the Midway area.

Although Nimitz knew where the Japanese planned to strike, his major concern was how to cope with the vast armada assembled for that purpose. There were only two carriers available for the battle, *Enterprise* and *Hornet,* and even the addition of the *Yorktown* after its rapid repair did not alter the situation very much, since the Japanese task force had at least eight carriers, to say nothing of the eleven battleships in the armada. The Pacific Fleet had no battleships thanks to the destruction wrought by the attack on Pearl Harbor six months earlier. In contrast with the even balance of forces in the Battle of the Coral Sea, the Battle of Midway was a contest between two grossly disproportionate fleets. That the United States held its own was due to the foreknowledge of the Japanese plan and the skillful deployment of limited resources.

The American fleet was ordered to a station north of Midway, out of the range of Japan's carrier-based reconnaissance craft. Thus, the Japanese approached Midway and prepared to launch their attack, completely unaware of the presence of the three American carriers. Nimitz, on the other hand, had been able to follow the movement of the Japanese armada through intercepted messages and reconnaissance aircraft based on the island. As the Japanese fleet drew near to the point of attack, the Americans moved in to launch an attack of their own.

On 4 June Admiral Nagumo ordered 108 carrier-based aircraft to attack military installations on Midway. An additional 100 planes were sent aloft to search for and destroy any Allied aircraft sighted in the area. The first raid was devestating, and the admiral immediately ordered a second attack aimed at knocking out aerodromes on the island. Shortly after Japanese fighter-

Top: The destruction of the aircraft carrier USS *Lexington:* 8 May 1942.
Above: Last stages of the destruction of the *Lexington.* All hands abandoned ship and not a man was lost.

Survivors from the *Lexington.*

Top: The Japanese scored a direct hit on the USS *Yorktown.* **Above:** Fleet Admiral Ernest J. King, Commander-in-Chief and Chief of Naval Operations. **Right:** The deck of the sinking *Yorktown.*

bombers were refueled and sent up to carry out this second strike, American ships were spotted some 200 miles northeast of Midway.

At first Nagumo believed that the American force was limited to two cruisers with a destroyer escort, but later reports confirmed the presence of at least one aircraft carrier in the group. This presented a problem. With most of his carrier-based aircraft flying over Midway, Nagumo could do little to counter an American attack on his ships unless he changed course; to do so, however, would jeopardize the raid over the island. In haste, Nagumo chose to risk sacrificing the Midway raid in favour of saving his task force. This choice proved to be correct, for at the very moment when the admiral ordered his fleet to change course, the Americans were zeroing in on him with dive bombers from their carriers. When the first group of American planes reached the area where Nagumo's task force was supposed to be, it was not there; by the time the Japanese fleet was spotted, Nagumo was ready to attack.

The first wave of American dive-bombers was practically destroyed, the Japanese shooting down thirty-five of the forty-one planes. A second attack proved more successful. Two minutes after the last of the six surviving aircraft left the vicinity of Nagumo's task force, thirty-seven more planes, launched from the *Enterprise* and *Yorktown,* found their mark. Not suspecting the presence of more than one American aircraft carrier, Nagumo and his lieutenants had assumed that the worst was over and were totally unprepared for the second wave of attackers. Nagumo's flagship, the carrier *Akagi,* was hit and the ship was abandoned shortly thereafter. The carriers *Kaga* and *Soryu* were also hit and destroyed. Only the *Hiryu* remained intact, and she was able to retaliate by sending planes to destroy the *Yorktown* before she was destroyed. By day's end, the Americans had mauled Nagumo's fleet with the loss of only one major ship.

The destruction of Nagumo's carriers ended the attack on Midway. Although his superior, Admiral Yamamoto, considered recalling the Japanese task force in the Aleutians and engaging the American fleet, this idea was quickly abandoned; on 5 June the Battle of Midway was called off, and the Japanese fleet steamed off to the west. Thus ended the most important naval confrontation of the Pacific War.

The victory in the Battle of Midway proclaimed a momentum which Allied military leaders were anxious to exploit. Although the defeat of Germany still had the highest priority, Nimitz and MacArthur were eager to take the offensive if a plan could be devised which would not hamper the effort in Europe. Both men were agreed that the time was right for launching a counter-offensive, but how this could be done, where it would take place, and who would command the venture remained unresolved questions.

Nimitz, reflecting the position of the Navy, was eager to have his service play the major role in any new offensive. He was supported by Admiral King, Commander-in-Chief of the United States Fleet, who had been reluctant to accept the importance of Roosevelt's 'Germany first' strategy which placed the Navy in a supporting but

Admiral Nagumo, Japanese commander in the Battle of Midway.

Below: Japanese aircraft carrier *Hiryu* off Midway; it was the only one remaining intact after the battle.
Bottom: General Douglas MacArthur of the US Army, Commander-in-Chief of Allied Forces in the Southwest Pacific, on an inspection tour.

secondary role. General MacArthur, on the other hand, was anxious to avenge the earlier defeat of the Army, and would hear of no plan in which his forces did not play at least an equal role with those under Nimitz's command.

To avoid protracted debate about jurisdiction over the proposed counteroffensive, a compromise was worked out by the Joint Chiefs of Staff and presented to Nimitz and MacArthur on 2 July. According to this plan, the offensive would be carried out in three stages. During phase one Nimitz would be responsible for the occupation of the eastern Solomons, particularly Tulagi and Guadalcanal, and the Santa Cruz Islands. Phase two would see MacArthur's forces completing the occupation of the Solomons and landing along the New Guinea coast. In the final phase MacArthur's forces would advance to Rabaul, Japan's major base in the southwest Pacific.

Like most compromises, this satisfied no one. MacArthur balked at the over-cautiousness of the scheme. Nimitz resented the role assigned MacArthur's forces during the second and third stage of the operation. Nevertheless, they had no choice but to accept the compromise if there was to be any positive action in the Pacific theatre; their superior officers would not tolerate a prolonged conflict between egocentric field commanders.

While Allied leaders ironed out the details of the counter-offensive, American intelligence reported a Japanese build-up on Guadalcanal, including the construction of an air strip at Lunga Point. If the Japanese succeeded in fortifying the island, it would be difficult if not impossible to execute the American offensive. It was necessary, therefore, to commence action immediately and to focus attention on Guadalcanal as opposed to other islands in the Solomon and Santa Cruz chains. Nimitz modified his plans and prepared to land Marines on the island as soon as possible.

Responsibility for coordinating the landings on Guadalcanal was given to Vice-Admiral Robert Ghormley and Rear Admiral Frank Fletcher. Major General Alexander Vandegrift commanded the 1st Marine Division which was to make the landing on 7 August. On the morning of the 7th, the fleet gathered off Guadalcanal and began an all day bombardment of supposed Japanese installations on the island. Some 10,000 Marines were put safely ashore later in the day. The landing was unopposed since the majority of the Japanese troops on the island were construction workers who fled into the jungle before the Marines' advances. A simultaneous landing on Tulagi proved equally successful.

The Japanese responded to the American landing by attempting to reinforce their own garrison on Guadalcanal. Admiral Mikawa, commander of the Japanese garrison at Rabaul, immediately sent a task force of seven ships (five heavy cruisers, two light cruisers) to survey the situation and engage the American force under Admiral Fletcher's command. The Japanese successfully navigated the 'Slot' between the chains of the Solomons and surprised the American fleet off Savo Island on the evening of 7 August, sinking four American cruisers and badly damaging a fifth before withdrawing. Although they failed to follow up this triumph by attacking troop

Left: US Marines clamber down the side of a transport as they approach Guadalcanal. **Right:** The Japanese underestimated the size and ferocity of the US Marines in Guadalcanal.

ships further south, the destruction of a substantial part of Fletcher's task force forced the Americans to withdraw their ships and aided the reinforcement of Japanese forces on Guadalcanal.

The Japanese underestimated the size of the American force on Guadalcanal, and consequently did not adequately reinforce their own garrison on the island, although they could have done so at the time. It was believed that the Marine force landed near Lunga Point numbered no more than 2000 men and that 4000 Japanese troops in addition to the garrison of 2200 already on the island would be sufficient to dispose of the Americans. Thus two troop convoys carrying approximately 3000 men were despatched from Rabaul on 17 August. When they landed near Lunga Point on the 18th, they were decimated by the Americans who outnumbered them several times over. A second Japanese landing several days later was hardly more successful.

The Japanese command at Rabaul was also anxious to lure the remnants of Admiral Fletcher's task force into a naval confrontation. When the second band of reinforcements left Rabaul on 19 August, their troop convoy was accompanied by a large force of carriers and battleships. Mikawa intended using one of the carriers, the *Ryujo*, as bait in the hope that Fletcher would pursue the craft into a trap from which there would be no escape. Fortunately Allied intelligence once again came to the rescue and what had been planned as an American rout was turned into a modest victory for the Allies.

Admiral Ghormley plotted the movement of the Japanese task force, moving three carriers (*Enterprise, Saratoga* and *Wasp*) south of Guadalcanal. The *Ryujo* was sighted and destroyed on 24 August and two additional Japanese carriers were seen; when they launched their planes, the Americans were prepared. The Japanese lost over eighty planes in the effort to sink the task force while only one American ship, the *Enterprise*, had

been hit when the engagement was broken off on the evening of the 24th.

After the disastrous attempt to dislodge the Americans from Lunga Point, Japanese authorities stepped up the effort to reinforce the remaining Japanese forces on Guadalcanal. The 'Tokyo Express' brought reinforcements to the island on a regular nightly basis during late August and September; by the beginning of October, the Japanese had brought their troop strength on Guadalcanal to over 22,000 and numerically were just about equal to the Marine garrison.

The Japanese launched a second offensive against the Americans on 24 October, this time moving overland through the dense jungle and tropical forest. The result, however, proved no different from their first attempt. After sustaining heavy casualties, the attack was broken off pending further reinforcement. A third attack was beaten back early in November. This was the last Japanese land offensive on Guadalcanal; by the end of November their forces had been depleted while the Americans had been steadily reinforced and now enjoyed a numerical superiority which permitted them to take the offensive. Although the Japanese stubbornly continued to fight, they were short of supplies and suffering from malaria. It would only be a matter of time before they were cleared from the island.

More important than the fighting on Guadalcanal was the naval confrontation between the United States and Japan in the waters surrounding the island during October and November. On 26 October the two fleets clashed in the Battle of the Santa Cruz Islands. Two weeks later they met again in a three-day battle (13–15 November) which has become known as the Naval Battle of Guadalcanal. Both navies sustained heavy losses in these contests but on balance, the United States Navy emerged victorious. Rather than risk another confrontation with the Americans, the Japanese government ordered the evacuation of

Guadalcanal on 4 January 1943. After more than four months of struggle and the loss of over 25,000 men and more than a dozen capital ships, the Battle for Guadalcanal was over.

The New Guinea Campaign

Having disposed of the Japanese in the southern Solomons, it was MacArthur's turn to shoulder the burden of the counter-offensive. While the battle for Guadalcanal was still in progress, his American and Australian forces had begun a campaign in the Papuan peninsula of New Guinea to prevent the Japanese from seizing Port Moresby, thus interrupting Allied supply lines and disrupting industrial production in Australia. This contest, a prerequisite for the assault on Rabaul, was still in progress when the Battle for Guadalcanal ended. Until it was concluded, there could be no pressing on with the counter-offensive.

To reach Port Moresby, the Japanese would have to either take the city through an amphibious operation or advance across the Owen Stanley mountains from Lae and Salamaua. Since an attempt at the former had been repulsed in July 1942, the Japanese were forced to adopt the latter approach, i.e., a trek through the mountains. Although the peaks were high and the terrain rugged, the Japanese succeeded in crossing the mountains through narrow foot paths, and on 12 August they took Kokoda and its small airstrip. From Kokoda they tried to seize Allied installations at Milne Bay but were pushed back instead to the Buna-Gona area.

A joint Australian-American force sought to dislodge the Japanese from their foothold on the northern coast of Papua in November, but the Japanese had dug in and built bunkers out of earth reinforced with sheet iron or steel drums. Although they lacked supplies, food, and medicine, they were able to keep the Allies at bay for over two months. MacArthur was so distressed by this that at the end of November he personally

ordered a change in the Allied command in this area in the hope that more spirited commanders would end the engagement so that the Allies could get on with the assault on Rabaul. Still, the Japanese were able to hold their position until the beginning of 1943; the last men were withdrawn on 22 January.

With Guadalcanal and the Papuan peninsula secured, the Allies could move on to Rabaul, Japan's major station in the southwest Pacific. In the compromise plan of 2 July 1942, the Joint Chiefs of Staff had proposed that the assault would follow immediately upon the seizure of the Solomons and the neutralization of Japanese positions in New Guinea. Although New Guinea had been partially secured by the end of 1942, of the Solomons, only Guadalcanal was controlled by the Allies. So before the attack on Japan's primary base could begin, the offensive in the Solomon Islands would have to be completed. The fierce resistance put up by the Japanese in Guadalcanal and New Guinea had shown, however, that this part of the campaign would take longer than had been anticipated and require a greater expenditure of force than had been originally allotted. In short, it was necessary to rewrite plans for the completion of the offensive.

In plotting a revision of their scheme the Joint Chiefs of Staff again encountered the problem of securing the cooperation of both the Army and Navy. Neither MacArthur nor Admiral Halsey had enough men to execute the scheme alone, nor would a one-track approach to Rabaul have been in the best interests of the Allies. Even if MacArthur or Halsey could have engineered an attack without the cooperation of the other, a two-pronged assault with the eventual convergence of Allied forces on Rabaul would confuse the Japanese and had a greater chance of success.

Operation Cartwheel, the revised plan for the attack on Rabaul, called for a dual effort. General MacArthur's Southwest Pacific forces were to

Seen from the flight deck of the USS *Enterprise* during the Battle of Santa Cruz: US destroyer rips off a round of anti-aircraft fire to protect the rear of the *Enterprise*.

Right: Paratroops and C-47s pave the way for one of the leapfrogging campaigns on the north coast of New Guinea.

Right: Admiral William F. (Bull) Halsey with Vice-Admiral John S. McCain aboard Halsey's flagship USS *New Jersey*.
Far right: Australian patrol in the jungle of New Guinea.

attack and take the Trobriand Islands, the Lae-Salamaua area in New Guinea and the western-most portion of New Britain, the island on which which Rabaul was located. Meanwhile, Admiral Halsey's South Pacific force was to seize the rest of the Solomon Islands, particularly Bougainville, from which they would be ready to attack New Britain. Both ventures would require amphibious assaults supported by aerial drops, following which new airfields would be hacked out of the jungle. The terrain would be difficult, the weather un-cooperative, and the risk of malaria and other tropical diseases immense.

Preparations for Operation Cartwheel began in March 1943, but the offensive was not launched until 30 June, when forces commanded by Halsey and MacArthur landed simultaneously at Wood-lark, Kiriwina, Nassau Bay (New Guinea), and New Georgia. The Trobriands were taken with no difficulty but MacArthur encountered stiff resistance when the landing party at Nassau Bay pushed on toward Lae and Salamaua. It was two weeks before the Americans could link up with Australian forces pushing toward Salamaua from the south, and even then the Japanese were not easily dislodged. It was only through a ruse that MacArthur succeeded in throwing the Japanese off balance and this involved the capture of Lae. Salamaua was not taken until 16 September, but from that point on, the New Guinea campaign proceeded as planned.

Admiral Halsey's South Pacific force encountered equally stiff resistance in the campaign in the Solomons. The landings at New Georgia were carried off without incident, but the Americans soon came under heavy fire from the Japanese defenders. The purpose of the landing in New Georgia was to capture the Japanese airbase at Munda Point, from which American aircraft could then be sent over Bougainville. A direct assault on the air base had been ruled out as too dangerous, so Halsey and his lieutenant, Rear Admiral Richard Kelly Turner, proposed a series of landings followed by an overland trek to the Munda Point base, a difficult task due to the rugged terrain and dense jungle cover. Munda Point did not fall to the Allies until 5 August, thirty-six days after the first landings were made.

New Georgia was secured by mid-August, but the campaign had proved more costly and time-consuming than the Joint Chiefs had anticipated. If the Japanese continued to offer as much resistance as they had in New Georgia and New Guinea, the offensive would drag on indefinitely and Allied casualties would soar. Shortly after the New Georgia campaign was concluded the Joint Chiefs unveiled a new scheme.

The alternative plan called for Allied troops to leapfrog over or around the fiercely defended Japanese bases. By substituting a flexible policy the Allies would gain valuable time and save lives. Japanese bases which they had passed would not prove menacing, as the garrisons would be isolated; once the Allies established forward air bases in front of the sites, they could be neutralized through aerial attack.

Leapfrogging was begun immediately and proved so successful that the principle was ultimately applied in the decision to skip over the Japanese base on Rabaul in favor of a less costly landing elsewhere. But this decision was not made until the end of 1943, and in the meantime the Allies faced some hard fighting, particularly on Bougainville, where they landed at the beginning of November.

The Bougainville landing was made at Empress

Left: Native stretcher bearers rest in a coconut grove while carrying American wounded from the front lines near Buna.

Far left: Australians take cover against Japanese shelling on New Guinea.
Left: US soldiers fire into a Japanese dugout near Buna.

Bay on 1 November. Halsey intended building a bridgehead deep enough to allow construction of an air field which could be used to attack Japanese bases at Rabaul and elsewhere in the South Pacific, and then to neutralize the Japanese garrison on the island. Although the Japanese had as many as 55,000 men on Bougainville, they were located at the southern end of the island and did not pose an immediate threat to the landings; when Halsey's Marines tried to expand their perimeter, however, they met with strong resistance.

Bougainville was too close to New Britain for the Japanese to accept the American landing lightly, nor could they permit Halsey to supplement his original landing force unmolested. Accordingly on 2 November, the day after the first landing, a Japanese task force of seven ships was sent to the area to prevent the landings. Halsey ordered Admiral Spruance to engage this task force, and on 5 November Spruance's Fifth Fleet attacked the Japanese, forcing them to abandon the waters between Rabaul and Bougainville. From then on the Japanese Navy did not menace the Allied operation on Bougainville. Although Japanese forces continued to occupy the southern portion of the island, they were unable to dislodge the Americans from their beachhead which had been expanded to a ten-mile wide enclave by the end of the year.

After Bougainville, Operation Cartwheel entered its final phase. Rabaul had been the original goal of the Allied advance, but as the year ended, the Chiefs of Staff decided that successful operations elsewhere had neutralized Rabaul and that it would not be necessary to attack the installation. Instead, a minor landing would be made to secure an air field on the western tip of New Britain and the Allies would increase their forces on New Guinea in order to clear out the remaining Japanese pockets on that large island.

Divisions of the United States Sixth Army landed in western New Britain at the end of December and quickly succeeded in establishing a beachhead and constructing an airfield. The Japanese, whose forces were concentrated on the other end of the island, hardly resisted the landings. Additional units of the Sixth Army were then ordered to New Guinea where they made landings at Saidor on 2 January 1944 and linked up with Australian forces on the island. The Huon Peninsula was cleared by the end of April and the Japanese were in retreat. At this point, with New Guinea secured and Rabaul neutralized, Operation Cartwheel was complete.

Next, Allied leaders began to plan an attack on the Philippines. The Admiralty, Marshall, and Gilbert islands had been successfully occupied, Truk and Rabaul neutralized. Only some cleaning up chores remained in the southwest Pacific. MacArthur believed that he could complete these by the end of the summer and begin an invasion of Mindanao, the largest of the southern Philippine islands, by November 1944. He was particularly anxious to return to the islands to avenge the humiliation suffered by the Americans and their Filipino comrades some two years earlier. It was with pleasure, therefore, that he prepared for the attack.

CHAPTER SIXTEEN
Defeat in Southeast Asia

By the end of May 1942, six months after the war began with the West, the goals that the Japanese high command had set for itself had all been accomplished. On the Allied side, however, the picture was thoroughly depressing. All but the French had lost their empires in Southeast Asia and with these, substantial amounts of natural resources that would be sorely needed to fight the war ahead. When Allied leaders decided on a Europe first strategy, they made an initial defeat in Asia inevitable.

Almost immediately after their first defeat, the colonial powers began to plan for the reconquest of their former territories. The British were primarily concerned with the recovery of Burma as part of an overall plan to recover their empire. On this basis, all of Burma would have to be recaptured and used as a base to attack Thailand, Malaya, and finally the Netherlands East Indies. To the Americans, however, this plan meant moving away from one of their major goals, the supplying of Chinese Nationalist armies. As an alternative, they suggested a more modest drive through north Burma in order to sustain Chinese forces and enable them to launch coordinated land and air attacks on the Japanese. These basic differences in strategic thinking were to plague Allied planners throughout the war.

With only limited measures available for Southeast Asia, the British, despite their strategic priorities, could make no more than a tentative stab eastward on the Arakan front in 1942. The backbone of this thrust was formed by the very troops that had already been defeated in Burma, since the few reinforcements allocated to Southeast Asia were still in India, untrained in jungle warfare. The drive could not be sustained; the Burma Road remained closed, and China was completely isolated except for one remote route to Russia. The airlift over the 'Hump' kept China in the war but was insufficient to meet her needs.

Plans for establishing a Southeast Asia Command (SEAC) had been laid during the Casablanca Conference in January 1943 and the Washington meeting (code name: 'Trident') in May of the same year, but it was not until the Quebec Conference between Winston Churchill and Franklin D. Roosevelt in August that a commander was designated and the command officially confirmed. Since Southeast Asia was considered to be a British responsibility it was agreed that an Englishman would command with American representation, and Lord Louis Mountbatten was appointed Supreme Commander.

The American representative to SEAC was Lieutenant General Joseph Stilwell. He wore several hats. As a member of Mountbatten's staff, he was Deputy Commander of SEAC. He was also Commanding General in the China-Burma-India theatre of operations (CBI) with command of all American forces in the region, Chief of Staff to Generalissimo Chiang Kai-shek, thus commanding all Chinese forces in Southeast Asia, and in addition he managed Lend-Lease aid to China. When General Slim became commander of the British 14th Army (subordinate to the 11th Army commanded by General Sir George Giffard), Stilwell's forces should have come under the command of Giffard, if not under Slim. But Stilwell, in his capacity as the commander of Chinese and American forces and as Chief of Staff to Chiang refused to do so. As Deputy Supreme Commander of SEAC, he was second only to Mountbatten himself; eventually his area of operations in northern Burma was organized into the Northern Combat Area Command (NCAC),

Above: Lord Louis Mountbatten, Supreme Commander of Southeast Asia Command.

Left: Lieutenant-General Sir William Slim.

Opposite top: The Japanese conquest of Burma was complete by mid-1942. **Opposite far left:** The British destroyed most of the major bridges in Burma before they evacuated. **Opposite right:** Vinegar Joe Stilwell, US representative to SEAC, enjoying his breakfast of C-rations on Christmas morning in Burma, 1943.

Merrill's Marauders enter Burma, accompanied by Burmese volunteers.

but it operated as a quasi-autonomous command, dependent upon the 14th Army for logistical and administrative supply and keeping Slim advised of its activities, but retaining near-independent freedom of action.

Meanwhile the Japanese were building up their organization and strength. By November 1943, the Japanese Army, Southern Region had the following formations under its command: the Burma Area Army, based in Rangoon with four divisions under 15th Army and two others on the Arakan front under 28th Army; the Siam Garrison Army (Bangkok) with two divisions; and the 25th Army in the Netherlands East Indies with

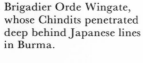

Brigadier Orde Wingate, whose Chindits penetrated deep behind Japanese lines in Burma.

seven divisions. In addition the Indo-China Garrison Army in Saigon had approximately three divisions, while the 3rd Air Army provided air support (approximately 400 aircraft) for the entire region, with headquarters in Singapore and one of its two divisions located at Rangoon and Moulmein.

Assuming that a Japanese division numbered 10,000 men, there were at least 60,000 combat troops deployed in Burma alone with another 100,000 men in the Southeast Asia operational area. Four of the six divisions in Burma had participated in the original conquest of the country. Now, though each had contributed units to Pacific campaigns, they were still in first-class fighting condition and had the psychological advantage of facing enemies that they had defeated before.

Mountbatten and Slim had a monumental task before them – that of getting the defeated troops into fighting trim. The retreat across Burma into India had obviously weakened the men physically, but the psychological effects were probably worse. Tired, hungry, beset with the constant fear of being cut off by the enemy, the troops had replaced an earlier contempt for the fighting qualities of the Japanese with overawe. The Japanese infantryman seemed almost super-human, able to survive in the jungle, outflank the British, live on a bag of rice, slip into friendly lines to snipe or to stab and then disappear. The short-range Arakan offensive in mid-1943 merely served to accentuate the difficulties in trying to defeat an experienced enemy in impossible terrain. In addition, the British commanders had to contend with a serious tropical disease problem, especially scrub typhus, which resulted in a number of fatalities.

In November 1943 plans were made to start offensive operations against the Japanese in Burma in late 1943-early 1944. Basically SEAC's job was to tie up as many Japanese troops as possible to prevent their employment in the Pacific, and to reopen land routes to China. At first the Combined Chiefs of Staff had favored a companion amphibious assault, but their landing craft were withdrawn to Europe to support the Italian and Normandy operations.

On land, the Allied plan called for an attack on the central front in Arakan accompanied by a northern thrust by Stilwell's Chinese and a newly arrived American formation, later to be known as Merrill's Marauders. Stilwell's group would link up with an attack southward from China by Chinese forces to open the Ledo road to Yunnan. This two-pronged attack once again reflected the basic difference between British and American thinking. To the Americans, the northern advance was vital for securing the route to China. To the British, the job would be better performed by the central front attack which would lead to the well-established old Burma Road while helping to secure Mandalay and Rangoon and getting back all of Burma for the British as well. The result was, of course, a compromise.

Wingate's Chindits

The narrative would be incomplete without mentioning the Long Range Penetration Groups (LRP) of the remarkable Brigadier Orde Wingate. Wingate, who had given the Italians an extremely hard time in Ethiopia, advocated the landing of large forces behind enemy lines, there to harass their lines of communications and disrupt their logistical network. He had already led one raid in 1942, but the group was not evacuated by air and had to make it out in small groups; over one-third of the original force did not survive. Militarily it had been a failure, but psychologically it had made the Japanese nervous about rear area security.

Now, with increased air transport capability and improved techniques, Wingate was ready to try again, but he received only a tepid response despite Mountbatten's personal enthusiasm. Field Marshal Slim had reservations because he was convinced that the Japanese, unlike the Italians would not be bullied into a withdrawal. If they fought back, a force deep in enemy territory would have to evacuate by air prematurely, thereby disrupting other plans, or be gradually annihilated. Also, the mere act of transporting Wingate's *Chindits* would use more aircraft and fuel than Slim considered reasonable for the expected dividends. In the end Wingate was granted an airlift but not as many men as he had wanted. Nevertheless he eventually got 12,000 men into Burma where they acted as flank security for Stilwell's NCAC attack as well as disturbing the enemy's peace of mind.

The Americans had a counterpart for Wingate. The 5307th Composite Unit, variously known as the 'Galahad' Force, the 5307th Provisional Regiment and 'Merrill's Marauders' (after their commander, Brigadier General Frank Merrill), were Stilwell's Long Range Penetration Group, but they entered Burma by land. It was a gallant force of volunteers; by the end of the war, casualties from combat and illness made it virtually non-existent as a fighting outfit.

Meanwhile the Japanese were doing some assessing of their own. The first *Chindit* operation in 1942, while not quite alarming them, had pointed out disturbing possibilities for the future, and the first Arakan campaign, abortive as it was, at least proved that the British were thinking about

Left: The RAF drops supplies to the Chindits in northern Burma. **Below:** Members of Wingate's Jungle Penetration Force. **Bottom:** Gurkhas and men of the West Yorkshire Regiment advance under cover of forward tanks.

Burma. The war in the Pacific was not going well. First Guadalcanal, then Attu in the Aleutians, Tarawa, New Guinea and other south and central Pacific Islands had fallen to American forces. The sea battles of Midway and the Coral Sea had turned back the once-invincible Japanese Navy and the island garrisons in the Pacific were becoming more and more difficult to supply and reinforce. The interior shipping lanes of the Outer Zone were coming under increasing enemy interference.

Clearly the oil-producing southern regions had to be preserved under Japanese control, sea communications from these regions to the Home Islands had to be kept open at all costs, and the American offensive in the Pacific had to be contained. There was not much that the Imperial land forces could do in Southeast Asia about the last two objectives, but if Burma was to be a shield for the oil-producing regions, it must be kept intact.

One look at a map of eastern India would reveal the importance of the Imphal-Kohima region of Assam province as a logical staging area for any British offensive; an attack should be launched elsewhere to confuse them and draw off troops from Imphal. Ironically, since the British also considered a multi-front attack into Burma, the respective British and Japanese offensives in the Arakan may be seen as mutually diversionary.

So, at the very end of November 1943, the British launched a two-pronged attack. In Arakan they met dogged resistance; once again, Japanese had to be dislodged individually from foxholes and tunnels. The process was slow, painful and bloody, but the British now held several advantages. First, they had found that in the areas where tanks could be employed, Japanese tanks were no match for the American and British models. Second, the Allies had achieved air superiority and cleared the skies of the enemy. Now it would be Japanese that would have to hide from strafing planes. Third, improved air supply techniques meant that British troops no longer needed to rely on roads. Last, the British had finally learned not to be upset when encircled by the enemy. They would merely sit tight, wait for air supply and let the enemy wear itself out.

Despite all these advantages, some have termed the British effort an 'avoidance of defeat' rather than a victory. A superior force had found that it took over a month to reduce an enemy strongpoint about 80 square miles in area. The Japanese had holed up in tunnels and previously prepared positions and it took the bayonet and flame-thrower to get them out. By 1 February 1944, when the last enemy redoubt had been reduced, there were already signs of a Japanese counter-offensive. On 4 February 1944 the Japanese 28th Army, led by General Sakurai, attacked the Arakan front. Progress was good and the 7th Indian Division found itself surrounded, but instead of withdrawing as in the past, the 7th held its position and relied on air supply; the Japanese, optimistically expecting to break through British lines and feast on captured stores, had only brought a ten-day supply of food. The climax came on February 14 when the Japanese launched an allout attack, including the use of night infiltrators

Top left: Moving toward Kohima through dense jungle. **Left:** A formation of RAF Thunderbolt fighters make a sweep over Burma.

and suicide squads. It was a waste of brave men, for the 7th continued to hold. By 24 February they had been joined by the 5th Indian Division, and another division (26th Indian) was closing in on Japanese remnants. By the beginning of March, the British had resumed their offensive on the Arakan front and were advancing toward the east.

For the first time in the Burma campaign the Japanese had been defeated in a setpiece battle, with over 5000 casualties in February 1944 alone. The British had failed to retreat as they had in the past, and when their positions could not be easily overrun, the Japanese supply system's failings came back to haunt them.

The Japanese invasion of Assam carried with it political hopes as well as military ones. It was no secret that the British were having trouble with Mahatma Gandhi, and it was hoped that the advance to Imphal would not only ruin British plans for retaking Burma, but would create further problems by the establishment of a Japanese-sponsored Indian state under Sri Subbhash Chandra Bose.

The Indian National Army
Bose had sought refuge in Nazi Germany and attempted to raise a National Army there. In 1943 he arrived in Singapore, where he established his *Azad Hind* government and raised an *Azad Hind Fouj* (Indian National Army) from the Indian prisoners taken during the earlier Malayan and Singapore campaigns. Apparently he was quite successful, for two divisions were organized and sent to the Imphal front with the Japanese 15th Army in 1944. They did not, however, see much service due to internal dissension and Japanese distrust; eventually they were withdrawn, and in the later British drive toward Rangoon many were captured or surrendered.

The British realized that Imphal would be an important Japanese target for it would be useful, not only as a forward base for the invasion of India, but as a means of isolating China and Stilwell's forces in northern Burma. General Slim planned to draw the enemy onto the large plain in front of the city where his superior armor and air power could be used to best effect; consequently, the Japanese attack on Imphal was not only anticipated, but actually desired as a chance to destroy several enemy divisions.

The Japanese were expected to follow their usual tactics and try to surround Imphal; this expectation was reinforced when the Japanese 33rd Division cut the road south of the city a week before the main attack began. But in the north the Japanese 31st Division, instead of turning toward Imphal, launched a major attack on Kohima and isolated it from the rest of the Imphal line. Kohima was vital to the British because it was only a stone's throw from Dimapur, a stop on the Bengal-Assam railway which carried all their supplies and reinforcements to the front. Luckily, whether through lack of knowledge or simply inflexibility, the Japanese did not go on to take Dimapur although it was virtually undefended.

Instead, the battle settled down to a bloody personal conflict which was often resolved in hand-to-hand combat. Soon, despite air lifts, the food supply in the city was down to two weeks'

Above left: The Japanese ambushed this armored column in Burma in early 1945. **Above:** The complex river systems of Burma did not stop the British drive north.

reduced rations with a one-week supply of gasoline; ammunition too was nearly exhausted. The Japanese, however, were in an even more precarious situation. Their offensive troops travelled lightly, hoping to exist on captured stores, and their supply lines could not support a sustained offensive. Air transport just kept the British alive and gradually the balance tipped in their favour. By April 1944 they were able to launch local counterattacks; by mid-May the defenders of Kohima were able to break out of the encirclement; and by the end of the month Imphal was free as well.

Even with all hope for victory gone, the Japanese hung on grimly, so that every hole had to be cleared, every 'dead' man confirmed. The Japanese command did not actually acknowledge its failure until mid-July, and the last Japanese soldier did not quit Indian soil until mid-August. They left behind 53,500 of the 84,300 men that had started the offensive, among them 30,000 or more killed or wounded. The British forces had 16,700 casualties, one-quarter of which occurred at Kohima.

Aside from general Japanese weaknesses, such as their supply and intelligence systems, the fact that the British did not fall for the diversion and thus had ample time to deal with the Arakan threat and then send troops to the relief of Imphal, presented the Japanese with an impossible inferiority in manpower and weapons. The Japanese penchant for continuing to use the same tactics and carry on with missions that were no longer valid resulted in a needless waste of lives. But one of the most important intangible factors was the new spirit of the Allied side. They had found out that the Japanese, tenacious and formidable, could be defeated.

While this fighting was going on, Stilwell's Chinese and Merrill's Marauders were finding the going rough in the north. Nevertheless, in August 1944, the key city of Myitkyina fell. Its capture facilitated an air route to China without the hazards of the Hump, provided a waterway to support the central Burma front, and moved the Allies a step closer to opening land routes to China.

With India's safety insured, there came a discussion as to future strategy which once again centred on two alternatives. The first plan called for a continued drive through central Burma toward Mandalay; the other entailed an amphibious landing near Rangoon. Due to requirements in Europe, however, which showed no signs of lessening despite the successful landing at Normandy, the second plan (code name 'Dracula') was cancelled.

Although the Japanese were steadily pushed back, there was no rout; instead they contested the advance wherever possible and staged a number of fierce counterattacks. But Allied air power was too much for them; only a few individual snipers stayed behind until they were killed.

As SEAC proceeded into Burma they faced political as well as military problems. Some members of the Burma Defense Army (BDA), a nationalist group organized by the Japanese, had contacted the British underground organization, Force 136, in 1944. At the end of the year the question of supplying them with arms arose and was opposed by some members of Mountbatten's staff on the grounds that they were suspected of having some contact with Communist groups. Mountbatten himself, however, saw no point in discriminating between the BDA and other minority groups that were already being supplied by the British; he finally sent them

Opposite: Bombs from a RAF Liberator head down toward Japanese Headquarters at Kyaukse. **Left:** The largest floating Bailey bridge, constructed by the 14th Army.

On the road to
Mandalay . . .

weapons on an individual rather than a group
basis with the proviso that his action implied no
future political commitment. He also insisted that
it be made clear to the Burmese people that their
liberators were the British, Indians, Americans
and Chinese – not the BDA.

In one of the most extraordinary ruses of all
time, some 5000 members of the BDA left
Rangoon on 16 March 1945, ostensibly to help the
Japanese fight the British; on 28 March they rose
in revolt and renamed themselves the Burma
National Army (BNA). They served with little
significance during the rest of the war.

The Japanese, now forced to tighten their
perimeter, were being pushed back toward the
southern tip of Burma, near Pegu. The honor of
forcing down along approximately the same route
as the original invasion fell to the 17th Indian
Division, first to feel the Japanese fury in 1942,
now webbed into one of the world's finest fighting
forces. Mandalay fell to the British in March and
Rangoon was recaptured on 3 May. Japan
surrendered on 15 August 1945, after two atomic
bombs were dropped on her cities, and on 13
September formally signed the surrender agreement with SEAC at Singapore.

Opposite left: Welsh
soldiers before the un-
damaged Bahe Pagoda,
January 1945. **Opposite
center:** Operation
"Nipoff" – General Ichida
directs the repatriation of
Japanese soldiers in
Rangoon. **Left:** Japanese
staff officers arrive in
Rangoon to discuss
surrender arrangements.

CHAPTER SEVENTEEN
The Defeat of Germany

The Allies had gained a secure foothold on Europe after the Normandy landings, but there was still bloody fighting ahead. Twenty days after the landing on the beaches, the port of Cherbourg was taken following four days of combat; the Germans had systematically destroyed every port facility, but skilled Allied engineers were able to return them to full use by August. Meanwhile, two gigantic artificial harbors called Mulberries were towed across the Channel and badly needed supplies flowed over them to the expanded beachheads.

By 26 July the Allies had broken out of Normandy and were enveloping the rest of France in a series of moves which, despite vigorous counterattacks, the Germans were unable to contain. On 15 August Operation Anvil the invasion of southern France, was begun near Cannes against relatively light German resistance. While these forces headed north to link up with the Normandy troops the French underground, the *Maquis,* offered valuable assistance. Within two weeks Marseilles, Toulon and Nice were liberated. In their turn, the Normandy forces caught the bulk of the German forces in France in a huge pocket, taking 50,000 prisoners and killing 10,000 Germans. The way to Paris was open.

The liberation of Paris was a sensitive issue. It was not directly essential to military operations, and its relief would mean the expenditure of valuable fuel and ammunition, but it was a symbol to the people of France. In the city itself, as the news spread that the Allies were getting closer, the people were preparing for an uprising against the German garrison.

General Eisenhower was reluctant to move toward the city, but his hand was forced when, on 19 August French underground forces launched general attacks against the German garrison. It was feared that unless Allied forces moved toward the city to relieve the Maquis, they would be annihilated by the Germans and the civilian population would suffer bitter reprisals.

The German garrison commander, General von Choltitz, was in a dilemma. He had received orders from Hitler to defend Paris to the death; if he could not hold the city, he was to reduce it to ashes. The task was extremely distasteful to him and in the end, through underground intermediaries, he agreed to surrender to the Allies. The French General LeClerc and his Second Armored Division were chosen to be the first Allied unit to enter Paris after four years of German occupation and the next day, 26 August,

Charles de Gaulle walked proudly down the boulevards of Paris past ecstatic crowds. The celebration lasted three days, but then the enemy threatened to counterattack; American troops marched in parade formation right from the city streets into combat.

Since the beginning of the Normandy invasion, the Germans had lost over 500,000 men including 200,000 bottled up in by-passed areas. The remnants of formations still in condition to fight now headed back toward the Siegfried Line, which was in effect the last major German defensive barrier. The Allies, with over two million troops on the continent, pushed forward with a series of spearheads, cutting off German positions as they forged ahead. Their advance was swift; Brussels was liberated on 3 September and Antwerp on the following day. Grown over confident, the Allies tried a bold gamble to shorten the war by trying to outflank the Siegfried Line using airborne troops.

In what turned out to be the biggest airborne operation of the war, over 20,000 men were

Opposite: German industry was decimated before the final thrust into the Reich.

Captured German soldier is marched into captivity during the street fighting which preceded the liberation of Paris.

dropped into Holland on 17 September 1944, the Americans in the vicinity of Eindhoven and Nijmegen and the British further north at Arnhem. Their mission was to seize key communications centers and secure bridges across the Maas and Waal Rivers. The Americans made good progress, though with some difficulty. But at Arnhem on the Lower Rhine, 8000 British paratroops ran into serious trouble. The Germans had evidently prepared for such an airborne assault, and the paratroops in the sky were shot as easily as clay pigeons. Once on the ground, they found that their relief forces were bogged down by bad weather.

For nine days and nights the British paratroops were steadily decimated by the furious German bombardment. Food began to run short, and ammunition was rationed. Eventually, the high command gave up and ordered them to break for their own lines. Of the 8000 men, barely 2000 escaped. In terms of the larger picture it was no disaster, but in view of the loss of large numbers of highly trained airborne troops, it was a minor catastrophe. It also showed that the Germans were still willing to fight and would have to be ground into defeat.

After the Nijmegen–Arnhem operation, a disagreement occurred between General Omar Bradley and Field Marshal Montgomery. Montgomery wanted a single concentrated attack toward the Ruhr north of the Ardennes forests, but General Bradley felt that American firepower, especially Patton's mobile Third Army, could best be utilized in a two-pronged attack, one north toward the Ruhr, one south toward the Saar basin. This would force the enemy to divide his dwindling forces against two major attacks. Eventually, Bradley won his point, and the offensive did indeed proceed on two fronts. But the November weather intervened to slow down American mobility, and the campaign began to drag despite vigorous local attacks.

As the momentum of the offensive began to slacken, the Allies were faced with the problem of replacing the men lost since the landings. Some infantry divisions were attacking with only three-quarters of their authorized combat strength, since due to administrative difficulties, replacements were slow in reaching the front-line units. Then, on 16 December 1944, the Germans launched their last counter-offensive on the western front. The Battle of the Bulge was about to begin.

The Battle of the Bulge

Even as Hitler was recuperating from the bomb blast in the Wolf's Lair, the idea of a counter-offensive on the western front was being conceived. Planning began in September 1944 when the Germans quietly started to mass over 250,000 men. This was a pitiful number compared to the Wehrmacht when the war began, and the men could not measure up in quality to the original soldiers, but it was still a sizable force, stiffened by fanatical SS units, well-equipped, dedicated Nazis. Coupled with it were some 1000 tanks, the last armored reserve in the West, or anywhere else for that matter.

Von Runstedt was brought out of retirement to

Left: Civilians flee for safety when German snipers open fire on de Gaulle and his staff as they entered the Notre Dame.
Left center: General Dietrich von Choltitz surrenders in the Gare Montparnasse. **Left lower center:** Warm welcome for British soldiers in Paris.
Bottom left: Brussels gave the Allies an equally enthusiastic welcome.

Right: Small bands of Germans caused crowds to panic in the Place de la Concorde, even after they surrendered the city.
Below: Hitler and Mussolini view the devastation caused by the explosion of a bomb in the Fuehrer's conference room
Below center: German prisoners and Belgian collaborators were locked in cages in the Antwerp Zoo. Here a German joins his comrades in the lions cage. **Below right:** Soldiers of the Waffen SS during the breakthrough at the Bulge.

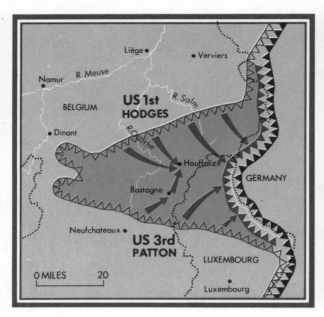

Above: Generals Patton and Bradley. Patton's 3rd Army saved the day for the Allies at Bastogne. **Top right:** Bastogne held and the German attack ground to a halt. **Opposite:** Bastogne after the Bulge was broken.

25 PDR Gun. Range: 13,400 yds. Armament: 3.45 in. caliber 24¼ lbs. shell. Crew: 7. Weight: 1 ton. 1460 lbs.

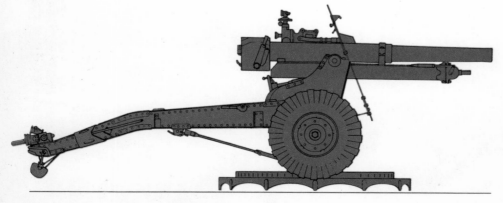

command this counter-offensive, but the plan was really Hitler's own brainchild. 'Operation Autumn Fog' was to collect all available men and supplies for one powerful strike in the Ardennes; they would penetrate Allied lines, break into open country and drive toward Antwerp. The attack would be made when bad weather was forecast, so that Allied aircraft would be restricted.

In early December Hitler called a conference to finalize plans for the operation. Gone was the self-assured and arrogant Fuehrer of the old days. He was visibly hampered by the bomb injuries, and seemed nervous, with his left hand twitching from time to time. When he spoke, he was hesitant, but his determination to defeat the West was unshaken.

The professional officers gathered to hear the plan were not unanimous in their reactions. General von Manteuffel questioned the distant objective of Antwerp with the forces available, and von Runstedt continued his contempt and distrust of the Austrian corporal, though he was entrusted with the plan's execution. But the surviving generals had largely been cowed by the purges after the bomb plot and Hitler was adamant.

A major cause for concern was air cover, and here Hitler seemed to be dealing in fantasy. In answer to a question, he claimed that the Luftwaffe was 'being deliberately held back. Goering has reported that he has 3000 fighters available. . . . Discount 1000 and that still leaves 2000'. It is doubtful if by that time the entire Luftwaffe had even half of that number in operational planes of all types.

On the Allied side, there had been reports of movement of the Sixth SS Panzer Army toward Cologne with another group slightly to the rear. The openness of these movements led Allied intelligence officers to speculate on the possibility of a feint and a major attack against what must be, in light of restricted German resources, a limited objective. An attack on Antwerp, in view of the distance, was considered too ambitious; it was estimated that the Germans had suffered over 100,000 casualties in November, not counting prisoners, and it was assumed that von Runstedt would probably husband his remaining manpower to try to blunt the Allied drive toward the Rhine.

The Ardennes sector was held by two fresh, untried American divisions in the north and two veteran, but badly mauled divisions in the south. It was considered to be generally unsuitable for tanks, being closely wooded with narrow, circuitous roads all but impassable in snow. The two new divisions were assigned to this area because it was considered to be a 'quiet' sector where the green troops could gain some battle experience fairly easily. The two veteran divisions were here to 'rest' from their ordeal in the Huertgen Forest a month before.

On 16 December 1944 when the German counter-offensive smashed into them, the impact upon the Americans was something like that at Pearl Harbor. In less than forty-eight hours penetrations, some more than fifteen miles deep, were made in Allied lines across a fifty-five mile front. The first blows swept away unsuspecting outposts; stubborn pockets of resistance were by-passed. To add to the confusion, the Germans employed troops disguised as American soldiers speaking perfect 'American' English. Though the tactic ultimately failed, it caused Americans at the front anxious moments and stragglers and strangers wandered at their own peril.

The operation gained momentum in the center, taking advantage of bad weather and Allied confusion over German objectives. For a while, it was reminiscent of the early Blitzkrieg days and a deep cut, some 45 miles wide and 65 miles deep, was gouged out of the Allied positions. But despite the stunning blows, Allied troops fought back everywhere. The lines buckled, but the Germans never were able to break completely

Above: Benito Mussolini hangs by his heels in Milan. **Opposite:** US troops march through the remains of Saarbrücken: 20 March 1945.

Scraping the bottom of the barrel, Hitler called upon children to defend his crumbling regime.

through the defenses. In the center, they struck for the town of Bastogne in Belgium, a key road center in the southern Ardennes. Bastogne would give the Germans three different approach routes, but if it was retained by the Allies it would be an ideal jumping off point to smash the German attack. An American armored division, the 10th, fought a delaying action, trading lives for time; eventually von Runstedt was able to outflank them, but by that time the 101st Airborne Division was solidly entrenched in the city center.

Bastogne was surrounded, but resisted valiantly; German artillery pounded it with merciless accuracy, but the paratroops grimly held on. Even as they expended their energy against this one lone town and division, they themselves were being squeezed on both sides of the bulge, and as the weather began to clear, 5000 Allied aircraft ranged over the entire area to destroy anything German that moved. Despite the fact that by December 26 the German attack ground to a halt, Hitler continued to throw in new divisions, most of them filled with ill-trained recruits.

By January 1945 it was clear that the bold gamble had failed. The Russians had started a gigantic offensive against the Germans and Hitler was forced to transfer all available forces to the eastern front. Within a month, all the ground gained had been lost.

If his goals had been limited, Hitler could conceivably have delayed the Allied drive toward the Rhine, though in 1944 Germany did not possess the power to defeat the Allies permanently. But by striving for the long-distance objectives of Antwerp and the other Channel ports without sufficient strength, the Germans squandered away any reserve that might have been used against either the Russian offensive or subsequently in the defence of Germany beyond the Rhine. As it was, the Battle of the Bulge achieved a one month delay, but left the road into Germany from the West a wide thoroughfare.

The counter-offensive left 120,000 Germans killed, wounded, captured or missing; over 1000 planes and 500 tanks were destroyed as well. The Americans sustained nearly 80,000 casualties. Though British troops were involved in the north, it had been primarily an American show, and it had put to rest once and for all the Hitler myth that Americans could not withstand pressure.

On New Year's Day, 1945, Adolf Hitler went on the air to give the German people renewed pledges of ultimate victory for the Reich and destruction for 'defeatists'. He repeated the vow that Germany 'will never capitulate', and called upon the German people for continued sacrifice for 'survival, . . . culture, . . . for prosperity'. As he spoke, British, American and Russian armies totalling more than 10 million men were pressing in upon the German nation. In the east three Russian thrusts headed for Berlin, Czechoslovakia was invaded, and East Prussia was isolated. These moves forced the transfer of all available forces from the West at top speed, but most of the men were already exhausted from the Ardennes offensive. From the air Allied bombers pulverized the German armament industry.

Across the Rhine

The shortage of manpower had now put older men, sub-teen striplings and infirm males into uniform as the Germans desperately sought to build up the Rhine defenses. The western Allies headed for the Rhine, sweeping up the last pockets of German resistance, and the Germans made ready to demolish all the bridges across this last major defensive barrier in the West. While the British and Americans brought up river crossing craft, the Americans had not had to cross any body of inland water under hostile fire since the American civil war. No one had successfully crossed the Rhine into Germany since Napoleon in 1805. All the bridges were supposedly blown up and the Germans sat and waited on the east side of the river where the steep ground gave them excellent observations and fields of fire.

Then on 7 March 1945, the Allies had a lucky break. A small American patrol approached the ancient medieval town of Remagen, located between Bonn and Coblenz, and found that the bridge was largely intact, despite the fact that explosive charges had been placed on it. Indeed one had already exploded. The small group hurried across under fire and reported the situation. As quickly as possible, more Americans were fed across; engineers reinforced the bridge so that tanks and trucks could cross, and within 24 hours more than 8000 men were on the other side. Two more emergency bridges were built alongside.

The Luftwaffe tried unsuccessfully to destroy the bridges from the air. One more span did eventually collapse sweeping a number of Americans to their death, but the Rhine had been nullified as a defense. Eighteen days later, all Allied offensive forces were across. Germany proper was defenseless.

After clearing the Rhine barrier, the Allies

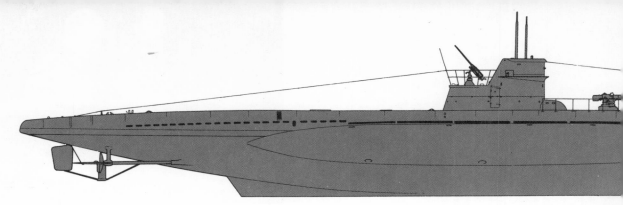

Right: VII C 'U' Boat
Length: 220¼ ft. Beam:
20¼ ft. Draught: 15¾ ft.
Maximum speed: 17/7½
knots. Armament:
1 × 3.5 in., 1 × 37 mm.
A.A., 2 × 20 mm. A.A.,
5 × 21 in. Torpedo tubes,
14 × torpedo. Crew: 44
Displacement: 769/871 tons.

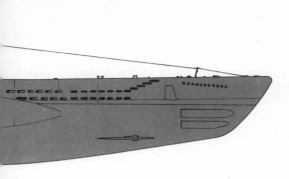

General Jodl signs the unconditional surrender of the Third Reich.

encircled the industrial heartland of Germany, reducing the Ruhr valley to a hollow shell with intensive bombing raids. Once more Hitler ordered his troops to stand and fight to the death; once more they were encircled or outflanked. By 1 April 1945 the entire Ruhr area had been enveloped, trapping German forces in an 80-mile circle. More than 400,000 were taken prisoner.

Twenty-one German divisions had been devoured by the Allied juggernaut and the Third Reich was buckling in the center, while to the south, another Allied Army thrust east into Germany. Mannheim fell on 29 March, Nuremberg on 20 April and Munich on 30 April. Thirsting for revenge, Free French forces overwhelmed Stuttgart and Karlsruhe near the Swiss border. But the fastest moving of all was Patton's Third Army. His precision machine was a military wonder: engineers cleared minefields and barriers while tank-infantry teams followed close behind and artillery pulverized resistance ahead. Supporting units kept the equipment repaired and replenished. Few Germans could stand in the way, and his advance guard closed in on Czechoslovakia on 23 April.

On 12 April 1945 President Franklin D. Roosevelt died. If Hitler rejoiced over his death, he found in the successor, Harry S. Truman, an equally relentless enemy. In a short speech Truman called for the 'unconditional surrender' of Germany.

British and Canadian troops swung north into Holland, toward the German coast. In the east Vienna fell on 13 April as on both fronts Allied armies scooped up thousands of dazed German soldiers. The streamline, efficient Wehrmacht was a thing of the past; animal-drawn transport cluttered the roads, and fighting units were scattered or simply disappeared. Then on 25 April 1945 small American and Russian patrols faced each other curiously at the town of Torgau on the Elbe River, some 75 miles south of Berlin. The confrontation was soon built into a full-fledged linkup slashing Germany in two.

That same day, Benito Mussolini attempted to escape into Switzerland with his mistress. Allied armies were converging upon Milan and the erstwhile dictator was now a broken man, frightened and despised. A group of Italian Communist partisans came upon him and, in a burst of machine-gun fire, ended the life of the man who had 'made Italian trains run on time'. His corpse along with those of his mistress and a number of other Fascists were publicly displayed in Milan and then buried in a potter's field.

Yet Hitler continued to believe that salvation was imminent. He now planned to direct the defence of northern Germany from Berlin while assigning Heinrich Himmler to defend the south. The Russians were rapidly approaching Berlin from the east and the city was studded with pillboxes and minefields, but the Nazis continued to scrawl slogans on the walls declaring their intention to fight to the death.

Allied airpower seemed about to pound the city into dust. Russians attacked from the east, northeast and southeast and their artillery crashed into the metropolitan heartland. German citizens cringed in terror, but the Nazis rounded up every able-bodied male from twelve to eighty for a last-ditch stand. By 23 April Russian forces held the center of the city and on 2 May 1945, all formal or organized resistance ceased.

There has been much speculation over the eventual fate of Adolf Hitler. As the Allies moved through Germany, the top Nazi leadership had begun to disintegrate. Some, like Goebbels, would commit suicide rather than face Allied retribution. Others, such as Goering, would be captured and then cheat the executioner by taking their own lives. More, such as Martin Bormann, would never be found. Some would even seek to find their own accommodation with the Allied authorities, as in the case of Himmler.

But the Fuehrer himself steadfastly refused to leave Berlin for any other sanctuary or headquarters. Almost to the end, he continued to study war maps, call conferences, and move nonexistent armies about. More and more he lapsed into fits of rage over the incompetence of subordinates or the 'ingratitude' of the German people. His health had been steadily deteriorating during the last days until he looked like some grim caricature out of a nightmare. He was bent and stooped and his left leg dragged, both souvenirs from the bomb plot; he was pale and hollow-eyed and ate less and less, becoming reluctant to leave his dank bunker and suffering from loss of sleep.

As one of his final acts, Hitler expelled Goering and Himmler from the Nazi Party and named Admiral Karl Doenitz to be the next leader of the Third Reich. On 15 April 1945 his mistress Eva Braun appeared at the bunker. They were married on 29 April with Russian artillery shells and rockets as their marital symphony. Although the facts have not been completely proved, it is generally accepted that on 30 April Hitler shot himself, while Eva Braun took poison. The bodies were burned in the courtyard, but the remains have never been found.

Admiral Doenitz attempted to continue as the head of government by offering to surrender to the Western Allies only. This was rejected, and on 7 May 1945 Nazi Germany unconditionally surrendered. The European phase of World War Two came to an end.

Opposite top: Frankfurt-am-Main was wiped out. **Opposite bottom:** The Anhalter Station in Berlin, like the rest of the city, was heavily hit. **Below:** Red flag over Berlin.

CHAPTER EIGHTEEN
Japan Subdued

Opposite top: The first wave of marines hits the Saipan beach. **Opposite bottom:** Marines take cover after their landing on Guam.

General Douglas MacArthur led his forces through a series of amphibious landings along along the northern New Guinea coast in preparation for his conquest of the Philippines.

Before MacArthur could begin his drive to liberate the Philippines, he still had to do some cleaning up in the Southwest Pacific. In April 1944 Allied forces took Hollandia in Dutch New Guinea. In May they pressed on to Biak and Wakde. Wakde was taken two days after the first Allied landings (19 May) but Biak proved more difficult. Allied forces were landed on the island on 27 May but it was not secured until the end of August, although an Allied air base had been constructed a month before the battle was over.

The battle for Biak would have been more difficult still if the Japanese had not decided to cancel a planned assault on Allied forces in the area in favor of sending what remained of the Japanese fleet against them in the Philippine Sea where landings on Saipan and Guam were imminent. The Saipan landing had actually begun while Biak was still being contested, on 16 June. When Allied leaders learned that Japan intended to engage Admiral Spruance's task force, the Guam landing was postponed and the US Navy prepared to meet the Japanese in one of the last major contests in the naval war in the Pacific.

The Battle of the Philippine Sea began on 19 June 1944. Unlike previous naval engagements in the Pacific, the American task force outnumbered its Japanese rival by more than two to one ships. More important, the American group that engaged the Japanese in the Philippine Sea was well seasoned. Whereas the Japanese had sustained heavy losses in personnel and equipment, particularly aircraft, by the summer of 1944, which forced them to rely on improperly trained seamen and fliers, the United States task force was experienced and able. The battle, therefore, proved to be an uneven match. By the time the Japanese retreated on 21 June, they had lost at least three carriers and more than 300 aircraft, a loss that the Imperial Japanese Navy could ill afford to sustain.

After the defeat of the Japanese fleet the capture of Saipan was only a matter of time. Had it not been for the fierce resistance of the Japanese garrison on the island, the Marines would have wrapped things up in a few days but as it happened, the campaign took several weeks. The Japanese did not surrender until 8 July and even then pockets of resistance still had to be cleaned out. Perhaps the term 'surrender' is misleading since the commander of the Japanese force on Saipan, General Yoshio Saito, ordered his men to fight to the death and fought to his own death beside them. Given this suicidal resistance and the

difficult terrain of the island, the Marines sustained unusually heavy losses before the island was secured with 3400 dead and over 14,000 wounded. Japanese casualties have been estimated at more than 24,000, one of their worst disasters of the war. Tojo was forced to resign as Premier shortly after this dreadful toll was announced in Tokyo.

The neutralization and conquest of Saipan had hardly been completed when the Allies attacked Guam and Tinian. Following a massive bombardment of Japanese installations, Guam was invaded on 21 July, and Tinian on 24 July. Both campaigns were efficiently and rapidly completed; the Stars and Stripes flew over Tinian by 3 August, and Guam was subdued by the 10th. Army engineers and Seabees lost no time in constructing and expanding air bases on the two islands, giving the Allies bases within easy flying time from Formosa and the islands from which to launch their B-29 strikes. For Japan, the end was near.

'I Shall Return'

The successful conclusion of the Marianas campaign opened the way for MacArthur to return to the Philippines. The only unsettled question was whether the thrust through the Philippines should be part of the major effort to subdue Japan or given second priority. For once, all major commanders in the Pacific theatre were in agreement; MacArthur was joined by Admiral Halsey and other senior naval officers who argued against a diversion of Allied efforts to China or Formosa. The campaign in the Philippines was quickly given top priority.

MacArthur's plans were already made when the Joint Chiefs gave their official blessing to the venture; all that remained to be done was to co-ordinate with the Navy and fix a date and place for the invasion. MacArthur and his associates had originally considered Mindanao the most likely target of an Allied attack on the islands of Leyte and Luzon. Morotai, Peleliu, and Ulithi, with their bases and refueling stations had to be captured first, however. The scheme was submitted to the Joint Chiefs in late August and was immediately approved.

By mid-September Morotai and Ulithi were in Allied hands, but Peleliu there was tough fighting and heavy resistance. Although the major landing target, an air field, was secured on 12 October, the island was not cleared until the middle of November. Nevertheless, MacArthur would not be deflected from his primary goal; re-occupation of the Philippines. Preparations

Above: Homage to the Emperor before certain death. **Right:** Kamikaze attacks on American ships caused considerable damage **Center right:** One or two direct hits by Japanese suicide planes could put an aircraft carrier out of commission. **Bottom right** USS *Franklin* lists badly after having received a direct hit.

for the invasion of the Philippines went on without interruption, and the Allies were ready by mid-October.

On 20 October 1944 America returned to the Philippines when units of the United States Sixth Army were landed in Leyte. The Japanese responded by sending what was left of their Combined Fleet to stop them. Four days after the Leyte landing the two sides met in the final major naval engagement of the Pacific war, the Battle of Leyte Gulf.

The Japanese divided their fleet, sending one group north through the Surignao Strait to Leyte Gulf, and another south from San Bernadino. If all went according to plan, the two halves of the fleet would converge upon the American task force in the gulf and suicide pilots, *Kamikazes*, would destroy American troop ships and their escorts. Surprise was essential, but on 23 October Admiral Kurita's Centre Task Force was spotted by American submarines as it was moving south through the Palawan Passage Strait. When Kurita reached the Sibuyan Sea the following morning, Admiral Mitscher was waiting. American aircraft sunk a battleship, the *Musashi*, three cruisers, and several smaller ships, and he was forced to withdraw. Japan's Southern Force fared little better.

On 25 October ships of the United States Seventh Fleet opened fire on the Southern Task Force as it tried to move from the Strait of Surigao into Leyte Gulf. The Seventh Fleet was deployed in a fifteen-mile line blocking the entrance into the Gulf, and the Japanese could reach it only by steaming through the American line. This they declined to do, although Admiral Mishimura made a more concerted effort to breach the line than did his partner, Admiral Shima. The Japanese lost several destroyers in the contest but managed to withdraw from the battle area with no additional losses.

Encouraged by the withdrawal of the Center Task Force, Admiral Halsey was anxious to pursue the retreating Japanese to find and attack Admiral Ozawa's decoy fleet which had been sent south from the Japanese Islands to draw the Americans away from the Philippines. With Kurita in retreat and the Seventh Fleet engaging the Southern Task Force, Halsey felt it was safe to leave the escort carriers of the Seventh Fleet near the San Bernadino Straits while his Third Fleet sought out Ozawa's task force. This proved to be a great mistake; no sooner had Halsey's task force left Leyte Gulf than Kurita appeared with his fleet. By the time Halsey got word of this, he was 150 miles north of the area and could have done little to rescue the fleet carriers even if he had thought such a mission possible, which he did not.

Although Kurita's reappearance was alarming, Halsey had overestimated the damage done to the Japanese armada in the contest off the Palawan Passage on the 24th, and did not think it presented any danger which American naval forces in the Gulf of Leyte could not handle. Unfortunately he was mistaken. When Kurita appeared in front of the carriers of the Seventh Fleet on 25 October, he had four battleships, a half dozen heavy cruisers, and several destroyers under his command, while the Americans could

Left: Tons of equipment and thousands of men reinforced the invaders of Luzon. Below left: The first wave of invaders heads toward the beaches of Luzon.

Japanese held areas until August 1945

19.2.45

Allied (U.S.) attack and date of attacks

muster only six carriers and their destroyer escorts. By the end of the day one American carrier and two destroyers had been laid to rest. But at least the carrier fleet was not annihilated, so the incident was not an unmitigated disaster for the Americans.

While Admiral Sprague battled Kurita's task force, Halsey found and engaged Admiral Ozawa's fleet 200 miles northeast of Luzon. Here the Americans more than made up for their losses further south; planes from American carriers flew hundreds of sorties and when the battle was over, four Japanese carriers lay at the bottom of the Pacific. Had Halsey not belatedly sent a small task force under Admiral Lee to the rescue of the Seventh Fleet carriers in Leyte Gulf, Ozawa's force would have been completely decimated. Nevertheless, the Japanese sustained heavy losses in the Battle of Cape Engano which, at this stage of the war, they could ill afford.

Back to Bataan

With the Imperial Navy neutralized, Japan's only hope of maintaining her position in the Philippines was to foil the American invasion effort. This would be no easy task, for their only advantage lay in the topography of the area and their fierce determination to resist to the last man if necessary. While this would not suffice in the end, it would considerably delay the capture of Leyte, forcing MacArthur to re-assess his plans for using the island as a jumping-off point in the attempt to recapture Luzon.

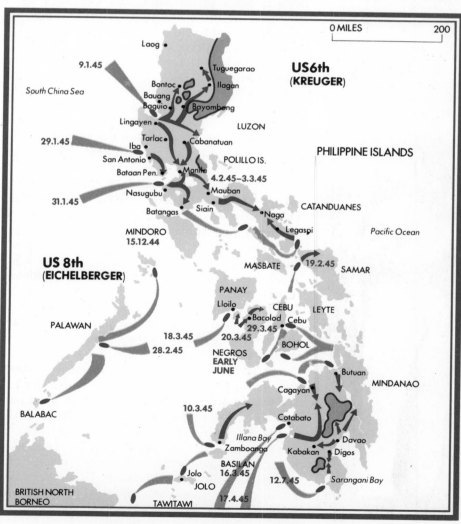

American troops move into the devastated Intramuros section of Manila.

MacArthur reads the proclamation of the liberation of Leyte.

Soon after the initial landings on Leyte, the Americans encountered additional obstacles. Rain-soaked roads proved unable to bear the weight of heavy armored vehicles which quickly bogged down in the mud, and airfields proved unusable for much the same reason. While the landing force was stuck in this mire, the Japanese were able to reinforce their garrison on the island; by the middle of December 45,000 men had been put ashore.

MacArthur and Halsey had intended using Leyte as a major site for air bases from which Japanese installations elsewhere in the Philippine Islands could be attacked, but this plan had to be modified. Carriers of the United States Third Fleet were ordered to stations in the Gulf of Leyte so that these attacks could be launched using carrier-based as opposed to land-based aircraft. This posed two problems which had not been originally anticipated. First, the carriers were themselves targets for Japanese *kamikaze* squadrons, and second, carrier-based aircraft were necessarily smaller than land based bombers, carried smaller payloads and were less effective.

There was no way to protect against *kamikaze* attacks. Suicide pilots, sealed into their aircraft, and determined to crash their planes which were loaded with bombs into Allied ships, presented a threat hitherto unheard of in modern warfare. The Third Fleet suffered the loss of two carriers and several other ships before Halsey ordered part of it to withdraw to the Caroline Islands at the end of November. By that time, however, things were going better on Leyte and the Americans considered plans for the invasion of Luzon.

Leyte was finally secured on 25 December 1944, although the Japanese continued to resist the Americans in isolated pockets until the following spring. While the mopping-up progressed on Leyte, the major action of the Philippine campaign, the invasion of Luzon, began. On 9 January American forces landed in the Lingayen Gulf.

Although the landing of the Sixth Army at Lingayen was easily accomplished, General Yamashita, the commanding general of Japanese forces in the Philippines, could not permit the landing party to proceed inland without contest. Japanese forces were deployed in front of the landing sites to resist the four American divisions put ashore during the first day of the Allied offensive, but the effort failed. While I Corps of the Sixth Army pushed the Japanese into the mountains of the Gulf, other units raced south toward Clark Field and Manila.

The Sixth Army encountered heavy opposition as it pushed toward Manila. Thanks to the establishment of air fields on Mindoro the Allied were able to check the effectiveness of Japanese air power over Luzon, but the going on the ground was extremely tough. The distance between the landing sites on the Lingayen Gulf and Manila was only 110 miles, but it took over a month to cover. True to their tradition, the Japanese fought bravely and often to the last man; since there were about 170,000 Japanese on Luzon, General Krueger's advance was necessarily slow.

As Krueger's forces pushed toward Manila, MacArthur prepared to seal the escape route through the Bataan Peninsula by landing a second Allied force close to that area on 29 January. A third force was airlifted and dropped 40 miles south of Manila on 31 January. Together, the three groups proceeded toward Manila, converging on the city, at the beginning of February by which time General Yamashita had abandoned it. Although Japanese army forces had been withdrawn to the mountains, the Manila was still defended by units of the Japanese Navy under the command of Admiral Iwabachi, who refused to obey Yamashita's order declaring Manila an open city and continued to resist the Americans for another month. With several thousand men under his command, Iwabachi turned the battle for Manila into a house to house confrontation, resulting in great damage to the city during the final stage of the campaign. By 4 March, when the city was finally cleared, much of it had been destroyed.

The capture of Manila marked the end of Japanese control in the Philippine Islands. Within weeks, the Bataan Peninsula was cleared and Corregidor was retaken. By the beginning of April Allied shipping was using the port of Manila again, and military leaders were considering their next move against Japan. Although isolated pockets of Japanese resistance were not eliminated until August 1945, shortly before the war's end, they presented no clear or present danger to the American position in the Philippines. MacArthur had returned.

Iwo Jima

It had originally been thought that once the Philippines were subdued the Allied would carry the war to Formosa and/or the China coast, but the success of the Philippine venture encouraged military planners to consider a direct attack against the Japanese home islands. Such a move would end the war more rapidly at a minimal cost in men and equipment, and the plan was generally well received by MacArthur, Halsey and their associates and quickly accepted by the Joint Chiefs of Staff.

The Joint Chiefs felt that if an attack on Japan was to be successful the Allies would have to capture Iwo Jima, Okinawa, and the Bonin Islands first. With these bases secure the Allies could launch a major aerial bombardment of the Japanese islands, pulverizing the major cities with their powerful B-29 bombers and destroying any remaining industrial capacity.

Iwo Jima was to be the first target, and even before Manila was captured, preparations were made for the invasion of this small volcanic island. The head of the American force assigned to capture Iwo Jima was to be Admiral Spruance, the new commander of the Fifth Fleet which for this venture included three Marine divisions. The date for the landing was set for 19 February 1945.

From 8 December 1944 to 19 February 1945, Allied aircraft bombed Japanese installations on Iwo Jima daily in order to soften Japan's defences on the island. This represented the single most prolonged bombing action of the war but the results did not seem to justify the effort; when the Marines landed on 19 February, they found most of the Japanese positions intact and the Japanese garrison ready and willing to engage them. Although Iwo Jima had been considered a relatively easy target, it was to prove to be one of the most costly and difficult battles for the Americans in the Pacific war.

Iwo Jima had not been a major Japanese station and until the summer of 1944 would have been relatively easy for the Allies to take. By September 1944, this situation had changed. As it became clear to the Japanese that the Allies would soon be pressing their homeland, the Japanese garrison on Iwo Jima was quickly reinforced to a strength of approximately 25,000 men, for Japan's military leaders understood as clearly as the Allies the value of the island as a long-range bomber base. Every effort was made to prepare for the American attack, including the construction of an elaborate network of caves and tunnels which would be difficult if not impossible to destroy.

When the Americans landed, they were greeted by mortar fire and an almost constant artillery barrage. Unlike earlier amphibious operations in which the Allies were able to establish a beachhead and quickly fan out to attack their targets, the Marine attack force at Iwo Jima was pinned down on the beaches and sustained exceptionally heavy losses (2500 killed or wounded) on the very first day of the operation. Nor was the first day an exception; in the slow march from the beaches to the inner island, losses continued to be very large. Even with the aid of aerial reconnaisance and naval bombardment, the Americans could not dislodge the Japanese from their fortifications without incurring heavy casualties.

Iwo Jima was not secured until 26 March 1945. During the nearly six weeks that the attack was in progress, the Marines sustained 26,000 casualties. Nearly one-third of the American forces were

killed or wounded; of the approximate 25,000 Japanese, 21,000 lay dead when the campaign ended and only a few hundred prisoners were taken alive. The remaining several thousand Japanese troops took to the hills where they held out until the end of May. All in all, almost the entire Japanese garrison was lost, making this one of Japan's worst defeats of the war.

By the beginning of April, American bombers were flying regular missions from their new bases on Iwo Jima. The Allies had achieved their goal but they paid a high price for it, and the fierce resistance on Iwo Jima gave Allied military commanders food for thought about the invasion of Japan proper. If the Japanese could fight so hard for a tiny volcanic island, what might the Allies expect when they landed in Kyushu or Honshu?

Okinawa

While the Battle for Iwo Jima was still in progress the Allies prepared to invade Okinawa, largest of the Ryukyu Islands, on 1 April 1945. Okinawa was even more strategically important than Iwo Jima, located mid-way between Japan and Formosa only 360 miles from the China coast. Its large size, approximately 480 square miles, would make it difficult to secure and require an even larger effort than the Iwo Jima campaign in which the Americans landed 80,000 men. Nevertheless, if Okinawa was captured, the door would be open to Japan itself. Conversely, if it was not taken, it would be difficult, if not impossible, for the Allies to press the war to the Japanese islands. In short Okinawa, the Allies believed, would be one of the most crucial operations of the war.

To insure success the American command massed a huge invasion force consisting of four

Wounded marine is evacuated from Iwo Jima.

Top: Midget submarines in a wrecked drydock at Kure. **Above:** The American fight against fanatical opposition was relentless. **Opposite:** The Japanese fought to the bitter end. **Opposite bottom:** Raising the flag on Mount Suribachi—a costly victory on Iwo Jima.

Army divisions and three Marine divisions, a total of over 280,000 men. Accompanying the troop ships and guarding them from aerial attack was a task force under the command of Admiral Mitscher, consisting of a fast carrier group plus some escort craft. Supporting the United States Navy was a British task force under the command of Admiral Sir Bruce Fraser which included two battleships, several heavy cruisers and four additional aircraft carriers. Never had the Allies massed a larger armada in support of an amphibious operation.

The Japanese also steeled themselves for the contest. Their garrison on the island numbered slightly over 100,000 men dug into caves and other sturdy defenses and supported by hundreds of gun emplacements and artillery pieces. As if this were not enough, the Japanese massed over 2000 *kamikaze* aircraft for suicide attacks against the Allied flotilla. Rarely had the Allies encountered such a horrifying array.

On 1 April 1945 the first wave of American troops were landed on Okinawa. Unlike the landing on Iwo Jima, it was carried off without any overt resistance, and a five-mile beachhead was carved out within hours after the first troops sloshed ashore. By the end of the day this beachhead had been widened to almost ten miles and still there was no sign of the Japanese. Indeed, the enemy was not sighted at all until three days after the first landings.

Until 13 April American ground forces advanced with little or no difficulty but in the air and on the sea, it was a different story. *Kamikaze* pilots systematically attacked Allied ships, sinking a dozen destroyers and damaging several others. In addition, the Allied armada encountered a new obstacle, a floating suicide squad. The capital ship *Yamato* had been sent to the waters off

Okinawa accompanied by a small escort force, with only enough fuel to drive her to the scene of the battle where she was to employ at sea the same dastardly tactics used by the *kamikaze* pilots. The mission was a true sign of the desperation of the Japanese, but might have proved quite devastating if American aircraft had not spotted the battleship and followed her approach. When the *Yamato* reached the battle area on 7 April she was attacked by 280 carrier-based aircraft and sent to the bottom. The Allied fleet reigned supreme and was never again challenged. The stage was now set for the land contest.

Two weeks after the original landing, the Japanese began their counter-attack. Japanese forces were concentrated in the southern part of the island. Thus, while the Marines had little difficulty pushing into the Motobu Peninsula, their peers in the south had a very difficult time. Despite an unusually heavy and continuous bombardment of Japanese positions in the south of Okinawa, the Americans could not dislodge them from their bunkers and caves. Aerial attack and artillery bombardment proved an ineffective substitute for infantry.

For three months American Marines and infantrymen slogged their way through the hot, humid and muddy Okinawan terrain, encountering zealous and often fanatic opposition reminiscent of the suicide missions of the *kamikazes* and the ill-fated *Yamato*. The battle was finally over on 21 June 1945, by which time both sides had sustained casualties that paled those suffered on Iwo Jima. According to official reports, the Americans lost almost 50 000 men, the Japanese over 110,000. Again the Allied command had to stop and think. If the Japanese sacrificed 110,000 men for the defense of Okinawa, how many would die to defend their homeland?

The Atomic Decision

Allied leaders were not ready to invade the Japanese islands. For months American bombers flying from their new bases in the Pacific had attacked targets in Japan with the ultimate aim of demoralizing the Japanese people, destroying Japan's industrial base, and disrupting Japanese agriculture. Yet despite the fact that the Japanese had taken a terrible pounding, the Allies were still uncertain about an invasion of the home islands even though they knew that the Soviets were prepared to join them in the effort once the European war was over. If the horrendous losses suffered on Iwo Jima and Okinawa were an

Top: The Japanese finally surrendered in late June after having lost over 110,000. **Center:** B–29s over Yokohama. **Above:** By mid-1945 American bombing laid waste to most of Japan's industrial machine. **Right:** The new Big Three continued the Potsdam Conference: Attlee, Truman and Stalin. **Opposite:** Hiroshima: 6 August 1945.

indication of what would happen during an invasion of Japan, not even the presence of the Soviets would diminish the disaster that would befall the Allies. It was not unnatural, then, for Allied and particularly American commanders to welcome any feasible alternative to the loss of two million men wounded or killed in the last phase of the war against Japan. Fortunately, or perhaps unfortunately, there was an alternative the use of atomic weapons.

American scientists, aided by refugees from Nazi Germany and Fascist Italy, had long labored on the ultimate destructive device at a series of secret sites in the United States. In the spring of 1945 they had perfected this device and were ready to test it. By the time President Truman attended the Potsdam Conference in July, there was every evidence that the new weapon could be deployed against Japan, and Truman said as much without going into great detail in a conversation with Churchill in 14 July. Churchill analyzed the implications of this new development in the following manner:

'We seemed suddenly to have become possessed of a merciful abridgement of the slaughter in the East and of a far happier prospect in Europe. . . . To avert a vast indefinite butchery, to bring the war to an end, to give peace to the world, to lay healing hands upon its tortured people by a manifestation of overwhelming power at the cost of a few explosions, seemed after all our toils and perils, a miracle of deliverance.'

Whatever has been said about the use of the atomic bombs on Japan, few people at the time would have differed from the point made by Churchill that 'there was never a moment's discussion as to whether the atomic bomb should be used or not'. Whatever the moral debate triggered by the destruction wrought by these horrible devices, for the moment they offered an alternative to the loss of two million men. Allied leaders felt this was an alternative they could not afford to refuse, and plans were made to test the new weapon against Japan, to bring the Japanese government to its senses. It only remained to decide where and when the devices would be used.

Was there an alternative to the use of the atomic bombs against Japan other than a land invasion of the Japanese islands? There may have been. By the summer of 1945 Japanese leaders attempted to feel the Allies out about a possible peace settlement, using the Soviets as intermediaries. The Allies did not know how serious these feelers were because the Soviets did not convey the message clearly; nor were they necessarily better informed about the terrible damage already done in Japan. The Japanese may have been ready to concede defeat, even unconditional surrender, but some of the Allied leaders did not know this, or if they did, they chose to ignore it in favour of extracting the last pound of flesh from the Japanese. In any case, the evidence indicates that, whatever the state of informed opinion in the Allied camp, most civilian and military leaders favored use of the new weapon.

After a considerable secret debate, plans were made for use of the new weapons against Japan. On 6 August 1945 the first atomic bomb ever to be used in warfare was dropped on Hiroshima,

leveling the city and killing over 80,000 people. Three days later, on 9 August, a second atomic bomb was dropped on Nagasaki. The following morning the Japanese sued for peace.

Ironically, the Russians entered the war just as the Japanese were seeking an acceptable way to end it. Even the two atomic bombings of Japan had not resulted in a mentality of surrender among Japan's leaders. Although the Imperial Council agreed that the war must be brought to an end, the Emperor's advisers remained divided on what terms they would be willing to accept for ending the war. It was only as a result of direct intervention by Hirohito that the stalemate was resolved. Fearing that the Allies might drop more atomic weapons on Japan and continue their regular bombing raids, the Emperor announced on 14 August 1945 that his government would accept the terms for ending the war that the Allies had articulated at Potsdam. These included: 1) unconditional surrender of Japan's armed forces; 2) surrender of all territories other than the Japanese islands over which Japan had acquired control since 1895; 3) militarism would be eliminated in Japan; 4) to accomplish this, the Allies would occupy Japan.

Unconditional Surrender

Hirohito's decision was communicated to the Swiss, who immediately forwarded his message to the United States. It was received by President Truman and Prime Minister Attlee on 14 August, less than twenty-four hours after the Emperor's announcement to the Imperial Conference. Formal surrender ceremonies were held on board the *USS Missouri* on 2 September 1945. After more than seven years, the war was finally over. In accepting Japan's surrender on behalf of the Allies, General MacArthur expressed the hope that 'a better world would emerge out of the blood and carnage of the past . . .'. Considering that tens of millions of people had lost their lives in the conflict, this was surely not too much to ask.

World War II was the greatest war in history: greatest in scope and in fighting, on every continent; greatest in numbers of dead; greatest in its horror – the concentration camps, genocide, the atomic blasts, the fire raids, the Blitz – and, above all, the greatest ideological war of modern times. Wars of religion are nothing new. But wars of the modern religion, nationalism, are probably the most fierce, made all the more devastating by the 'advances' of perverted science. The war was a war of rival ideologies – fascism versus communism, democracy versus dictatorship – as well as a war between rival national myths. In the perspective of over twenty-five years, the war, if it was fought to rid the world of dictatorships, was a failure. If it was fought to suppress the economic and political might of Germany and Japan, it was also a failure. It succeeded only in weakening the democracies and economies of Western Europe for a time, which allowed the nations of the Third World to add their national myths to a world still ridden with nationalistic fervor. It is, undoubtedly, pessimistic to conclude that World War II accomplished little, and that the men who struggled in it died in vain. But perhaps that is the legacy of all wars.

Above: Postwar Japan.
Right: Unconditional surrender on the *Missouri* 2 September 1945.

The Legacy of World War II

Index

Page numbers in *italics* refer to illustrations

POST WAR WORLD

COMMUNIST STATES